Lecture Notes in Artificial Intelligence   8854

Subseries of Lecture Notes in Computer Science

LNAI Series Editors

Randy Goebel
University of Alberta, Edmonton, Canada
Yuzuru Tanaka
Hokkaido University, Sapporo, Japan
Wolfgang Wahlster
DFKI and Saarland University, Saarbrücken, Germany

LNAI Founding Series Editor

Joerg Siekmann
DFKI and Saarland University, Saarbrücken, Germany

Juan Luis Navarro Mesa   Alfonso Ortega
António Teixeira   Eduardo Hernández Pérez
Pedro Quintana Morales   Antonio Ravelo García
Iván Guerra Moreno   Doroteo T. Toledano (Eds.)

Advances in Speech and Language Technologies for Iberian Languages

Second International Conference, IberSPEECH 2014
Las Palmas de Gran Canaria, Spain, November 19-21, 2014
Proceedings

 Springer

Volume Editors

Juan Luis Navarro Mesa
Eduardo Hernández Pérez
Pedro Quintana Morales
Antonio Ravelo García
Iván Guerra Moreno
ETSIT, Las Palmas de Gran Canaria, Spain
E-mail: {juanluis.navarro, eduardo.hernandez,
pedro.quintana, antonio.ravelo}@ulpgc.es
E-mail: iguerra@idetic.eu

Alfonso Ortega
University of Zaragoza, Spain
E-mail: ortega@unizar.es

António Teixeira
University of Aveiro, Portugal
E-mail: ajst@ua.pt

Doroteo T. Toledano
Autonomous University of Madrid, Spain
E-mail: doroteo.torre@uam.es

ISSN 0302-9743   e-ISSN 1611-3349
ISBN 978-3-319-13622-6   e-ISBN 978-3-319-13623-3
DOI 10.1007/978-3-319-13623-3
Springer Cham Heidelberg New York Dordrecht London

Library of Congress Control Number: 2014955401

LNCS Sublibrary: SL 7 – Artificial Intelligence

Typesetting: Camera-ready by author, data conversion by Scientific Publishing Services, Chennai, India

Printed on acid-free paper

Springer is part of Springer Science+Business Media (www.springer.com)

Preface

The Spanish Thematic Network on Speech Technology (RTTH) and the ISCA-Special Interest Group on Iberian Languages (SIG-IL) are pleased to present the selected papers of IberSpeech 2014, Joint VIII Jornadas en Tecnologías del Habla and IV Iberian SLTech Workshop, held in Las Palmas de Gran Canaria, Spain, November 19–21. The Organizing Committee of IberSpeech believes and trusts that we have achieved the quality that the researchers in advances in speech and language technologies for Iberian languages value. To ensure this quality, each article was reviewed by at least three members of the Scientific Review Committee, who provided feedback to improve the final version of the articles in this book.

The conference has become mature as different editions have been organized, starting in Vigo 2010 with FALA and continuing in Madrid 2012 with the new denomination: IberSpeech. This new edition is a step forward the support of researchers in Iberian languages. IberSpeech is a joint event resulting from the merging of two conferences, the "Jornadas en Tecnología del Habla" and the Iberian SLTech Workshop. The first has been organized by the "Red Temática en Tecnologías del Habla" (Spanish Speech Technology Thematic Network, http://www.rthabla.es) since 2000. This network was created in 1999 and currently includes over 200 researchers and 30 research groups in speech technology all over Spain. And the second, was organized by the Special Interest Group on Iberian Languages (SIG-IL, http://www.il-sig.org/) of the International Speech Communication Association (ISCA). The Iberian SLTech Workshop had its first edition in Porto Salvo, Portugal, in 2009.

As a result, IberSpeech is one of the most important research meetings in the field of speech and language processing focusing on Iberian languages, attracting many researchers (about 140 in the 2014 edition), mainly from Spain, Portugal, and from other Iberian-speaking countries in Latin America. We have also attracted the interest of several research groups from all around the world, including China, United Kingdom, France, Japan, Hungary, Israel, Norway, Czech Republic, and Germany.

Although the main focus is on Iberian languages and the Iberian region, the conference is not restricted to these topics. Proof of this are the ALBAYZIN Technology Competitive Evaluations, organized in conjunction with the conference, which in this edition have attracted the interest of several research groups. The ALBAYZIN Technology Competitive Evaluations have been organized alongside with the conference since 2006, promoting the fair and transparent comparison of technology in different fields related to speech and language technology. In this edition we have two different evaluations: Audio Segmentation and Search on Speech. The organization of each one of these evaluations requires the preparation of development and test data, providing data along with a clear set of rules to the participants, and gathering and comparing results from participants. This organization was carried out by different groups of researchers and is crucial for the success in participation that we are envisaging. Although results from the evaluations cannot be included in this volume due to timing restrictions, we would like to express our gratitude to the organizers and also to the participants in the evaluations.

We had 60 submitted papers and, after a strict peer-reviewing process, only 29 were selected for publication in this volume of Springer *Lecture Notes in Artificial Intelligence*. This selection was based on the scores and comments provided by our Scientific Review Committee, which includes over 79 researchers from different institutions mainly from Spain, Portugal, Latin America, USA, UK, Hungary, and Czech Republic, to whom we also would like to express our deepest gratitude. Each article was reviewed by at least three different reviewers and authors have had time to address the comments before submitting the camera-ready paper. The articles are organized into four different topics:

- Speech Production, Analysis, Coding and Synthesis
- Speaker and Language Characterization
- Automatic Speech Recognition
- Speech and Language Technologies in Different Application Fields

Besides the excellent research articles included in this volume, the conference had the pleasure of having two extraordinary keynote speakers: Dr. Pedro Gómez Vilda (Departamento de Arquitectura y Tecnología de Sistemas Informáticos de la Universidad Politécnica de Madrid, Spain) and Dr. Roger K. Moore (Department of Computer Science University of Sheffield, UK).

We would also like to thank Springer, and in particular Alfred Hoffmann, for the possibility of publishing this volume, his suggestions in order to increase the spread of the international scope of IberSpeech 2014, his help and great work in preparing it.

Finally, we would like to thank all those whose effort has made possible this conference, the members of the local Organizing Committee, the technical and program chairs, the reviewers and so many people who gave their best to achieve a successful conference.

November 2014   Juan Luis Navarro Mesa
                                                 Alfonso Ortega Giménez
                                                 António Teixeira

Organization

General Chairs

Juan Luis Navarro Mesa — Universidad de Las Palmas de Gran Canaria, Spain

Alfonso Ortega Giménez — Universidad de Zaragoza, Spain

António Teixeira — Universidade de Aveiro, Portugal

Technical Chairs

Carmen García Mateo — Universidade de Vigo, Spain

Doroteo Torre Toledano — Universidad Autónoma de Madrid, Spain

Rubén San-Segundo Hernández — Universidad Politécnica de Madrid, Spain

Program Chairs

Eduardo Hernández Pérez — Universidad de Las Palmas de Gran Canaria, Spain

Pedro Quintana Morales — Universidad de Las Palmas de Gran Canaria, Spain

Jesús Alonso Hernández — Universidad de Las Palmas de Gran Canaria, Spain

Publication Chair

Sofía Martín González — Universidad de Las Palmas de Gran Canaria, Spain

Demos Chairs

Javier Hernando Pericas — Universidad Politécnica de Cataluña, Spain

Rubén San-Segundo Hernández — Universidad Politécnica de Madrid, Spain

Daniela Braga — Voicebox Technologies, Portugal

Awards Chairs

Javier Hernando Pericas — Universidad Politécnica de Cataluña, Spain

Inma Hernaez Rioja — Universidad del País Vasco, Spain

Daniela Braga — Voicebox Technologies, Portugal

Evaluation Chairs

Antonio Ravelo García	Universidad de Las Palmas de Gran Canaria, Spain
Carlos Travieso González	Universidad de Las Palmas de Gran Canaria, Spain

Local Organizing Committee

Universidad de Las Palmas de Gran Canaria

Jesús B. Alonso Hernández
Juan M. Caballero Suárez
Fidel Cabrera Quintero
Elena García Quevedo
Iván D. Guerra Moreno
Eduardo Hernández Pérez
Sofía I. Martín González
Manuel M. Medina Molina
Juan Luis Navarro Mesa
Pedro J. Quintana Morales
Antonio G. Ravelo García
Carlos Travieso González

Evaluations and Scientific Review Committee

Albayzin Evaluation Commitee

Juan Luis Navarro Mesa	Universidad de Las Palmas de Gran Canaria, Spain
Alfonso Ortega Giménez	Universidad de Zaragoza, Spain
António Teixeira	Universidade de Aveiro, Portugal
Rubén San-Segundo Hernández	Universidad Politécnica de Madrid, Spain

Scientific Review Committee

Alberto Abad	L2F/Spoken Language Systems Laboratory, Portugal
Jesús B. Alonso Hernández	Universidad de Las Palmas de Gran Canaria, Spain
Olatz Arregi Uriarte	Euskal Herriko Unibertsitatea, Spain
Plínio Barbosa	Universidade Estadual de Campinas, Portugal

Daniela Braga	Voicebox, Portugal
Juan M. Caballero Suárez	Universidad de Las Palmas de Gran Canaria, Spain
Fidel Cabrera Quintero	Universidad de Las Palmas de Gran Canaria, Spain
Valentín Cardeñoso Payo	Universidad de Valladolid, Spain
Paula Carvalho	Universidade de Lisboa, Portugal
María José Castro Bleda	Universitat Politécnica de Valencia, Spain
Jan Cernocky	BTU (Brno), Czech Republic
Chin Hui Lee	Georgia Tech, USA
Ricardo de Cordoba Herralde	Universidad Politécnica de Madrid, Spain
Carmen de la Mota Gorriz	Universitat Autònoma de Barcelona, Spain
Laura Docío Fernández	Universidade de Vigo, Spain
Daniel Erro Eslava	Euskal Herriko Unibertsitatea, Spain
David Escudero Mancebo	Universidad de Valladolid, Spain
Rubén Fernandez Pozo	Universidad Politécnica de Madrid, Spain
Javier Ferreiros López	Universidad Politécnica de Madrid, Spain
Julián Fierrez Aguilar	Universidad Autónoma de Madrid, Spain
Javier Franco Pedroso	Universidad Autónoma de Madrid, Spain
Ascensión Gallardo Antolín	Universidad Carlos III de Madrid, Spain
Carmen García Mateo	Universidade de Vigo, Spain
Elena García Quevedo	Universidad de Las Palmas de Gran Canaria, Spain
Juan Ignacio Godino Llorente	Universidad Politécnica de Madrid, Spain
Pedro Gómez Vilda	Universidad Politécnica de Madrid, Spain
Iván D. Guerra Moreno	Universidad de Las Palmas de Gran Canaria, Spain
Annika Hamalainen	Microsoft (MLDC), Portugal
Inma Hernaez Rioja	Euskal Herriko Unibertsitatea, Spain
Eduardo Hernández Pérez	Universidad de Las Palmas de Gran Canaria, Spain
Francisco Javier Hernando Pericas	Universitat Politècnica de Catalunya, Spain
Lluís Felip Hurtado Oliver	Universitat Politécnica de Valencia, Spain
Eduardo Lleida Solano	Universidad de Zaragoza, Spain
María Teresa López Soto	Universidad de Sevilla, Spain
Ramón López-Cózar Delgado	Universidad de Granada, Spain
Jordi Luque Serrano	Telefónica I+D, Spain
José B. Mariño Acebal	Universitat Politècnica de Catalunya, Spain
Sofía I. Martín González	Universidad de Las Palmas de Gran Canaria, Spain

Carlos David Martínez Hinarejos	Universitat Politécnica de Valencia, Spain
Manuel M. Medina Molina	Universidad de Las Palmas de Gran Canaria, Spain
Hugo Meinedo	Microsoft (MLDC), Portugal
Helena Moniz	INESC, Portugal
Juan Manuel Montero Martínez	Universidad Politécnica de Madrid, Spain
Nicolas Morales Mombiela	Nuance
Antonio Moreno Sandoval	Universidad Autónoma de Madrid, Spain
Climent Nadeu Camprubi	Universitat Politècnica de Catalunya, Spain
Juan Luis Navarro Mesa	Universidad de Las Palmas de Gran Canaria, Spain
Eva Navas Cordón	Euskal Herriko Unibertsitatea, Spain
Géza Nemeth	BME, Hungary
Juan Nolazco Flores	Tecnológico de Monterrey, Mexico
Alfonso Ortega Giménez	Universidad de Zaragoza, Spain
Antonio Miguel Peinado Herreros	Universidad de Granada, Spain
Carmen Peláez Moreno	Universidad Carlos III de Madrid, Spain
José Luis Pérez Córdoba	Universidad de Granada, Spain
Ferrán Pla Santamaría	Universitat Politécnica de Valencia, Spain
Paulo Quaresma	Universidade de Évora, Portugal
Pedro J. Quintana Morales	Universidad de Las Palmas de Gran Canaria, Spain
Daniel Ramos Castro	Universidad Autónoma de Madrid, Spain
Andreia Rauber	Universidade Católica de Pelotas, Portugal
Antonio G. Ravelo García	Universidad de Las Palmas de Gran Canaria, Spain
José Adrián Rodríguez Fonollosa	Universitat Politècnica de Catalunya, Spain
Eduardo Rodríquez Banga	Universidade de Vigo, Spain
Luis Javier Rodríquez Fuentes	Microsoft (MLDC), Portugal
Joan Andreu Sánchez Peiró	Universitat Politécnica de Valencia, Spain
Emilio Sanchís Arnal	Universitat Politécnica de Valencia, Spain
Rubén San-Segundo Hernández	Universidad Politécnica de Madrid, Spain
Diana Santos	University of Oslo, Norway
Kepa Sarasola Gabiola	Euskal Herriko Unibertsitatea, Spain
Encarnación Segarra Soriano	Universitat Politécnica de Valencia, Spain
Mário Silva	Universidade de Lisboa, Portugal
Alberto Simões	ESEIG/IPP, Portugal
Richard Stern	Carnegie Mellon University, USA

António Teixeira	Universidade de Aveiro, Portugal
Javier Tejedor Noguerales	Universidad de Alcalá de Henares, Spain
Doroteo Torre Toledano	Universidad Autónoma de Madrid, Spain
Isabel Trancoso	IST/University of Lisbon & INESC-ID, Portugal
Carlos Travieso González	Universidad de Las Palmas de Gran Canaria, Spain
María Amparo Varona Fernández	Euskal Herriko Unibertsitatea, Spain
Aline Villavicencio	Federal University of Rio Grande do Sul, Portugal

Table of Contents

Speech Production, Analysis, Coding and Synthesis

Speaker and Language Characterization

Automatic Speech Recognition

Speech and Language Technologies in Different Application Fields

Analysis and Synthesis of Emotional Speech in Spanish for the Chat Domain

A Parametric Approach

Yesika Laplaza and Juan María Garrido

Grup de Lingüística Computacional (GLiCom)
Departament de Traducció i Ciències del Llenguatge
Universitat Pompeu Fabra, Barcelona, Spain
yesika.laplaza@gmail.com, juanmaria.garrido@upf.edu

Abstract. This paper presents the results of the analysis of a set prosodic parameters considered relevant for the expression of emotion in Spanish on a corpus of read aloud chat messages, and explores the application of the obtained results to generate emotional synthetic speech using a novel parametric approach. The obtained results show that the analysed parameters seem to be relevant for the differentiation among the considered emotions, but that its use in parametric synthesis does not offer yet the desired quality level, although better in any case than using corpus-based techniques.

Keywords: prosody, emotions, TTS.

1 Introduction

Emotional speech is a hot research topic both in the fields of Phonetics and Speech Synthesis. The description of the phonetic cues involved in the acoustic expression of emotions has been the goal of many literature for many languages, including Spanish (see [1,2,3,4,5,6] among other), and it is interesting not only for theoretical reasons, but also for the use of this information in the generation of synthetic speech with emotional content. However, most of the work done in this field has been focused only on the description of basic emotions, and not on the emotions used in real-world applications of TTS.

The automatic generation of emotional synthetic speech has been attempted using several approaches, such as 'classical' corpus-based techniques, HMM synthesis, or parametric techniques. The parametric approach implies the modelling of a set of relevant acoustic phonetic parameters from an analysis (manual or automatic) of natural speech, which will be later used in the generation phase. Several attempts have been described in the literature to generate synthetic speech using parametric modelling of prosodic features ([4] and [7], for example, in the case of Spanish), and for the moment they offer only discrete results, but they have also some advantages, such as that it is not necessary to collect large amounts of data to obtain the values for the generation process.

J.L. Navarro Mesa et al. (Eds.): IberSPEECH 2014, LNAI 8854, pp. 1–10, 2014.

This paper presents the results of the analysis of a set prosodic parameters consi-dered relevant for the expression of emotion in Spanish on a corpus of read aloud chat messages, and explores the application of the obtained results to generate emotional synthetic speech using a novel parametric approach. Reading aloud chat messages is a possible application of TTS that demands, among other aspects, the modeling of emo-tional content that goes beyond the classical set of basic emotions.

2   Acoustic Analysis

The acoustic analysis phase involved the study of a set of prosodic parameters related to pitch, duration and intensity. Pitch parameters include F0 height and range, (re-ferred here as global pitch parameters, because they describe the general evolution of F0 along utterances), two features described in the literature as being relevant for the expression of emotions ([2], [4] and [6], for example), but also pitch patterns (local parameters), whose use in emotional speech has been much less described in the lite-rature ([1], [6]). Durational parameters include speech rate, a feature widely consi-dered as relevant for the expression of emotions in the previous literature ([3], [5], [7], among many other studies) and duration of the prepausal vowel, a temporal features less analyzed in previous studies. And finally, intensity, another feature considered as relevant for the expression of emotions in the literature ([2], for example), has also been measured.

2.1   Corpus

The analysed corpus is made up of 525 utterances, extracted from a corpus of real written chat messages previously collected ([8]), which were read by a professional actor imitating the different intended emotions. This corpus contains 25 examples of each of the 21 different considered emotional labels (21x25=525), which are detailed in table 1. This set of labels was established after the analysis of the annotation of the emotional and expressive meanings in the reference chat corpus which was carried out by an human expert (the 21 labels appearing most frequently in the annotated corpus were used), and represent isolated and mixed emotions, physiological states and speech acts.

Table 1. Set of emotional labels represented in the corpus

Isolated emotions		Mixed emotions	Physiological states	Speech acts
Admiration	Rejection	Mockery/rejection	Agitation	Greeting
Affection	Resignation	Anger/rejection		Farewell
Joy	Positive surprise	Joy/greeting		
Mockery	Sadness			
Disappointment				
Fun				
Doubt				
Anger				
Negative surprise				
Interest				
Pride				

2.2   Method

The corpus was phonetically transcribed, time aligned and prosodically annotated using different automatic tools. Phonetic transcription and alignment was done using the aligner included in the Cerevoice Voice Creation kit [9]. Annotation of prosodic units (syllables, intonation units) was carried out using SegProso, a Praat-based tool described in [10].

This annotated material was used as input for the analysis phase, which was also carried out automatically using a set of Praat, R and Bash scripts. F0 contours were processed using MelAn, an automatic tool for stylisation, annotation and modelling of F0 ([11]). The tool gives as output two kinds of pitch patterns from the annotated corpus provided as input: a set of global patterns, describing the global shape of F0 contours, in the form of two reference lines predicting the evolution of F0 height of peaks (P line) and valleys (V line) along the contours; and a set of local patterns, in the form of a listing of the most frequent F0 patterns appearing in the provided corpus. Local patterns are identified with symbolic labels expressing the height, container syllable and position within the syllable of every inflection point making up the pattern, following the conventions described in [12] and [13].

The rest of acoustic parameters was automatically processed using Praat and R scripts developed by the authors. For each parameter, separate mean values for each considered emotional labels were calculated, and an ANOVA test was applied to check if there were significant differences among emotional labels. The difference between the mean value obtained for each emotional label and the neutral mean value was also calculated, in the form of a deviation coefficient.

2.3   Results

Global Pitch Parameters: F0 Height and Range. Table 2 presents mean values for the initial and final points of the reference lines for each considered emotion calculated with MelAn, which have been used in this work to analyse the F0 height parameter. These results show that all the emotions have higher mean values than the neutral sentences. Surprise, anger, fun, mockery/rejection agitation and joy are the emotions showing highest values. The results of the ANOVA analysis indicate that these differences among emotions are statistically significant, both for initial (F=17.21, p=0 for P points; F=11.3, p=0, for V points) and final (F=6.8, p=0 por P points; F=11.08, p=0, for V points) values.

Table 3 presents mean values for the F0 range at the beginning and end of the reference lines, calculated as the difference between the initial and final points of P and V lines, respectively. The results show that some emotions (positive surprise, agitation, anger, fun, mockery/rejection, joy, pride and anger/rejection) have a higher initial F0 range than neutral, that is, in general, those with a positive degree of activation, and some other (admiration, rejection, mockery, affection, resignation, sadness, interest, disappointment and doubt) have a lower range (mostly those with a negative degree of activation). Final range behaves in general in the same way, but some exception can be observed, such as positive surprise or pride, with a mean range lower than the neutral, and on the other side, interest and doubt, with final ranges higher the neutral, probably due in this case to the fact that sentences of these emotion labels were mostly questions. The ANOVA test showed also in this case that the differences were statistically significant both for initial (F=6.006, p=0) and final (F=3.27, p=0) range.

Table 2. Mean values for initial and final points and slopes of the upper (P) and lower (V) reference lines for each considered emotional label and the neutral condition

Emotional label	Cases	Mean initial P value (Hz)	Mean final P value (Hz)	Mean initial V value (Hz)	Mean final V value (Hz)
Positive surprise	2	208.64	131.35	119.82	120.41
Agitation	10	203.39	135.75	146.78	95.25
Fun	16	193.28	133.44	149.86	98.27
Anger	13	182.37	116.26	131.40	85.79
Mockery/Rejection	16	178.85	119.98	135.42	96.37
Joy	17	174.76	134.64	132.32	96.13
Anger/Rejection	6	174.01	128.30	134.03	87.38
Pride	19	171.38	82.87	126.50	72.39
Mockery	13	161.64	121.05	131.59	92.50
Admiration	1	160.93	92.08	128.58	77.34
Neutral	363	158.91	90.57	120.27	69.18
Rejection	20	150.39	100.13	119.34	75.93
Resignation	11	135.53	95.14	110.21	83.06
Affection	13	135.28	101.03	108.11	75.29
Disappointment	19	126.41	97.12	105.19	77.66
Sadness	22	123.77	85.56	99.28	72.34
Interest	1	122.80	168.60	100.95	-7.97
Doubt	16	121.73	134.45	103.10	93.96

Table 3. Mean values for initial and final range (difference between initial and final values of the P and V reference lines) for each considered emotional label and the neutral condition

Emotional label	Case	Mean initial range (Hz)	Mean final range (Hz)
Positive surprise	2	88.81	10.93
Agitation	10	56.61	40.49
Anger	13	50.96	30.46
Fun	16	43.42	35.16
Mockery/Rejection	16	43.42	25.96
Joy	17	42.44	38.50
Pride	19	41.79	12.17
Anger/Rejection	6	39.98	40.91
Neutral	363	38.66	21.71
Admiration	1	32.34	14.74
Rejection	20	31.04	24.20
Mockery	13	30.05	28.54
Affection	13	27.16	25.73
Resignation	11	25.32	12.07
Sadness	22	24.48	13.21
Interest	1	21.85	79.20
Disappointment	19	21.21	19.46
Doubt	16	18.62	40.49

Local Pitch Parameters: Pitch Patterns. MelAn generates separate full pattern lists for each of the four considered stress group (SG) types: initial, interior, non-sentence final and sentence final. The obtained data show a large variety of patterns used in both conditions, neutral and emotional. This section presents a comparison of the most frequent patterns between neutral and emotional sentences for each type of SG. Only data for the SG of one and two syllables, the most frequent ones in the analysed corpus, are presented here.

Table 4. Most frequent pitch patterns in the 1-syllable and 2-syllable initial SG, both for neutral and emotional speech

Number of syllables of the SG	1		2	
Condition	Pattern	Cases	Pattern	Cases
Neutral	VI0_PM0	75	VI0_PM0	32
	VI0	35	PI0	30
	PI0	30	PI0_PI1	29
	VM0	24	VI0_PI1	26
	PM0	20	VI0	23
Emotional	VI0	9	VI0_PI1	6
	VI0_PM0	7	VI0_PM0	5
	VI0_VF0	5	PI0	3
	PI0	3	VI0	3
	PI0_PM0	3	VI0_VF1	3
			VM0_PI1	3

Tables 4 and 5 present the most frequent patterns for initial and internal SG, respectively, made up of one and two syllables. An analysis of the tables shows that most frequent pitch patterns are quite the same in neutral and emotional conditions: VI0_PM0 (initial low inflection point at the beginning of the stressed syllable, followed by a high inflection point near the centre of the syllable nucleus), VI0 (a single initial low inflection point at the beginning of the stressed syllable) and PI0 (a single initial high inflection point at the beginning of the stressed syllable) appear in all the lists, although not exactly in the same position; and VI0_PI1 (initial low inflection point at the beginning of the stressed syllable, followed by a high inflection point near the beginning of the poststressed syllable) appears among the most frequent patterns of the 2-syllable SG.

Table 5. Most frequent pitch patterns in the 1-syllable and 2-syllable internal SG, both for neutral and emotional speech

Number of syllables of the SG	1		2	
Condition	Pattern	Cases	Pattern	Cases
Neutral	VI0_PM0	169	VI0_PM0	226
	0	149	0	188
	PM0	107	PI1	135
	PI0	95	PM0	126
	VF0	47	PI0	114
Emotional	VI0	9	VI0_PI1	6
	VI0_PM0	7	VI0_PM0	5
	VI0_VF0	4	PI0	3
	PI0	3	VI0	3
	PI0_PM0	3	VI0_VF1	3

Table 6 presents the most frequent patterns for final (non sentence-final) and final (sentence-final), for one and two-syllable SG. It can be observed that in this case, there is more difference between the patterns used in neutral and emotional conditions. In the case of non-sentence final patterns, there are some patterns appearing in both conditions in 1 syllable SG (VI0_PM0_VF0, PI0_VF0 and PF0), but 2-syllable patterns are not coincident. In the case of sentence-final patterns, there are also some falling patterns appearing in both conditions (VF0, VI0_VF0, VM1, PI0_VM1), but emotional speech seems to show more variety in the type of used patterns, with some circumflex (VI0_PM0_VF0) and rising patterns (VI0_PF0, VI0_PM0_PF0) also among the most frequent ones. This tendency is confirmed is a full analysis of the sentence-final patterns of the corpus, classified by type, is carried out.

Table 6. Most frequent pitch patterns in the 1-syllable and 2-syllable final (non-sentence final and sentence final) SG, both for neutral and emotional speech

	Non-sentence final		Sentence final	
Condition	**1 syllable**	**2 syllable**	**1 syllable**	**2 syllable**
Neutral	VI0_PM0_PF0	PI0_VI1_VM1	VF0	PI0_VI1_VM1
	VI0_PM0_VF0	0	VI0_VF0	VM1
	VI0_PF0	PM0_VI1_VM1	PI0_VM0	VI1_VM1
	PI0_VF0	PI0_VI1_VF1	VM0	PI0_VF0_VM1
	PF0	VI1_PM1	VI0_VM0	PI0_VM1
Emotional	0	PI0_VM1	VF0	VM1
	VF0	VI0_PI1_VF1	VI0_PF0	VI0_VM1
	VI0_PM0_VF0	PM0_VM1_PF1	VI0_PM0_VF0	PI0_VM1
	PF0	PM1_VF1	VI0_VF0	VF1
	PI0_VF0	VI0_PF0_VM1_VF1	VI0_PM0_PF0	PI1_VM1

Duration Parameters. Table 7 presents the results obtained for speech rate and duration of the prepausal vowel. The analysis of the data reveals, in the case of speech rate, a tendency of the emotions showing positive activation (joy, agitation, anger) to show higher speech rate than the neutral, and emotions with negative activation (resignation, negative surprise, interest, doubt) to be expressed with a slower speech rate, although important exceptions are also observed (sadness, with a higher speech rate than the neutral, for example). In any case, the results of the ANOVA test indicate that the observed differences among emotional labels are statistically significant ($F=7.33$, $p=0$). In the case of the duration of the prepausal vowel, almost any of the analysed emotional labels show higher durations than the neutral, which can be interpreted that this cue is a general emotional mark. The ANOVA test also indicated that this parameter is statistically significant ($F=12.009$, $p=0$).

Intensity. Table 8 presents the results obtained for mean intensity. The data indicate that there are differences among the different considered emotional labels (statistically significant according to the ANOVA test: $F=13.52$, $p=0$), with some of them showing higher mean amplitude and intensity than the neutral (resignation, joy and interest are the one showing the highest mean amplitude), and some other with a mean amplitude below the neutral (admiration, agitation and anger/rejection showing the lowest values). In this case, however, it does not seem to exist any correlation between activation and this parameter.

Table 7. Mean values for speech rate and duration of the prepausal vowel for each considered emotional label and the neutral condition

Emotional label	Cases	Mean speech rate (words/min.)	Emotional label	Cases	Mean duration prepausal vowel (ms.)
Joy	21	14.499	Doubt	25	0.225
Sadness	26	14.056	Positive surprise	2	0.22
Agitation	12	13.672	Anger/Rejection	20	0.194
Disappointment	27	13.513	Affection	31	0.191
Mockery	30	13.484	Rejection	24	0.189
Admiration	7	13.432	Interest	3	0.187
Anger	22	13.404	Resignation	41	0.186
Neutral	4.694	13.147	Pride	28	0.186
Rejection	24	13.121	Agitation	12	0.185
Interest	3	12.949	Fun	18	0.185
Positive surprise	2	12.933	Mockery/rejection	21	0.184
Negative surprise	5	12.929	Disappointment	27	0.182
Affection	31	12.824	Negative surprise	5	0.182
Resignation	41	12.688	Anger	22	0.173
Mockery/rejection	21	12.526	Mockery	30	0.166
Anger/Rejection	20	12.266	Sadness	26	0.160
Pride	28	12.233	Admiration	7	0.151
Fun	18	11.859	Neutral	4.694	0.149
Doubt	25	11.167	Joy	21	0.144

Table 8. Mean values for intensity for each considered emotional label and the neutral condition

Emotional label	Cases	Mean intensity (dB)
Resignation	41	71.683
Joy	21	71.347
Interest	3	71.234
Doubt	25	70.865
Disappointment	27	70.709
Sadness	26	70.465
Rejection	24	70.002
Mockery	30	69.707
Mockery/rejection	21	69.644
Negative surprise	5	69.576
Fun	18	69.539
Anger	22	69.401
Pride	28	69.347
Neutral	4.694	69.250
Positive surprise	2	69.195
Affection	31	69.083
Admiration	7	68.640
Agitation	12	68.499
Anger/Rejection	20	67.932

2.4   Discussion

The results just presented seem to indicate that all the analysed parameters play a role in the acoustic expression and differentiation of the emotional labels analysed here. Differences observed in F0 height and range, speech rate, duration of the prepausal vowel and intensity have been revealed to be statistically significant. These results are similar to the ones presented in [2], [4] and [6], with a different set of emotional labels. In the case of the pitch pattern, main differences seem to focus in the final patterns, rather than in initial and internal. Emotional sentence-final patterns seem to show a wider variety of pattern types (rising, falling and circumflex) than the neutral ones, with a strong preference for the falling patterns.

3   Parametric Synthesis

The data obtained in the acoustic analysis phase were used in a synthesis experiment to test to what extent it is possible to generate synthetic speech using these parameters by means of parametric techniques, and to obtain a quality level at least similar to the one obtained using other techniques such as corpus-based unit selection. The parametric approach applied here includes the use of F0 analysis-synthesis tools based in the F0 modelling framework described in [12,13]. Due to the difficulty of evaluating all the 21 considered emotional labels, only four basic emotions (joy, anger, positive surprise and sadness), plus neutral, were chosen for the experiment.

3.1   Synthesis Procedure

The corpus previously described was used to build a synthetic voice compatible with the Cerevoice TTS system [9], containing both neutral and emotional units. Cerevoice is a corpus-based TTS engine that allows the generation of emotional speech by the addition to the input text of a set of XML tags indicating the intended emotion. This tagging procedure was used to generate a reduced set of synthesised stimuli (5 utterances with emotion-neutral semantic content) expressing the four selected emotions plus the neutral (5 utterances x 5 emotional conditions = 25 stimuli).

These stimuli were later processed using a set of Praat-based scripts to modifiy the considered acoustic parameters. For the modification of the F0 paramenters, a modified version of ModProso [14], a Praat-based tool to replace the original F0 contour by a 'synthetic' contour predicted from symbolic pitch pattern labels of the form of the one generated by MelAn. Other Praat scripts were also used for the modification of the natural durations and intensity of the input speech waves according to the predictions of the data obtained in the analysis phase. The goal of this procedure was to simulate the effect of the parametric prediction of the selected parameters in the generation of synthetic speech without a previous implementation in the TTS engine.

4   Evaluation

Two different perception experiments were carried out with the stimuli obtained using the described synthesis procedure, the first one to evaluate the degree of discrimination of the different emotions, and the second one to compare the identification of the emotions using the stimuli directly obtained with the TTS system and the stimuli with the parametric modification of the prosodic parameters. In the first experiment, the subjects were asked to select the emotional label that according to their perception best fits every synthetic stimulus, from a closed set of labels ('joy', 'anger', 'surprise', 'sadness', 'neutral' and 'other'). In the second one, the subjects had to listen to pairs of versions of the same synthesised stimuli, one with parametric modification of prosody and the other one without it (then with the prosody assigned by the corpus-based TTS), and they had to say which of the two best expressed the intended emotion. Both experiments were carried out using a web platform which hosted the synthetic stimuli. 22 subjects ran the first experiment, and 21 the second one.

4.1 Results

The results of the emotion identification experiment are presented in table 9. The analysis of the table reveals that all the target emotions were mostly identified as neutral. The emotions best identified are suprise and sadness (0.18 and 0.29, respectively). Mean score for the whole set of emotions was 0.24.

Table 10 presents the results of the second experiment. It shows that, in general, subjects preferred the parametric version to the corpus-based one, especially for joy and anger, and even the neutral style.

Table 9. Confusion matrix for the results of the first experiment (normalised 0-1 scale)

	Joy	Anger	Surprise	Sadness	Neutral	Other
Joy	0.08	0.06	0.13	0.3	0.33	0.09
Anger	0.1	0.09	0.14	0.1	0.47	0.1
Surprise	0.22	0.07	0.18	0.15	0.31	0.08
Sadness	0	0.16	0.03	0.29	0.48	0.05
Neutral	0.11	0.18	0.05	0.03	0.58	0.06

Table 10. Results of the second experiment (normalised 0-1 scale)

Emotional label	Corpus-based	Parametric
Joy	0.29	**0.71**
Anger	**0.83**	0.17
Surprise	**0.62**	0.38
Sadness	0.26	**0.74**
Neutral	0.05	**0.95**
TOTAL	0.40	**0.60**

5   Conclusions

This paper has presented the results of an acoustic analysis of some prosodic parameters in a corpus of read aloud chat messages, in order to see to what extent they vary depending of the expressed emotion, and some synthesis experiments aimed at evaluating the use of these data for the parametric generation of emotional synthetic speech. The results of the acoustic analysis have shown the existence of significant differences in the acoustic expression of the analysed emotions. The synthesis experiments seem to indicate that, although the quality of the speech obtained with parametric method tested here is still far from being excellent, it seems to offer better results than traditional corpus-based techniques in a context of poor training data, as in this case.

References

1. Navarro, T.: Manual de entonación española. Hispanic Institute on the United States, New York (1944)
2. Rodríguez, A., Lázaro, P., Montoya, N., Blanco, J.M., Bernadas, D., Oliver, J.M., Longhi, L.: Modelización acústica de la expresión emocional en el español. Procesamiento del Lenguaje Natural 25, 159–166 (1999)
3. Montero, J.M., Gutiérrez-Arriola, J., Colás, J., Enríquez, E., Pardo, J.M.: Analysis and Modelling of Emotional Speech in Spanish. In: Proceedings of the 14th International Conference of Phonetic Sciences, pp. 957–960 (1999)
4. Montero, J.M.: Estrategias para la mejora de la naturalidad y la incorporación de variedad emocional a la conversión texto a voz en castellano. Ph. D thesis, ETSI Telecomunicación, UPM (2003)
5. Martínez, H., Rojas, D.: Prosodia y emociones: datos acústicos, velocidad de habla y percepción de un corpus actuado. Lengua Y Habla 15, 59–72 (2011)
6. Garrido, J.M.: Análisis de las curvas melódicas del español en habla emotiva simulada. Estudios de Fonética Experimental XX, 205–255 (2011)
7. Francisco, V., Gervás, P., Hervás, R.: Analisis y síntesis de expresión emocional en cuentos leídos en voz alta. Procesamiento del Lenguaje Natural 35, 293–300 (2005)
8. Laplaza, Y.: Síntesis del habla con emociones en el dominio de las conversaciones virtuales. Ph D. Thesis. Pompeu Fabra University, Barcelona (2013)
9. Garrido, J.M., Bofias, E., Laplaza, Y., Marquina, M., Aylett, M., Pidcock, C.: The CEREVOICE speech synthesiser. In: Actas de las V Jornadas de Tecnología del Habla, pp. 126–129 (2008)
10. Garrido, J.M.: SegProso: A Praat-Based tool for the Automatic Detection and Annotation of Prosodic Boundaries. In: Proceedings of TRASP 2013, pp. 74–77 (2013)
11. Garrido, J.M.: A Tool for Automatic F0 Stylisation, Annotation and Modelling of Large Corpora. In: Speech Prosody 2010 (2010)
12. Garrido, J.M.: Modelling Spanish Intonation for Text-to-Speech Applications. Ph.D. Thesis, Universitat Autònoma de Barcelona, Bellaterra (1996)
13. Garrido, J.M.: La estructura de las curvas melódicas del español: propuesta de modelización. Lingüística Española Actual XXIII(2), 173–209 (2001)
14. Garrido, J.M.: ModProso: A Praat-Based tool for F0 Prediction and Modification. In: Proceedings of TRASP 2013, pp. 38–41 (2013)

Developing a Basque TTS
for the Navarro-Lapurdian Dialect

Eva Navas[1], Inma Hernaez[1], Daniel Erro[1,2],
Jasone Salaberria[3], Beñat Oyharçabal[3], and Manuel Padilla[3]

[1] Aholab (UPV/EHU), ETSI Bilbao, Alda. Urquijo s/n, Bilbao, Spain
[2] IKERBASQUE, Alda. Urquijo, 36-5, Bilbao, Spain
[3] IKER UMR 5478, 15 Place Paul Bert, 64100 Bayonne, France
{eva,inma,derro}@aholab.ehu.es

Abstract. The paper presents a new TTS system for the Navarro-Lapurdian dialect based on a standard Basque TTS. A phonetically balanced recording corpus of 4000 sentences has been designed and two speakers have recorded it. The voice has been built using a high quality speech coder in the context of HMM based speech synthesis. The new dialectal TTS system has been compared in a subjective evaluation with the existing TTS system for standard Basque and with a mixed system that applies the phonetic transcription rules of the dialect, but uses the speech generation module of the standard Basque system. The adaptation of the front-end module with the inclusion of new phonetic transcription rules and new sounds is not enough to get a system that works better than the standard Basque system. The results with the dialectal new voice indicate that users prefer the new dialectal system to the standard Basque one.

Keywords: Dialectal TTS, Minoritarian Language, Basque TTS.

1 Introduction

Speech synthesis is a well known speech technology that has reached good quality for many of the majority languages. This technology is developed even for some minority languages, and recently there have been some attempts at developing it for dialectal speech in Swedish [1], Austrian German [2], Tianjin [3] and Northern Sotho [4]. All these works apply statistical parametric speech synthesis based in Hidden Markov Models (HMM) [5]. In statistical parametric systems average models are trained from acoustically similar natural units, building decision trees with linguistic features. HMM based speech synthesis technique provides high stability and flexibility to create new voices through adaptation or interpolation techniques [6]. This speech synthesis technique is based on databases of natural speech and even though the size of the database is not critical, it benefits from a large size phonetically rich corpus in the generation of high quality synthetic speech. The development of such a speech corpus is especially important for languages with limited resources and many dialects. Basque language has about

J.L. Navarro Mesa et al. (Eds.): IberSPEECH 2014, LNAI 8854, pp. 11–20, 2014.
© Springer International Publishing Switzerland 2014

1.050.000 speakers and 5 main dialects. One of these dialects is the Navarro-Lapurdian which is the main dialect spoken in Labourd and Lower Navarre, the two historical provinces of the French Basque Country. As such, this dialect gets some influence from the French dominant language. There are 73.000 Basque speakers in the French part of the Basque Country (30.5% of the population) [7].

There are text to speech synthesis (TTS) systems for standard Basque like for instance AhoTTS [8] and Nuance Vocalizer[TM], but not for any Basque dialect. The goal of this work was to develop a new TTS system for the Navarro-Lapurdian dialect, based on AhoTTS. The typical structure of a TTS system includes two different modules: the front-end or linguistic module, that normalizes the input text and assigns phonetic transcriptions to each word and the back-end or synthesizer that generates the synthetic speech from the linguistic representation provided by the first module.

In the next section of the paper the modifications made in the linguistic module are explained. Then, section 3 describes the design and recording of the natural speech database needed to create the TTS system. Section 4 presents the steps followed to obtain the synthetic voice and the evaluation of the system is detailed in section 5. Finally some conclusions are presented in section 6.

2   Adaptation of the Linguistic Module

The multilingual TTS system AhoTTS includes a linguistic module for standard Basque that has been adapted to the Navarro-Lapurdian Basque dialect by including new phones, new transcription rules and reviewing the existing ones. This linguistic module performs text normalization and grapheme to phoneme conversion by means of rules, whereas it uses a specific lexicon and some simple disambiguation rules for POS tagging.

The Basque dialect spoken in the Labourd and Lower Navarre region has some phonetic differences compared to standard Basque. For instance, while palatalization of /n/ and /l/ is common when preceded by an /i/ in standard Basque, this phenomenon is not observed in Navarro-Lapurdian dialect.[1] There are also new sounds like /h/ which is not pronounced in standard Basque but is realized as a laryngeal unvoiced fricative in the Northern dialect. However, the loss of the aspirated consonant has begun in the Navarro-Lapurdian dialect too. One of the biggest changes concerns the realization of the grapheme rr. It is realized as a voiced alveolar rhotic trill(/rr/) in Standard Basque, but this consonant has an uvular articulation (/R/) in present-day Navarro-Lapurdian.

One of the most problematic aspects in the development of the system is the fact that in the Navarro-Lapurdian Basque dialect it is very common to find French proper nouns that are uttered following the French pronunciation rules. To properly consider them, it is in fact necessary to add the whole French

---

[1] All phone codes are expressed in SAMPA. Basque SAMPA
http://aholab.ehu.es/sampa_basque.htm;
French SAMPA http://www.phon.ucl.ac.uk/home/sampa/french.htm.

sound system to the Basque one. Although important for a real application of the TTS, our goal in this first prototype has intentionally been focused on the developments for Basque. As an intermediate solution, the most essential French phonemes were taken into account, namely /a~/, /e~/, /o~/, /y/, /2/, /v/ and /Z/. No French phonetic transcription rules were developed, so to correctly get the transcription of the French proper nouns a dictionary with their corresponding phonetic transcription was manually prepared. The selected French phonemes only appear in these transcriptions made by dictionary.

3 Recording the Speech Database

3.1 Preparing the Recording Corpus

Standard Basque is a minority language with little text material available to build corpora [9] and this resource scarcity problem is even more serious when dealing with a Basque dialect like Navarro-Lapurdian Basque. The TTS we wanted to build was supposed to have an unrestricted domain, therefore we tried to get texts from as many sources as possible. More than 90MB of plain text were collected from different domains: 45MB from Herria magazine, 9MB from 19th century books and 42MB from 20th century books. The texts from oldest books were available in a modern spelling, so they were suitable to be part of the recording corpus.

This initial text corpus was automatically cleaned to avoid problematic sentences (for instance, sentences that contained foreign words whose anomalous transcription could distort the phonetic analysis). Then the phonetic transcription was obtained by means of the modified version of the linguistic module of AhoTTS system, described in section 2.

The final recording corpus was devised to include about 4000 sentences. To select this subset of sentences from the huge initial text corpus a greedy algorithm [10] has been used. The conditions applied to select the final sentences were to maximize the diphone coverage according to their frequency of appearance in the collected data, limiting the number of words per sentence to less than 15 to keep the corpus easily readable. To ensure that French phones appeared in the corpus, 200 sentences of the final corpus were separately selected from the part of the initial text corpus that contained French proper nouns. All

Table 1. Main characteristics of the recording text corpus, compared to a Standard Basque corpus [11]

Number of...	Navarro-Lapurdian Corpus	Standard Basque Corpus
Sentences	3999	3799
Words	38776	38544
Distinct phonemes	42 (35+7)	35 (34+1)
Distinct diphonemes	1079	583

extracted sentences were proofread, discarding the invalid ones (e.g. sentences with grammatical errors) and correcting some misspellings. This selection and correction process was repeated up to five times until obtaining the final recording corpus described in Table 1. For the sake of comparison, Table 1 also includes the data corresponding to a similar corpus developed for standard Basque [11]. Compared to standard Basque, the Navarro-Lapurdian Basque corpus considers a larger number of phonemes, but it is important to notice that only 35 of them actually belong to the Basque dialect. The rest correspond to the seven French phonemes added to the phoneset with the aim of getting a better pronunciation of French proper nouns. As five of these extra phonemes are vowels also the number of diphones grows heavily. Table 2 shows the most frequent diphones in the developed corpus and compares them to the most frequent diphones in the standard Basque corpus. We can see that both corpus share the most common diphones.

3.2 Selection of the Speakers

The selection of the speakers was made after a careful casting that included 3 male and 3 female speakers, all of them radio professional speakers. They were asked to read some texts taken from the same big text corpus that was used to extract the sentences to be recorded. The speakers were selected according to their ability to comply with the phonetic transcription rules agreed for Navarro-Lapurdian Basque and to the quality of the transcoded voice obtained using their speech signals. This quality was assessed in an informal subjective evaluation performed at the lab.

Table 2. Most frequent diphones in the recording corpus, compared to a Standard Basque corpus [11]

Navarro-Lapurdian Corpus		Standard Basque Corpus	
Diphone	Number	Diphone	Number
e-n	5196	e-n	4666
a-n	4754	t-a	3645
t-a	4635	a-n	3224
t-e	3461	k-o	3138
a-k	3316	t-e	3956
k-o	3040	a-k	2571

3.3 Recording Process

Recordings were made in a professional radio studio that belongs to *Gure Irratia*, a Basque radio station established in the Navarro-Lapurdian region in 1981. A pop filter was placed between the speaker and the main microphone in order to reduce the airflow pressure. Each session was monitored from the outside with the help of headphones.

To complete the recordings 6 sessions were necessary for the female speaker and 5 sessions for the male speaker. In order to reduce the inter-session variability (e.g. differences in voice quality, rhythm, tone, etc.) several preventive measures were followed. The position of the microphone in the studio and the distance from the speaker to the microphone were kept almost constant during the whole recording process. Speakers were given some instructions about how to conduct their readings to reduce voice fatigue over long sessions on consecutive days. They were asked to speak effortlessly and in a volume they could sustain for a long period of time. At the beginning of each session the average amplitude of the input signal was adjusted to get a similar level to that of the last recording session. The speakers were allowed to hear a couple of sentences from past recordings so that they could maintain the rhythm and tone. In the middle of the recording, if the speaker had deviated in excess from the reference point, new instructions were transmitted to the voice talent. Regarding the style, the speakers were asked to use a natural reading style. Additional instructions about how to pronounce some French and Basque proper nouns were made, in order to make the canonical transcriptions and the real pronunciations match as much as possible.

4   Synthetic Voice Generation

In order to get high quality synthetic voices, the analysis and accurate annotation of the recorded corpora constitutes a decisive step. However, getting a high labelling accuracy usually implies a hard working and time consuming hand annotation process. In the creation of the synthetic voice for Navarro-Lapurdian Basque dialect, we decided to apply an automatic labelling process with little or no manual intervention. Prior to the voice building step, a normalization of the recorded signals and a segmentation process were performed as explained next.

4.1   Normalization

First, all the waveform files were down-sampled to 16kHz and their power was normalized. This normalization process is important to avoid excessive volume differences among recording sessions of the same voice. The normalization was performed per waveform following this procedure: voiced portions of each signal were automatically determined with the help of Praat [12]. The mean power was then fixed to -25dV as specified in ITU-T-P.56 [13]. If this normalization process led to the saturation of the signal, problematic segments were automatically detected and properly attenuated within a rectangular window. The boundaries of this window were the nearest zero crossing values outwards the problematic region itself. This simple approach reduced the excessive volume at the beginning of some utterances while preserving the natural power envelope of the sentences.

4.2 Segmentation

The sentences from the recording corpus were manually reviewed and corrected so they matched the actual sentences uttered by each of the speakers. Pauses were also included and punctuation signs were added or deleted to match the pauses made by the speaker. Finally, a customized lexicon for each speaker was constructed to include the pronunciations that did not comply with the considered transcription rules.

Feeding the phonetic transcriptor described in section 2 with the corrected text files and using the corresponding customized lexicon, sequences of phonemes and orthographical pauses were generated. This phoneme sequences along with the normalized signals were used to perform an automatic speaker dependent segmentation based on forced alignment. The HTK toolkit [14] was used during the segmentation process. First, tied-state triphone models were trained from a plain start, without the insertion of short pauses at word boundaries. Finally, the segmentation boundaries of the phonemes adjacent to pauses were refined by means of a simple but effective algorithm that uses power envelope and durational outliers.

4.3 Voice Building

First, speech signals were analysed with AhoCoder, a high-quality vocoder developed in our lab [15]. Then, proper linguistic labels were prepared [16] and the HTS system [17] was used to train HMM models. At present, only the female voice has been built.

During the synthesis process discontinuities between voiced sounds were observed, mainly at word boundaries. To minimize the impact of this problem, unvoiced threshold has been reduced from 0.5 (default value) to 0.2 so that more frames are considered voiced.

5 Subjective Evaluation

The evaluation of TTS systems is usually made by subjective tests where real users give their opinion about different aspects of the system. With this evaluation we wanted to get information about the convenience of adapting the linguistic module and recording a voice for generating dialectal synthetic speech. Therefore, three different systems, all of them based on AhoTTS and sharing the lexicon, have been included in the evaluation:

- The standard Basque system (identified as standard in Figures 2 and 3)
- The dialectal system developed in the work described in this paper (dialectal)
- A mixed system (mixed) that uses the modified linguistic module described in section 2 and the back-end of the standard Basque TTS.

5.1 Development of the Mixed System

To build the mixed system, only the adaptation of the linguistic module is needed, no recordings have to be made and no text corpus has to be prepared. But, as the phoneset is different in standard Basque and Navarro-Lapurdian Basque dialect, it is necessary to map the phones of the dialect to those of the standard that are closest to them. With this purpose, a blind phonetic clustering has been made. A Gaussian Mixture Model (GMM) with a single gaussian has been trained with 12 MFCC parameters for each phone using the dialectal synthesis speech database and a female speech database in standard Basque AhoSyn [11]. These models are useful to represent the phonetic characteristics of each phone in a compact way and have been used to cluster the phones applying regression trees. Figure 1 shows the dendrogram obtained for the clustering of the vowels. The vowels of standard Basque are indicated with the prefix "S" just before the corresponding SAMPA code and for the vowels considered in the dialectal system the prefix "D" has been used. For instance, we can see in Figure 1 that the dialectal vowels /e~/, /2/ and /e/ are closer to the standard /e/ sound than to any other, so these three phones that will be produced at the output of the dialectal linguistic module, will be mapped to standard /e/ to be synthesized by the standard back-end in the mixed system. In the same way the rest of the vowels and the new consonant sounds have been mapped to sounds in the standard Basque phoneset. As a result of this blind clustering procedure, /R/ sound has been mapped to /G/ and /h/ to /x/. In the case of nasal vowels, an /n/ phone has been inserted after the mapped vowel to preserve the nasality.

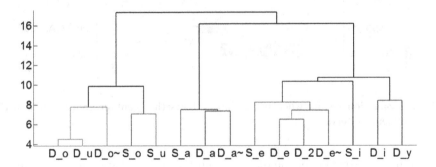

Fig. 1. Dendrogram for vowel sounds

5.2 Results of the Evaluation

In this work a comparative evaluation has been designed. The evaluators have to listen through a WEB interface to two different synthetic versions of a sentence and choose the one that they like most. A five point scale has been used, grading from -2 to 2, where -2 means "I clearly prefer the first speech signal", -1 "I slightly prefer the first speech signal", 0 "I cannot decide, I think both of them are equivalent", 1 "I slightly prefer the second speech signal" and 2 "I clearly prefer the second speech signal".

Two different types of sentences have been included in the evaluation: half of the sentences were written completely in Basque and the other half contained French proper nouns. In this way we can determine if the presence of French nouns influences the preference of the users for one system or the other.

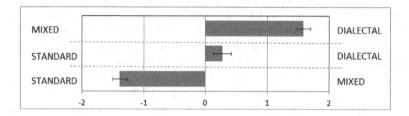

Fig. 2. Evaluation results when using Basque texts without French proper nouns, with 95% confidence intervals

Twenty six people, all native of Navarro-Lapurdian Basque dialect, have participated in the evaluation. The results are shown in Figure 2 for Basque texts without French nouns and in Figure 3 for texts with French proper nouns.

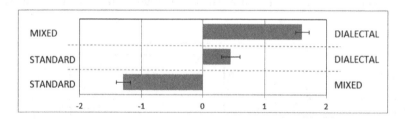

Fig. 3. Evaluation results when using Basque texts that contain French nouns with 95% confidence intervals

The users clearly prefer the dialectal and the standard systems to the mixed system to read any kind of text. The dialectal system is also preferred to the standard Basque one for both types of texts, but the difference is not as large as the one got in the comparison with the mixed system. This may be due to the high quality of the standard Basque voice, for which the segmentation of the database has been manually reviewed. Besides, due to the dominant position of standard Basque in the media, people from the Labourd and Lower Navarre region are used to standard Basque so that it sounds good to them even if it does not correspond to their dialect. As the 95% confidence intervals do not include the value 0 in any case, all these preferences are significant. Figure 4 shows the distribution of scores given to the TTS systems when using Basque

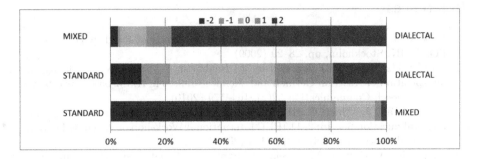

Fig. 4. Distribution of scores for Basque texts without French proper nouns

texts without French proper nouns. In the comparison between Standard and dialectal Basque systems, 40% of the people preferred the dialectal one and only 20% chose the standard Basque system. The slight preference seen in Figure 2 is due to the almost 40% of people that were not capable to decide between them.

6   Conclusions

A new TTS system for the Navarro-Lapurdian dialect has been developed, using the standard Basque TTS system AhoTTS as a base. More than 90MB of plain Navarro-Lapurdian Basque texts have been collected and 4000 phonetically balanced sentences have been selected to form the recording corpus. To build the voice a high quality speech coder in the context of HMM based speech synthesis has been used. The new dialectal TTS system has been compared in a subjective evaluation with the existing TTS system for standard Basque and with a mixed system that applies the phonetic transcription rules of the dialect, but uses the speech generation module of the standard Basque system. The adaptation of the front-end module with the inclusion of new phonetic transcription rules and new sounds is not enough to get a system that works better than the standard Basque system, at least using the blind phone clustering applied in this work. It is possible that using a knowledge-based linguistic approach for the phone mapping provides better results. If no recordings can be made, it is more advisable to use the standard Basque system. But the results with the dialectal new voice indicate that users prefer the dialectal system to the standard one.

Acknowledgments. The authors want to thank Iñaki Sainz for his hard work on the project, Josu Landa who collected and provided the dialectal texts to build the recording corpus and also all the people that has taken part in the subjective evaluation. This work has been partially funded by L'Eurorégion Aquitaine-Euskadi under the project IPARRAHOTSA, the Spanish Ministry of Economy and Competitiveness (SpeechTech4All project, TEC2012-38939-C03-03) and the Basque Government (Ber2tek project, IE12-333).

References

1. Beskow, J., Gustafson, J.: Experiments with Synthesis of Swedish Dialects. In: FONETIK, Stockholm, pp. 28–29 (2009)
2. Pucher, M., Schabus, D., Yamagishi, J., Neubarth, F., Strom, V.: Modeling and interpolation of Austrian German and Viennese dialect in HMM-based speech synthesis. Speech Communication 52(2), 164–179 (2010)
3. Hu, Q., Tao, J., Zhao, C.: HMM-based Tianjin Dialect speech synthesis using bilateral question Set. In: 2011 IEEE International Workshop on Machine Learning for Signal Processing, Beijing, pp. 1–4 (2011)
4. Langa, R., Manamela, J., Gasela, N.: Synthesis of dialect speech for an under-resourced language. In: SATNAC, Western Cape (2012)
5. Yoshimura, T., Tokuda, K., Masuko, T., Kobayashi, T., Kitamura, T.: Simultaneous modeling of spectrum, pitch and duration in HMMbased speech synthesis. In: EUROSPEECH, Budapest, pp. 2347–2350 (1999)
6. Zen, H., Tokuda, K., Black, A.W.: Statistical parametric speech synthesis. Speech Communication 51, 1039–1064 (2009)
7. Basque Government: Fifth Sociolinguistic Survey: Basque Autonomous Community, Navarre and Iparralde, http://www.euskara.euskadi.net/r59-738/en/contenidos/informacion/sociolinguistic_research2011/en_2011/2011.html
8. Hernaez, I., Navas, E., Murugarren, J.L., Etxebarria, B.: Description of the AhoTTS Conversion System for the Basque Language. In: 4th ISCA Tutorial and Research Workshop (ITRW) on Speech Synthesis, paper 202, Perthshire (2001), http://sourceforge.net/projects/ahottsmultiling/
9. Hernaez, I., Navas, E., Odriozola, I., Sarasola, K., Diaz de Ilarraza, A., Leturia, I., Diaz de Lezana, A., Oyharçabal, B., Salaberria, J.: The Basque language in the digital age/Euskara aro digitalean. METANET White Paper Series. Springer (2012)
10. Sesma, A., Moreno, A.: CorpusCrt 1.0: Diseño de corpus orales equilibrados. Technical report, UPC (2000) (in Spanish)
11. Sainz, I., Erro, D., Navas, E., Hernaez, I., Sanchez, J., Saratxaga, O.I.: Versatile Speech Databases for High Quality Synthesis for Basque. In: LREC, Istanbul, pp. 3308–3312 (2012)
12. Boersma, P., Weenink, D.: Praat: doing phonetics by computer (Computer program). Version 5.1.38 (2010), http://www.praat.org/ (retrieved June 2, 2010)
13. International Telecommunication Union (ITU-T): Recommendation ITU-T P.56, Objective measurement of active speech level (2011), https://www.itu.int/rec/T-REC-P.56-201112-I/en
14. Young, S., Evermann, G., Gales, M., Hain, T., Kershaw, D., Moore, G., Odell, J., Ollason, D., Povey, D., Valtchev, V., Woodland, P.: The HTK Book, version 3.4 (2006)
15. Erro, D., Sainz, I., Navas, E., Heráaez, I.: HNM-Based MFCC+f0 Extractor Applied to Statistical Speech Synthesis. In: ICASSP, Florence, pp. 4728–4731 (2011)
16. Erro, D., Sainz, I., Luengo, I., Odriozola, I., Sanchez, J., Saratxaga, I., Navas, E., Hernaez, I.: HMM-based Speech Synthesis in Basque Language using HTS. In: FALA, Vigo, pp. 67–70 (2010)
17. Zen, H., Nose, T., Yamagishi, J., Sako, S., Black, A.W., Masuko, T., Tokuda, K.: The HMM-based speech synthesis system (HTS) version 2.0. In: SSW 2006, Bonn, pp. 294–299 (2006)

Fine Vocoder Tuning for HMM-Based Speech Synthesis: Effect of the Analysis Window Length

Agustin Alonso[1], Daniel Erro[1,2], Eva Navas[1], and Inma Hernaez[1]

[1] AHOLAB, University of the Basque Country (UPV/EHU), Bilbao, Spain
{agustin,derro,eva,inma}@aholab.ehu.es
[2] IKERBASQUE, Basque Foundation for Science, Bilbao, Spain

Abstract. This paper studies how the length of the window used during spectral envelope estimation influences the perceptual quality of HMM-based speech synthesis. We show that the acoustic differences due to variations in the window length are audible. The experiments reveal an overall preference towards short analysis windows, although longer windows seem to alleviate some artifacts related to training data scarcity.

Keywords: Vocoder, statistical parametric speech synthesis, harmonic analysis, window length.

1 Introduction

Vocoders are one of the essential parts of a hidden Markov model (HMM) based speech synthesis system [1,2]. During training, they provide the parameter vectors from which HMMs are learnt. During synthesis, the system generates the most likely sequence of parameter vectors given the input specifications and the trained models [3]; then, vectors are converted into waveforms by the vocoder.

Many different vocoders have been proposed in the context of HMM-based speech synthesis, especially since the appearance of HTS [4]. The first HTS releases contained a simple vocoder based on Mel-cepstral (MCEP) analysis [5]. It generated speech from parameters by filtering an f0-dependent pulse-or-noise excitation through a filter built from the MCEP coefficients (the so called MLSA filter [6]). This vocoder was later improved by means of mixed excitation models [7,8,9,10]. Recent HTS releases include a much more sophisticated vocoder [11] based on STRAIGHT toolkit [12]. Vocoders dealing with explicit vocal tract plus glottal source models [13,14,15] or sinusoidal models [16,17, 18] have also been studied.

Speech parameter extraction (through vocoders) and statistical modeling of parameter vector sequences have been traditionally seen as separate training steps. One of the recent trends in HMM-based synthesis is combining these two steps in several ways [19,20,21,22], under the assumption that they can benefit from each other.

This work addresses the interaction between vocoding and modeling by studying a simple parameter which often goes unnoticed: the length of the window used during spectral envelope analysis. Without loss of generality, we use a MCEP vocoder based

J.L. Navarro Mesa et al. (Eds.): IberSPEECH 2014, LNAI 8854, pp. 21–29, 2014.
© Springer International Publishing Switzerland 2014

on harmonic analysis [18], which allows the window length to be as small as two signal periods thanks to least-squares based analysis procedures [23]. As spectral analysis often relies on the assumption of local stationarity, methods requiring a short analysis window length [24] are advantageous in the sense that they allow accurate analysis at high temporal resolution. However, statistical models are not capable of capturing all the small local variations between frames. This means that using a too short analysis window may provide useless information while resulting in more heterogeneous adjacent frames and worse subsequent statistical modeling. On the contrary, if analysis windows are reasonably longer, the acoustic information that HMMs are able to capture is preserved while potentially irrelevant inter-frame variations are likely to get blurred. At the same time, however, the use of longer windows indirectly implies increasing the oversmoothing effect, which may be annoying to some listeners. This work aims at clarifying the role played by the analysis window length (if any) under the standard settings of an HTS-based system (5 ms frame shift, 5-state left-to-right context-dependent HMMs, log-f_0 + MCEP + excitation-related coefficients). To address this question we have conducted a set of objective and subjective experiments from the point of view of both parametric analysis/resynthesis and statistical parametric synthesis. We will show that the results of our experiments reveal some interesting trends to be taken into account by system designers.

The remainder of this paper is structured as follows. Section 2 gives a brief overview of how spectral information is extracted from speech signals. Section 3 studies the influence of the window length on objective resynthesis scores. Section 4 shows its influence on objective scores related to statistical modeling. In section 5, two specific configurations of the vocoder are compared via perceptual tests. The general conclusions of this study are summarized in section 6.

2   Vocoder Description

The vocoder we have used in our experiments was extensively described in [18]. For a better understanding of what is next, this section gives a brief overview of how it parameterizes and reconstructs speech signals. Basically, this vocoder (as many others do) handles information at three different levels: (i) fundamental frequency, (ii) spectral envelope and (iii) degree of harmonicity of the excitation. These three information streams are parameterized through log-f_0, MCEP coefficients and maximum voiced frequency (MVF), respectively.

Fundamental frequency estimation is based on autocorrelation maximization with dynamic programming smoothing followed by a refinement based on quasi-harmonic analysis. MVF is estimated according to the sinusoidal likeness of the spectral peaks near the harmonic positions. Since these two analysis modules do not play a relevant role in this study, we omit further details about them (interested readers should refer to [18]) and focus on spectral envelope analysis.

Assuming a full-band harmonic model of speech (harmonics are assumed to be present even within theoretically noisy bands), spectral envelope is locally estimated by interpolating between the harmonic log-amplitudes. Both amplitudes and phases are previously yielded by a least squares based harmonic analyzer [23]:

$$\{A_i^{(k)}, \varphi_i^{(k)}\} = \arg\min \sum_{n=-L/2}^{L/2} w^2[n](s[n+kN] - h^{(k)}[n])^2 \qquad (1)$$

$$h^{(k)}[n] = \sum_{i=1}^{I^{(k)}} A_i^{(k)} \cos(i\omega_0^{(k)} n + \varphi_i^{(k)}) \qquad (2)$$

where k is the frame index, N is the frame shift (samples), $w[n]$ is an analysis window of length L, $I^{(k)}$ is the local number of harmonics within the band $(0, f_s/2)$, and ω_0 is equal to $2\pi f_0/f_s$. Phase information is discarded immediately after harmonic analysis. Interpolation between harmonic log-amplitudes and MCEP parameterization are carried out simultaneously thanks to Mel regularized discrete cepstrum technique [25][23][18], which searches for the MCEP vector $\mathbf{c}$ that optimizes the system

$$\mathbf{M} \cdot \mathbf{c} = \mathbf{a}$$

$$\mathbf{M} = \begin{bmatrix} 1 & m_{1,1} & \cdots & m_{1,p} \\ 1 & m_{2,1} & \cdots & m_{2,p} \\ \vdots & \vdots & \ddots & \vdots \\ 1 & m_{I,1} & \cdots & m_{I,p} \end{bmatrix}, \quad \mathbf{c} = \begin{bmatrix} c_0 \\ c_1 \\ \vdots \\ c_p \end{bmatrix}, \quad \mathbf{a} = \begin{bmatrix} a_1 \\ a_2 \\ \vdots \\ a_I \end{bmatrix} \qquad (3)$$

$$m_{i,q} = 2\cos(q \, \mathrm{mel}(i\omega_0)), \quad a_i = \log(A_i / 2\sqrt{f_0})$$

where $\mathrm{mel}(\cdot)$ applies the Mel frequency scale to the input linear frequency (rad). The frame index k has been omitted from eq. (3) for clarity.

After HMM-driven parameter generation, speech is reconstructed by overlapping frames of the form

$$s^{(k)}[n] = h^{(k)}[n] + e^{(k)}[n] \qquad (4)$$

Unlike the analysis module, the resynthesis module assumes a harmonics plus noise signal model. In the synthetic version of $h^{(k)}[n]$, given again by eq. (2), $I^{(k)}$ is the number of harmonics between 0 and the local MVF, the synthetic amplitudes $\{A_i^{(k)}\}$ are obtained by resampling the MCEP envelope at multiples of the local f_0 (this can be seen as a direct application of eq. (3)), and the synthetic phases $\{\varphi_i^{(k)}\}$ result from combining the resampled minimum-phase envelope given by the MCEP coefficients and a linear-in-frequency term that controls inter-frame coherence. Finally, $e^{(k)}[n]$ is a time-windowed high-pass noise shaped by the MCEP coefficients and bandlimited by the local MVF [18].

The performance of this vocoder has been shown to be comparable with that of well known state-of-the-art systems [18], while it allows varying the length of the analysis window $w[n]$, L, for values greater than two fundamental periods [23] – this reasonable lower bound is imposed by the underlying harmonic analysis procedure (eq. (1)).

3   Window Length and Resynthesis

As already mentioned in section 1, when local stationarity is assumed there is a close relationship between the length of the analysis window, L, and the resynthesis accuracy, especially for sounds exhibiting rapid variations over time. However, informal listening tests reveal that small variations in L have small perceptual consequences. To quantify this effect for many different voices without the need for unmanageable perceptual tests, we have used an objective measure called PESQ (ITU-T/P.862) [26]. Given a natural speech signal and its transcoded version, PESQ predicts the mean opinion score (MOS) that the latter would achieve in a subjective listening test. Since PESQ is waveform-sensitive, we compared the natural signals with their harmonic reconstruction (eq. (2)) using the phases yielded by the harmonic analyzer (eq. (1)) and the amplitudes resulting from MCEP fitting and resampling (eq. (3)). Unvoiced frames were analyzed/synthesized at $f_0 = 100$ Hz. Comparisons were made for 53 voices taken from various speech synthesis and recognition databases.

Fig.1 shows the PESQ-MOS for different window lengths. Since the absolute window length is related to the pitch period, we calculate separate average scores for female and male voices. The maximum PESQ-MOS is reached for 2–2.5 periods in male voices and for 2.5–3 periods in female voices. Overall, PESQ penalizes longer windows. Although short windows seem to be penalized too, we believe this is due to the fact that PESQ analysis itself uses fixed-length windows of 32ms [26], thus not being capable of discriminating perceptually relevant details below this limit. From now on, we will consider that resynthesis benefits from short analysis windows as expected.

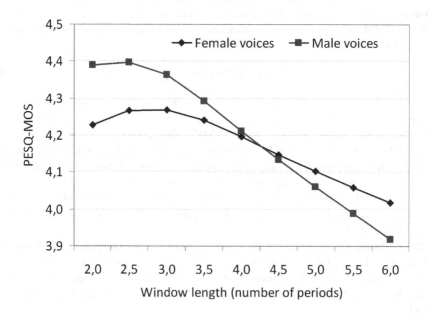

Fig. 1. Gender-dependent PESQ-MOS for different windows length

4   Window Length and Statistical Modeling

The next experiment aims at determining the optimal window length from the point of view of statistical modeling. We used the first training steps of HTS [4] to learn monophone HMMs from 500 short utterances of two different voices sampled at 16 kHz frequency: one female voice in Basque and one male voice in Spanish. The reason why monophone models were considered instead of context-dependent ones is avoiding the effect of unequal context clustering for different window lengths. After training the monophone models, we computed the average log-likelihood of the vectors in the training dataset.

The results shown by Fig. 2 indicate that the model fits the training data best when the analysis window is made longer. Longer windows imply some degree of time-domain smoothing thus reducing the variability of the parameters within the phone. A maximum is reached at 3.5 periods for the male voice and 5.5-6 periods for the female voice. Taking into account that the average pitch of the speakers is 100 and 170 Hz respectively, this maximum corresponds to a constant window length of 35 ms approximately. Beyond this value, the analysis window is apparently long enough as to capture the features of adjacent phones, which produces poorer modeling.

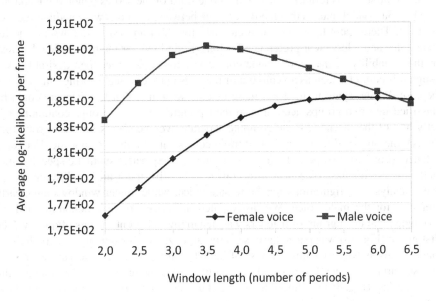

Fig. 2. Average log-likelihood per frame given a monophone HMM for different window lengths

5   Subjective Evaluation

Until now, we have shown that an accurate capture of the perceptually relevant speech signal characteristics requires a short analysis window, while accurate statistical modeling requires significantly longer windows. However, we have yet no hints about the relevance of these aspects with regard to the perceptual quality or naturalness of the resulting synthetic waveforms. Hence, our next experiment is a perceptual test where we assess the relative performance of the synthesizer when the training data are analyzed at two different window lengths: (i) two periods (short analysis window, suitable for resynthesis) and (ii) optimal number of periods according to Fig. 2 (suitable for accurate statistical modeling). We trained two HTS voices using the whole training dataset of the same voices as in section 4: 2k short utterances from the female voice and 1.2k utterances from the male voice. A total of 22 evaluators were asked to listen to 10 randomly selected pairs of synthetic utterances and to choose among 5 possible scores: "strong preference" for any of the two utterances, "slight preference" for any or "no preference". Both utterances in each pair were equivalent except for the window length used during analysis and training. They were presented in random order to the listeners. A comparative MOS (CMOS) was calculated by assigning an integer score between -2 and 2 to each option and averaging all individual scores. Negative scores denote preference for two-period windows, positive scores denote preference for longer windows, and 0 denotes no preference.

The resulting CMOSs and their corresponding 95% confidence intervals are shown in Fig. 3. First, let us remark that less than one third of the scores denoted uncertainty (see Fig. 3a), which means that the differences between methods were audible most of the time. There seem to be a clear preference for short analysis windows for the female voice and a less clear preference for longer windows for the male voice. However, the variability of the scores made confidence intervals larger than desirable. Although this could be seen as a symptom of inconsistent individual scoring, this was not the case. While trying to interpret these results, we found that the listeners could be classified into two groups according to their preferences, both groups containing exactly half of the listeners. If we compute separate average scores for each group (see Fig. 4), the observed trends are found to be consistent and almost opposite. For some listeners (Fig. 4a), two-period windows produce clearly better synthetic speech, especially for the female voice. For some others (Fig. 4b), there are no differences between analysis configurations for the female voice, while longer windows are clearly preferred for the male voice. We investigated the causes of this dichotomy and we concluded that each group of listeners was penalizing different aspects of quality. The first group (Fig. 4a) was particularly sensitive to buzziness or tonality effects. Indeed, longer analysis windows imply a loss of inter-frame variability, which in turn results in less variable – thus buzzier and less natural – synthetic speech. By contrast, the second group (Fig. 4b) was more tolerant to buzziness. Leaving buzziness aside, these listeners did not find a criterion for discrimination in the female case. However, for the male voice, there were some subtle discontinuities in a few phonetic transitions which we believe related to a lower amount of training data and a less accurate phonetic labeling. According to the perception of the second group of listeners, long analysis windows alleviate the negative impact of the mentioned discontinuities (at the expense of some extra buzziness to which they were not very sensitive).

As a summary, short analysis windows lead to higher synthesis quality – less buzzy synthetic speech – while the smoothing effect produced by longer analysis windows can alleviate artifacts resulting from small amounts of training data. Although these findings should be reinforced by considering more voices and languages, they provide a possible explanation for the different performance of theoretically similar vocoders. We expect these conclusions to hold also for parameterizarions other than MCEP.

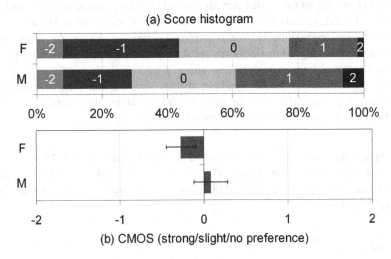

Fig. 3. Results of the listening test: (a) Score distribution (b) CMOS with 95% confidence interval. F: female voice; M: male voice. -2/-1=strong/slight preference for 2periods; 0=no preference; 2/1=strong/slight preference for 3.5/5./5 periods.

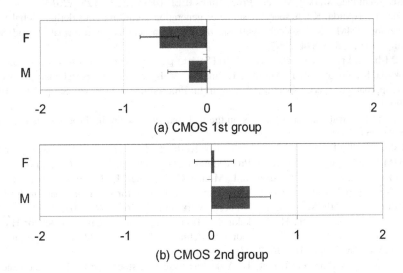

Fig. 4. Results of the listening test (CMOS with 95% confidence interval) for two separate groups of listeners F: Female voice; M: Male voice

6   Conclusions

We have shown that the choice of the window length used during spectral envelope estimation is not a trivial issue in the design of an HMM-based synthesizer. On the one hand, short windows (about two signal periods) provide locally accurate acoustic analysis. On the other hand, models fit the training data better if the window length is increased up to 35 ms approximately. When artificial voices are trained for these two configurations, the resulting synthetic signals are distinguishable by listeners. Under the test conditions reported here, a compromise arises: longer analysis windows produce less variable, less natural and buzzier synthetic speech, which is annoying to some listeners; however, they also alleviate the negative impact of training data scarcity or inaccurate labeling, which might be interesting depending on the circumstances.

Acknowledgements. This work was supported in part by the Spanish Ministry of Economy and Competitiveness (SpeechTech4All, TEC2012-38939-C03-03), the Basque Government (Ber2tek, IE12-333), and Eurorregion Aquitaine-Euskadi (Iparrahotsa, 2012-004).

References

1. Zen, H., Tokuda, K., Black, A.W.: Statistical parametric speech synthesis. Speech Communication 51(11), 1039–1064 (2009)
2. Tokuda, K., Nankaku, Y., Toda, T., Zen, H., Yamagishi, J., Oura, K.: Speech synthesis based on hidden Markov Models. Proceedings IEEE 101(5), 1234–1252 (2013)
3. Toda, T., Tokuda, K.: A speech parameter generation algorithm considering global variance for HMM-based speech synthesis. IEICE Transactions on Information and System E90-D(5), 816–824 (2007)
4. HHM-based Speech Synthesis System (HTS), http://hts.sp.nitech.ac.jp/
5. Tokuda, K., Kobayashi, T., Masuko, T., Imai, S.: Mel-generalized cepstral analysis - a unified approach to speech spectral estimation. In: Proceedings ICSLP, vol. 3, pp. 1043–1046 (1994)
6. Imai, S.: Cepstral analysis synthesis on the mel frequency scale. In: Proceedigns ICASSP, pp. 93–96 (1983)
7. Yoshimura, T., Tokuda, K., Masuko, T., Kobayashi, T., Kitamura, T.: Mixed excitation for HMM-based speech synthesis. In: Proceedings Eurospeech, pp. 2263–2266 (2001)
8. Gonzalvo, X., Socorro, J.C., Iriondo, I., Monzo, C., Martinez, E.: Linguistic and mixed excitation improvements on a HMM-based speech synthesis for Castilian Spanish. In: Proceedings of the 6th ISCA Speech Synthesis Workshop, pp. 362–367 (2007)
9. Maia, R., Toda, T., Zen, H., Nankaku, Y., Tokuda, K.: An excitation model for HMM-based speech synthesis based on residual modeling. In: Proceedings 6th ISCA Speech Synthesis Workshop, pp. 131–136 (2007)
10. Drugman, T., Wilfart, G., Dutoit, T.: A deterministic plus stochastic model of the residual signal for improved parametric speech synthesis. In: Proceedings Interspeech, pp. 1779–1782 (2009)

11. Zen, H., Toda, T., Nakamura, M., Tokuda, K.: Details of the Nitech HMM-based speech synthesis system for the Blizzard Challenge 2005. IEICE Transactions on Information and System E90-D(1), 325–333 (2007)
12. Kawahara, H., Masuda-Kasuse, I., de Cheveigne, A.: Restructuring speech representations using a pitch-adaptive time-frequency smoothing and an instantaneous-frequency-based F0 extraction: possible role of a repetitive structure in sounds. Speech Communication 27, 187–207 (1999)
13. Cabral, J.P., Renals, S., Richmond, K., Yamagishi, J.: Glottal Spectra Separation for Parametric Speech Synthesis. In: Proceedings Interspeech, pp. 1829–1832 (2008)
14. Lanchantin, P., Degottex, G., Rodet, X.: A HMM-based speech synthesis system using a new glottal source and vocal-tract separation method. In: Proceedings ICASSP, pp. 4630–4633 (2010)
15. Raitio, T., Suni, A., Yamagishi, J., Pulakka, H., Nurminen, J., Vainio, M., Alku, P.: HMM-based Speech Synthesis Utilizing Glottal Inverse Filtering. IEEE Transactions on Audio Speech and Language Processing 19(1), 153–165 (2011)
16. Banos, E., Derro, D., Bonafonte, A., Moreno, A.: Flexible harmonic/stochastic modeling for HMM-based speech synthesis. In: Proceedings V Jornadas en Tecnologías del Habla, pp. 145–148 (2008)
17. Shechtman, S., Sorin, A.: Sinusoidal model parameterization for HMM-based TTS system. In: Proceedings Interspeech, pp. 805–808 (2010)
18. Erro, D., Sainz, I., Navas, E., Hernaez, I.: Harmonics plus noise model based vocoder for statistical parametric speech synthesis. IEEE Journal of Selected Topics in Signal Processing (in press)
19. Toda, T., Tokuda, K.: Statistical approach to vocal tract transfer function estimation based on factor analyzed trajectory HMM. In: Proceedings ICASSP, pp. 3925–3928 (2008)
20. Wu, Y.J., Tokuda, K.: Minimum generation error training by using original spectrum as reference for log spectral distortion measure. In: Proceedings ICASSP, pp. 4013–4016 (2009)
21. Ling, Z.H., Deng, L., Yu, D.: Modeling spectral envelopes using restricted Boltzmann machines and deep belief networks for statistical parametric speech synthesis. IEEE Transactions on Audio Speech and Language Processing 21(10), 2129–2139 (2013)
22. Hojo, N., Yoshizato, K., Kameoka, H., Saito, D., Sagayama, S.: Text-to-speech synthesizer based on combination of composite wavelet and hidden Markov models. In: Proceedings of the 8th ISCA Speech Synthesis Workshop, pp. 129–134 (2013)
23. Stylianou, Y.: Harmonic plus noise models for speech, combined with statistical methods, for speech and speaker modification. Ph.D. thesis, École Nationale Supèrieure de Télécommunications, Paris (1996)
24. Erro, D., Sainz, I., Navas, E., Hernaez, I.: Efficient spectral envelope estimation from harmonic speech signals. IET Electronics Letters 48(16), 1019–1021 (2012)
25. Cappé, O., Laroche, J., Moulines, E.: Regularized estimation of cepstrum envelope from discrete frequency points. In: Proceedings WASPAA, pp. 213–219 (1995)
26. Rix, A.W., Beerends, J.G., Hollier, M.P., Hekstra, A.P.: Perceptual evaluation of speech quality (PESQ) – a new method for speech quality assessment of telephone networks and codecs. In: Proceedings ICASSP, pp. 749–752 (2001)

Quantitative Analysis of /l/ Production from RT-MRI: First Results

Samuel Silva[1], Paula Martins[2], Catarina Oliveira[2], and António Teixeira[1]

[1] DETI/IEETA, University of Aveiro, 3810–193 Aveiro, Portugal
[2] ESSUA/IEETA, University of Aveiro, 3810–193 Aveiro, Portugal
{sss,pmartins,coliveira,ajst}@ua.pt

Abstract. Lateral consonants are complex and variable sounds. Static MRI provides relevant information regarding /l/ geometry, but does not address dynamic properties. Real-time MRI is a well suited technique for dealing with temporal aspects. However, large amounts of data have to be processed to harness its full potential. The main goal of this paper is to extend a recently proposed quantitative framework to the analysis of real-time MRI data for European Portuguese /l/. Several vocal tract configurations of the alveolar consonant, acquired in different syllable positions and vocalic contexts, were compared. The quantitative framework revealed itself capable of dealing with the data for the /l/, allowing a systematic analysis of the multiple realisations. The results regarding syllable position effects and coarticulation of /l/ with adjacent vowels are in line with previous findings.

Keywords: laterals, quantitative analysis, RT-MRI.

1 Introduction

Lateral consonants are articulatorily complex and variable sounds. In several languages, the /l/ is associated with two canonical allophones (light /l/ in syllable onset, and dark /l/ in coda position). The most important articulatory distinction between them is a greater tongue dorsum retraction in the dark /l/ than in the light variety [9,20]. In terms of interarticulator timing, in syllable-onset position, tongue tip constriction of /l/ tends to occur earlier than, or in simultaneous with, tongue dorsum gesture, while in final syllable position roughly the reverse situation occurs [20,5,3]. Previous 3D MRI studies [9,22,7,10] provide a detailed characterisation of the 3D geometry of /l/. This information is of the utmost relevance, but further data is needed regarding other temporal properties.

Methods such as real-time magnetic resonance imaging (RT-MRI) [14] provide data regarding the position and coordination of the different articulators, over time [6]. Furthermore, they offer the possibility to improve the studies based on information gathered from static sustained productions by avoiding/reducing the hyperarticulation effect [4]. Processing the large amounts of image data resulting from these methods poses challenges that need to be addressed to harness their full potential. The identification and extraction of notable structures (e.g.,

J.L. Navarro Mesa et al. (Eds.): IberSPEECH 2014, LNAI 8854, pp. 30–39, 2014.

vocal tract profile [2,15]) is one important first challenge. What to do with the extracted data, in order to perform a systematic analysis, is one of the challenges that follows.

To that purpose, the authors have recently proposed a quantitative framework [18] to support the comparison between vocal tract configurations (e.g., of different sounds). Recently, the framework was extended to consider data from multiple speakers [17] and multiple realisations of each utterance [16].

In recent years, our team has been dedicated to the characterisation of the articulatory properties of the EP /l/, using different instrumental techniques (EMA and MRI), in order to bring some new light into the controversial question whether the Portuguese /l/ is categorically associated with two positional allophones or not [7,10,11].

The goals of the work presented here are threefold: first, to test the processing and analysis pipeline to deal with real-time MRI data concerning laterals; second, to assess how the quantitative framework, previously presented, can be used to assess different aspects concerning the production of laterals, and how it should evolve to address its specificities; and third, to gather additional insight regarding laterals, which might improve our knowledge regarding their production and guide future research.

The remainder of this article is organised as follows: section 2 provides details regarding the corpus, methods used to acquire, process and analyse the vocal tract data concerning the EP alveolar lateral, /l/; section 3 presents first results of applying the quantitative framework to the analysis of laterals' data; finally, section 4 briefly discusses the overall aspects of the presented work and how it might evolve, and presents final remarks.

2   Methods

Speech production studies, using RT-MRI, can be described by a set of stages: 1) images (and audio) are acquired, considering a corpus and a set of speakers; 2) the resulting data is processed to annotate specific segments (e.g., sounds) and extract relevant features (e.g., vocal tract outline); and 3) the data is analysed and interpreted, providing insight on the studied phenomena and, eventually, providing clues on how to improve future research. Taking into consideration the work presented in this article, a brief account of the methods used at each of these stages is provided.

2.1   Corpus and Image Acquisition

The MRI experiment was carried out using a 3.0 T MR scanner (Magneton Tim Trio, Siemens) equipped with high performance gradients. A standard 12-channel head and neck phased array coils and parallel imaging (GRAPPA) were used.

Images were acquired at the midsagittal plane of the vocal tract using an Ultra-Fast RF-spoiled Gradient Echo (GE) pulse sequence with a slice thickness of 8 mm and the following parameters: TR/TE/FA = 72ms/1.02ms/5°, Bandwidth = 1395 Hz/pixel, FOV(mm^2)= 210 x 210, reconstruction matrix of (128 x 128) elements, yielding a frame rate of 14 frames/second.

The described acquisition protocol was mainly used to gather data regarding EP oral and nasal vowels [21]. Nevertheless, at the end of the study, a few acquisitions were performed with the participants uttering multiple realisations of several words containing the alveolar lateral /l/ in different word positions (onset, intervocalic and coda) and vocalic contexts ([a,i,u]). Table 1 presents the acquired corpus. A total of 24 tokens per syllable position were recorded.

Table 1. Corpus acquired using RT-MRI (orthographic form and IPA transcription) for lateral /l/

Pos.	IPA	Word	Pos.	IPA	Word	Pos.	IPA	Word
	/la/	**laca** (hair spray)		/alɐ/	**sala** (room)		/al/	**sal** (salt)
onset	/li/	**litro** (liter)	intervoc.	/ili/	**bilis** (bile)	coda	/il/	**til** (tilde)
	/lu/	**lupa** (magnifier)		/ulu/	**pulo** (jump)		/ul/	**sul** (south)

Audio was recorded simultaneously with the RT images, inside the MR scanner, at a sampling rate of 16000 Hz, using a fiberoptic microphone. The audio was annotated manually, using Praat [1], identifying the segments containing the /l/ and adjacent vowels, e.g., [lakɐ], [biliʃ] and [sul]. Since the audio is synchronised with the image sequences [21], it is possible to determine the images corresponding to the annotated intervals.

Data was collected for two female speakers, CM and SV, aged 21, phonetically trained, with no history of hearing or speech disorders. An MRI screening form and informed consent was obtained before the study to comply with security and ethics rules.

2.2 Vocal Tract Segmentation

The vocal tract was segmented from the image sequences using an evolution of the active appearance models (AAM) based method presented in [15]. This method allows unsupervised segmentation of the vocal tract for the full image sequences. Based on the audio annotation, the frames of interest can be selected, for analysis. Figure 1 presents the extracted vocal tract profiles of speaker CM during the production of [salɐ]. The lingual contact along the midsagittal line and the retraction of tongue dorsum towards the velum are clearly observed in frames 8-9, corresponding to the /l/ articulation.

2.3 Quantitative Vocal Tract Configurations Comparison

The authors have proposed a framework to support the quantitative comparison between vocal tract configurations [18]. This framework adopts a set of measures to compare different features of the vocal tract and represents the resulting data

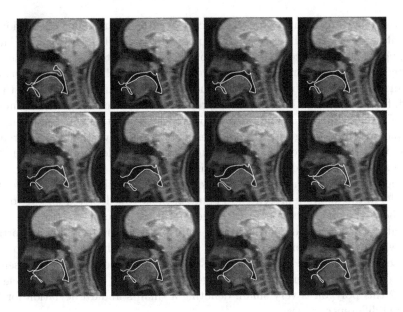

Fig. 1. Image frames, for speaker CM, acquired along the production of [saɫɐ], depicting the extracted vocal tract contour

in a difference diagram. At this moment, the framework considers the difference for seven features: tongue back (TB), velum (VEL), tongue dorsum (TD), tongue tip (TT), lip aperture (LA), lip protrusion (LP) and pharyngeal wall (Ph). The differences, for each of the features, are computed using various methods. For example, for the tongue back, tongue dorsum, velum and pharingeal wall, the Pratt index is used [12] to compare contour segments.

Figure 2 shows, at the centre, a set of superimposed contours for [a] and [i] and the corresponding diagram depicting the mean differences (considering the multiple cross-comparisons possible) computed using the proposed framework.

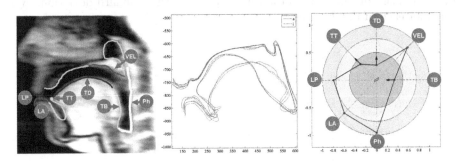

Fig. 2. From left to right: vocal tract contour depicting several regions of interest; superimposed contours for the vocal tract configurations assumed in multiple realisations of [a] and [i]; and the corresponding difference diagram with the differences represented.

In the diagram, each feature is associated with a particular orientation in the unitary circle. The differences are expressed between 0 and 1, with the latter standing for no difference. In order to provide an easier interpretation of the represented values, three circular coronas are presented: the first, in green, between 0.75 and 1; the second, in yellow, for values between 0.5 and 0.75; and the third, in red, for values bellow 0.5. These are proposed to represent "no meaningful difference", "mild difference" and "strong difference" respectively. Considering the example presented in figure 2, the difference diagram shows that the differences among the two vowels concern the tongue back, tongue dorsum and tongue tip.

The arrows, presented for each value inside the yellow and red circular coronas, depict the direction in which the movement occurred, for that feature. For example, in the diagram presented in figure 2, the arrow depicted for the tongue back shows that it moved forward (to the left) from [a] to [i].

Finally, when cross-comparing among multiple contours, it is also important to provide a measure of the variability affecting the difference data. To that purpose, for each of the difference values, the standard deviation is represented by the corresponding vertex of the orange polygon at the centre of the circle. In figure 2 this polygon is very small, denoting a small standard deviation for the gathered difference values.

What has been presented so far provides a quantitative method to (cross-) compare among static vocal tract configurations. By computing these differences between the vocal tract configurations assumed over time, for two utterances, it is possible to assess how and when they differ. Figure 3 shows the representation of the differences found, over time, between vowel [ẽ] and its oral congener [ɛ]. To the left, a difference diagram is presented for the differences found between the initial vocal tract configurations, for both utterances and, on the right, the difference diagram for the vocal tract configurations at the end of the utterance. In the middle, a plot shows a curve for each of the vocal tract features considered. Similarly to what is done for the difference diagram, three coloured horizontal bars are shown to help interpret the values. In the diagram, notice two notable aspects: a mild difference is found at the velum, justified by the comparison between an oral and a nasal vowel; and the difference gradually grows, over time [8]. The bottom plot, at the centre, presents the standard deviation, over time, for each of the features.

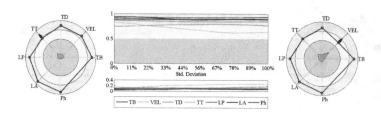

Fig. 3. Diagram depicting the differences computed, over time, between [ẽ] and [ɛ]

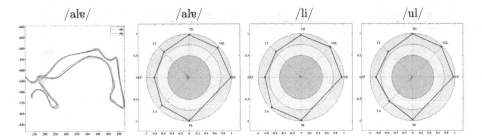

Fig. 4. Variability among multiple realisations of /l/. Each diagram obtained considering data for a single speaker and the same syllable position and vocalic context. From left to right, for speaker SV, contours for all realisations of /alɐ/ and corresponding difference diagram and, for speaker CM, difference diagrams for all realisations of /li/ and /ul/.

Due to the limited space, the description provided regarding the quantitative framework is, necessarily, brief. For additional details regarding the framework, in particular regarding the methods used to compute the differences, the reader is forwarded to [18]. For details regarding the application of the framework to assess articulatory differences, by considering multiple realisations of the same utterance, the reader is forwarded to [17,16].

3   Results

The quantitative framework for comparing vocal tract configurations was used to analyse both static and dynamic aspects of the production of /l/.

3.1   Comparison at One Time Point

A first analysis was performed by comparing the frames where alveolar contact for the production of /l/ was established. The frames of interest were automatically selected by the algorithm.

Aiming at gathering initial information on the validity of the method and on the consistency of the productions, the first aspect assessed concerned how multiple realisations of /l/ compared to each other. Figure 4 shows several difference diagrams for /l/ in different word positions and vocalic contexts. As can be observed, for each case, no notable differences occur, being all differences in the outer (green) circular corona.

To investigate the usually reported syllable position effects on the /l/, figure 5 presents vocal tract profiles and the corresponding difference diagram for the /l/ in different positions, in [i] context, for speaker CM. It additionally shows difference diagrams regarding positional effects for speaker SV. For both speakers, there are no noticeable differences between the /l/ in initial and final position, regardless of the vowel considered. The major adjustments occur between intervocalic and the other word positions analysed, in [i] context.

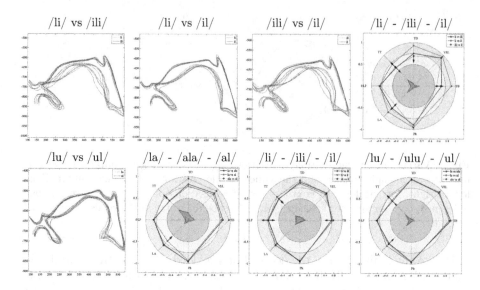

Fig. 5. Syllable positional effects. On the top row, for speaker CM, the contours for the pairs /li/ vs /ili/, /li/ vs /il/ and /ili/ vs /il/, followed by the difference diagram for the three comparisons. On the bottom row, for speaker SV, the contours for /lu/ vs /ul/, and the difference diagrams for all considered vowels.

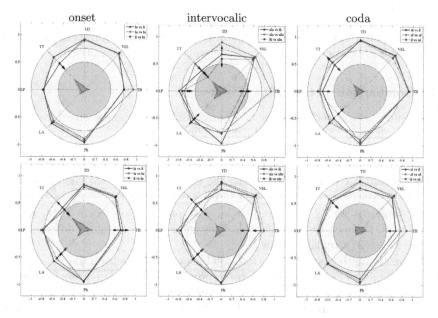

Fig. 6. Vocalic context. Difference diagrams for the influence of vocalic context, for each word position, for speakers CM (top) and SV (bottom).

As it is also relevant to investigate the influence of the vocalic context on the /l/, figure 6 shows that /l/ is not immune to the effect of adjacent vowel, but these effects are similar in initial and final position, for both speakers. In intervocalic context, the coarticulation of /l/ with the vowel is more noticeable.

3.2 Dynamic

Regarding dynamic aspects, the top row of figure 7 shows, on the left, the vocal tract contours along the production of [sal], illustrating the data available for analysis and, on the right, a difference diagram, depicting the overall data for the comparison among the multiple realisations of /alɐ/. It shows that the multiple realisations follow the same pattern (all lines are in the green region), with some variability at the start, for the tongue tip and, at the middle, for lip aperture. On the bottom row, figure 7 depicts the differences found along one realisation of /il/ and /ul/, using the first frame of each utterance as reference. This shows how the vocal tract differences evolve, along the production, from the initial vocal tract configuration. Noteworthy are the differences at the tongue tip and lip aperture, for both, and at the tongue back for /il/.

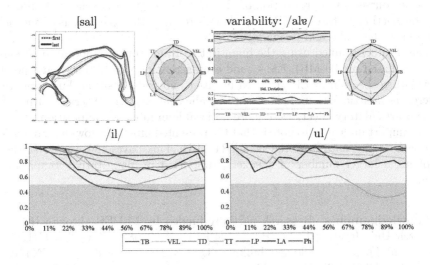

Fig. 7. Top row: left, vocal tract contours obtained during the production of [sal]; right, diagrams depicting differences found, over time, for all realisations of /alɐ/. Bottom row: differences computed along the production of /il/ and /ul/ using the first frame of each as reference.

4   Conclusions

Considering the three goals set for our work, these have been successfully attained. The segmentation method provided very good results with only some minor issues, resulting from the noisy nature of the images. For example, when the tongue back was near the pharyngeal wall, that segment of the vocal tract profile tended to slightly diverge. During analysis, those few segmentations that were not correct were detected and manually removed from the data.

Regarding the quantitative framework, overall, it allows dealing with the data for the laterals, easily encompassing, in the analysis, data from multiple realisations. All the analysis is run, unsupervised, generating figures with the considered contours, for debugging, and the difference diagrams. Selection of the data to analyse is performed based on the audio annotations. By changing them, e.g., using different criteria to annotate the VCV segments, a new analysis can be performed.

A few aspects of using the quantitative framework, to analyse laterals, motivate some ideas that might be explored. For example, the way the tongue tip differences are computed, results in very large differences being reported for small spatial differences. On one hand, this is an important characteristic, since it enhances the visibility of such differences, but it might help to test different approaches, possibly based on the sounds involved: comparing the tongue tip position between [a] and [u] might be treated differently than comparing between two realisations of /l/, or additional features might be computed [19].

Regarding dynamic information, one important aspect would be to analyse the time course of the production of /l/, in order to quantify relative timing of the constriction gestures of EP /l/ [19]. This requires that the data is annotated using both the audio and image frames [13].

The results obtained using the quantitative framework corroborate previous findings, based on 3D MRI, EMA (and even acoustic) data [7,10,11], and point to a dark realisation of EP /l/ both in onset and coda position. Furthermore, differences in articulation of /l/, due to vocalic context, were observed, although these coarticulatory effects were more noticeable in intervocalic position.

One important aspect to note is that the presented pipeline allows a systematic approach to the data acquired using RT-MRI. This paves the way to studies involving a larger number of speakers, supported in quantitative comparable data.

Acknowledgements. Research partially funded by FEDER through IEETA Research Unit funding FCOMP-01-0124-FEDER-022682 (FCT-PEst-C/EEI/-UI0127/2011), project Cloud Thinking (QREN Mais Centro, ref. CENTRO-07-ST24-FEDER-002031) and Marie Curie Actions IRIS (ref. 610986, FP7-PEOPLE-2013-IAPP).

References

1. Boersma, P., Weenink, D.: Praat: doing phonetics by computer (computer program). version 5.3.42 (June 2014), http://www.praat.org/
2. Bresch, E., Katsamanis, A., Goldstein, L., Narayanan, S.: Statistical multistream modeling of real-time MRI articulatory speech data. In: Proc. Interspeech, Makuhari, Japan, pp. 1584–1587 (2010)

3. Browman, C.P., Goldstein, L.: Gestural syllable position effects in American English. In: Producing Speech: Contemporary Issues, pp. 19–33 (1995)
4. Engwall, O.: A revisit to the application of MRI to the analysis of speech production - testing our assumptions. In: Proc. ISSP, Sydney, Australia, pp. 43–48 (2003)
5. Gick, B.: Articulatory correlates of ambisyllabicity in English glides and liquids. In: Local, J., Ogden, R., Temple, R. (eds.) Papers in Laboratory Phonology VI: Constrains on Phonetic Interpretation, pp. 222–236. Cambridge University Press, Cambridge (2003)
6. Hagedorn, C., Proctor, M.I., Goldstein, L.: Automatic analysis of singleton and geminate consonant articulation using Real-Time Magnetic Resonance Imaging. In: Proc. Interspeech, Florence, Italy, pp. 409–412 (2011)
7. Martins, P., Oliveira, C., Silva, A., Teixeira, A.: Articulatory characteristics of European Portuguese Laterals: An 2D and 3D MRI Study. In: FALA 2010, Vigo, Spain (2010)
8. Martins, P., Oliveira, C., Silva, S., Teixeira, A.: Velar movement in European Portuguese nasal vowels. In: Proc. IberSpeech — VII Jornadas en Tecnología del Habla and III Iberian SLTech Workshop, Madrid, Spain, pp. 231–240 (2012)
9. Narayanan, S., Alwan, A., Haker, K.: Toward articulatory-acoustic models for liquid approximants based on MRI and EPG data. Part I. The laterals. Journal of the Acoustical Society of America (JASA) 101(2), 1064–1077 (1997)
10. Oliveira, C., Martins, P., Marques, I., Couto, P., Teixeira, A.: An articulatory and acoustic study of European Portuguese. In: Proc. 17th Int. Congress of Phonetic Sciences (ICPhS 2011), Hong Kong (2011)
11. Oliveira, C., Teixeira, A., Martins, P.: Towards an articulatory characterization of European Portuguese /l/. In: Proc. 3rd ExLing, Athens, Greece (2010)
12. Pratt, W.K.: Digital Image Processing. Wiley-Interscience (2007)
13. Proctor, M., Goldstein, L., Lammert, A., Byrd, D., Toutios, A., Narayanan, S.: Velic Coordination in French Nasals: a Real-time Magnetic Resonance Imaging Study. In: Proc. Interspeech, Lyon, France, pp. 577–581 (2013)
14. Scott, A.D., Wylezinska, M., Birch, M.J., Miquel, M.E.: Speech MRI: Morphology and function. Physica Medica (in press, 2014)
15. Silva, S., Teixeira, A.: AAM based vocal tract segmentation from real-time MRI image sequences. In: Proc. RecPad, Lisbon, Portugal (2013)
16. Silva, S., Teixeira, A.: RT-MRI based dynamic analysis of vocal tract configurations: Preliminary work regarding intra- and inter-sound variability. In: Proc. ISSP, Cologne, Germany, pp. 399–402 (2014)
17. Silva, S., Teixeira, A.: Systematic and quantitative analysis of vocal tract data: Intra- and inter-speaker analysis. In: Proc. ISSP, Cologne, Germany, pp. 403–406 (2014)
18. Silva, S., Teixeira, A., Oliveira, C., Martins, P.: Towards a systematic and quantitative analysis of vocal tract data. In: Proc. Interspeech, Lyon, France, pp. 1307–1311 (2013)
19. Smith, C.: Complex tongue shaping in lateral liquid production without constriction-based goals. In: Proc. ISSP, Cologne, Germany, pp. 413–416 (2014)
20. Sproat, R., Fujimura, O.: Allophonic variation in English /l/ and its implications for phonetic implementation. Journal of Phonetics 21, 291–311 (1993)
21. Teixeira, A., Martins, P., Oliveira, C., Ferreira, C., Silva, A., Shosted, R.: Real-time MRI for Portuguese: database, methods and applications. In: Caseli, H., Villavicencio, A., Teixeira, A., Perdigão, F. (eds.) PROPOR 2012. LNCS (LNAI), vol. 7243, pp. 306–317. Springer, Heidelberg (2012)
22. Zhou, X.: An MRI-Based articulatory and acoustic study of American English liquid souns /r/ and /l/. PhD thesis, University of Maryland, USA (2009)

Statistical Text-to-Speech Synthesis of Spanish Subtitles

S. Piqueras, M.A. del-Agua, A. Giménez,
J. Civera, and A. Juan

MLLP, DSIC, Universitat Politècnica de València,
Camí de Vera s/n, 46022, València, Spain
{spiqueras,mdelagua,agimenez,jcivera,ajuan}@dsic.upv.es

Abstract. Online multimedia repositories are growing rapidly. However, language barriers are often difficult to overcome for many of the current and potential users. In this paper we describe a TTS Spanish system and we apply it to the synthesis of transcribed and translated video lectures. A statistical parametric speech synthesis system, in which the acoustic mapping is performed with either HMM-based or DNN-based acoustic models, has been developed. To the best of our knowledge, this is the first time that a DNN-based TTS system has been implemented for the synthesis of Spanish. A comparative objective evaluation between both models has been carried out. Our results show that DNN-based systems can reconstruct speech waveforms more accurately.

Keywords: video lectures, text-to-speech synthesis, accessibility.

1 Introduction

The proliferation of online video lecture repositories over recent years is a phenomenon hard to ignore. In particular, in the field of education, universities around the world are making a huge effort in the recording and publication of video lectures. Some of the most successful online video lecture repositories are TED talks [21], VideoLectures.NET [28], Coursera [2], and Khan Academy [4], to name just a few.

These repositories are opened on a global scale, but their monolingual content creates a language barrier that is difficult to overcome, driving away many potential users. Although the most popular video lectures in these repositories are manually transcribed and translated by dedicated users in a collaborative effort, manual subtitling cannot keep pace with the increasing rhythm of video generation on the long term. This subtitling process becomes even more cumbersome when dealing with talks that include highly specialized vocabulary.

Recent advances in automatic speech recognition (ASR) [7] and machine translation (MT) [5,13,15] have pushed the scientific community to tackle more challenging subtitling tasks related to large video lecture repositories. Indeed, current state-of-the-art ASR and MT systems can provide accurate enough subtitles that can be manually revised with minimum effort, saving time and money.

J.L. Navarro Mesa et al. (Eds.): IberSPEECH 2014, LNAI 8854, pp. 40–48, 2014.

In particular, the trans**Lectures** project [20] is aiming to develop high quality, cost-effective solutions for the transcription and translation of massive online repositories. This project has so far resulted in the release of the open-source trans**Lectures** -UPV toolkit [22]. Nevertheless, the availability of subtitles may not be enough to fully exploit video visualisation, since users are forced to split their attention between subtitles and lecture slides. In addition, visually impaired users cannot benefit from subtitles. In these cases, it would be much more convenient to be able to listen to the lecturer in the user's own language.

A text-to-speech (TTS) synthesizer is a system capable of generating an artificial speech track for a given text. State-of-the-art TTS systems usually employ one of two approaches: unit selection [11] or statistical parametric speech synthesis [34]. The TTS system presented here is based on the latter, as it is usually regarded as the most reliable synthesis approach when it comes to intelligibility [12], which is a key factor in our problem. However, the current reference Spanish TTS system publicly available only provides pre-trained HMM-based models [17].

In this work, two statistical TTS systems for Spanish are presented. The first of them is based on the conventional HMM acoustic modeling [30], while the second system implements state-of-the-art deep neural networks (DNN) for acoustic modeling [33]. These TTS systems were objectively evaluated on a real-life video-lecture repository. To the best of our knowledge, this evaluation has never been performed for the Spanish language. The best performing TTS system is intended to be applied to the generation of Spanish audio tracks on large video lecture repositories. The TTS-generated voice will be seamlessly integrated into the original video in order to allow users to concentrate on the video lecture content, keeping them from having to read subtitles.

The rest of this paper is organized as follows. Firstly, an overview of a TTS system is depicted in Section 2. Then, TTS systems, both HMM-based and DNN-based, are described in Section 3. Next, results on the objective evaluation with both TTS systems are reported in Section 4. Finally, concluding remarks and future research lines are wrapped up in Section 5.

2   System Overview

In Figure 1 we provide an overview of the modules that make up our TTS system. We describe the modules involved in our system from the moment the subtitle file is received to the point the speech output is ready to be embedded.

In the first step, the subtitle file is divided into segments according to its timestamps. This division allows us to process large transcription files in parallel, and we will later concatenate the segments appropriately. Furthermore, silences between segments will not be passed to the synthesizer, so the generation is more efficient.

Segments are processed by the linguistic analysis module that has been developed for this work. The words are split into syllables, which are then converted to phonemes with a rule-based grapheme-to-phoneme algorithm. As Spanish

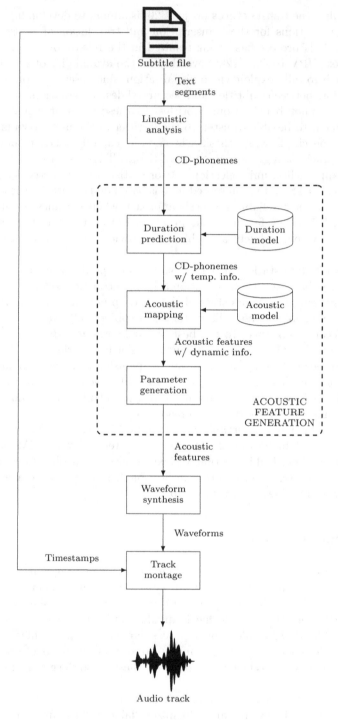

Fig. 1. System overview

orthography is highly phonemic, this conversion is carried out without much loss. Please note that while this approach can deal appropriately with Spanish words, it does not cover foreign words (e.g. proper nouns of people). The module also extracts contextual information of each phoneme, syllable and word, and then employs it to create context-dependent (CD) phonemes [31]. We have not included some of the higher-level features, which are used in other speech synthesizers, such as POS tagging, stress marks or ToBI endtones.

Next, an acoustic feature generation module converts the CD-phonemes into an acoustic parameter sequence. It is currently divided into three parts, which correspond to the duration generation module, the acoustic mapping module and the parameter generation module. These modules will be described in detail in Section 3.

The acoustic parameter sequence is then post-processed with a spectral enhancement algorithm and then sent to the vocoder to generate the audio segments. The vocoder's task is to reconstruct the speech waveforms from the acoustic parameter sequence. Our system uses a harmonics-plus-noise model based vocoder [8], and makes use of the free implementation provided by their authors [1]. In this vocoder, the spectral parameters are the Mel-frequency cepstral coefficients ($mfcc$), while the excitation parameters are the logarithm of the fundamental frequency ($\log F_0$), which determines the pitch, and the maximum voiced frequency (mvf).

The track montage module uses temporal annotations included in the subtitle file to create a new track by concatenating silence and synthesized audio segments. This track may later be embedded in the multimedia file as a side track, in order to allow the user to select their preferred language.

3   Acoustic Modeling

In this section, the two main approaches to acoustic modeling investigated in this work, HMM and DNN, are described in detail. The reader familiar with ASR should note that in TTS, in contrast to ASR, the acoustic modeling process tackles the reverse problem of mapping acoustic features to CD-phonemes.

3.1   HMM-Based

The conventional approach to acoustic modeling in speech synthesis is to perform the acoustic mapping through context-dependent Hidden Markov Models with explicit duration, also known as Hidden Semi-Markov Models (HSMMs). In the generation step, first the state durations for each phoneme are predicted by a Gaussian distribution model. Then, an HMM model is selected. Finally, the means and variances of the output acoustic parameter vector are generated by the HMM model. In order to avoid the discontinuities that would arise from a maximum likelihood approach, the acoustic parameter sequence is smoothed with the introduction of dynamic features and the use of the maximum likelihood parameter generation (MLPG) algorithm [24].

As CD-phonemes often have high dimensionality, training a CD-HMM for each possible combination of text analysis features is unrealistic and would result into poorly estimated HMMs. By way of solution, context clustering techniques at a state-level are used. Clustering is performed by means of binary decision trees. In the training phase, the Minimum Description Length (MDL) criterion is used to construct these decision trees [19]. The size of the trees can be controlled through the penalty term α (where α is typically set to 1). As the spectral and excitation parameters have different context dependency, separate trees are built for each one. This approach allows our model to handle unseen contexts.

An extra problem emerges from the modelization of the non-continuous parameters log F_0 and *mvf*. These parameters are defined in the regions known as "voiced", and undefined in the regions known as "unvoiced". Log F_0 has been modeled with a multi-space probability distribution [25], while the *mvf* parameter was added as an extra stream and modeled with a continuous distribution, as suggested in [8]. The *mvf* values were interpolated in the unvoiced frames.

3.2   DNN-Based

DNNs have been successfully applied to acoustic modeling in ASR tasks [10]. DNNs map frame features, including textual and temporal features, to acoustic features in a feed-forward approach. The textual information is composed of binary features, such as *is-current-syllable-accented*, and numerical features, such as *number-of-phonemes-in-current-word*. Four temporal features are defined, corresponding to the position of the current frame (forward and backward) in the current phoneme, the duration of the phoneme and the duration of the whole segment. Similar to the HSMMs method, the duration of the phonemes is predicted by an external Gaussian model. However, in contrast to HMM models, all the parameters for every possible CD-phoneme will be generated by the same network. This joint modeling procedure results in a more robust estimation, which produces better generalization [33].

In order to deal with the voiced/unvoiced (V/UV) discontinuity problem, a continuous explicit modeling approach has been used for both log F_0 and *mvf*. An extra bit of the output is used to classify the frame as voiced or unvoiced. To produce smoother parameter trajectories, the output includes dynamic information (first and second derivatives) of the parameter sequence. The network output is assumed to be the mean vector of a Gaussian posterior distribution, and is combined with a precomputed variance vector to generate the acoustic feature vector through the MLPG algorithm used in HMM synthesis. A single variance for each output is estimated from all the training samples.

4   Experimental Results

In this section, the corpus employed in our experiments is described. Then, the evaluation measures are presented along with the experimental setup. Finally, comparative results between HMM-based and DNN-based TTS systems are reported and discussed.

4.1 Corpus Description

The data used for our experiments has been extracted from the poli[Media] repository, which contains over 2,000 hours of video lectures. poli[Media] is a recent, innovative service for the creation and distribution of multimedia educational content at the UPV [16,27] mostly in Spanish, but also in Catalan and English. It is primarily designed to allow UPV lecturers to record their courses in short videos lasting up to 10 minutes, accompanied by time-aligned slides.

The production process of a poli[Media] repository has been carefully designed to achieve both a high rate of production and a fine quality, comparable to a TV production but at a lower cost. However, this repository was not specifically recorded with synthesizer training in mind, and so audio conditions are far from perfect. Furthermor, the recordings contain speaker hesitations, unfinished words and various noises (i.e. coughs).

The complete poli[Media] repository has been automatically transcribed using the open-source ASR system called transLectures-UPV toolkit [22]. In order to train this ASR system, a set of 100 hours of video lectures were manually transcribed. From this set, a subset of 40 videos with 2320 utterances by a single male native Spanish speaker was selected. After removing the silences from the videos, 6 hours of speech remain for our experiments.

From this subset, 49 utterances were used for testing purposes. The remaining 2271 utterances were used to train the HMM-based system. In the case of the DNN-based system, 2171 utterances were devoted to pretraining and fine-tuning stages, while 100 utterances were reserved as a validation set in order to avoid overfitting. Phoneme alignments were automatically performed by the best acoustic model deployed in the transLectures project at month 24 [26].

4.2 Evaluation Measures

The comparative evaluation of our TTS systems was performed in terms of well-known objective error measures. These measures are mean Mel-cepstral distortion [14] (MMCD), voiced/unvoiced error rate and root mean squared error (RMSE) in log F_0. In the latter case, the RMSE was only computed for the frames where the system had correctly guessed whether the frame was voiced or unvoiced. Phoneme durations were set to match those from the natural speech, rather than being generated by the Gaussian model described in Section 3.

It should be noticed that while these objective values are frequently used in the TTS research field to compare the performance of the acoustic models, they do not perfectly correlate with the naturalness of the synthesized speech [23].

4.3 Experimental Setup

For training purposes, audio was extracted from the video and downsampled from 44100Hz to 16000Hz. Every 5 milliseconds, 40 Mel-cepstral coefficients, log F_0 and maximum voiced frequency values were extracted using AhoCoder tools [1]. The *mvf* parameter was interpolated in the unvoiced regions for both models, while the log F_0 was interpolated for the DNN explicit voicing. The acoustic parameter vectors were then augmented with the information of the first and second derivatives. The textual analysis information was the same for both models.

The HMM system was composed of 5-state, no-skip models with diagonal co-variance matrices. A total of 1017 different questions were used for the construction of the decision trees. For comparison purposes, we trained 3 HMM-based systems modifying the parameter α which controls the number of nodes of the decision trees (with $\alpha = 0.5$, 1.0 and 2.0). The training was performed using the most recent stable version (2.2) of the the HMM-based Speech Synthesis System (HTS) [3].

In the case of the DNN-based system, the number of neurons in the input layer was 169, while the number of neurons in the output layer was 127, corresponding to 39 *mfcc* plus energy, log F_0, *mvf*, first and second derivatives and the V/UV bit. Inputs to the DNN were normalized to have zero mean and one variance, while outputs were normalized between 0.01 and 0.99. Different neural network sizes were tested by changing the number of hidden layers (1, 2, 3 or 4) and the number of neurons per layer (128, 256, 512 or 1024). The sigmoid activation function was used in the hidden and output layers. Neural networks with more than one hidden layer were pretrained using a discriminative approach [18], and then fine-tuned with a stochastic minibatch backpropagation algorithm [6]. The error criterion in both steps was the mean squared error (MSE). The training was performed with a CUDA-based GPU implementation, part of a development version of the trans**Lectures** toolkit.

4.4   Results and Discussion

Table 1 shows the objective evaluation measures computed for each DNN configuration, together with the results of the best HMM model. For every DNN configuration, the optimal number of neurons per layer has been selected so that the evaluation measure is optimized. We can see that DNN-based systems systematically achieve better results in every measure than HMM-based systems. The optimal number of layers is unclear, since the evaluation measures exhibit different behaviour. The V/UV error rate performs better when using simpler architectures, while the spectral parameters benefit more from a complex architecture.

Table 1. Comparison between HMM-based and DNN-based acoustic models

System	# layers	RMSE log F_0	MMCD	V/UV Error rate
HMM	-	0.190	6.987	13.35
DNN	1	0.183	6.792	12.08
	2	0.183	6.702	12.27
	3	0.184	6.678	12.36
	4	0.184	6.679	12.42

5   Conclusions and Future Work

We have presented a novel text-to-speech system for the synthesis of Spanish subtitles in video lectures. We have reviewed the statistical speech synthesis framework and discussed why it is appropriate for our task. We have described the whole system and presented two different approaches to performing acoustic mapping: HMM-based and DNN-based. We have performed a series of experiments to compare the performance of both approaches. Objective measures show that the best DNN systems consistently outperform the HMM systems.

Currently, our next steps include the training of a female Spanish voice and the integration of the system in the UPV video lecture platform poli[Media]. Once integrated, subjective evaluation of the intelligibility and naturalness of the voices will be carried out. Future work also includes the exploration of other network topologies [9], incorporating variance modeling into the DNNs [32], cross-lingual speaker adaptation [29] and a more in-depth linguistic analysis.

Acknowledgments. The research leading to these results has received funding from the European Union Seventh Framework Programme (FP7/2007-2013) under grant agreement no 287755 (trans**Lectures**) and ICT Policy Support Programme (ICT PSP/2007-2013) as part of the Competitiveness and Innovation Framework Programme (CIP) under grant agreement no 621030 (EMMA), and the Spanish MINECO Active2Trans (TIN2012-31723) research project.

References

1. Ahocoder, `http://aholab.ehu.es/ahocoder`
2. Coursera, `http://www.coursera.org`
3. HMM-Based Speech Synthesis System (HTS), `http://hts.sp.nitech.ac.jp`
4. Khan Academy, `http://www.khanacademy.org`
5. Axelrod, A., He, X., Gao, J.: Domain adaptation via pseudo in-domain data selection. In: Proc. of EMNLP, pp. 355–362 (2011)
6. Bottou, L.: Stochastic gradient learning in neural networks. In: Proceedings of Neuro-Nîmes 1991. EC2, Nimes, France (1991)
7. Dahl, G.E., Yu, D., Deng, L., Acero, A.: Context-dependent pre-trained deep neural networks for large-vocabulary speech recognition. IEEE Transactions on Audio, Speech, and Language Processing 20(1), 30–42 (2012)
8. Erro, D., Sainz, I., Navas, E., Hernaez, I.: Harmonics plus noise model based vocoder for statistical parametric speech synthesis. IEEE Journal of Selected Topics in Signal Processing 8(2), 184–194 (2014)
9. Fan, Y., Qian, Y., Xie, F., Soong, F.: TTS synthesis with bidirectional LSTM based recurrent neural networks. In: Proc. of Interspeech (submitted 2014)
10. Hinton, G., Deng, L., Yu, D., Dahl, G.E., Mohamed, A.R., Jaitly, N., Senior, A., Vanhoucke, V., Nguyen, P., Sainath, T.N., et al.: Deep neural networks for acoustic modeling in speech recognition: The shared views of four research groups. IEEE Signal Processing Magazine 29(6), 82–97 (2012)
11. Hunt, A.J., Black, A.W.: Unit selection in a concatenative speech synthesis system using a large speech database. In: Proc. of ICASSP, vol. 1, pp. 373–376 (1996)

12. King, S.: Measuring a decade of progress in text-to-speech. Loquens 1(1), e006 (2014)
13. Koehn, P.: Statistical Machine Translation. Cambridge University Press (2010)
14. Kominek, J., Schultz, T., Black, A.W.: Synthesizer voice quality of new languages calibrated with mean mel cepstral distortion. In: Proc. of SLTU, pp. 63–68 (2008)
15. Lopez, A.: Statistical machine translation. ACM Computing Surveys 40(3), 8:1–8:49 (2008)
16. poliMedia: The polimedia video-lecture repository (2007), http://media.upv.es
17. Sainz, I., Erro, D., Navas, E., Hernáez, I., Sánchez, J., Saratxaga, I.: Aholab speech synthesizer for albayzin 2012 speech synthesis evaluation. In: Proc. of Iber-SPEECH, pp. 645–652 (2012)
18. Seide, F., Li, G., Chen, X., Yu, D.: Feature engineering in context-dependent dnn for conversational speech transcription. In: Proc. of ASRU, pp. 24–29 (2011)
19. Shinoda, K., Watanabe, T.: MDL-based context-dependent subword modeling for speech recognition. Journal of the Acoustical Society of Japan 21(2), 79–86 (2000)
20. Silvestre-Cerdà, J.A., et al.: Translectures. In: Proc. of IberSPEECH, pp. 345–351 (2012)
21. TED Ideas worth spreading, http://www.ted.com
22. The transLectures-UPV Team.: The transLectures-UPV toolkit (TLK), http://translectures.eu/tlk
23. Toda, T., Black, A.W., Tokuda, K.: Mapping from articulatory movements to vocal tract spectrum with Gaussian mixture model for articulatory speech synthesis. In: Proc. of ISCA Speech Synthesis Workshop (2004)
24. Tokuda, K., Kobayashi, T., Imai, S.: Speech parameter generation from hmm using dynamic features. In: Proc. of ICASSP, vol. 1, pp. 660–663 (1995)
25. Tokuda, K., Masuko, T., Miyazaki, N., Kobayashi, T.: Multi-space probability distribution HMM. IEICE Transactions on Information and Systems 85(3), 455–464 (2002)
26. transLectures: D3.1.2: Second report on massive adaptation, http://www.translectures.eu/wp-content/uploads/2014/01/transLectures-D3.1.2-15Nov2013.pdf
27. Turró, C., Ferrando, M., Busquets, J., Cañero, A.: Polimedia: a system for successful video e-learning. In: Proc. of EUNIS (2009)
28. Videolectures.NET: Exchange ideas and share knowledge, http://www.videolectures.net
29. Wu, Y.J., King, S., Tokuda, K.: Cross-lingual speaker adaptation for HMM-based speech synthesis. In: Proc. of ISCSLP, pp. 1–4 (2008)
30. Yamagishi, J.: An introduction to HMM-based speech synthesis. Tech. rep. Centre for Speech Technology Research (2006), https://wiki.inf.ed.ac.uk/twiki/pub/CSTR/TrajectoryModelling/HTS-Introduction.pdf
31. Yoshimura, T., Tokuda, K., Masuko, T., Kobayashi, T., Kitamura, T.: Simultaneous modeling of spectrum, pitch and duration in HMM-based speech synthesis. In: Proc. of Eurospeech, pp. 2347–2350 (1999)
32. Zen, H., Senior, A.: Deep mixture density networks for acoustic modeling in statistical parametric speech synthesis. In: Proc. of ICASSP, pp. 3872–3876 (2014)
33. Zen, H., Senior, A., Schuster, M.: Statistical parametric speech synthesis using deep neural networks. In: Proc. of ICASSP, pp. 7962–7966 (2013)
34. Zen, H., Tokuda, K., Black, A.W.: Statistical parametric speech synthesis. Speech Communication 51(11), 1039–1064 (2009)

Unsupervised Accent Modeling for Language Identification

David Martínez González, Jesús Villalba López, Eduardo Lleida Solano,
and Alfonso Ortega Gimenez

ViVoLab Speech Technologies Group, University of Zaragoza, Spain
{david,villalba,lleida,ortega}@unizar.es
http://www.vivolab.es

Abstract. In this paper we propose to cluster iVectors to model different accents within a language. The motivation is that not all the speakers
of the same language have the same pronunciation style. This source of
variability is not usually considered in state-of-the-art language identification systems, and we show that taking it into account helps. For each
language, the iVector space is partitioned according to the similarity of
the iVectors, and each cluster is considered a different accent. Then, a
simplified probabilistic linear discriminant analysis model is trained with
all the accents, and during the test, each utterance is evaluated against
all of them. The highest score of each language is selected to make decisions. The experiment was carried out on 6 languages of the 2011 NIST
LRE dataset. For the 30 s condition, the relative improvement over the
baseline was of 11%.

Keywords: Language identification, accent modeling, iVector, agglomerative hierarchical clustering, PLDA.

1 Introduction

One of the most important problems in language identification (LID) is that
features contain, not only language, but many other types of information. For
example, we can find variability due to the communication channel, to the speech
message, to the speaker voice characteristics, or to his/her state of mood. Therefore, we need to find methods for keeping only the language information and
taking off all the information which is not related with the language.

One important source of variability within a language is accent. It is defined
as a way of pronouncing a language associated to a particular country, area, social class, or person. In a standard LID system, this variability can be harmful.
However, in the speech recognition community there have been efforts to model
and compensate this factor with successful results [1], and we think that LID
systems can also take advantage of the same idea. A similar approach was presented in [2], where several models per language were trained in a phonotactic
LID system. Each model reflected specific characteristics, like a foreign accent or
a dialect. They clustered the data in a supervised way with labels. The multiple
scores of a given language were combined with a linear fusion.

J.L. Navarro Mesa et al. (Eds.): IberSPEECH 2014, LNAI 8854, pp. 49–58, 2014.
© Springer International Publishing Switzerland 2014

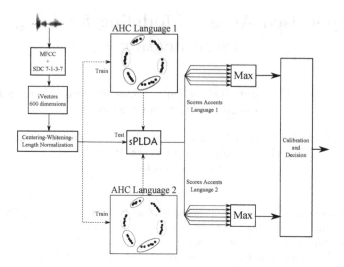

Fig. 1. Architecture of a LID system with accent modeling

In our approach, we partitioned the iVector space [3] in an unsupervised way and assumed each cluster within a language as belonging to a different accent. Once we detected all the accent clusters, a simplified probabilistic linear discriminant analysis (sPLDA) classifier [4,5] was used to make language decisions.

The paper is organized as follows: in Section 2, we describe the new classifier based on accent modeling; in Section 3, the experiments and results are presented; and in Section 4, we discuss the results and draw conclusions.

2   System Architecture

The main idea of this paper is that there are different accents within a language, and a single unimodal model will not capture this variability. In our proposal, we first clustered the iVectors of each language according to their proximity. Then, we considered that each cluster represents a different accent. Next, a sPLDA model was trained with those labels, and finally, all the accent models were evaluated against the test utterance. For each language, the highest score was selected, and decisions were made with them. The classification method is similar to the speaker identification problem. The system architecture is depicted in Figure 1 for two target languages.

2.1   Feature Extraction

The speech signal was processed in frames of 25 ms long and shifted every 10 ms. 7 mel-frequency cepstral coefficients (MFCC) including C0 were extracted at each frame. Vocal tract length normalization (VTLN), cepstral mean and variance normalization (CMVN), and RASTA filtering were applied over the MFCCs. Then, shifted delta cepstra (SDC) were computed over the MFCCs with configuration 7-1-3-7, to obtain a final vector of 56 dimensions at each frame.

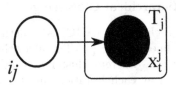

Fig. 2. Graphical model of the iVector approach

2.2 iVector Extraction

Joint factor analysis (JFA) allows coding all the acoustic information contained in an utterance in a single fixed-length low-dimension vector [3]. The MFCCs of utterance j are assumed to follow a Gaussian mixture model (GMM) distribution with mean supervector, $\mathbf{M}_j$, modeled as

$$\mathbf{M}_j = \mathbf{m}_0 + \mathbf{T}\mathbf{i}_j, \qquad (1)$$

where $\mathbf{m}_0$ is the universal background model (UBM) mean, $\mathbf{T}$ is a low-rank factor loading matrix, which spans a subspace containing all types of variability in the signal, including language, and $\mathbf{i}_j$, commonly known as iVector, is a segment-specific vector lying in this subspace, modeled with standard normal prior. Unlike traditional factor analysis [6], where the latent variable $\mathbf{i}$ is different for every frame within an utterance, in the iVector approach, it is tied to the whole utterance. Figure 2 shows the corresponding graphical model, with T_j being the total number of frames of utterance j, and x_t^j the MFCC of frame t of utterance j.

iVectors are the new features used to make classification. Simple classifiers can be built upon iVectors, thanks to their low-dimensionality. One of the most successful consists of a Gaussian distribution trained for each target language with maximum likelihood [7].

2.3 Centering, Whitening, and Length Normalization

Length normalization of iVectors was found necessary in order to make the clustering work successfully. The normalization consists in dividing each iVector by its module, so the resulting vector is unit-length. This step was very useful in [8] to remove biases between training, development, and test datasets.

Previous to the normalization, iVectors must be centered and whitened. The centering means the subtraction of the global mean of all training iVectors to each iVector, so they end up centered at the origin of coordinates. The whitening is a decorrelation transformation that converts the global covariance of the training iVectors into the identity matrix. After these two operations, iVectors are uncorrelated and lying evenly distributed around the origin. After length normalization, they are placed in the unit hypersphere, evenly distributed around the origin. If no centering and whitening were applied, they would be concentrated in a small region of the unit hypersphere, without any discriminative power for classification.

2.4 Agglomerative Hierarchical Clustering

Agglomerative hierarchical clustering (AHC) is a method for grouping similar vectors according to a defined metric [9]. The algorithm follows a bottom-up strategy, where every file is a different cluster at the beginning, and the two closest vectors are grouped at each iteration, until a total of K clusters are formed, with K being defined by the user.

In our problem, the cosine distance was used as similarity metric. Each time a new cluster was built, it was represented by the average of the iVectors belonging to that cluster. The clustering algorithm was run for each language separately. At the end, we assumed that each cluster represented a different accent, but note that the partition is unsupervised. The interesting idea is that iVectors with similar acoustic characteristics are grouped together.

2.5 Simplified Probabilistic Linear Discriminant Analysis

Once a set of K clusters or accents were found for each language, a single sPLDA model was trained with them. During the test phase, each utterance was evaluated against all the accents, and for each language, the score of the most similar one was selected by a *Max* block (see Figure 1). Thus, one score per target language passed to the calibration block.

sPLDA assumes that iVectors are generated according to a model $\mathcal{M}$ [4,5]. Then, the iVector $\mathbf{i}_j$ of utterance j can be written as

$$\mathbf{i}_j = \mu + \mathbf{V}\mathbf{y}_s + \epsilon, \tag{2}$$

where μ is a language independent term, $\mathbf{V}$ is a low-rank factor loading matrix, $\mathbf{y}_s$ is the n_y-dimension accent factor of accent s, and ϵ is a channel offset. The following prior distributions are assumed

$$\mathbf{y} \sim \mathcal{N}(\mathbf{y}|\mathbf{0}, \mathbf{I}). \tag{3} \qquad\qquad \epsilon \sim \mathcal{N}(\epsilon|\mathbf{0}, \mathbf{W}^{-1}), \tag{4}$$

with $\mathbf{W}$ the within-class precision matrix. The training of this generative model is performed with the EM algorithm.

To evaluate the model, we calculate the ratio between the posterior probabilities of enrollment and test iVectors, under the hypothesis that they belong to the same accent, $\mathcal{S}$, and under the hypothesis that they belong to different accents, $\mathcal{D}$,

$$R(\mathbf{i}_{\text{enr}}, \mathbf{i}_{\text{test}}, \mathcal{M}) = \frac{P(\mathbf{i}_{\text{enr}}, \mathbf{i}_{\text{test}}|\mathcal{S}, \mathcal{M})}{P(\mathbf{i}_{\text{enr}}, \mathbf{i}_{\text{test}}|\mathcal{D}, \mathcal{M})} = \frac{Q(\mathbf{i}_{\text{enr}}, \mathbf{i}_{\text{test}})}{Q(\mathbf{i}_{\text{enr}})Q(\mathbf{i}_{\text{test}})}, \tag{5}$$

where

$$Q(\mathbf{i}) = \frac{P(\mathbf{y}_0|\mathcal{M})}{P(\mathbf{y}_0|\mathbf{i}, \mathcal{M})}. \tag{6}$$

Note that the enrollment iVectors are the unsupervised accents found in training. For simplicity, $\mathbf{y}_0$ is chosen to be equal to $\mathbf{0}$, $P(\mathbf{y}_0|\mathcal{M})$ is given in Eq. (3), and $P(\mathbf{y}|\mathbf{i}_s, \mathcal{M}) = \mathcal{N}(\mathbf{y}|\mathbf{L}^{-1}\gamma, \mathbf{L}^{-1})$ as shown in [4,5], where

$$\mathbf{L} = \mathbf{I} + N_s \mathbf{V}^T \mathbf{W} \mathbf{V}, \tag{7} \qquad\qquad \gamma = \mathbf{V}^T \mathbf{W} \mathbf{F}_s. \tag{8}$$

$\mathbf{N}_s$ is the zeroth order statistic for accent s, that is, the number of observations of accent s, and $\mathbf{F}_s$ is the first order statistic,

$$\mathbf{F}_s = \sum_{j=1}^{\mathbf{N}_s} \mathbf{i}_{js}. \tag{9}$$

2.6 Calibration

The calibration block consists of a generative Gaussian backend followed by a discriminative multiclass logistic regression. The Gaussian backend consists in a Gaussian distribution for each target language trained over the scores given by the *Max* blocks. The means are the means of the scores of each language, and the covariance is shared among all Gaussian models, and it is equal to the within class covariance matrix of all the scores. The multiclass logistic regression transforms the scores coming from the Gaussian backend into meaningful log-likelihoods by optimizing an objective function called *multiclass C_{llr}*. The multiclass logistic regression also allows fusing several systems at the same time of the calibration. Once we apply this transformation, cost-effective Bayes decisions can be taken. MultiFocal toolkit is used to train and test the calibration backend [10].

3 Experiments

3.1 Experimental Setup

In this part, we show results of our new classification paradigm based on accent modeling, and compare it with the traditional state-of-the-art techniques. The experiments were conducted over 6 languages of the 2011 NIST LRE evaluation dataset: English, Farsi, Hindi, Mandarin, Russian, and Spanish. The reason of this selection is that those are the 6 languages for which we could collect 20 h of training data and 1 h of development data. We wanted an experimental scenario where training and development data were balanced among target languages. The databases with hours of speech and number of utterances used for training, development, and test are reflected in Tables 1, 2, and 3, respectively. VOA3 received an especial processing explained in [11]. The evaluation data is composed of conversational telephone speech (CTS) and broadcast narrowband speech (BNBS) [12]. In order to cover both types of channel, in training, VOA3 is BNBS and the rest of datasets (LRE03-05-07, CALLFRIEND, OHSU, SRE04-06-08) are CTS, and in development, VOA3 and part of LRE09 are BNBS, and the other part of LRE09 and LRE07e are CTS.

The iVector extractor included a 2048-component UBM, and a 600-dimension total variability subspace. The train dataset was used to train the iVector extractor, to obtain the centering and whitening transformation, and to find the accents by AHC. Finally, the sPLDA parameters were trained with them. They were also used as enrollment data in the test phase, as commented in Section 2.5. The development data was used to train the Gaussian backend and the discriminative calibration.

Table 1. Training Data

Language	Total #	Total hrs	CTS #	CTS hrs	BNBS #	BNBS hrs
English	1412	21.67	1280	19.86	132	1.81
Farsi	1375	19.12	830	14.45	545	4.67
Hindi	1376	21.89	1153	17.51	223	4.38
Mandarin	1357	21.31	1068	19.99	289	1.32
Russian	1367	21.89	680	17.44	687	4.45
Spanish	1473	20.94	1173	17.64	300	3.30

Table 2. Development Data

Language	Total #	Total hrs	CTS #	CTS hrs	BNBS #	BNBS hrs
English	300	0.97	98	0.37	202	0.60
Farsi	300	0.95	65	0.23	235	0.72
Hindi	300	0.96	79	0.31	221	0.65
Mandarin	310	1.00	102	0.39	208	0.61
Russian	300	0.92	90	0.33	210	0.59
Spanish	310	0.95	65	0.23	245	0.72

Table 3. 2011 NIST LRE Test Data

Language	total.3 #	total.3 hrs	total.10 #	total.10 hrs	total.30 #	total.30 hrs	cts.3 #	cts.3 hrs	cts.10 #	cts.10 hrs	cts.30 #	cts.30 hrs	bnbs.3 #	bnbs.3 hrs	bnbs.10 #	bnbs.10 hrs	bnbs.30 #	bnbs.30 hrs
English	452	0.29	683	1.71	221	1.44	121	0.06	121	0.22	121	0.75	331	0.22	562	1.49	100	0.69
Farsi	405	0.24	406	0.81	404	2.68	197	0.12	197	0.40	197	1.33	208	0.12	209	0.41	207	1.35
Hindi	418	0.26	621	1.54	215	1.44	70	0.04	70	0.13	70	0.45	348	0.22	551	1.41	145	0.99
Mandarin	432	0.26	504	1.18	360	1.34	259	0.15	259	0.50	259	1.64	173	0.11	245	0.68	101	0.70
Russian	441	0.28	441	0.95	441	3.10	139	0.08	139	0.28	139	0.91	302	0.20	302	0.67	302	2.19
Spanish	419	0.25	419	0.86	419	2.82	231	0.13	231	0.44	231	1.45	188	0.12	188	0.42	188	1.37

3.2 Results of the LID with Accent Modeling Classifier

The results in Figures 3, 4, and 5 are shown for the 30 s, 10 s, and 3 s tasks, respectively, in terms of C_{avg}, an error metric defined in [13]. Results are reported over the evaluation dataset. In this experiment, we investigated the influence of the number of accents per language, K, and of the dimension of the accent subspace in the sPLDA model, n_y. Note that in order to find a subspace of n_y dimensions, we need a minimum of n_y accents. Therefore, since we have 6 target languages, and the variable K indicates the number of accents per language, the relationship $6K \geq n_y$ must hold. Our baseline was an iVector system with Gaussian classifier [7]. Except for the classifier, the rest was identical to the proposed system. It can be observed that the general behavior of the two classifiers was similar. However, we can find some improvements with the new approach for the 30 s and 3 s tasks. In the 30 s task, with an accent subspace of 5 dimensions and 25 accents, we reduced the result of the baseline from $100 \cdot C_{avg} = 0.36$ down to 0.32, what means a 11% relative improvement. In the 10 s task, the best result obtained by our proposal was again with $n_y = 5$, but with 10 accents, and it was equal to the baseline. In the 3 s task, the best result was obtained again with $n_y = 5$ and 10 accents, and the relative improvement over the baseline was about 1%. If we study the behavior of our proposal more in depth, we can see that for the 30 s task, the results were stable for a range of subspace dimensions between 5 and 200, from 1 to 100 accents. For the 10 s task, stable results were obtained with the subspace of 5 dimensions from 1 to 25 accents, and if we focus on the 25-dimension subspace, stability was achieved from 5 to 150 accents. In the case of the 3 s task, stable results with the 5-dimension subspace were obtained from 1 to 25 accents. With the 25-dimension subspace, as good results as with the 5-dimension subspace were only obtained with 5 accents.

We think that AHC is especially helpful because it allows making an evaluation over a model better fitted to our test utterance, and it can compensate for

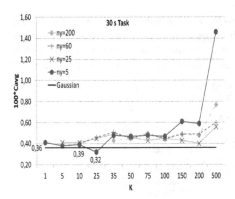

Fig. 3. $100 \cdot C_{avg}$ for the 30 s task

Fig. 4. $100 \cdot C_{avg}$ for the 10 s task

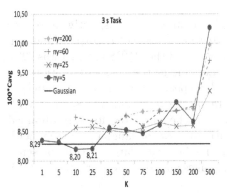

Fig. 5. $100 \cdot C_{avg}$ for the 3 s task

Table 4. Fusion of LID with accent modeling ($n_y = 5$, $K = 25$) and Gaussian iVector classifiers

| | Results in $100 \cdot C_{avg}$ | | |
Task	LID with accents	Gaussian	Fusion
30 s	**0.32**	0.36	0.35
10 s	1.84	1.83	**1.76**
3 s	8.21	8.29	**8.20**

undesired effects like channel variability. Note that the case of clustering only on 1 accents is like having the Gaussian classifier but differently trained and tested.

Table 4 shows the fusion of both classifiers, LID with accent modeling with $n_y = 5$ and $K = 25$, and Gaussian. The fusion only helped for the 10 s condition, which improved a 3.8% over the Gaussian classifier.

3.3 Channel Dependency

In Table 5, we show the confusion matrix of the results for the 3 s task obtained with the LID with accent modeling classifier with $n_y = 5$ and $K = 25$. We have split the results of each language to show the rates of the CTS and BNBS channels separately. In rows, we find the language spoken in either CTS or BNBS channel, and in columns, the decided language. The numbers are percentages of decisions made for the language of that column. For the 30 s and 10 s tasks (tables not shown here), both channels obtained similar confusion rates, with almost perfect recognition in the case of 30 s, and between 85% and 95% in the case of 10 s. However, for the 3 s task, it can be seen that the accuracy was

Table 5. Confusion matrix in % of detections for the 3 s task ($n_y = 5$, $K = 25$). Rows: language spoken in the test utterance with transmission channel; columns: decision made by our system. Note that rows do not have to sum 1 because this is a detection task, and more than one, one or zero languages can be decided for each utterance.

	engl	fars	hind	mand	russ	span
engl-CTS	**72.73**	5.79	2.48	2.48	0.83	2.48
engl-BNBS	**82.48**	2.11	1.81	0.91	0.60	1.51
fars-CTS	4.57	**71.07**	2.54	5.58	1.02	2.54
fars-BNBS	0.48	**69.23**	2.88	7.69	2.88	0.96
hind-CTS	1.43	4.29	**54.29**	10.00	4.29	5.71
hind-BNBS	1.72	8.62	**52.59**	3.16	6.90	6.90
mand-CTS	2.32	6.95	4.25	**67.18**	2.70	1.54
mand-BNBS	0.58	4.62	2.31	**77.46**	0.00	2.89
russ-CTS	3.60	3.60	3.60	2.16	**68.35**	0.72
russ-BNBS	1.32	2.32	3.97	1.32	**78.15**	2.32
span-CTS	5.63	5.63	10.82	5.63	3.90	**44.59**
span-BNBS	1.06	3.72	5.85	0.53	2.66	**72.87**

lower. In general, both channels obtained similar numbers, slightly better for BNBS, with maximum differences about 10% in the case of English, Mandarin, and Russian. However, for Spanish, the accuracy of the BNBS channel was 72%, whereas for the CTS channel it was 44%. Looking at the data distribution, the most remarkable difference that we find with respect to the rest of the languages, is that Spanish had no CTS LRE09 data in the development. Spanish CTS data was mainly confused with Hindi (11%). The worst results were obtained for Hindi, which was confused evenly with the rest of languages except with English. The major differences of Hindi in the data were larger SRE08 presence in the training dataset than the rest of languages and also a low presence of CTS LRE09 in the development.

3.4   Comparison with the iVector System Submitted to the 2011 NIST LRE

Last, we compare the results obtained with our new approach, with $n_y = 5$ and 25 accents, with the iVector system submitted to the 2011 NIST LRE by our group. As major differences, in the system submitted to the 2011 NIST LRE a Gaussian classifier was used, as the baseline presented above, and the training and development datasets included 61 and 60 languages, respectively, and many more hours. This comparison is shown in Table 6 for the 30 s task. In this case, results are shown in terms of the metric defined for the 2011 NIST LRE, where C_{avg} was computed for pairs of languages, and the overall evaluation metric included the average cost of the worst N_l pairs, with N_l being the number of target languages. The worst N_l pairs were selected according to the *minimum* cost, whereas the final average cost was computed over the *actual* cost of those N_l pairs. As additional information, we also show the average *actual* cost of all the pairs (15 in our case). As we can see, the results were very good with both systems. There were some pairs for which the result was improved with our proposal, whereas for other pairs there was an increase in the cost. The most remarkable case was the Hindi-Spanish pair, which was improved by our new

Table 6. Comparison of the 30 s task results between the system based on iVectors with a LID with accent modeling classifier ($n_y = 5$, $K = 25$) and balanced training and development data, and the system submitted to the 2011 NIST LRE based on iVectors with Gaussian classifier and very large training and development datasets

Lang1	Lang2	LID with accent modeling			2011 NIST LRE system		
		Position	$100 \cdot C_{min}$	$100 \cdot C_{act}$	Position	$100 \cdot C_{min}$	$100 \cdot C_{act}$
fars	hind	1	**0.60**	**0.73**	2	**0.73**	**0.73**
engl	hind	2	**0.45**	**0.70**	10	0.00	0.23
fars	span	3	**0.24**	**0.36**	9	0.12	0.12
fars	russ	4	**0.24**	**0.24**	8	0.12	0.25
hind	russ	5	**0.23**	**0.58**	5	**0.35**	**0.58**
engl	mand	6	**0.14**	**0.14**	3	**0.45**	**0.59**
engl	fars	7	0.12	0.12	4	0.35	0.58
fars	mand	8	0.12	0.25	6	0.25	0.40
hind	span	9	0.12	0.48	1	1.17	1.43
engl	russ	10	0.00	0.23	11	0.00	0.00
engl	span	11	0.00	0.36	12	0.00	0.00
hind	mand	12	0.00	0.23	7	0.14	0.14
mand	russ	13	0.00	0.14	13	0.00	0.00
mand	span	14	0.00	0.00	14	0.00	0.00
russ	span	15	0.00	0.12	15	0.00	0.24
		$100 \cdot C_{avg} 6pairs$		**0.46**	$100 \cdot C_{avg} 6pairs$		0.72
		$100 \cdot C_{avg} 15pairs$		**0.31**	$100 \cdot C_{avg} 15pairs$		0.35

system from $100 \cdot C_{avg} = 1.43$ to $100 \cdot C_{avg} = 0.48$. It is also interesting to observe that the average of the 6 worst pairs was improved with the new approach by a 36%. We believe that the improvement is due to the new classifier, which as we have seen, slightly improves over the Gaussian classifier, and to the training and development datasets, which were specifically designed for those languages. Although in general it is better to use data of as many languages as possible, for this case, where our 6 target languages were not very confusable, it seems beneficial to have used data from only those 6 target languages.

4   Discussion and Conclusions

In this paper, we present a new approach to classify iVectors in a LID system. Our proposal is to model the different accents that exist in a language. Accents arise due to different geographic, social, cultural, or even personal backgrounds in the speakers of a language. First, we clustered the iVectors of each language in an unsupervised way and identified the accents of each language. Then, an sPLDA model was trained with them. During the evaluation, each accent was treated as a target speaker in a speaker identification system, and the highest score of each language was selected. Finally, scores were calibrated and decisions about the spoken language were made. It is shown that this recognizer worked at least as well as the state-of-the-art Gaussian classifier for the 10 s task, and better than it for the 3 s and 30 s tasks. In our experiments, 10-25 accents per language were optimal. We believe that one of the reasons of the success of this technique is that, with AHC, each test utterance is evaluated over a model better fitted to it, trained with data belonging to a smaller part of the subspace. In fact, the idea of this approach is similar to a GMM classifier that creates different modes on the iVector space. However, for small training datasets, the GMM classifier did not perform better than a single Gaussian [7], but it did with larger training datasets [14]. Therefore, the LID with accent modeling classifier can be seen as a good solution to create different modes when there is not enough data to train a GMM. Nonetheless, we think that it would also increase the performance if it were trained on larger datasets. Additionally, it is also shown that the system was well designed for our 6 target languages, as it performed better than the iVector-based system submitted to the 2011 NIST LRE, trained on a much larger dataset including many more languages.

Acknowledgments. This work was funded by the Spanish Government and the European Union (FEDER) under projects TIN2011-28169-C05-02 and IN-NPACTO IPT-2011-1696-390000.

References

1. Humphries, J.J., Woodland, P.C., Pearce, D.: Using Accent-Specific Pronunciation Modelling for Robust Speech Recognition. In: Fourth International Conference on Spoken Language Processing, Philadelphia, PA, USA, pp. 2324–2327 (1996)
2. Glembek, O., Matejka, P., Burget, L., Mikolov, T.: Advances in Phonotactic Language Recognition. In: Interspeech, Brisbane, Australia (2008)
3. Dehak, N., Kenny, P., Dehak, R., Dumouchel, P., Ouellet, P.: Front-End Factor Analysis for Speaker Verification. IEEE Transactions on Audio, Speech, and Language Processing 19(4), 788–798 (2011)
4. Brümmer, N., de Villiers, E.: The Speaker Partitioning Problem. In: Odyssey 2010: The Speaker and Language Recognition Workshop, Brno, Czech Republic, pp. 194–201 (2010)
5. Villalba, J., Lleida, E.: Handling iVectors from Different Recording Conditions Using Multi-Channel Simplified PLDA in Speaker Recognition. In: ICASSP, Vancouver, BC, Canada, pp. 6763–6767 (2013)
6. Bishop, C.M.: Pattern Recognition and Machine Learning. Springer (2006)
7. Martínez, D., Plchot, O., Burget, L., Ondrej, G., Matejka, P.: Language Recognition in iVectors Space. In: Interspeech, Florence, Italy (2011)
8. Garcia-Romero, D., Espy-Wilson, C.: Analysis of i-Vector Length Normalization in Speaker Recognition Systems. In: Interspeech, Florence, Italy, pp. 249–252 (2011)
9. Avilés-Casco, C.V.: Robust Diarization for Speaker Characterization. PhD thesis, Universidad de Zaragoza (2011)
10. Brümmer, N.: FoCal Multi-Class: Toolkit for Evaluation, Fusion and Calibration of Multi-Class Recognition Scores (2007)
11. Martínez, D., Villalba, J., Ortega, A., Lleida, E.: I3A Language Recognition System Description for NIST LRE 2011. In: NIST Language Recognition Evaluation, Atlanta, GE, USA (2011)
12. The 2011 NIST Language Recognition Evaluation Plan (LRE 2011). Technical report (2011)
13. The 2009 NIST Language Recognition Evaluation Plan (LRE 2009). Technical report (2009)
14. Lopez-Moreno, I., Gonzalez-Dominguez, J., Plchot, O., Martínez, D., Gonzalez-Rodriguez, J., Moreno, P.: Automatic Language Identification Using Deep Neural Networks. In: ICASSP, Florence, Italy (2014)

Global Speaker Clustering towards Optimal Stopping Criterion in Binary Key Speaker Diarization

Héctor Delgado[1], Xavier Anguera[2], Corinne Fredouille[3],
and Javier Serrano[1]

[1] CAIAC, Autonomous University of Barcelona, Barcelona, Spain
[2] Telefonica Research, Barcelona, Spain
[3] University of Avignon, CERI/LIA, France
{hector.delgado,javier.serrano}@uab.cat, xanguera@tid.es,
corinne.fredouille@univ-avignon.fr

Abstract. The recently proposed speaker diarization technique based on binary keys provides a very fast alternative to state-of-the-art systems with little increase of Diarization Error Rate (DER). Although the approach shows great potential, it also presents issues, mainly in the stopping criterion. Therefore, exploring alternative clustering/stopping criterion approaches is needed. Recently some works have addressed the speaker clustering as a global optimization problem in order to tackle the intrinsic issues of the Agglomerative Hierarchical Clustering (AHC) (mainly the local-maximum-based decision making). This paper aims at adapting and applying this new framework to the binary key diarization system. In addition, an analysis of cluster purity across the AHC iterations is done using reference speaker ground-truth labels to select the purer clustering as input for the global framework. Experiments on the REPERE phase 1 test database show improvements of around 6% absolute DER compared to the baseline system output.

Keywords: speaker diarization, binary key, ILP, cluster purity.

1 Introduction

Speaker diarization is the task of segmenting an audio file into speaker homogeneous segments. It is well known the importance of speaker diarization as a pre-processing tool for many speech-related tasks which take advantage of dealing with speech signals from a single-speaker. For instance, speech recognition can benefit of speaker diarization to adapt acoustic models to target speakers. Furthermore, searching speech utterances spoken by target speakers within big audiovisual content repositories is increasingly becoming very popular and challenging. Before identifying such speakers by means of speaker identification technology, they must be previously separated adequately. Here, speaker diarization systems should be accurate and fast enough in order to process big quantities of data in a reasonable time period.

J.L. Navarro Mesa et al. (Eds.): IberSPEECH 2014, LNAI 8854, pp. 59–68, 2014.
© Springer International Publishing Switzerland 2014

Most state-of-the-art systems perform a combination of Gaussian Mixture Model (GMM) as speaker models, Bayesian Information Criterion (BIC) as a measure for cluster merging and stopping criterion, and Viterbi decoding for data assignment. All the mentioned algorithms are applied iteratively, imposing a high computational load which results in too long processing times [1] (above 1xRT, being xRT the Real Time factor) for some real-life applications.

The recently proposed speaker diarization approach based on binary key speaker modeling [1] provides a fast system (over 10 times faster than real time) with little performance decrease. DER scores of around 27% with a real time factor of 0.103 xRT were reported using all the NIST RT databases. This technique provides a fast alternative to the use of parallel computing, but using a single CPU. Later, the approach was extended and successfully applied to process TV broadcast audio in [2].

Both works report on the weakness of the stopping criterion being used, which usually does not provide the optimum clustering in terms of DER. Indeed, [2] demonstrates that the diarization system is able to produce better clusterings than the one returned by the stopping criterion. This indicates that improving stopping criterion will systematically produce a gain in performance.

Lately, a global optimization framework to speaker clustering was introduced in [7]. Contrary to classic AHC, the framework tries to find the optimum clustering in a global way, instead of relying on greedy, local-maximum-made decisions as AHC does. Given the weakness of the optimum clustering selection algorithm used in the binary key speaker diarization system, it seems reasonable to think that such an approach, which is able to implicitly determine the optimum number of clusters, can provide an effective alternative to the faulty stopping criterion.

This work follows this direction in order to evaluate the effectiveness of the global clustering technique integrated in the binary key speaker diarization system. First, the approach is adapted to be used in our case. Second, an analysis of cluster purity of the binary key system is performed. And third, the global clustering approach is tested in our system by using the extracted result of the first analysis. Preliminary results show that the global clustering approach outperforms the clustering originally returned by the system stopping criterion. However, it also suffers some robustness issues among test audio files since the global clustering parameters need to be tuned for each input file.

The paper is structured as follows: Section 2 describes the baseline binary key speaker diarization system. Section 3 gives an explanation of the global speaker clustering and proposes an adaptation suitable for the binary key system. Section 4 describes the experimental setup and results. Section 5 concludes and proposes future work.

2   Overview of the Binary Key Speaker Diarization System

The implementation of the binary key diarization system used in this work is described in [2]. First, an acoustic processing block aims at transforming the acoustic input data into a suitable binary representation. Secondly, the binary processing block takes the binary data from the previous stage to perform an Agglomerative Hierarchical Clustering (AHC) but, unlike the classic approach, all operations are performed in the binary domain. This results in a significant gain in execution time, compared with state-of-the-art agglomerative systems.

As said above, the acoustic processing block transforms the acoustic feature vectors into binary vectors called binary keys. The key element for this transformation is a UBM-like acoustic model, called KBM (binary Key Background Model), which is trained using the own test input data, but in a particular way. A single Gaussian is trained every n seconds (with some overlap), so that at the end a pool of several hundreds of Gaussians is obtained. Proceeding in this way, it is guaranteed that the overall acoustic space of speakers is covered by the pool of Gaussians. The next step consists in taking a subset of N components from the pool so that the selected Gaussians are as complementary and discriminant between them as possible. To achieve that, the Gaussians are selected iteratively by calculating the KL2 (symmetric Kullback-Leibler) divergence between the already selected components and the remaining ones, and the most dissimilar component is selected. The process is repeated until having N components.

Once the KBM is trained, any set or sequence of input feature vectors can be converted into a Binary Key (BK). A BK $v_f = \{v_f[1], ..., v_f[N]\}, v_f[i] = \{0, 1\}$ is a binary vector whose dimension N is the number of components in the KBM. Setting a position $v_f[i]$ to 1 (TRUE) indicates that the ith Gaussian of the KBM coexists in the same area of the acoustic space as the acoustic data being modeled. The BK can be obtained in two steps. Firstly, for each feature vector, the best N_G matching Gaussians in the KBM are selected (i.e., the N_G Gaussians which provide higher likelihood for the given feature), and their identifiers are stored. Secondly, for each component, the count of how many times it has been selected as a top component along all the features is calculated. Then, the final BK is obtained by setting to 1 the positions corresponding to the top M Gaussians at the whole feature set level, (i.e., the Mth most selected components for the given feature set). Note that this method can be applied to any set of features, either a sequence of features from a short speech segment, or a feature set corresponding to a whole speaker cluster.

The last step before switching to the binary process block is the clustering initialization. This is done at the acoustic level in order to have an initial rough clustering as a starting point. Taking advantage of the KBM trained before, an initial set of N_{init} clusters is build by using the first N_{init}th Gaussians in the KBM. The input data are divided into small segments (e.g., 100ms) and they are assigned to the cluster whose Gaussian provides the highest likelihood.

The binary block implements an AHC clustering approach. However, all operations are done with binary data, which makes the process much faster than with classic GMM-based approaches. First, BKs for the initial clusters are calculated using the method explained in section 2. Then, the input data are reassigned to the current clusters. Data are first divided into fixed length segments and BKs are calculated for all them. Note that these BKs keys will be used along the iterations of the AHC, so they can be stored and reused. Next, the segments are assigned by comparing their BKs with all current cluster BKs. The similarity metric is given by equation 1.

$$S(v_{f1}, v_{f2})) = \frac{\sum_{i=1}^{N}(v_{f1}[i] \wedge v_{f2}[i])}{\sum_{i=1}^{N}(v_{f1}[i] \vee v_{f2}[i])} \qquad (1)$$

where $\wedge$ indicates the boolean AND operator, and $\vee$ indicates the boolean OR operator. This is a very fast, bit-wise operation between two binary vectors.

Once data are redistributed, BKs are trained for the new clusters. Finally, similarities between all cluster pairs are obtained using equation 1 and the cluster pair with the highest score is merged, reducing the number of clusters by one.

The iterative process is repeated until a single cluster is reached, storing all the partial clusterings. At the end of the process, the final clustering is output by using a modification of the T-test T_S metric proposed in [6]. After the computation of intra-cluster and inter-cluster similarity distributions between segments for each clustering C^i, the selected clustering is the one which maximizes T_S, given by equation 2.

$$T_s = \frac{m_1 - m_2}{\sqrt{\frac{\sigma_1^2}{n_1} + \frac{\sigma_2^2}{n_2}}} \qquad (2)$$

where m_1 , σ_1 , n_1 , m_2 , σ_2 and n_2 are the mean, standard deviation and size of intra-cluster and inter-cluster distance distributions, respectively.

3   Global Speaker Clustering

As it has been reported in [1], the final clustering selection (i.e., the stopping criterion) based on the T-test distance does not return the optimum clustering (differences in performance of around 7-8% absolute DER with the REPERE database [2]).

Recently an alternative approach to the classic AHC was presented in [7]. The main argument against AHC is the greedy nature of the technique, which uses local optimums to decide which cluster pair should be merged in each iteration. If an erroneous merging is produced, the error will likely be propagated through the iterations, resulting in impure clusters and, consequently, in loss of performance. Following these thoughts, the proposed alternative clustering method addresses the clustering as a global process, reformulated as a problem of Integer Linear Programming (ILP), in order to minimize a certain objective function, subject to a set of constraints, in a global manner.

The authors of [7] propose to apply this global clustering method immediately after a first BIC-based AHC stage. At this point, it is assumed that the resulting clusters are pure, i.e., each cluster contains speech from a single speaker. However, more than one cluster may refer to a given speaker. This can occur because a given speaker who is speaking over different acoustic conditions (e.g. background music, background noise) may be modeled by different clusters by the system. It is at this point where the ILP clustering can be used to obtain a final clustering where the several clusters referring to the same speaker are merged together in a single cluster. Additionally, to deal with channel variability, each input cluster is represented by an i-vector. Thus, given an input clustering of N clusters, a set of N i-vectors is obtained. From here on, the clusters are treated as single points.

Given the N points, the goal is to group them into K clusters while minimizing the objective function and meeting the constraints (refer to section 3.1). Some of the N points can act as "centers" of new clusters. The remaining ones (e.g., the ones not selected as centers) must be associated to one of the centers. In the end, there will be as many clusters as centers. Intuitively, the objective function consists in minimizing the number K of clusters and the dispersion of the points within each cluster. Regarding the constraints, each point which is not a center can be associated with only one center and its distance to the center must be short enough (below a given threshold).

3.1   Adaptation of ILP Clustering to the Binary Key Diarization System

In order to adapt the technique to our framework, some modifications are proposed. First, the points of the problem will be BKs instead of i-vectors. Second, unlike the original work, no channel compensation is applied.

The ILP clustering formulation has been adapted to our framework (refer to [3] for the original formulation), and it is defined as:
Minimize

$$\sum_{k=1}^{N} x_{k,k} - \frac{1}{D} \sum_{k=1}^{N} \sum_{j=1}^{N} d(k,j) x_{k,j} \tag{3}$$

Subject to

$$x_{k,j} \in \{0,1\} \qquad\qquad \forall k, \forall j \tag{4}$$

$$\sum_{k=1}^{N} x_{k,j} = 1 \qquad\qquad \forall j \tag{5}$$

$$d(k,j) x_{k,j} \leq \delta \qquad\qquad \forall k, \forall j \tag{6}$$

Eq. 3 is the objective function to be minimized. As said above, the aim is to minimize the number of clusters and the dispersion of the BKs within each cluster. The binary variable $x_{k,k}$ is equal to 1 if the BK k is a center. The distance $d(k,j)$ between BKs k and j is calculated as $1 - S(k,j)$, where $S(k,j)$ is given by eq. 1 (section 2). D is a normalization factor equal to the longest distance $d(k,j)$ for all k and j. The binary variable $x_{k,j}$ is set to 1 if BK j is associated with center k. Eq. 5 ensures that each BK j is associated with only one center k. Finally, each BK j associated with a center k must have a distance shorter than a threshold.

The proposed ILP clustering requires an input clustering to start the process. This input clustering will be the result of applying a given number of iterations of the AHC binary key diarization system. Each cluster will be represented as a BK, extracted following the method for BK computation explained in section 2. Ideally, the input clusters should be as pure as possible, since the ILP clustering method is not able to re-allocate misclassified data, so the errors will be propagated to the resulting clusters. For this reason, an analysis of cluster purity across the AHC iterations is conducted previous to the application of the global clustering (section 4.2).

4   Experiments and Results

This section describes experimental setup and results for two different experiments. Firstly, a study of cluster purity across the iterations of the baseline AHC is performed. Secondly, the resulting purest clusterings from the first experiment are taken to be used as input clusters to test the ILP global clustering.

As the aim of this work is mainly to analyze speaker clustering and stopping criterion, it has been decided to use perfect SAD labels. That is, the speaker ground-truth labels have been used to extract the speech activity and to discard nonspeech content. In this way, the analysis can focus on speaker clustering without the effects of additional noise (false alarm speech) and not loosing useful speaker time (miss speech).

Both tests are evaluated on the REPERE phase 1 test dataset of TV data [4]. This database was developed in the context of the REPERE Challenge [5]. It consists of a set of TV shows from several French TV channels.

Previous to experiment descriptions, the experimental setup is explained in the next subsection.

4.1   Experimental Setup

Parameters and settings of the various modules of the binary key speaker diarization system are described here.

Regarding audio processing, the provided single channel is used without further treatment. Next, feature extraction is performed. Standard 19-order MFCCs are computed using a 25ms window every 10ms.

For training the KBM, single Gaussian components are obtained using a 2s window in order to have sufficient data for parameter estimate. Window rate is set according to the input audio length, in order to obtain an initial pool of 2000 Gaussians. Then, 896 components are selected to conform the final KBM following the method described in section 2.

With regard to binary key estimate parameters, the top 5 Gaussian components are taken in a frame basis, and the top 20% components at segment level.

The clustering initialization is done by using the first N_{init} Gaussian components in the KBM as cluster models. Two different values of N_{init} are tested in the experiments: 25 and 50. Then, 100ms segments are assigned to the different clusters to obtain the first rough, over-segmented clustering.

Finally, in the AHC stage, BKs keys are computed for each 1s segment, augmenting it 1s before and after, totaling 3s.

In order to evaluate performance, the output labels are compared with the reference ones to compute the DER. Since the proposed system does not handle overlap speech, regions with more than one active speakers are ignored in the score computation (note that this is only for evaluation, so that overlapped speech regions are included during the complete diarization process). In addition, as perfect SAD is being used and overlap speech is not being evaluated, false alarm and miss errors are virtually equal to zero, so the analysis can focus only on speaker errors.

4.2   Search of the Purest Clustering

The aim of this analysis is to study the evolution of the cluster purities among the iterations of the diarization system. By using the reference speaker labels, one can determine how much speaker time in the cluster belongs to the different speakers in the reference. In a given cluster there is always a majority speaker, who is the one with most speaker time within the cluster. Considering this speaker as the "main" speaker, the cluster purity can be calculated as the ratio between the cluster time assigned to the main speaker and the total cluster time. However, purity of clusters of different sizes does not affect, globally speaking, in the same way to the system. Due to this fact, the calculation of a time-weighted purity measure is proposed instead by taking into account cluster sizes. The final time-weighted cluster purity is calculated as the cluster purity multiplied by the cluster length, and divided by the total duration of the test audio (after removing nonspeech content). Finally, the time-weighted purity for a whole clustering can be obtained as the average of the time-weighted purity of all clusters in the clustering.

Normally, the purity should start to increase after a few iterations of AHC and will start to decrease when the number of clusters is lower than the actual number of speakers. In table 1, clustering purity is shown for two different clusterings: the one providing highest purity ("highest purity columns") and the one producing lowest DER ("sysOut purity" columns). The experiment is repeated for 25 and 50 initial clusters (N_{init}). Generally, purities reach the optimum in early iterations of the AHC (with a number of clusters significantly higher than the optimum clustering), although the exact iteration is showed to be quite dependent on the show. In addition, optimum purities are higher in the case of 50 initial clusters compared to 25 initial clusters. With regard to the system output, as it could be expected, purity is, in general, inversely proportional to DER. Finally, overall DER of system output with $N_{init} = 25$ (9.47%) is slightly lower than for $N_{init} = 50$ (10.60%). It seems that each of the two configurations works better for certain shows.

Table 1. Results of cluster purity analysis broken down into shows. #spk is the number of actual speaker of each show. N_{init} indicates the number of initial clusters. Column "highest purity" shows purity and number of clusters (#C) of the optimum clusterings in terms of time-weighted overall purity, whilst column "sysOut purity" shows purity and number of clusters of the optimum clusterings in terms of DER.

Show ID	#spk	$N\_init = 25$						$N\_init = 50$					
		Highest purity			SysOut purity			Highest purity			SysOut purity		
		#C	Purity	DER	#C	Purity	DER	#C	Purity	DER	#C	Purity	DER
BFMTV_BFMStory_1	6	19	0.910	24.60	8	0.883	4.37	45	0.923	51.49	6	0.865	6.42
BFMTV_BFMStory_2	18	18	0.891	18.43	18	0.891	18.43	41	0.941	33.32	31	0.913	21.00
BFMTV_BFMStory_3	10	19	0.951	29.77	13	0.937	7.25	35	0.962	33.19	11	0.915	5.58
BFMTV_BFMStory_4	6	11	0.962	11.05	6	0.952	1.59	20	0.963	14.82	6	0.950	1.78
BFMTV_CultureEtVous_1	5	14	0.950	52.13	4	0.891	10.11	21	0.970	52.04	3	0.881	8.88
BFMTV_CultureEtVous_2	6	10	0.925	27.16	4	0.776	21.09	23	0.956	43.30	4	0.780	20.63
BFMTV_CultureEtVous_3	16	22	0.904	63.80	5	0.744	24.44	29	0.851	62.16	4	0.702	23.68
BFMTV_CultureEtVous_4	9	22	0.890	54.37	2	0.640	33.07	41	0.902	70.80	3	0.650	30.63
BFMTV_CultureEtVous_5	6	21	0.905	72.06	3	0.823	9.90	20	0.917	65.02	3	0.823	9.90
BFMTV_CultureEtVous_6	12	18	0.870	52.70	5	0.700	25.37	29	0.890	57.79	5	0.720	21.15
BFMTV_CultureEtVous_7	14	18	0.839	43.19	6	0.701	31.22	34	0.850	68.51	9	0.758	26.67
LCP_CaVousRegarde_1	7	23	0.925	70.01	4	0.823	15.46	48	0.957	82.51	6	0.883	12.11
LCP_CaVousRegarde_2	5	7	0.938	8.00	4	0.903	3.11	14	0.951	9.28	4	0.917	2.64
LCP_CaVousRegarde_3	5	21	0.950	40.21	6	0.836	19.28	37	0.950	55.75	15	0.886	21.94
LCP_EntreLesLignes_1	5	15	0.919	24.07	10	0.909	11.34	19	0.958	19.64	19	0.958	19.64
LCP_EntreLesLignes_2	5	27	0.932	28.44	6	0.891	4.92	26	0.949	24.37	6	0.891	4.44
LCP_EntreLesLignes_3	5	15	0.945	29.45	3	0.823	14.74	26	0.935	29.45	3	0.823	14.74
LCP_LCPInfo13h30_1	16	21	0.890	23.69	14	0.882	10.04	39	0.938	26.83	20	0.902	13.19
LCP_LCPInfo13h30_2	12	18	0.951	16.77	11	0.890	10.87	41	0.953	34.64	23	0.918	17.40
LCP_LCPInfo13h30_3	10	13	0.905	24.55	7	0.871	12.28	27	0.921	24.67	11	0.841	17.10
LCP_PileEtFace_1	3	14	0.921	25.17	3	0.821	8.24	16	0.955	19.52	6	0.921	10.91
LCP_PileEtFace_2	3	15	0.954	29.25	3	0.864	8.11	31	0.960	72.58	2	0.853	8.28
LCP_PileEtFace_3	3	9	0.910	11.18	3	0.797	6.89	24	0.932	37.36	3	0.808	6.89
LCP_PileEtFace_4	3	7	1.000	6.81	6	0.988	3.95	17	1.000	21.56	8	0.988	7.59
LCP_PileEtFace_5	3	18	0.936	53.94	3	0.912	4.20	4	0.936	3.67	4	0.936	3.67
LCP_TopQuestions_1	8	22	0.987	35.89	8	0.976	1.36	12	0.989	7.42	9	0.981	2.11
LCP_TopQuestions_2	5	15	0.985	23.41	3	0.914	8.13	20	0.985	29.11	6	0.959	4.09
LCP_TopQuestions_3	6	11	0.973	21.53	5	0.948	5.17	14	0.973	13.34	5	0.948	5.17
Overall	-	-	-	-	-	-	9.47	-	-		-	-	10.60

4.3   Experiments on ILP Clustering

As stated above, the ILP clustering needs an input set of clusters to work with. Ideally, this input clustering should be as pure as possible, as the technique is not able to recover incorrectly assigned speech. The previous experiment shows that the exact number of iterations to get the purest clustering is dependent on the show. This fact results in a lack of robustness among different audio data. To avoid this issue, in this experiment the clusterings with highest purity of the previous experiment have been selected as input for the current one.

Figure 1 depicts DER of the ILP clustering in function of the threshold θ. For comparison purposes, DER of the baseline system output and optimum clusterings are also plotted. For the initial clustering obtained with $N_{init} = 25$, optimum DER is obtained for $\theta = 0.63$, while for the one of $N_{init} = 50$ is obtained for $\theta = 0.66$. Although the previous analysis shows that the average cluster purity for the case of $N_{init} = 50$ is higher, DER of clustering obtained from $N_{init} = 25$ is slightly lower (15.1% versus 16,26%). This may be due to the higher number of clusters to be merged. As it can be seen, the ILP method outperforms the baseline system with T-test stopping criterion for a range of values of θ, obtaining a gain of around 6% absolute DER with the best configuration. However, performance still

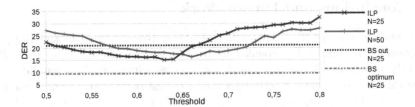

Fig. 1. Overall DER trend of the ILP clustering while varying the threshold θ for N_{init} equal to 25 and 50. Overall DER of the baseline system output (BS out) and optimum clusterings (BS optimum) are also provided for comparison.

Table 2. Results of ILP clustering experiments using the purest clusterings from table 1 for N_{init} equal to 25 and 50 as inputs. For each show, values of the optimum threshold θ_{opt}, resulting number of clusters #C, and DER are shown. The actual number of speakers per show #spk is also provided.

Show ID	#spk	N_init = 25			N_init = 50		
		θ_{opt}	#C	DER	θ_{opt}	#C	DER
BFMTV_BFMStory_1	6	0.63	5	4.52	0.78	6	7.17
BFMTV_BFMStory_2	18	0.50	18	18.17	0.61	24	21.44
BFMTV_BFMStory_3	10	0.57	11	6.42	0.63	11	4.51
BFMTV_BFMStory_4	6	0.62	7	1.78	0.65	7	1.69
BFMTV_CultureEtVous_1	5	0.77	2	18.57	0.82	3	20.35
BFMTV_CultureEtVous_2	6	0.81	3	13.79	0.73	5	17.42
BFMTV_CultureEtVous_3	16	0.77	4	30.31	0.77	6	55.28
BFMTV_CultureEtVous_4	9	0.83	4	39.64	0.89	14	30.56
BFMTV_CultureEtVous_5	6	0.77	4	38.63	0.75	4	33.24
BFMTV_CultureEtVous_6	12	0.76	4	25.74	0.85	4	22.68
BFMTV_CultureEtVous_7	14	0.77	4	29.73	0.82	4	26.48
LCP_CaVousRegarde_1	7	0.69	4	9.61	0.79	5	12.05
LCP_CaVousRegarde_2	5	0.63	4	3.11	0.73	4	2.60
LCP_CaVousRegarde_3	5	0.69	9	19.58	0.74	7	19.31
LCP_EntreLesLignes_1	5	0.63	11	10.08	0.50	19	19.64
LCP_EntreLesLignes_2	5	0.68	5	3.41	0.75	4	9.27
LCP_EntreLesLignes_3	5	0.77	3	15.39	0.76	3	15.00
LCP_LCPInfo13h30_1	16	0.52	15	10.07	0.65	13	10.42
LCP_LCPInfo13h30_2	12	0.53	11	15.26	0.56	22	11.40
LCP_LCPInfo13h30_3	10	0.57	6	13.76	0.57	17	13.59
LCP_PileEtFace_1	3	0.77	2	12.28	0.76	4	10.32
LCP_PileEtFace_2	3	0.74	3	7.15	0.77	2	8.28
LCP_PileEtFace_3	3	0.70	5	8.22	0.73	4	8.82
LCP_PileEtFace_4	3	0.63	6	2.94	0.77	3	1.35
LCP_PileEtFace_5	3	0.74	2	4.98	0.50	4	3.67
LCP_TopQuestions_1	8	0.63	8	1.60	0.63	9	1.01
LCP_TopQuestions_2	5	0.72	4	2.89	0.77	4	2.36
LCP_TopQuestions_3	6	0.66	5	2.79	0.64	7	4.30
Overall	-	-	-	9.57	-	-	10.20

does not reach that of the optimum clustering of the baseline system manually selected(5.63% absolute higher).

In order to demonstrate the dependence of threshold θ on the show, additional results are provided in table 2. Here, DER is shown for the optimum value of θ for each show. Obtained results are quite similar to the ones of the baseline system with optimum clustering manually selected. The reading of these results could be twofold. On one hand, the technique presents a lack of robustness since the number of iterations and threshold must be tuned for each input audio file. On the other hand, even if the threshold is not tuned in a per-show basis, the proposed adaptation of the ILP clustering outperforms the baseline system stopping criterion.

5   Conclusions and Future Work

This work focuses on the exploration of alternative methods to the stopping criterion of the binary key speaker diarization approach presented in [2]. The recently presented global framework for speaker clustering is a candidate to solve this drawback, as the technique implicitly estimates the optimum number of clusters. As this approach needs an input clustering as pure as possible, an analysis of cluster purity of the binary key AHC approach was carried out in order to select the optimum clustering in terms of purity. Then, the original ILP framework was adapted to our needs by replacing the i-vector with the binary key and was tested and compared with the baseline system on the REPERE phase 1 test database. Experiment results show an improvement of performance with respect to the baseline system, but also present some robustness issues according to the audio file being processed. It is thought that an in-depth analysis of the relation between system parameters (number of previous AHC iterations, threshold) and audio nature (audio length, number of speakers) could lead to some guidelines in order to tune system parameters for optimizing the system to the input audio. Finally, DER rates are still high and applying some kind of channel compensation could help to improve performance.

Acknowledgements. This work is part of the project "Linguistic and sensorial accessibility: technologies for voiceover and audio description", funded by the Spanish Ministerio de Economía y Competitividad (FFI2012-31023). This work was partially done within the French Research program ANR Project PERCOL (ANR 2010-CORD-102). This article is supported by the Catalan Government Grant Agency Ref. 2014SGR027.

References

1. Anguera, X., Bonastre, J.F.: Fast speaker diarization based on binary keys. In: 2011 IEEE International Conference on Acoustics, Speech and Signal Processing (ICASSP), pp. 4428–4431 (May 2011)
2. Delgado, H., Fredouille, C., Serrano, J.: Towards a complete binary key system for the speaker diarization task. In: INTERSPEECH (2014)
3. Dupuy, G., Rouvier, M., Meignier, S., Estéve, Y.: I-vectors and ILP clustering adapted to cross-show speaker diarization. In: INTERSPEECH (2012)
4. Giraudel, A., Carré, M., Mapelli, V., Kahn, J., Galibert, O., Quintard, L.: The REPERE Corpus: a multimodal corpus for person recognition. In: Proceedings of the Eight International Conference on Language Resources and Evaluation (LREC 2012), Istanbul, Turkey (May 2012)
5. Kahn, J., Galibert, O., Quintard, L., Carre, M., Giraudel, A., Joly, P.: A presentation of the REPERE challenge. In: 2012 10th International Workshop on Content-Based Multimedia Indexing (CBMI), pp. 1–6 (June 2012)
6. Nguyen, T.H., Chng, E., Li, H.: T-test distance and clustering criterion for speaker diarization. In: INTERSPEECH (2008)
7. Rouvier, M., Meignier, S.: A global optimization framework for speaker diarization. In: ODYSSEY (2012)

Unsupervised Training of PLDA
with Variational Bayes

Jesús Villalba and Eduardo Lleida*

ViVoLab, Aragon Institute for Engineering Research (I3A),
University of Zaragoza, Spain
{villalba,lleida}@unizar.es

Abstract. Speaker recognition relays on models that need a large amount of labeled development data. This models are successful in tasks like NIST SRE where sufficient data is available. However, in real applications, we usually do not have so much data and the speaker labels are unknown. We used a variational Bayes procedure to train PLDA on unlabeled data. The method consisted in a generative model where both the unknown labels and the model parameters are latent variables. We experimented on unlabeled NIST SRE data. The trained models were evaluated on NIST SRE10. Compared to cosine distance, unsupervised PLDA improved EER by 28% and minimum DCF by 36%.

Keywords: speaker recognition, PLDA, unsupervised training, variational Bayes, AHC.

1 Introduction

The i-vector approach provides a method to map a speech utterance to a low dimensional fixed length vector while retaining the speaker identity [1]. We can model the i-vector distributions with advanced techniques like probabilistic linear discriminant analysis (PLDA). PLDA is a generative model that decomposes i-vectors into a speaker specific part and a channel noise. PLDA models need to be trained on labeled databases with large number of speakers and sessions per speaker. Unfortunately, in most applications data is scarce and, in many cases, labels are unknown. We intend to train PLDA in this latter case.

There are previous works that intended to reduce dataset shift to be able to use the same PLDA model in different domains. i-Vector length normalization makes the distributions of different datasets closer. For example, between NIST datasets [2] or between different languages [3]. Bayesian evaluation of likelihood ratios also helps with dataset shift, because the predictive distributions that result, if the amount of training data is small, are heavy-tailed [4, 5].

We presented a variational Bayes (VB) method to adapt a full-rank PLDA model from one domain to another with scarce development data [6], where

---

* This work has been supported by the Spanish Government and the European Union (FEDER) through projects TIN2011-28169-C05-02 and INNPACTO IPT-2011-1696-390000.

J.L. Navarro Mesa et al. (Eds.): IberSPEECH 2014, LNAI 8854, pp. 69–78, 2014.

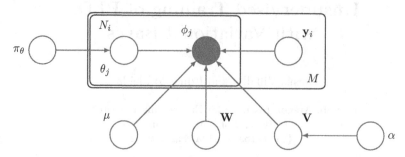

Fig. 1. BN for unsupervised SPLDA

speaker labels were known. Our method was compared with others–parameter or objective function weighting– in the context of the *Domain adaptation challenge* proposed in the 2013 JHU workshop on speaker recognition[1] [7].

The adaptation challenge also promoted adapting models using unlabeled data. We adapted a simplified PLDA model from Switchboard data to NIST SRE [8]. The speaker labels and model parameters were hidden variables whose posterior distributions were iteratively estimated by a VB procedure. In this paper, we intend to evaluate if this procedure is useful to train PLDA from scratch, instead of doing model adaptation. That is, we will not use any labeled data.

Recently, more works about unsupervised adaptation have appeared in relation with the challenge. In [9], agglomerative hierarchical clustering (AHC) is used to obtain the speaker labels of the development set. The clustering is based on the pair-wise scores between i-vectors, computed with an out-of-domain PLDA model. A threshold on the scores, which are unsupervisedly calibrated [10], stops the cluster merging. In [11], several clustering methods were compared (AHC, Markov, infomap). Another approach consists in adding a term accounting for dataset shift to the PLDA model. We can find several flavors of this method [12, 13].

2 Unsupervised SPLDA

2.1 Model Description

Simplified probabilistic linear discriminant analysis (SPLDA) is a linear generative model that assumes that an i-vector ϕ_j of speaker i can be written as:

$$\phi_j = \mu + \mathbf{V}\mathbf{y}_i + \epsilon_j \tag{1}$$

where μ is a speaker independent term, $\mathbf{V}$ is a low rank eigenvoices matrix, $\mathbf{y}_i$ is the speaker factor vector, and ϵ_j is the within class variability term. We put a standard normal prior on $\mathbf{y}_i$ and normal with zero mean and precision $\mathbf{W}$ on ϵ_j.

---

[1] http://www.clsp.jhu.edu/workshops/archive/ws13-summer-workshop/
groups/spk-13/

Figure 1 depicts the Bayesian network of this model where the labels θ of the training data are hidden. θ partitions N i-vectors into M speakers. θ_j is a latent variable comprising a 1–of–M binary vector with elements θ_{ji} with $i = 1, \ldots, M$. Note that the distribution of each speaker is assumed to be Gaussian with mean $\mu + \mathbf{V}\mathbf{y}_i$ and precision $\mathbf{W}$. The set of all the speakers forms a GMM where θ corresponds to the component occupations. The conditional distribution of θ given the mixture weights π_θ is

$$P\left(\theta|\pi_\theta\right) = \prod_{j=1}^{N} \prod_{i=1}^{M} \pi_{\theta_i}^{\theta_{ji}} . \tag{2}$$

We put a Dirichlet prior on the weights:

$$P\left(\pi_\theta|\tau_0\right) = \mathrm{Dir}(\pi_\theta|\tau_0) = C(\tau_0) \prod_{i=1}^{M} \pi_{\theta_i}^{\tau_0 - 1} \tag{3}$$

where, by symmetry, we choose the same τ_0 for all the components, $C(\tau_0)$ is the normalization constant,

$$C(\tau_0) = \frac{\Gamma(M\tau_0)}{\Gamma(\tau_0)^M} \tag{4}$$

and Γ is the Gamma function.

2.2 Model Priors

We chose the model priors based on Bishop's paper about VB PPCA [14]. We introduced a *hierarchical* prior $P\left(\mathbf{V}|\alpha\right)$ over $\mathbf{V}$ through a conditional Gaussian distribution of the form:

$$P\left(\mathbf{V}|\alpha\right) = \prod_{q=1}^{n_y} \left(\frac{\alpha_q}{2\pi}\right)^{d/2} \exp\left(-\frac{1}{2}\alpha_q \mathbf{v}_q^T \mathbf{v}_q\right) \tag{5}$$

where $\mathbf{v}_q$ are the columns of $\mathbf{V}$ and n_y is the speaker factors dimension. Each α_q controls the inverse variance of the corresponding $\mathbf{v}_q$. If a particular α_q has a posterior distribution concentrated at large values, the corresponding $\mathbf{v}_q$ will tend to be small, and that direction of the latent space will be effectively "switched off".

We defined a prior for α:

$$P\left(\alpha\right) = \prod_{q=1}^{n_y} \mathcal{G}\left(\alpha_q|a_\alpha, b_\alpha\right) \tag{6}$$

where $\mathcal{G}$ denotes the Gamma distribution.

We placed a Gaussian prior for the mean μ:

$$P\left(\mu\right) = \mathcal{N}\left(\mu|\mu_0, \beta^{-1}\mathbf{I}\right) . \tag{7}$$

Low values of a_α, b_α and β make the priors less informative and vice versa.

Finally, we put informative Wishart priors on $\mathbf{W}$,

$$P\left(\mathbf{W}\right) = \mathcal{W}\left(\mathbf{W}|\mathbf{\Psi}_0, \nu_0\right) . \tag{8}$$

2.3   Variational Bayes with Deterministic Annealing

We approximated the joint posterior of the latent variables by a factorized distribution of the form:

$$P\left(\mathbf{Y}, \theta, \pi_\theta, \mu, \mathbf{V}, \mathbf{W}, \alpha | \mathbf{\Phi}\right) \approx q\left(\mathbf{Y}\right) q\left(\theta\right) q\left(\pi_\theta\right) \prod_{r=1}^{d} q\left(\tilde{\mathbf{v}}_r'\right) q\left(\mathbf{W}\right) q\left(\alpha\right) \qquad (9)$$

where $\tilde{\mathbf{v}}_r'$ is a column vector containing the rth row of $\tilde{\mathbf{V}} = [\mathbf{V} \quad \mu]$. If $\mathbf{W}$ were diagonal the factorization $\prod_{r=1}^{d} q\left(\tilde{\mathbf{v}}_r'\right)$ would not be necessary because it would arise naturally. However, for full $\mathbf{W}$, we have to force the factorization to make the problem tractable.

We computed these factors by using Variational Bayes [15] with deterministic annealing (DA) [16]. The formula to update a factor q_j is

$$\ln q_j^*\left(\mathbf{Z}_j\right) = \mathrm{E}_{i \neq j}\left[\kappa \ln P\left(\mathbf{\Phi}, \mathbf{Z}\right)\right] + \mathrm{const} \qquad (10)$$

where $\mathbf{Z}$ abbreviates the set of all hidden variables, $\mathbf{Z}_j$ are the hidden variables corresponding to the jth factor, and κ is the annealing factor; expectations are taken with respect to all the factors $i \neq j$. We could prove that Equation (10) optimizes the VB lower bound

$$\mathcal{L} = \mathrm{E}\left[\ln P\left(\mathbf{\Phi}, \mathbf{Z}\right)\right] - \mathrm{E}\left[\ln q\left(\mathbf{Z}\right)\right)\right] = \ln P\left(\mathbf{\Phi}\right) - \mathrm{KL}\left(q\left(\mathbf{Z}\right) \| P\left(\mathbf{Z} | \mathbf{\Phi}\right)\right) \qquad (11)$$

where expectations are taken with respect to the variational posterior $q\left(\mathbf{Z}\right)$. $\mathcal{L}$ is an approximation of the marginal likelihood of the data $\ln P\left(\mathbf{\Phi}\right)$, which becomes equality when approximated posterior is equal to the true posterior. Annealing modifies the VB objective in a way that helps to avoid local maxima. We must set $\kappa < 1$ at the beginning and increase it in each iteration until $\kappa = 1$. The full VB equations can be found in our report [17].

2.4   Initialization with AHC

The speaker labels were initialized with Agglomerative hierarchichal clustering (AHC) [18]. AHC is a greedy bottom-up approach. Initially, each i-vector is its own cluster and, then, clusters are progressively merged using a similarity criterion–We used cosine distance. Thus, we started with the pair-wise score matrix between all the development i-vectors. Then, to merge two clusters, A and B, we tried tree linkage criteria: average, complete and single. The linkage criterion determines the similarity between the clusters A and B, $s(A, B)$, as a function of the pair-wise scores between their elements $s(a, b)$. Thus,

$$s_{\mathrm{avg}}(A, B) = \frac{1}{|A||B|} \sum_{a \in A} \sum_{b \in B} s(a, b) \qquad (12)$$

$$s_{\mathrm{complete}}(A, B) = \min\left\{s(a, b) | a \in A, b \in B\right\} \qquad (13)$$

$$s_{\mathrm{single}}(A, B) = \max\left\{s(a, b) | a \in A, b \in B\right\}. \qquad (14)$$

2.5   Model Selection

To select the best model, i.e., the best number of speakers M; we used the same method that in our previous work [8]. We ran the AHC+VB algorithm several times, each time hypothesizing a different M. We assumed that the best model is the one that obtains the largest VB lower bound $\mathcal{L}(M)$. To fairly compare lower bounds for different M, the Dirichlet prior on the speaker weights needs to be such that the product $M\tau_0$ is constant. To select the value of that constant, we tried several values and chose the one that maximized the sum $\sum_M \mathcal{L}(M)$.

3   Experiments

3.1   Experimental Setup

We trained PLDA on an unlabeled version of NIST SRE04-08. The i-vectors for this task were provided by the JHU HLT-COE in the 2013 JHU workshop on speaker recognition [11]. The training data consisted of 33125 segments from 3789 speakers. To perform faster experiments, we also created a subset of 500 speakers. The adapted models were evaluated on the NIST SRE10 det5 (tel-tel) extended condition.

The i-vectors were 600 dimensional. They were extracted using 20 MFCC + Δ with short time mean and variance normalization. The UBM and i-vector extractor were gender independent and used 2048 Gaussians. We applied centering, whitening and length normalization to the i-vectors [2]. The parameters needed for centering and whitening were trained on all NIST SRE data since speaker labels are not required.

The SPLDA models were gender independent with speaker factors of dimension $n_y = 400$ when training with 500 speakers; and $n_y = 600$ when training with all the speakers. Given the results in our previous work [8], we put informative priors on the model parameters. Our priors were based on the average total variance of the data s_0^2–average across dimensions. From our previous work, we assumed that the average variance of the speaker space was approximately 15% of s_0^2 and the channel variance was the remaining 85%. Thus, we computed s_0^2 from the training data. Then, for α (prior of the inverse eigenvalues), we placed a wide prior with mode $1/(0.15s_0^2)$ by setting $a_\alpha = 2$ and $b_\alpha = 0.15s_0^2$. For $\mathbf{W}$, we used a Wishart prior with expectation $1/(0.85s_0^2)\mathbf{I}$ by setting $\nu_0 = 602$ and $\Psi_0 = 1/(0.85s_0^2\nu_0)\mathbf{I}$. Note that, for the Wishart prior to be proper, we need $\nu_0 > d$, this means that the prior will have an important influence on the posterior unless we have a number of training segments $N >> d$. We set $\tau_0 = 400/M$.

The expectations of the model parameters given the VB posteriors were used to compute the likelihood ratios of the evaluation set in the standard way.

3.2   Experiments Results

First, we focus on the results obtained by training the PLDA with 500 speakers. Figure 2 plots the EER and VB lower bound against the number of hypothesized speakers M. Each subfigure corresponds to one of the linkage criteria used in

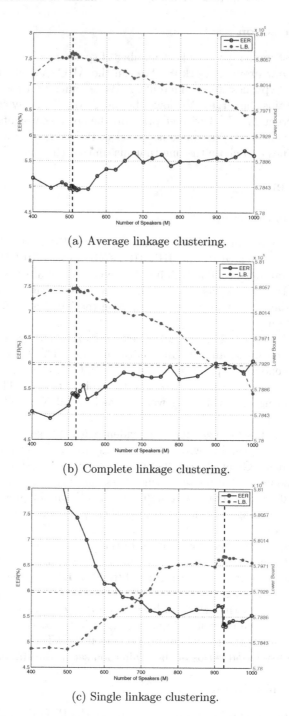

(a) Average linkage clustering.

(b) Complete linkage clustering.

(c) Single linkage clustering.

Fig. 2. EER(%)/$\mathcal{L}$ against the number of hypothesized speakers for different initialization methods and using a subset of 500 development speakers

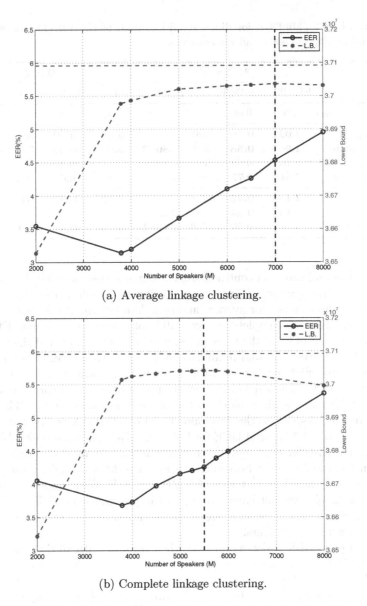

(a) Average linkage clustering.

(b) Complete linkage clustering.

Fig. 3. EER(%)/$\mathcal{L}$ against the number of hypothesized speakers for different initialization methods and using all the development speakers

the AHC initialization. The left y-axes show the scale of the EER, and the right y-axes show the scale of the lower bound. The horizontal dashed line indicates the baseline–cosine similarity– and the vertical dashed line indicates the point where $\mathcal{L}$ is maximum. Regarding the detection of the number of speakers in the development set, average and complete linkage criteria had their $\mathcal{L}$ maxima

Table 1. EER(%)/MinDCF for different initialization of the VB. The table blocks correspond to training 500 or all the speakers.

	M Actual				M Max $\mathcal{L}$			
	EER(%)	MinDCF	M	$\mathcal{L} \times 10^{-6}$	EER(%)	MinDCF	M	$\mathcal{L} \times 10^{-6}$
Baseline (Cosine)	5.96	0.66	-	-	5.96	0.66	-	-
Oracle labels	**3.02**	**0.50**	500	-	**3.02**	**0.50**	500	-
VB average link	**4.96**	**0.58**	500	5.8060	5.00	0.58	508	5.8066
VB complete link	5.16	0.60	500	5.8048	5.35	0.61	520	5.8054
VB single link	7.61	0.77	500	5.7830	5.37	0.61	925	5.7987
Oracle labels	**2.19**	**0.42**	3789	-	**2.19**	**0.42**	3789	-
VB average link	**3.14**	**0.44**	3789	36.977	4.53	0.47	7000	37.036
VB complete link	3.67	0.46	3789	**37.014**	4.25	0.47	5500	**37.041**

close to the actual value. In contrast, single linkage almost doubled the speakers. Nevertheless, the maximum $\mathcal{L}$ was a good criterion to select a model with low EER for the three cases. For average and complete linkage, it selected the point of minimum EER. For complete linkage it did not choose the minimum EER but a point quite near of it. In the three cases, it significantly improved the baseline.

Table 1 compares EER and minimum DCF for multiple cases. The table also shows the number of speakers and the $\mathcal{L}$ obtained in each case. The table has two column blocks. The left block shows results for the model corresponding to the actual M; and the right block to the model that maximizes $\mathcal{L}$. The upper block of rows correspond to the development set of 500 speakers. Average linkage obtained the lowest EER and DCF for both model selection methods (M actual and max. $\mathcal{L}$). Also for both methods average linkage obtained the highest $\mathcal{L}$, so we can use $\mathcal{L}$ to choose the best initialization. The Max $\mathcal{L}$ model improved the baseline by 16% and 12% in terms of EER and DCF. With respect to training with oracle labels, we still have a margin of improvement of 39% and 14% respectively. Single linkage was the worst initialization method so we discarded it for the following experiments.

Figure 3 plots EER and $\mathcal{L}$ against M when training with all the development speakers (3789). In this case, $\mathcal{L}$ was maximum for M much higher than its actual value–almost twice for average linkage. The reason is that, when we increase the number of speakers, we increase the probability of finding speakers with overlapping i-vector distributions and clustering becomes harder. Despite of that, the selected models outperformed the baseline. Average linkage obtained the best EER and DCF for the models with oracle M but complete linkage was better for the model maximizing $\mathcal{L}$. $\mathcal{L}$ was also higher for complete linkage. With respect to the baseline, EER improved by 28.7% and DCF by 36.4%. With respect to oracle model selection, we have a margin for improvement of 26% and 6% respectively; and with respect to oracle labels, margins of 48.5% and 10%. We can see that those margins are still very high. As we increase the amount of data, the margin between the unsupervised and supervised models also increases. As clustering becomes harder, there is a point where increasing the amount of unsupervised data is not beneficial.

4 Conclusions

We presented a method to train SPLDA models with unsupervised labels. We designed a generative model where labels and model parameters are hidden variables that are updated iteratively with a variational Bayes procedure. The speaker labels were initialized using AHC with different linkage criteria. The best criteria were average and complete linkage. The VB procedure was run several times, each time hypothesizing a different number of development speakers. We selected the model that maximized the VB lower bound.

We experimented training on unlabeled NIST SRE04-08 data. We evaluated the resulting model on the NIST SRE10 det5 condition. For training with 500 speakers, the algorithm was able to select almost the best model. Compared to cosine distance, EER improved by 16% and minimum DCF by 16%. For training with 3789 speakers, clustering becomes harder and we did not selected the best model. However, EER improved by 28% and DCF by 36%. Despite that these gains were significant, there is still a large margin of improvement to match the results of supervised training.

References

1. Dehak, N., Kenny, P., Dehak, R., Dumouchel, P., Ouellet, P.: Front-End Factor Analysis For Speaker Verification. IEEE Transactions on Audio, Speech and Language Processing 19(4), 788–798 (2011)
2. Garcia-Romero, D., Espy-Wilson, C.Y.: Analysis of I-vector Length Normalization in Speaker Recognition Systems. In: Proceedings of the 12th Annual Conference of the International Speech Communication Association, Interspeech 2011, Florence, Italy, pp. 249–252. ISCA (August 2011)
3. Vaquero, C.: Dataset Shift in PLDA based Speaker Verification. In: Proceedings of Odyssey 2012 - The Speaker and Language Recognition Workshop, Singapore, pp. 39–46. COLIPS (June 2012)
4. Villalba, J., Brummer, N.: Towards Fully Bayesian Speaker Recognition: Integrating Out the Between-Speaker Covariance. In: Proceedings of the 12th Annual Conference of the International Speech Communication Association, Interspeech 2011, Florence, Italy, pp. 505–508. ISCA (August 2011)
5. Villalba, J., Brummer, N., Lleida, E.: Fully Bayesian Likelihood Ratios vs i-vector Length Normalization in Speaker Recognition Systems. In: NIST SRE 2011 Speaker Recognition Workshop, Atlanta, Georgia, USA (December 2011)
6. Villalba, J., Lleida, E.: Bayesian Adaptation of PLDA Based Speaker Recognition to Domains with Scarce Development Data. In: Proceedings of Odyssey 2012 - The Speaker and Language Recognition Workshop, Singapore. COLIPS (June 2012)
7. Garcia-Romero, D., McCree, A.: Supervised Domain Adaptation for I-Vector Based Speaker Recognition. In: Proceedings of the IEEE International Conference on Acoustics, Speech and Signal Processing, ICASSP 2014, Florence, Italy, pp. 4075–4079. IEEE (May 2014)

8. Villalba, J., Lleida, E.: Unsupervised Adaptation of PLDA by Using Variational Bayes Methods. In: Proceedings of the IEEE International Conference on Acoustics, Speech and Signal Processing, ICASSP 2014, Florence, Italy. IEEE (May 2014)

9. Garcia-Romero, D., McCree, A., Shum, S., Brummer, N., Vaquero, C.: Unsupervised Domain Adaptation for I-Vector Speaker Recognition. In: Proceedings of Odyssey 2014 - The Speaker and Language Recognition Workshop, Joensuu, Finland, pp. 260–264. ISCA (June 2014)

10. Brummer, N., Garcia-Romero, D.: Generative Modelling for Unsupervised Score Calibration. In: Proceedings of the IEEE International Conference on Acoustics, Speech and Signal Processing, ICASSP 2014, Florence, Italy, pp. 1699–1703. IEEE (May 2014)

11. Shum, S., Reynolds, D.A., Garcia-Romero, D., McCree, A.: Unsupervised Clustering Approaches for Domain Adaptation in Speaker Recognition Systems. In: Proceedings of Odyssey 2014 - The Speaker and Language Recognition Workshop, Joensuu, Finland, pp. 265–272. ISCA (June 2014)

12. Aronowitz, H.: Inter Dataset Variability Compensation for Speaker Recognition. In: Proceedings of the IEEE International Conference on Acoustics, Speech and Signal Processing, ICASSP 2014, Florence, Italy, pp. 4030–4034. IEEE (May 2014)

13. Glembek, O., Ma, J., Matejka, P., Zhang, B., Plchot, O., Burget, L., Matsoukas, S.: Domain Adaptation Via Within-Class Covariance Correction in I-Vector Based Speaker Recognition Systems. In: Proceedings of the IEEE International Conference on Acoustics, Speech and Signal Processing, ICASSP 2014, Florence, Italy, pp. 4060–4064. IEEE (May 2014)

14. Bishop, C.: Variational principal components. In: Proceedings of the 9th International Conference on Artificial Neural Networks, ICANN 1999, Edinburgh, Scotland, pp. 509–514. IET (September 1999)

15. Bishop, C.: Pattern Recognition and Machine Learning. Springer Science+Business Media, LLC (2006)

16. Katahira, K., Watanabe, K., Okada, M.: Deterministic annealing variant of variational Bayes method. Journal of Physics: Conference Series International Workshop on Statistical-Mechanical Informatics (IW-SMI 2007), 95 (January 2008)

17. Villalba, J.: Unsupervised Adaptation of SPLDA. Technical report, University of Zaragoza, Zaragoza, Spain (2013)

18. Anderberg, M.R.: Cluster Analysis for Applications. Academic Press (1973)

On the Use of Convolutional Neural Networks in Pairwise Language Recognition

Alicia Lozano-Diez, Javier Gonzalez-Dominguez, Ruben Zazo,
Daniel Ramos, and Joaquin Gonzalez-Rodriguez

ATVS - Biometric Recognition Group
Universidad Autonoma de Madrid (UAM), Spain
{alicia.lozano,javier.gonzalez,daniel.ramos,joaquin.gonzalez}@uam.es,
ruben.zazo@estudiante.uam.es

Abstract. Convolutional deep neural networks (CDNNs) have been successfully applied to different tasks within the machine learning field, and, in particular, to speech, speaker and language recognition. In this work, we have applied them to pair-wise language recognition tasks. The proposed systems have been evaluated on challenging pairs of languages from NIST LRE'09 dataset. Results have been compared with two spectral systems based on Factor Analysis and Total Variability (i-vector) strategies, respectively. Moreover, a simple fusion of the developed approaches and the reference systems has been performed. Some individual and fusion systems outperform the reference systems, obtaining $\sim 17\%$ of relative improvement in terms of $minC_{DET}$ for one of the challenging pairs.

Keywords: Convolutional networks, CDNNs, pair-wise language recognition.

1 Introduction

Deep Neural Networks (DNNs) are a new paradigm within machine learning. They have shown to be successful in many tasks such as acoustic modelling [16,7,12,8] or speaker recognition [10,4].

Considering this, our work is focused on a related problem: the automatic language recognition (or Spoken Language Recognition, SLR) task. This problem has been addressed for many years by NIST Language Recognition Evaluations (LRE). Many of the state-of-the-art approaches to this problem are based on acoustic systems. For instance, GMM-based systems where a session variability compensation scheme via Factor Analysis (FA) is applied [6], and, also, i-vector approaches that have been proved to be successful to deal with the SLR task [18].

However, new approaches to the problem of SLR based on DNNs have been recently published [15,13]. We propose the use of convolutional deep neural networks (CDNNs), which is a less demanding approach in terms of memory and computational resources than the one proposed in [15]. Moreover, we have applied them to the pair-wise language recognition task, which has been one of

J.L. Navarro Mesa et al. (Eds.): IberSPEECH 2014, LNAI 8854, pp. 79–88, 2014.

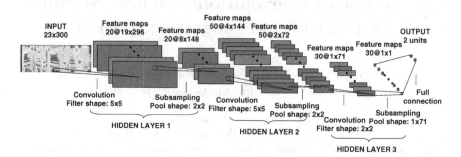

Fig. 1. Representation of architecture used in the experimental part of this work with three hidden layers of 20, 50 and 30 filters respectively (*Model 1*). The other model used (*Model 2*) has the same structure but with 12 filters in each layer.

the tasks proposed by NIST in their Language Recognition Evaluations (LRE). Besides, unlike [13], our proposal is based on the use of CDNNs as a complete system that is directly fed with filter-bank outputs. Figure 1 shows an example of structure used in the experimental part of this work.

The rest of this paper is organized as follows. In Section 2, the proposed system based on CDNNs is described. The reference systems are presented in Section 3 and the database and experimental framework used are exposed in Section 4. Finally, Sections 5 and 6 present the results and conclusions of this work.

2   Convolutional DNNs for Language Recognition

2.1   Convolutional DNNs Architecture

The proposal of this work is to develop a system based on convolutional networks applied to the problem of pairwise language recognition.

CDNNs are models based on the structure of the visual system and are composed of two kinds of layers: convolutional layers and subsampling layers [11]. The first ones act as a feature extractor where each unit is connected to a local subset of units in the layer below. Some units that are related because of their location share their parameters, allowing the network to extract the same features from different locations in the input. This also decreases the amount of parameters to tune. Subsampling layers reduce the size of the representations obtained by convolutional layers by applying a subsampling operation, and making the network, in some way, invariant to small translations and rotations [1]. Moreover, convolutional nets can be trained as a classic *feedforward* network, by using, for instance, supervised learning based on gradient descent algorithms [11].

All these features make them be easier to train and cheaper in terms of resources than other approaches within the *deep learning* paradigm. Then, we have used them as a complete system to perform pair language recognition. In particular, they have been trained in a supervised way to discriminate between two languages, which are considered challenging pairs due to their similarities. The database used has been a subset of the one provided by NIST in the LRE'09.

2.2   Proposed System: CDNN-Based System

The details of the CDNN-based system are as follows. The input of the network consists of a 2-dimensional *time-frequency* representation of the speech signal. In our case, 23 Mel-scale filter-bank outputs have been used to feed the network for each segment of 3 seconds of speech, normalized to have zero mean and unit variance for each coefficient over the whole training set. Those 3 seconds correspond with 300 frames, since windows of 20 ms of duration have been applied with 10 ms of overlap. Moreover, in order to suppress silences, a voice activity detector based on energy has been used. This last filtering process makes test segments contain less than 3 seconds of actual speech, which was a problem since the network input dimensions were fixed. It was solved by applying a *right padding* by using the first frames of the segment to fit this requirement.

Depending on the configuration of the network, two different models have been considered. Both of them have 3 hidden *convolutional-maxpooling* layers. Each of these layers are composed of two stages: 1) computation of the activation for each hidden unit in each feature map by convolving the input with a linear filter (*weights*), adding a bias term and applying the non-linear transformation *tanh* ($h = tanh(W * x + b)$); and 2) application of a sub-sampling phase based on partitioning the input into non-overlapping regions and choosing the maximum activation of each region. For both models, the shape of the linear filters is 5×5 for the first two hidden layers, and 2×2 for the third one. Regarding the maxpooling regions, they have a shape of 2×2 in the first two hidden layers, and 1×71 in the third one in order to have a single value as output of the last hidden layer. Then, the difference between the two mentioned models relies on the number of filters or *feature maps* considered for each hidden layer, which is related to the idea of how many different features want to be extracted in each layer. The first model (*Model 1*) has 12 filters in each layer and the second one (*Model 2*), has 20, 50 and 30 in each of the three mentioned hidden layers, respectively. All this information is summarized in Table 1.

Table 1. Configuration parameters for the developed models

Conf. Parameter	Model 1	Model 2
# Layers	3	3
# Filters/layer	[12, 12, 12]	[20, 50, 30]
Filter shapes	[(5, 5), (5, 5), (2, 2)]	[(5, 5), (5, 5), (2, 2)]
Pool shapes	[(2, 2), (2, 2), (1, 71)]	[(2, 2), (2, 2), (1, 71)]

As far as the output layer is concerned, it consists of a *fully-connected* layer that computes a *softmax* function according to the following expression:

$$P(Y = i|x, W, b) = softmax_i(Wx + b) = \frac{e^{W_i x + b_i}}{\sum_j e^{W_j x + b_j}}$$

where i is a certain class, and W and b are the parameters of the model (weights and bias, respectively).

The output value is considered as a score or likelihood measure of belonging to a certain language, between the two languages involved, since the performed experiments are based on *language-pairs*. The final score for a test segment is computed as the difference between the logarithms of each likelihood.

Regarding the training of the network, the algorithm that has been used is the stochastic gradient descent algorithm with a learning rate of 0.1 and based on *minibatches* of 500 samples each one. The cost function that the algorithm tries to optimize (minimize in this case) is the negative log-likelihood, defined as follows:

$$NLL(\theta, D) = -\sum_{i=1}^{|D|} \log P(Y = y^{(i)}|x^{(i)}, \theta)$$

where D is the dataset, θ represents the parameters of the model ($\theta = W, b$, weights and bias respectively), $x^{(i)}$ is an example, $y^{(i)}$ is the label corresponding to example $x^{(i)}$, and P is defined as the output of the *softmax* function defined above.

Also, an *"early stopping"* technique has been used during the training in order to avoid the *overfitting* problem, so the performance of the model is evaluated in a validation set, and if the improvements over that set are not considered relevant, the training stops.

All this development has been done by using Python and, specifically, *Theano* [2], following the ideas of [14].

3   Reference Systems: FA-GMM and i-Vector

In order to have a baseline to compare with, two different systems have been taken as reference and have been evaluated on the same datasets that the proposed method based on CDNNs.

The first one consists of a Factor Analysis GMM Linear Scoring (FA-GMM-LS) [6], which is a GMM system with linear scoring and session variability compensation applied in the statistic domain. The speech signal is represented by a parameterization consisting of seven MFCCs with CMN-Rasta-Warping concatenated to 7-1-3-7 SDC-MFCCs. Two Universal Background Models (UBMs) with 1024 Gaussian components were trained. One of them (UBM_{CTS}) was trained with Conversational Telephone Speech (hereafter, CTS). The other one (UBM_{VOA}) was train with data from VOA (Voice of America radio broadcasts through Internet), provided by NIST. Thereby, two different systems were developed, one for each UBM. Two session variability subspaces matrices were obtained (U_{CTS} and U_{VOA}). The subspaces were initialized with PCA (Principal Component Analysis) based on [9,20], taking into account just top-50 eigenchannels, and trained by using the EM algorithm.

The second reference system, the i-vector system, is based on GMMs where a Total Variability modeling strategy [3] is employed in order to model both language and session variability. Unlike FA, a *total space* represented by a low-rank T matrix jointly includes language and session variability. Moreover, a session variability compensation stage is applied directly to the low dimensional space driven by T by means of Linear Discriminant Analysis (LDA) and Within-Class Covariance Normalization (WCCN) [5].

The speech signal is represented as in the first reference system and the T matrix has been trained with CTS and broadcast data as well.

Both systems output a score for each test segment computed as the difference between the scores given for each of the two language models involved in each pair.

Moreover, as scores from reference and CDNN-based systems are in the same domain (real numbers), a simple sum fusion has been performed.

4   Database and Experimental Protocol

4.1   Database Description

The database used to perform the experiments has been that provided by NIST in LRE'09 [17].

LRE'09 database includes data coming from different audio sources: conversational telephone speech (CTS), used in previous evaluations, and broadcast data that contain telephone and non-telephone speech. That broadcast data consist of two corpora from past Voice of America (VOA) broadcast in multiple languages (VOA2 and VOA3). Some language labels of VOA2 might be erroneous since they have not been audited. More details can be found in [17].

Regarding evaluation data, segments of 3, 10 and 30 second of duration from CTS and broadcast speech data are available to test the developed systems. However, the experiments shown in this paper are only based on segments of 3 seconds (*short duration*).

We have selected five challenging pairs of languages for the experiments of this work: Bosnian-Croatian (BC), Farsi-Dari (FD), Hindi-Urdu (HU), Portuguese-

Table 2. Amount of data used for the experiments per language (in hours)

| | Amount of data (# Hours) | | |
	Training	Validation	Test
Bosnian	12.27	5.26	0.28
Croatian	9.16	3.92	0.29
Dari	25	10.72	1.07
Farsi	25	10.72	0.28
Hindi	25.9	11.10	0.51
Portuguese	11.79	5.05	0.32
Russian	20.27	8.69	0.66
Spanish	13.85	5.94	0.31
Ukrainian	15.89	6.81	0.31
Urdu	26.63	11.41	0.29

Spanish (PS) and Russian-Ukrainian (RU). These pairs are among the proposed tasks of the language-pair evaluation in the NIST LRE'09, since they are considered of particular interest due to their similarities. Indeed, all of them except Portuguese-Spanish are considered mutually intelligible.

The available datasets have been split into three separate subsets: training, validation and test. The first two datasets includes just broadcast data (VOA2 and VOA3) from the development data provided by NIST LRE'09. However, test segments come from CTS and VOA datasets and are the actual evaluation data of NIST LRE'09. The amount of data (in hours) per language used in the experiments is shown in Table 2.

4.2   Performance Evaluation

The performance of the systems has been evaluated according to the cost measure (C_{DET}) defined in the NIST LRE'09 evaluation plan [17]. This measure takes into account the false alarm and false rejection probabilities and the cost of a bad classification of the segment of speech. As this measure shows the cost with the optimal threshold, it corresponds with the minimum cost operating point, so we will refer to it as $minC_{DET}$ [19].

Furthermore, DET curves have been used in order to evaluate the performance of the systems in different operating points. In the legend of the DET curves shown in Section 5 the EER (in %) is also shown.

Apart from the performance evaluation of the individual systems considered in this work, the performance of fusion systems has been also included. Those fusion schemes consist of a score level fusion where both mentioned reference systems (FA-GMM and i-vector) and the corresponding CDNN-based model are involved. A simple sum of the scores output by each system involved in the fusion scheme has been used to obtain the final score for a certain segment of speech.

Table 3. Performance of individual (left) and fusion (right) systems ($minC_{DET} \times 100$)

	Individual Systems				Fusion Systems	
	Reference		CDNNs		Ref. Systems +	Ref. Systems +
	FA-GMM	i-vector	Model1	Model 2	Model1	Model 2
BC	34.45	37.24	34.89	37.76	**32.13**	35.48
FD	**33.81**	45.51	49.92	49.88	49.46	49.79
HU	43.30	41.93	36.09	37.72	**35.16**	36.90
PS	11.51	**9.15**	17.08	14.71	10.07	9.53
RU	35.29	**35.06**	45.69	44.53	41.72	42.50

5   Results

The experiments shown in this paper are based on the five challenging language pairs mentioned in Section 4.1. For each of these pairs, two different models (according to the configurations shown in Table 1) and the two reference systems described in Section 3 have been evaluated on the same test samples. Furthermore, the amount of data used for training the CDNN-based system (see Table 2) is approximately the same that the used for training the reference systems, although some languages datasets have been reduced in order not to have big differences between the datasets of the two languages involved in each experiment.

The performance of each individual system can be seen in the left side of Table 3. According to the results, CDNN-based models outperform the best reference systems in the case of Hindi-Urdu, with a relative improvement of ~14% in $minC_{DET}$. As it is shown in the right side of Table 3, by performing a simple sum-fusion of the reference systems and the CDNNs systems, the relative improvement yields up to ~ 17% for the Hindi-Urdu pair. For the Bosnian-Croatian experiment, the fusion system gives ~ 7% of relative improvement, and the performances of all individual systems are pretty similar for this pair.

By way of contrast, the models obtained for the language-pairs Farsi-Dari, Portuguese-Spanish and Russian-Ukrainian, even the fusion ones, give worse results than those yielded by the reference systems. Possible reasons might be that the configuration parameters used are not adequate for the available data or that the development dataset has not been adequately selected (with little variability among utterances).

Regarding the comparison between the two CDNN-models, although *Model 2* has more filters (*feature maps*) and, thereby, its capability to extract a better abstract representation of the input signal is bigger, just in three pairs it gives better results than *Model 1*. This might be caused by a lack of data or variability within them that leads to the problem of *overfitting*. More evidence of occurrence of that problem is that we have observed a big *gap* between validation and test errors.

Finally, Figure 2 shows the DET curves obtained for each language-pair according to the performance of both reference systems, the best CDNN system and the best fusion model. As it was observed with the $minC_{DET}$ performance

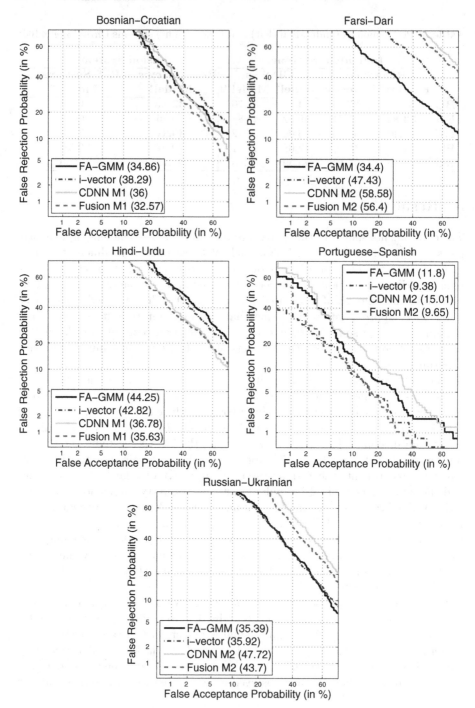

Fig. 2. DET curves corresponding to reference systems, the best CDNN system and the best fusion according to the EER for each language pair. The EER (in %) is shown in brackets.

measure, our individual approach outperforms the reference systems in the experiments with Hindi-Urdu, and the fusion one, in the Bosnian-Croatian pair. Relative improvements and general behaviour or the systems are similar to the one observed with $minC_{DET}$ measure.

6   Conclusions

Considering recent work, CDNNs can be considered a powerful tool to be applied to SLR tasks with a tractable amount of data. It can be considered one of the less costly approaches within the deep learning paradigm.

In this work, we have applied them to the problem of language-pair recognition. The proposed systems have been trained to discriminate between two languages, which are considered challenging due to their similarities. Results have been compared with the ones obtained from two spectral systems.

The proposed models manage to outperform the reference systems in two out of the five pairs considered. It should be pointed out that the test utterances have a duration of just 3 seconds of speech. Moreover, the CDNN systems are fed with the Mel-Filter bank outputs in blocks of 3 seconds. However, this can be considered an exploratory work and more configurations and different treatment of data should be studied.

Acknowledgments. This work has been developed within the project *CMCV2: Caracterización, Modelado y Compensación de Variabilidad en la Señal de Voz* (TEC2012-37585-C02-01), funded by *Ministerio de Economía y Competitividad,* Spain.

References

1. Bengio, Y.: Learning deep architectures for AI. Foundations and Trends in Machine Learning 2(1), 1–127 (2009), also published as a book. Now Publishers (2009)
2. Bergstra, J., Breuleux, O., Bastien, F., Lamblin, P., Pascanu, R., Desjardins, G., Turian, J., Warde-Farley, D., Bengio, Y.: Theano: a CPU and GPU math expression compiler. In: Proceedings of the Python for Scientific Computing Conference (SciPy) (June 2010), oral Presentation
3. Dehak, N., Kenny, P., Dehak, R., Glembek, O., Dumouchel, P., Burget, L., Hubeika, V., Castaldo, F.: Support vector machines and joint factor analysis for speaker verification. In: ICASSP, pp. 4237–4240 (2009)
4. Ghahabi, O., Hernando, J.: i-vector modeling with deep belief networks for multi-session speaker recognition. In: Proc. ODYSSEY (2014)
5. Gonzalez-Dominguez, J., Lopez-Moreno, I., Franco-Pedroso, J., Ramos, D., Toledano, D.T., Gonzalez-Rodriguez, J.: Atvs-uam nist sre 2010 system. In: Proceedings of FALA 2010 (November 2010)
6. Gonzalez-Dominguez, J., Lopez-Moreno, I., Franco-Pedroso, J., Ramos, D., Toledano, D.T., Gonzalez-Rodriguez, J.: Multilevel and session variability compensated language recognition: Atvs-uam systems at nist lre 2009. IEEE Journal on Selected Topics in Signal Processing (2010) (article in press)

7. Hinton, G., Deng, L., Yu, D., Dahl, G., Rahman Mohamed, A., Jaitly, N., Senior, A., Vanhoucke, V., Nguyen, P., Sainath, T., Kingsbury, B.: Deep neural networks for acoustic modeling in speech recognition. Signal Processing Magazine (2012)

8. Jaitly, N., Nguyen, P., Senior, A., Vanhoucke, V.: Application of pretrained deep neural networks to large vocabulary speech recognition. In: Proceedings of Interspeech 2012 (2012)

9. Kenny, P., Boulianne, G., Dumouchel, P.: Eigenvoice modeling with sparse training data. IEEE Transactions on Speech and Audio Processing 13(3), 345–354 (2005)

10. Kenny, P., Gupta, V., Stafylakis, T., Ouellet, P., Alam, J.: Deep neural networks for extracting baum-welch statistics for speaker recognition. In: Proc. ODYSSEY (2014)

11. LeCun, Y., Bottou, L., Bengio, Y., Haffner, P.: Gradient-based learning applied to document recognition. In: Intelligent Signal Processing, pp. 306–351. IEEE Press (2001)

12. Lee, H., Largman, Y., Pham, P., Ng, A.Y.: Unsupervised feature learning for audio classification using convolutional deep belief networks. In: Advances in Neural Information Processing Systems 22, pp. 1096–1104 (2009)

13. Lei, Y., Ferrer, L., Lawson, A., McLaren, M., Scheffer, N.: Application of convolutional neural networks to language identification in noisy conditions. In: Proc. ODYSSEY (2014)

14. LISA: Deep Learning Tutorial. University of Montreal,
http://deeplearning.net/tutorial/

15. Lopez-Moreno, I., Gonzalez-Dominguez, J., Plchot, O.: Automatic language identification using deep neural networks. In: Proc. ICASSP (2014)

16. Mohamed, A.R., Dahl, G.E., Hinton, G.: Acoustic modeling using deep belief networks. IEEE Trans. on Audio, Speech and Language Processing,
http://www.cs.toronto.edu/~hinton/absps/speechDBN_jrnl.pdf

17. NIST: The 2009 nist language recognition evaluation plan (2009),
http://www.itl.nist.gov/iad/mig/tests/lre/2009/LRE09_EvalPlan_v6.pdf

18. Penagarikano, M., Varona, A., Diez, M., Rodriguez-Fuentes, L.J., Bordel, G.: Study of different backends in a state-of-the-art language recognition system. In: INTERSPEECH (2012)

19. Van Leeuwen, D.A., Brummer, N.: Channel-dependent gmm and multi-class logistic regression models for language recognition. In: IEEE Odyssey 2006: The Speaker and Language Recognition Workshop, pp. 1–8. IEEE (2006)

20. Vogt, R., Sridharan, S.: Explicit modelling of session variability for speaker verification. Computer Speech & Language 22(1), 17–38 (2008)

Global Impostor Selection for DBNs in Multi-session i-Vector Speaker Recognition

Omid Ghahabi and Javier Hernando

TALP Research Center, Department of Signal Theory and Communications
Universitat Politecnica de Catalunya - BarcelonaTech, Spain
{omid.ghahabi,javier.hernando}@upc.edu

Abstract. An effective global impostor selection method is proposed in this paper for discriminative Deep Belief Networks (DBN) in the context of a multi-session i-vector based speaker recognition. The proposed method is an iterative process in which in each iteration the whole impostor i-vector dataset is divided randomly into two subsets. The impostors in one subset which are closer to each impostor in another subset are selected and impostor frequencies are computed. At the end, those impostors with higher frequencies will be the global selected ones. They are then clustered and the centroids are considered as the final impostors for the DBN speaker models. The advantage of the proposed method is that in contrary to other similar approaches, only the background i-vector dataset is employed. The experimental results are performed on the NIST 2014 i-vector challenge dataset and it is shown that the proposed selection method improves the performance of the DBN-based system in terms of minDCF by 7% and the whole system outperforms the baseline in the challenge by more than 22% relative improvement.

Index Terms: Speaker Recognition, Deep Belief Network, Impostor Selection, NIST i-vector challenge.

1 Introduction

Speaker recognition based on identity vectors (i-vector) [1] is widely accepted as the state-of-the-art in this field. To compensate undesired speaker and session variabilities, i-vectors are further post-processed with some techniques [1][2][3][4]. A common and successful paradigm for multi-session speaker recognition is based on i-vector and Probabilistic Linear Discriminant Analysis (PLDA) in which a combination of different sessions will be carried out either in the i-vector or score level [5][6] [7]. In the i-vector level, the available i-vectors per each target speaker are averaged and the resulting i-vector is compared with the test i-vectors. On the other hand, in the score level combination, each i-vector belonging to the given target speaker is compared separately with the test i-vectors and then obtained scores are combined.

To encourage research groups to deal with new challenges, the National Institute of Standard and Technologies (NIST) organizes from time to time speaker

J.L. Navarro Mesa et al. (Eds.): IberSPEECH 2014, LNAI 8854, pp. 89–98, 2014.

recognition evaluations and the participating sites present their results in the Speaker Odyssey Workshop. The most recent challenge is planned for modeling i-vectors in a multi-session enrollment task [8]. A large amount of unlabeled i-vectors are given as a development set and participating sites are not allowed to use their own data set to develop the systems. Thus the supervised variability compensation techniques like Within-Class Covariance Normalization (WCCN), Linear Discriminant Analysis (LDA), or the most effective one (PLDA) cannot be used easily in this challenge as they need speaker labels. Moreover, i-vectors are extracted from speech utterances with different durations which it makes the challenge more difficult.

Most of participating sites tried to develope some automatic speaker classifiers on the development i-vectors to label data and then to use supervised learning approaches [9] [10][11][12]. Some of them also tried to solve the unmatch condition between train and test i-vectors from the speech duration point of view [11][10] . We proposed a Deep Belief Network (DBN) based system [13] in which we could achieve notable results in comparison to the baseline and other individual systems [9][10] [11][12] without using the speech duration information or any automatic labeling technique. In this paper we propose a new global impostor selection method which achieves similar results as in [13], in the context of our DBN-based system, by using only the background dataset. Using just the background dataset is actually the advantage of the proposed method in comparison to other similar ones [14][15][16][13], as they use also the training dataset as a part of the selection method.

In our DBN-based system we take the advantage of unsupervised learning to model a global DBN to be used in an adaptation process and the advantage of supervised learning to model each target speaker discriminatively. As more than one i-vector sample are available per each target speaker in this case and each of them may be recorded from different session, DBNs will capture more speaker and session variabilities from the input data and will work better than in the single session task [16].

2   i-Vector Extraction

This section gives a brief overview on the i-vector framework developed in [1]. Given the centralized Baum-Welch statistics from all available speech utterances, the low rank total variability matrix ($\mathbf{T}$) is trained in an iterative process. The training process assumes that an utterance can be represented by the Gaussian Mixture Model (GMM) mean supervector,

$$\mathbf{m} = \mathbf{m}_u + \mathbf{T}\boldsymbol{\omega} \tag{1}$$

where $\mathbf{m}_u$ is the speaker- and session-independent mean supervector from the Universal Background Model (UBM), and $\boldsymbol{\omega}$ is a low rank vector referred to as the identity vector or i-vector. The supervector $\mathbf{m}$ is assumed to be normally distributed with the mean $\mathbf{m}_u$ and the covariance $\mathbf{TT}^t$, and the i-vectors have a standard normal distribution $\mathcal{N}(0,1)$. More details can be found in [1].

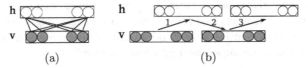

Fig. 1. RBM (a) and RBM training (b)

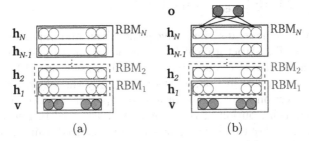

Fig. 2. Generative (a) and discriminative (b) DBNs

3 Deep Belief Networks

DBNs are originally probabilistic generative networks with multiple layers of stochastic hidden units above a layer of visible variables. There is an efficient greedy layer-wise algorithm for learning DBNs [17]. The algorithm treats every two adjacent layers as an RBM (Figs. 1a and 2a). The output of each RBM is considered as the input to its above RBM. RBMs are constructed from a layer of binary stochastic hidden units and a layer of stochastic visible units (Fig. 1a).

Training an RBM is based on an approximated version of the Contrastive Divergence (CD) algorithm [18][17] which consists of three steps (Fig. 1b). At first, hidden states ($\mathbf{h}$) are computed given visible states ($\mathbf{v}$), then given $\mathbf{h}$, $\mathbf{v}$ is reconstructed, and in the third step $\mathbf{h}$ is updated given the reconstructed $\mathbf{v}$. Finally, the change of connection weights is given as follows,

$$\Delta w_{ij} \approx -\alpha \left(\langle v_i h_j \rangle_{data} - \langle v_i h_j \rangle_{recon} \right) \tag{2}$$

where α is the learning rate, w_{ij} represents the weight between the visible unit i and the hidden unit j, $\langle . \rangle_{data}$ and $\langle . \rangle_{recon}$ denote the expectations when the hidden state values are driven respectively from the input visible data and the reconstructed data. Actually, the training process tries to minimize the reconstruction error between the actual input data and the reconstructed one. The parameter updating process is iterated until the algorithm converges. Each iteration is called an epoch. It is possible to perform the above parameter update after processing each training example, but it is often more efficient to divide the whole input data (batch) into smaller size batches (minibatch) and to do the parameter update by an average over each minibatch. More theoretical and practical details can be found in [18][17][19].

When the unsupervised learning is finished, by adding a label layer on top of the network and doing a supervised backpropagation training, it can be converted to a discriminative model (Fig. 2b). In other words, the unsupervised learning can be considered as a pre-training for the supervised stage. It has been shown [17] that this unsupervised pre-training can set the weights of the network to be closer to a good solution than random initialization and, therefore, avoids local minima when using supervised gradient descent.

4   i-Vector Modeling Using DBN

The main idea is to model discriminatively the target and impostor i-vectors by a DBN structure. The structure which was proposed for the first time in a single session enrollment task [16] and later in a multi-session one [13] will be used also in this paper. In this section, we describe briefly the whole structure used, and in the next section focus on the proposed impostor selection method which is the main new contribution of this paper. As illustrated in Fig. 3, the DBN structure is composed of three main parts namely balanced training, adaptation, and fine-tuning.

Like other discriminative methods, DBNs need also balanced positive and negative input data to achieve their best results. The balanced training part in the block diagram (Fig. 3) tries to use the information of all available impostors and decrease their population in a reasonable way. The decreasing is carried out in two steps, selecting the most informative ones and clustering. In [16] and [13] simple and effective selection methods are proposed. First, the n closest impostors to each target speaker are chosen according to their cosine distances. Then the closest impostors are accumulated over all target speakers and the k top ranked impostors are selected according to the number of times they are appeared in the accumulated set of impostors. In other words, the k impostors which are statistically closer to all target speakers are selected by this method. The selected impostors are clustered finally by the k-means algorithm using the cosine distance criterion.

In the multi-session task where more than one positive sample are available per each target speaker, we will choose the number of impostor cluster centroids in each minibatch the same as the number of available positive samples to make the training balanced. Hence, if the number of minibatches is set to three, for instance, and the number of positive samples per each speaker is five, the total number of impostor clusters will be 15. Actually, in each minibatch we will show the network the same positive samples as in other minibatches but different negative ones.

DBNs have the ability to be trained unsupervisingly [17][18] contrary to conventional neural networks that need labeled data to be trained. Thus a global model called Universal DBN (UDBN) [16] is trained by feeding many i-vectors from development background data. The training is carried out layer by layer using RBMs as described in section 3. UDBN parameters are adapted to the new data of each speaker including both target and impostor samples obtained in the balanced training part of Fig. 3. The adaptation is carried out by pre-training each network initialized by the UDBN parameters. It is shown [16] that the adaptation process outperforms both random and pre-training initializations.

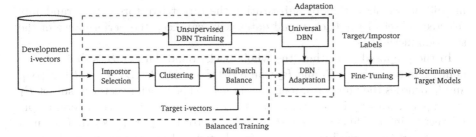

Fig. 3. Block-diagram of the DBN based speaker recognition system

Once the adaptation process is completed, a label layer is added on the top of the network and the stochastic gradient descent backpropagation is carried out as the fine-tuning process. The softmax will be the activation function of the top label layer. To minimize the negative effect of using random numbers used for initializing the top layer parameters, a pseudo pre-training process is performed by only one layer error backpropagating for a few iterations before a full backpropagation is carried out. If the input labels in the training phase are chosen as $(l_1 = 1, l_2 = 0)$ and $(l_1 = 0, l_2 = 1)$ for target and impostor i-vectors respectively, the final output score in the testing phase will be computed in a Log Likelihood Ratio (LLR) form as follows,

$$LLR = log(o_1) - log(o_2) \qquad (3)$$

where (o_1, o_2) represents the outputs of the top layer. LLR computation helps to gaussianize the true and false score distributions.

5 Global Impostor Selection

As it was mentioned in section 4, we need to decrease the number of impostors in an effective way to provide a balanced training for DBNs. In [16] and [13] we decreased the number of impostors in two steps, impostor selection and clustering. In this paper we will focus on the impostor selection step. A support vector based method was proposed in [14] to select the most informative impostors for the Support Vector Machine (SVM) speaker recognition. In that work, those impostors which are selected more frequently as the support vectors in the target SVM models are shown to be more informative. In [15] the authors are extended the method proposed in [14] by pooling the target dependent support vectors and the global selected ones. In [16] and [13] we proposed a method in which those impostors statistically close to all the target i-vectors are selected as the final impostors. We used cosine distance criterion as a similarity measure in our method. However, in all of these methods the target speakers play a main role in the selection process.

The idea in this paper is to develop an impostor selection method which uses only the development background data keeping the advantage of being global to all the target speakers. The base of the proposed method will be the same as in [16] but we show that by substituting the target i-vectors with a randomly selected subset of the background dataset we can keep the performance of the selection method.

In the proposed algorithm, the whole background dataset B is divided randomly into two subsets B_1 and B_2 where $B_1 \cup B_2 = B$, $B_1 \cap B_2 = \phi$, $|B_1| \ll |B_2|$, and $|.|$ denotes the number of members in a set. Then each i-vector in subset B_1 is compared with all i-vectors in subset B_2 using cosine distance criterion. The n i-vectors in B_2 which are closest to each i-vector in B_1 are selected. The number of times that each i-vector in B_2 is selected will be referred to as impostor frequency and is considered as a measure for the importance of that impostor in the whole background dataset B. To make the process statistically more reliable, we repeat the whole process several times (100 times in our experiments) and in each iteration we accumulate the impostor frequencies. We assume that higher impostor frequencies correspond to higher importance of those impostors in comparison to other ones in the background data. Thus we sort the impostor frequencies descendingly at the end and select the first k ones as the final impostors. It is worth noting that since the diagram of the sorted frequencies will be smooth enough due to the repetition of the selection process, we just select the first k impostors with the higher frequencies. In this way, there will be no need to use a threshold for selecting the impostors as it is proposed in [13].

The whole selection procedure can be summarized as follows.

1. Initialization
   (a) $t = 1$
   (b) $f_m = 0$, $1 \le m \le M$
2. Divide the background i-vector dataset $B = \{\omega_m, 1 \le m \le M\}$ into B_1 and B_2, where $B_1 = \{\nu_i, 1 \le i \le 1000\}$, $B_2 = \{\chi_j, 1 \le j \le M - 1000\}$, $B_1 \cup B_2 = B$, and $B_1 \cap B_2 = \phi$
3. For each $\nu_i \in B_1$
   (a) Compute $score\,(\nu_i, \chi_j)$, $1 \le j \le M - 1000$
   (b) Select the n i-vectors χ_j with the highest scores
   (c) Search for the corresponding indexes m of the selected i-vectors
   (d) For the selected i-vectors $f_m \leftarrow f_m + 1$
4. $t \leftarrow t + 1$
5. if $t \le 100$ go to 2
6. Sort f_m, $1 \le m \le M$ descendingly
7. Select the first k i-vectors as the final impostors,

where $score\,(\nu_i, \chi_j)$ is the cosine score between two i-vectors ν_i in set B_1 and χ_j in set B_2. The values of 1,000 and 100 are set arbitrary for the size of B_1 and the number of iterations, respectively. The parameters n and k will be determined experimentally in section 6.

6   Multi-session Experiments

The details of the database, the baseline and the DBN-based setups, and the obtained results are given in this section.

6.1   Baseline and Database

The experiments are carried out on the NIST 2014 i-vector challenge [8]. In this challenge contrary to other previous NIST evaluations, i-vectors are provided instead of speech signals. The i-vectors are computed from conventional telephone speech recordings in the SRE 2004 to 2012. The durations of speech utterances used to obtain i-vectors are different. They are sampled from a normal distribution with a mean of 40 s. The length of each i-vector is 600. Three sets of i-vectors are provided: unlabeled development, model, and test. The amounts of i-vectors in each set are respectively 36,572, 6,530, and 9,634. The number of target models is 1,306 and for each of them five i-vectors are available. Each model will be scored against all the test i-vectors and, therefore, 12,582,004 trials will be reported. Among all trials, 40% (progress subset) will be scored by NIST as a feedback to develop the system and 60% (evaluation subset) will be reserved for the final official evaluation. The performance is evaluated using a new Decision Cost Function (DCF) defined by NIST [8],

$$DCF(t) = (\#Miss(t)/\#Targets) + 100 \times (\#FalseAlarm(t)/\#NonTargets) \quad (4)$$

where t refers to the threshold for which the DCF is being computed. The minimum DCF obtained over all thresholds will be the official system score.

In the baseline system, average i-vectors obtained over the available i-vectors for each target speaker are scored against all test i-vectors using cosine distance classifier. However, before averaging and scoring some post-processing is carried out on i-vectors. The global mean and covariance are computed using unlabeled development data. All i-vectors are centered and whitened based on the global mean and covariance. Then the resulting i-vectors are length normalized. Length normalization is applied again on the average i-vectors obtained for each target speaker.

6.2   DBN-Based Setup

As in [16] DBNs with only one hidden layer are explored in this paper. The size of hidden layer is set to 400. Each minibatch will include five impostor centroids and five target samples. The impostor centroids in each minibatch are different than those in other ones, but they share the same target samples. The number of minibatches is set to three and, therefore, we will have 15 impostor centroids in total. The unlabeled development i-vectors provided by NIST are used for impostor selection. UDBN is trained with the same development i-vectors as in the impostor database. As the input i-vectors are real-valued normal distributed, a Gaussian-Bernoulli RBM [19][20] is employed. The learning rate (α), the number of epochs (NofE), and the minibatch size are set respectively to 0.02, 50, and 100 for UDBN training. A fixed momentum of 0.9 and a weight decay of 2×10^{-4} are also considered.

The adaptation process is carried out with $\alpha = 0.03$ and NofE=25. To decrease the probability of overfitting during the adaptation, it is performed on each minibatch separately and then the obtained network parameters are averaged.

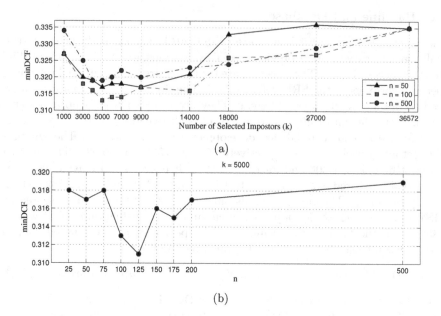

Fig. 4. Determination of the parameters n and k for the proposed global imposter selection method (a) finding the rough values (b) keeping parameter k fixed and seting parameter n

The softmax connection weights are initialized by $\mathcal{N}(0, 0.01)$ and pre-trained with $\alpha = 1$ and NofE=15 before the whole backpropagation is performed. The momentum is started by 0.4 and is scaled up by 0.1 after each epoch (up to 0.9). The whole backpropagation is then carried out with $\alpha = 1$, NofE=30, and a fixed momentum of 0.9. The weight decay for both top layer pre-tarining and the whole backpropagation is set to 0.0014.

6.3   Results

Figure 4a illustrates the variability of minDCF obtained by eq. 4 in terms of the two parameters n and k defined in sec. 5. We have selected three rough values for parameter n and have plotted the obtained minDCF values for different number of selected global impostors. The figure shows that for all three selected values for parameter n, the minimum value of minDCF is obtained by selecting the first 5,000 impostors with higher frequencies ($k = 5,000$). Moreover, the figure shows that a medium value of $n = 100$ archives better results in overall. Therefore, $n = 100$ and $k = 5,000$ are chosen as the rough values which the selection method can perform well. By keeping one parameter fixed and setting another one and vice versa we can set both parameters more accurately. Figure 4b illustrates the variation of minDCF in terms of parameter n when $k = 5,000$. It shows that $n = 125$ yields the best result when k is kept fixed. Our experimental results

Table 1. Performance comparison of the DBN-based system with the baseline. The results are obtained on the NIST 2014 i-vector challenge.

System	Impostors	minDCF
Baseline	-	0.386
DBN-based	Full Background	0.335
DBN-based	Global Selected	0.311
DBN-based	Global Selected + 200 closest Target-Dependent	0.300

show that keeping $n = 125$ and changing k does not achieve better results. Thus we set $n = 125$ and $k = 5,000$ for our impostor selection method.

Table 1 shows the importance of the proposed impostor selection method in comparison to when the whole background dataset is used before clustering in fig. 3. As it can be seen in this table the global impostor selection method helps the DBN system to be around 7% more efficient. The experimental results show that if we pool the global selected impostors with 200 closest background i-vectors to each target speaker and then cluster them all together for each target speaker independently, we will achieve better results (minDCF=0.300) although it would be more computationally expensive. The overall performance of our DBN-based system is also notable (22% relative improvement) in comparison to the baseline in the challenge.

7 Conclusion

The authors proposed a new global impostor selection method for a Deep belief Network (DBN) system in the multi-session i-vector speaker verification. The advantage of the proposed method is that only the background i-vector dataset is used in the selection process which make it suitable for using in the recent NIST i-vector challenge. The global selected impostors are further clustered and the cluster centroids are used as the final negative samples for discriminative DBN speaker models. The experimental results showed that the proposed impostor selection method increase the performance of the DBN system more than 7% in terms of minDCF and the final discriminative DBN models achieve a considerable performance in comparison to the conventional baseline system (more than 22% relative improvement).

Acknowledgement. This work has been partially funded by the Spanish Government projects TEC2010-21040-C02-01 and PCIN-2013-067.

References

1. Dehak, N., Kenny, P., Dehak, R., Dumouchel, P., Ouellet, P.: Front-End Factor Analysis for Speaker Verification. IEEE Transactions on Audio, Speech, and Language Processing 19, 788–798 (2011)
2. Prince, S., Elder, J.: Probabilistic Linear Discriminant Analysis for Inferences About Identity. In: IEEE 11th International Conference on Computer Vision, ICCV 2007 (2007)

3. Kenny, P.: Bayesian speaker verification with heavy tailed priors. In: IEEE Odyssey Speaker and Language Recognition Workshop (2010)
4. Brummer, N., Villiers, E.: The speaker partitioning problem. In: Proceedings of the Odyssey Speaker and Language Recognition Workshop, Brno, Czech Republic (2010)
5. Liu, G., Hasan, T., Boril, H., Hansen, J.: An investigation on back-end for speaker recognition in multi-session enrollment. In: 2013 IEEE International Conference on Acoustics, Speech and Signal Processing (ICASSP), pp. 7755–7759 (2013)
6. Larcher, A., Lee, K., Ma, B., Li, H.: Phonetically-constrained PLDA modeling for text-dependent speaker verification with multiple short utterances. In: 2013 IEEE International Conference on Acoustics, Speech and Signal Processing (ICASSP), pp. 7673–7677 (2013)
7. Larcher, A., Bonastre, J.-F., Fauve, B., Lee, K., Lvy, C., Li, H., Mason, J., Parfait, J.-Y.: ALIZE 3.0 Open Source Toolkit for State-of-the-Art Speaker Recognition. In: Proc. Interspeech, pp. 2768–2771 (2013)
8. The 2013-2014 Speaker Recognition i-vector Machine Learning Challenge (2014)
9. Khoury, E., El Shafey, L., Ferras, M., Marcel, S.: Hierarchical speaker clustering methods for the NIST i-vector Challenge. In: Odyssey: The Speaker and Language Recognition Workshop, pp. 254–259 (2014)
10. Novoselov, S., Pekhovsky, T., Simonchik, K.: STC Speaker Recognition System for the NIST i-Vector Challenge. In: Odyssey: The Speaker and Language Recognition Workshop, pp. 231–240 (2014)
11. Vesnicer, B., Zganec-Gros, J., Dobrisek, S., Struc, V.: Incorporating Duration Information into I-Vector-Based Speaker-Recognition Systems. In: Odyssey: The Speaker and Language Recognition Workshop, pp. 241–248 (2014)
12. Khosravani, A., Homayounpour, M.: Linearly Constrained Minimum Variance for Robust I-vector Based Speaker Recognition. In: Odyssey: The Speaker and Language Recognition Workshop, pp. 249–253 (2014)
13. Ghahabi, O., Hernando, J.: i-Vector Modeling with Deep Belief Networks for Multi-Session Speaker Recognition. In: Odyssey: The Speaker and Language Recognition Workshop, pp. 305–310 (2014)
14. McLaren, M., Baker, B., Vogt, R., Sridharan, S.: Improved SVM speaker verification through data-driven background dataset collection. In: IEEE International Conference on Acoustics, Speech and Signal Processing, ICASSP 2009, pp. 4041–4044 (2009)
15. Liu, G., Suh, J.-W., Hansen, J.: A fast speaker verification with universal background support data selection. In: 2012 IEEE International Conference on Acoustics, Speech and Signal Processing (ICASSP), pp. 4793–4796 (2012)
16. Ghahabi, O., Hernando, J.: Deep belief networks for i-vector based speaker recognition. In: 2014 IEEE International Conference on Acoustics, Speech and Signal Processing (ICASSP) (2014)
17. Hinton, G., Osindero, S., Teh, Y.-W.: A Fast Learning Algorithm for Deep Belief Nets. Neural Computation 18, 1527–1554 (2006)
18. Hinton, G., Salakhutdinov, R.: Reducing the Dimensionality of Data with Neural Networks. Science 313, 504–507 (2006)
19. Hinton, G.E.: A Practical Guide to Training Restricted Boltzmann Machines. In: Montavon, G., Orr, G.B., Müller, K.-R. (eds.) NN: Tricks of the Trade, 2nd edn. LNCS, vol. 7700, pp. 599–619. Springer, Heidelberg (2012)
20. Dahl, G., Yu, D., Deng, L., Acero, A.: Context-Dependent Pre-Trained Deep Neural Networks for Large-Vocabulary Speech Recognition. IEEE Transactions on Audio, Speech, and Language Processing 20, 30–42 (2012)

Phoneme-Lattice to Phoneme-Sequence Matching Algorithm Based on Dynamic Programming

Ciro Gracia[1,2], Xavier Anguera[1], Jordi Luque[1], and Ittai Artzi[3]

[1] Telefonica Research, Edificio Telefonica-Diagonal 00, 08019, Barcelona, Spain
[2] Universitat Pompeu Fabra, Department of Information and Communications Technologies, Barcelona, Spain
[3] Tel Aviv University, Tel Aviv, Israel
ciro.gracia@upf.edu, {xanguera,jls}@tid.es

Abstract. A novel phoneme-lattice to phoneme-sequence matching algorithm based on dynamic programming is presented in this paper. Phoneme lattices have been shown to be a good choice to encode in a compact way alternative decoding hypotheses from a speech recognition system. These are typically used for the spoken term detection and keyword-spotting tasks, where a phoneme sequence query is matched to a reference lattice. Most current approaches suffer from a lack of flexibility whenever a match allowing phoneme insertions, deletions and substitutions is to be found. We introduce a matching approach based on dynamic programming, originally proposed for Minimum Bayes decoding on speech recognition systems. The original algorithm is extended in several ways. First, a self-trained phoneme confusion matrix for phoneme comparison is applied as phoneme penalties. Also, posterior probabilities are computed per arc, instead of likelihoods and an acoustic matching distance is combined with the edit distance at every arc. Finally, total matching scores are normalized based on the length of the optimum alignment path. The resulting algorithm is compared to a state-of-the-art phoneme-lattice-to-string matching algorithm showing relative precision improvements over 20% relative on an isolated word retrieval task.

Keywords: phoneme lattice search, keyword search, speech recognition, information retrieval.

1 Introduction

The use of Phoneme Lattice-based Search (PLS) for efficient keyword search and retrieval has captured the attention of researchers during the last few years. For instance, the use of phoneme lattices for efficient representation of speech utterances has become popular in tasks like Spoken term detection (STD) [1] or Keyword spotting (KWS) [2]. Such tasks are oriented towards applications related to information retrieval which require the processing of large amounts of speech data. Some example of application include mining of the opinion and complains of customers in call center data [3], indexing of meetings or lectures [4] and browsing and retrieval of voice/video mail messages [5,6].

J.L. Navarro Mesa et al. (Eds.): IberSPEECH 2014, LNAI 8854, pp. 99–108, 2014.
© Springer International Publishing Switzerland 2014

Phoneme lattice-based search is based on a lattice representation of the set of phoneme alternatives decoded from the audio signal, used to compactly encode the acoustic signals as the N best decoding hypotheses. Although in 1-best decoding transcriptions the search for a keyword is a simple "grep" operation, it is found that errors on such transcript affect too negatively the retrieval performance. Encoding more than a single decoding hypothesis solves this problem in most part, although a graph or network structure is usually required for optimal encoding, making search and matching algorithms quite complex whenever we want to consider insertions and deletions. In this paper we propose an alternative indexing and search method targeted to phoneme lattices that simplifies prior approaches.

In general, PLS-based approaches [2,7] are a good alternative to previous proposed strategies [8,9] thanks to their flexibility, even where no prior knowledge about the searched words is provided, and thanks to their capacity to represent in a compact form multiple phoneme-sequences hypotheses between two time stamps in the utterance. In [7] the authors used a phoneme lattice-based approach for keyword search in a subset of the DARPA Resource Management (RM) task [10]. Their approach matches the keyword pronunciation against each lattice through dynamic programming, which takes into account phoneme recogniser insertions, deletions and substitutions by heuristically imposing a penalty on them. The authors also compared the lattice search with previous strategies like Keyword HMM [8], which makes use of the knowledge on the searched keywords to constrain a recognition network consisting on pre-trained HMM models per each word and a "garbage" model for the rest. PLS-based approaches can achieve significantly higher query speeds than HMM-based systems by first indexing the lattices for subsequent search.

In [11] the authors incorporate the benefits from Dynamic Programming sequence matching techniques aiming to decrease miss rates due to phoneme recognizer errors. Dynamic programming matches the keyword pronunciation against each lattice through a improvement on the Minimum Edit Distance (MED) where penalty substitutions are derived from a phoneme confusion matrix. The authors also employ HTK toolkit [12] for lattice generation, showing considerable improvements in terms of both keyword search accuracy and searching speed while maintaining low miss rate on a conversational telephone speech database.

In [13] the authors propose to derive substitution phoneme penalties for the MED distance from a phone confusion matrix. This leads to a considerable improvement in the accuracy of the keyword search algorithm. In order to build the confusion matrix, the authors used the ground truth transcription from a database to compare against an automatic transcription from a speech recognition system. In [14], spoken terms are searched in pruned phoneme lattices. A "term-dependent discriminative decision" technique is introduced which integrates multiple decisions into a classification posterior probability. Furthermore, the work addresses OOV detection through estimation of a posterior acoustic confidence.

In this paper we propose a novel PLS approach that integrates a dynamic programming matching algorithm first proposed in [15] for Minimum Bayes decoding on speech recognition systems. It is augmented with several improvements to perform a phoneme sequence to phoneme lattice matching in a fast and effective way. First, a self-trained phoneme confusion matrix for phoneme comparison is applied as phoneme penalties. Also, posterior probabilities are computed per arc, instead of using likelihoods and an acoustic matching distance is combined with the edit distance at every arc. Finally, combined matching scores are normalized based on the length of the optimum alignment path. We test our algorithm using a simple test scenario comparing multiple instances of words, designed to rapidly evaluate the capabilities of matching/search algorithms working with lattice representation. We show improvements of over 20% relative in a subset of the Switchboard word corpus [16] compared to results on the same task obtained by a state-of-the-art phoneme-lattice-to-string matching algorithm [1,15] .

2   Edit Distance Computation on Lattices

In this section we review the algorithm proposed in [15] to obtain an upper bound on the edit distance calculation between a phoneme string and a phoneme lattice, which we will later improve in this paper. This algorithm compares a sequence of phonemes $R = \{r_1, ..., r_Q\}$ (i.e. a phoneme string or sequence) against a phoneme lattice L in the context of the minimum Bayes risk decoding for the optimization of speech recognition systems. The lattice L is composed by nodes $n_i \in \{n_1, ..., n_N\}$ that encode time stamps in the acoustic signals. Each node n_i has a set of incoming $pre(n_i)$ and a set of outgoing $post(n_i)$ arcs. An arc a_j represents a decoding hypothesis for a certain time interval and is represented by: a starting node $s(a_j)$, an ending node $e(a_j)$, a hypothesis class label $w(a_j)$ and, typically, a pair of log-likelihoods from the acoustic model $l_a(a_j)$ and the language model $l_l(a_j)$. The algorithm uses the Levenshtein edit distance[17] to compare a sequence of phonemes R and a sequence of phonemes $W(S)$ obtained from the sequence of arc labels in the lattice path S.

As a lattice can be seen as set of decoded strings, each of the decoded strings can be compared with the reference string generating a corresponding edit distance. In addition, each of the decoded strings has an associated likelihood, provided by the recognition system. Given $S \in L$ a path in the lattice, the log-probability of the path $(log(p(S)))$ is defined from the total likelihood obtained from the arcs in S as shown in equation 1.

$$log(p(S)) = \sum_{n=1}^{|S|} l_a(S_n) + l_l(S_n) \tag{1}$$

Where $|S|$ is the total number of arcs in the path, $l_a(S_n), l_l(S_n)$ are the acoustic and language model log-likelihoods of phoneme S_n in the path. The exact edit distance between the phoneme lattice L and the phoneme string R, Edit-Distance(L, R), can be computed by equation 2.

$$\text{Edit-Distance}(L, R) = \frac{\sum_{S \in L} p(S) ED(W(S), R)}{\sum_{S \in L} p(S)} \tag{2}$$

where $ED(W(S), R)$ is the standard edit distance between two strings, in this case the sequence of phonemes of path S in the lattice and the phoneme string (note the difference with Edit-Distance(L, R) which indicates the distance between the whole lattice and a string). Given that computing Eq. 2 is very expensive, in [15] they propose an efficient way to obtain an upper bound to Equation 2 through a dynamic programming procedure shown in Algorithm 1.

Algorithm 1. $\hat{L}$ = Edit-Distance'(L,R)

1: $N \leftarrow |L|, Q \leftarrow |R|$
2: Initialize array $\alpha(1...N), \alpha'(1...N, 0...Q), \alpha'_{arc}(0..Q)$
3: $\alpha(1) \leftarrow 1, \alpha' \leftarrow 0$
4: **for** $q \leftarrow 1..N$ **do**
5:     $\alpha'(1, q) \leftarrow \alpha(1, q - 1) + loss(\epsilon, r_q)$
6: **end for**
7: **for** $n \leftarrow 2..N$ **do**
8:     $\alpha(n) \leftarrow \sum_{a \in pre(n)} \alpha(s(a)) p(a)$
9:     $\forall q, \alpha'(n, q) \leftarrow 0$
10:    **for** $a \in pre(n)$ **do**
11:        $\lambda(a) \leftarrow \frac{\alpha(s(a)) p(a)}{\alpha(n)}$
12:        **for** $q \leftarrow 0..Q$ **do**
13:            **if** $q = 0$ **then**
14:                $\alpha'_{arc}(q) \leftarrow \alpha'(s(a), q) + loss(w(a), \epsilon) + \delta$
15:            **else**
16:                $\alpha'_{arc}(q) \leftarrow \min \begin{cases} \alpha'(s(a), q - 1) + loss(w(a), r_q) \\ \alpha'(s(a), q) + loss(w(a), \epsilon) + \delta \\ \alpha'_{arc}(q - 1) + loss(\epsilon, r_q) \end{cases}$
17:            **end if**
18:            $\alpha'(n, q) \leftarrow \alpha'(n, q) + \lambda(a) \alpha'_{arc}(q)$
19:        **end for**
20:    **end for**
21: **end for**
22: $\hat{L} \leftarrow \alpha'(N, Q)$

---

3   Adaptation to Phoneme Lattice Search

In this section we describe four proposed improvements to Algorithm 1.

3.1   Single-Best-Path Alignment

The use of a phoneme lattices instead of the 1-best phoneme decoding in Algorithm 1 increases the probability of finding correct matches with the phonetic sequence given by the word transcription. Still, Algorithm 1 computes at each node the weighted average of all arcs reaching that node, making the final distance strongly dependent on the structure of the lattice. Different parameter configurations in the lattice pruning may produce different lattice densities, which can translate into very different resulting distances, driven by the least probable lattice paths. For this reason we avoid the definition of a final score as the average edit distance with respect to the whole lattice and, instead, we define it as the average edit distance between the query phoneme sequence and the closest phoneme path within the phoneme lattice. To do so, we redefine the α' term (Line 18 in Algorithm 1) as $\alpha'(n, q) \leftarrow \min(\alpha'(n, q), \alpha'_{arc}(q))$ to propagate only the best scoring path at each node. This modification allows us to retrieve the single best path with respect to the query instead of the single best sequence of nodes.

3.2   Combining Edit Distance with Acoustic Likelihoods

Algorithm 1 defines the distance between a phoneme lattice and a phoneme sequence as the average edit distance. The edit distance measures the dissimilarity, in terms of edit operations, between phonetic sequences but it does not take into account neither the acoustic nor the language model likelihoods associated to each phoneme in that path. This leads to situations in where phone sequences with little phonetic mismatch might be selected although they produced low global acoustic probability scores. This is a problem in very dense lattices where it is more probable that spurious matching paths exist.

In order to take into account the phoneme likelihood into the algorithm we define a new global score that combines both sources of information. To do so, we first define in Equations 3 and 4 the $\hat{\alpha}(n)$ and $\hat{\beta}(n)$ variables which represent the acoustic score of the best path starting and ending at a certain node in the lattice. Then, in Equation 5 we define $\lambda(a)$ as the ratio between the total acoustic score of the best path containing arc a and the score of the most likely path in the lattice. This score lies within the range $[0 - 1]$, becoming 1 when a belongs to the most likely path. Finally, Equation 6 combines the edit distance and acoustic scores and is used in replacement of line 14 in Algorithm 1.

$$\hat{\alpha}(n) = \begin{cases} 0, & \text{if } n = 1 \\ max_{a \in pre(n)}\{\hat{\alpha}(s(a)) + l_a(a) + l_l(a)\}, & \text{otherwise} \end{cases} \quad (3)$$

$$\hat{\beta}(n) = \begin{cases} 0, & \text{if } n = N \\ max_{a \in post(n)}\{\hat{\beta}(e(a)) + l_a(a) + l_l(a)\}, & \text{otherwise} \end{cases} \quad (4)$$

$$\lambda(a) \leftarrow exp(\hat{\alpha}(s(a)) + l_a(a) + l_l(a) + \hat{\beta}(e(a)) - \hat{\alpha}(N)) \quad (5)$$

$$\alpha'_{arc}(q) \leftarrow \alpha'(s(a), q) + \theta(loss(w(a), r_q) + \delta) + (1 - \theta)(1 - \lambda(a)) \quad (6)$$

Where the factor θ is used to weight the contribution between the edit distance and the acoustic score. We have experimentally set it to $\theta = 0.85$.

3.3   Phonetic Loss Function Estimation

Algorithm 1 uses a loss function $loss(a, b) \leftarrow (1 \leftarrow a = b, 0 \leftarrow a \neq b)$ based on the edit distance and driven by binary (i.e $\{0, 1\}$) decisions. Despite it being adequate for comparing general sequences of symbols its does not take into account any available domain knowledge. Similarly to [13], we improve the loss function by incorporating specific penalties for possible phoneme substitutions, insertions and deletions.

In order to define an appropriate loss function we apply a data driven approach. First we compute, for all words in the development set, all possible phoneme-level alignments between queries and lattices representing instances of the same word. Similarly, we also compute all possible phoneme-level alignments between instances of different words. Alignments are obtained through a back-tracking of the $\alpha'(n, q)$ matrix once Algorithm 1 has finished aligning all development data. With the alignment results we build two confusion matrices by accumulating the number of times the recognizer substituted the ith phoneme by the jth phoneme. If the value (i, j) in the matrix is greater than the value in (i, k), it means that the ith phoneme is more likely to be substituted by the jth phoneme than by the kth phoneme. The information in these matrices is used to specify lower penalty for phonemes that have been shown as frequently interchangeable due to variations in the pronunciation of the patterns and higher penalties for those representing mismatches. Formally, we define $C \in R^{|ph| \cdot |ph|}$ and $NC \in R^{|ph| \cdot |ph|}$ as square and symmetric matrices corresponding to the same-word and different-word confusion matrices,where $|ph|$ is the size of the phonetic alphabet. These matrices are normalized in order to obtain conditional probabilities. Equation 7 defines the final cost matrix: $COST \in R^{|ph| \cdot |ph|}$, containing the penalties associated to each of the possible substitutions,deletions, insertions and assignments of phoneme symbols.

$$COST(a, b) = 1 - \left(\frac{C(a, b)}{C(a, b) + NC(a, b)} \right)$$

$$loss(a, b) \leftarrow \begin{cases} COST(a, b), & \text{if } a \neq b \\ 0, & \text{otherwise} \end{cases} \tag{7}$$

3.4   Matching Scores Normalization

The last improvement proposed over Algorithm 1 involves the normalization of the total matching score. While originally no normalization is proposed by [15], we observed that scores obtained from matching phoneme sequences of different lengths were not directly comparable with each other. For this reason we experimented with several normalization factors to reduce such mismatch. In this paper use the length of the 1-best path over the lattice in combination with the length of the phoneme sequence has been found the most successful.

4   Experimental Evaluation

We test the proposed algorithm using an isolated word matching test for a set of word lattices and word phoneme sequences. The task is focused into evaluating the algorithm's retrieval capabilities using the phoneme sequences as queries to be searched into the lattices. Performance is measured by the percentage of lattices corresponding to the same word as the query word that are contained in the top N retrieval results (P@N, N being total number lattices from the query word present in the database). We compare P@N obtained with our algorithm to a state of the art spoken term detection algorithm proposed in [1] and to the original algorithm proposed in [15] and reviewed in Section 2 above.

4.1   Dataset

In order to evaluate the algorithm we use a subset of the Switchboard corpus as defined in [16]. In particular, we select all instances of 20 of the most repeated words both in the development and in the evaluation sets in [16]. Table 1 shows the selected words and the number of repetitions of each word we selected. Each word instance is extracted from the acoustic signal and decoded using the Kaldi Speech Recognition Toolkit [18], trained using the standard Switchboard recipe for English. For each instance we obtain a phoneme lattice and the first-best phoneme sequence, which will be used as the query in order to simulate an audio-to-audio search (alternatively one could use a grapheme-to-phoneme convertor on the text query for a standard spoken-term detection task).

Table 1. Frequencies of the 20 words selected for the experiment

Words	Development	Evaluation
anything	34	48
because	98	110
benefits	136	109
companies	42	40
company	66	64
everything	56	49
exactly	65	63
expensive	56	35
important	45	37
insurance	93	82
newspapers	57	45
plastic	57	63
probably	59	57
punishment	80	107
really	59	58
recycling	149	155
retirement	39	42
situation	50	35
something	56	71
vacation	39	61
Total	1336	1331

4.2   Experiments

Table 2 shows average P@N results for the development and evaluation sets for the two baseline systems and for the improvements proposed here. The first

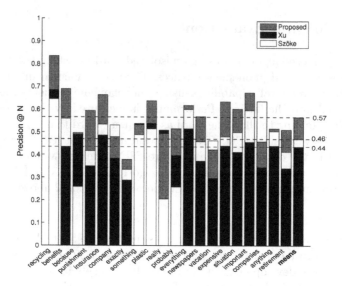

Fig. 1. Comparison of the methods for the development set

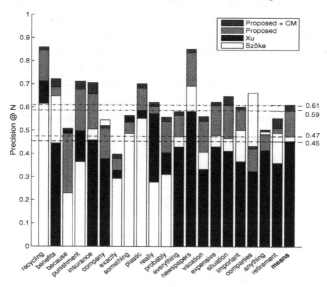

Fig. 2. Comparison of the methods for the evaluation set

improvement to [15] (SB) uses the single best scoring path in the lattice. The second improvement (SC) corresponds to the combination of Edit distance with the acoustic probability. Finally the third improvement (CM) uses the phoneme loss function estimated on the development set. The first values corresponds to the unweighted average p@N whereas the value between parentheses correspond to the weighted average P@N using the prior of each word class. We see how each proposed improvement gives an improvement in the P@N both in the development set as well as in the evaluation set. This achieves a 20% relative improvement in the development set and over a 28% improvement in the evaluation set in unweighted average P@N, and a 24% and 34% relative improvement in weighted average P@N.

In Figures 1 and 2 we evaluate in more detail the performance (unweighted P@N) of each word in the development and in the evaluation sets for some of the systems. We see that by itself, the algorithm in [15] usually obtains worse results than the algorithm in [1] (black bar is followed by the white region). On the contrary, by applying the proposed improvements an important gain is obtained over all baselines for most words (grey bars).

Table 2. unweighted P@N (weighted P@N) results for both systems averaged over all words, for development and evaluation sets

System	Development set	Evaluation Set
Szöke[1]	0.4697 (0.4773)	0.4752 (0.4737)
Xu[15]	0.4354 (0.4568)	0.4550 (0.4820)
Xu + SB	0.5432 (0.5771)	0.5713 (0.5956)
Xu + SB + SC	0.5653 (0.5938)	0.5883 (0.6108)
Xu + SB + SC + CM	0.5986 (0.6267)	0.6117 (0.6349)

5 Conclusions and Future Work

We present an algorithm based on dynamic programming for the task of phoneme sequence search on phoneme lattices. Our proposal extends an algorithm previously used in speech recognition by adapting it to the task of isolated word retrieval. The proposed improvements include modifying the optimization procedure to search for the single best scoring path in the lattice, adapting the scoring to balance it between path likelihood and phonetic mismatch and incorporating the estimation of a data driven loss function to exploit phoneme interactions present in the words pronunciations. The algorithm is evaluated on an isolated word retrieval task, obtaining very competitive results with previous state-of-the-art spoken-term detection methods obtaining over 20% relative improvement on a precision-at-N metric. Future work will focus on extending the algorithm to allow phonetic lattice to phonetic lattice search and retrieval. We plan to face the task of spoken term detection by adapting the algorithm to produce sub-sequence scores.

References

1. Szöke, I., Schwarz, P., Matjka, P., Karafit, M.: Comparison of keyword spotting approaches for informal continuous speech. In: Proceedings Eurospeech (2005)
2. Young, S.J., Brown, M., Foote, J.T., Jones, G.J., Sparck Jones, K.: Acoustic indexing for multimedia retrieval and browsing. In: IEEE International Conference on Acoustics, Speech, and Signal Processing, ICASSP 1997, vol. 1, pp. 199–202. IEEE (1997)

3. Nambiar, U., Faruquie, T., Subramaniam, L.V., Negi, S., Ramakrishnan, G.: Discovering customer intent in real-time for streamlining service desk conversations. In: Proceedings of the 20th ACM International Conference on Information and Knowledge Management, CIKM 2011, pp. 1383–1388. ACM, New York (2011), http://doi.acm.org/10.1145/2063576.2063776

4. Chelba, C., Acero, A.: Position specific posterior lattices for indexing speech. In: Proceedings of the 43rd Annual Meeting on Association for Computational Linguistics, ACL 2005, pp. 443–450. Association for Computational Linguistics, Stroudsburg (2005), http://dx.doi.org/10.3115/1219840.1219895

5. Foote, J.T., Faate, J.T., Brown, M., Jones, G., Young, S., Jones, K.S., Yaung, J.S.J.: Video mail retrieval by voice: Towards intelligent retrieval and browsing of multimedia documents (1995)

6. Foote, J.T., Jones, G.J.F., Jones, K.S., Young, S.J.: Talker-independent keyword spotting for information retrieval (1995)

7. James, D.A., Young, S.J.: A fast lattice-based approach to vocabulary independent wordspotting. In: IEEE International Conference on Acoustics, Speech, and Signal Processing, ICASSP 1994, vol. 1, pp. I–377. IEEE (1994)

8. Wilpon, J., Rabiner, L., Lee, C.-H., Goldman, E.: Automatic recognition of keywords in unconstrained speech using hidden markov models. IEEE Transactions on Acoustics, Speech and Signal Processing 38(11), 1870–1878 (1990)

9. Knill, K.M., Young, S.: Fast implementation methods for viterbi-based wordspotting. In: Proc. ICASSP, pp. 522–525 (1996)

10. Price, P., Fisher, W., Bernstein, J., Pallett, D.: The darpa 1000-word resource management database for continuous speech recognition. In: International Conference on Acoustics, Speech, and Signal Processing, ICASSP 1988, vol. 1, pp. 651–654 (April 1988)

11. Thambiratnam, K., Sridharan, S.: Dynamic match phone-lattice searches for very fast and accurate unrestricted vocabulary keyword spotting. In: Proc. ICASSP, vol. 5, pp. 465–468 (2005)

12. Young, S., Woodland, P.C., Byrne, W.J.: Htk version 3.4.1: User, reference and programmer manual (September 1993)

13. Audhkhasi, K., Verma, A.: Keyword search using modified minimum edit distance measure. In: IEEE International Conference on Acoustics, Speech and Signal Processing, ICASSP 2007, vol. 4, pp. IV–929–IV–932 (April 2007)

14. Wang, D.: Out of vocabulary spoken term detection. PhD thesis, Institute for Communicating and Collaborative Systems, School of Informatics, University of Edinburgh (2010)

15. Xu, H., Povey, D., Mangu, L., Zhu, J.: Minimum bayes risk decoding and system combination based on a recursion for edit distance. Computer Speech and Language 25(4), 802–828 (2011), http://www.sciencedirect.com/science/article/pii/S0885230811000192

16. Carlin, M.A., Thomas, S., Jansen, A., Hermansky, H.: Rapid evaluation of speech representations for spoken term discovery. In: INTERSPEECH, pp. 821–824 (2011)

17. Levenshtein, V.I.: Binary codes capable of correcting deletions, insertions and reversals. Soviet Physics Doklady 10, 707 (1966)

18. Povey, D., Ghoshal, A., Boulianne, G., Burget, L., Glembek, O., Goel, N., Hannemann, M., Motlicek, P., Qian, Y., Schwarz, P., Silovsky, J., Stemmer, G., Vesely, K.: The kaldi speech recognition toolkit. In: IEEE 2011 Workshop on Automatic Speech Recognition and Understanding, vol. 2(2), pp. 2–3. IEEE Signal Processing Society (December 2011), iEEE Catalog No.: CFP11SRW-USB

Deep Maxout Networks Applied to Noise-Robust Speech Recognition

F. de-la-Calle-Silos, A. Gallardo-Antolín,
and C. Peláez-Moreno

Department of Signal Theory and Communications,
Universidad Carlos III de Madrid,
Leganés (Madrid), Spain
fsilos@tsc.uc3m.es

Abstract. Deep Neural Networks (DNN) have become very popular for acoustic modeling due to the improvements found over traditional Gaussian Mixture Models (GMM). However, not many works have addressed the robustness of these systems under noisy conditions. Recently, the machine learning community has proposed new methods to improve the accuracy of DNNs by using techniques such as dropout and maxout. In this paper, we investigate Deep Maxout Networks (DMN) for acoustic modeling in a noisy automatic speech recognition environment. Experiments show that DMNs improve substantially the recognition accuracy over DNNs and other traditional techniques in both clean and noisy conditions on the TIMIT dataset.

Keywords: noise robustness, deep neural networks, dropout, deep maxout networks, speech recognition, deep learning.

1 Introduction

Machine performance in Automatic Speech Recognition (ASR) tasks is still far away from that of humans, and noisy conditions only compound the problem. Noise robustness techniques can be divided into two approaches: feature enhancement and model adaptation. *Feature enhancement* tries to remove noise from the speech signal without changing the acoustic model parameters while *model adaptation* changes these parameters to fit the model to the noisy speech signal. Apart from these techniques, the last years have witnessed an important leap in performance with the introduction of new acoustic models based on Deep Neural Networks (DNNs) in comparison with conventional Gaussian Mixture Model-Hidden Markov Model (GMM-HMM) ([7], [3]) ASR systems. Nevertheless, the performance of these kind of ASR systems in noisy conditions has not yet been fully assessed.

Deep Neural Networks can be applied both in the so-called *tandem* [16] and *hybrid* [15] architectures. In the first case, DNNs can be trained to generate bottleneck features which are fed to a conventional GMM-HMM back-end. In the second, DNNs are employed for acoustic modeling by replacing the GMMs into an HMM system. In this paper we adopt a DNNs hybrid configuration.

J.L. Navarro Mesa et al. (Eds.): IberSPEECH 2014, LNAI 8854, pp. 109–118, 2014.

DNN-HMM hybrid systems combine several features that make them superior to previous Artificial Neural Network (ANN)-HMM hybrid systems [11]: a) DNNs have a larger number of hidden layers leading to systems with many more parameters than the later. As a result, these models are less influenced by the mismatch between training and testing data but can easily suffer from overfitting if the training set is not big enough, b) the network usually models senones (tied states) directly (although there might be thousands of senones), and c) long context windows are used. Although conventional ANN also take into account longer context window than HMM or are able to model senones, the key to the success of the DNN-HMM is the combination of these components. DNN-HMM systems with these properties are often named Context-Dependent Deep Neural Network HMM (CD-DNN-HMM).

However, the most remarkable difference with traditional neural networks is that a *pre-training* stage in needed to reduce the chance that the error back-propagation algorithm employed for training falls into a poor local minimum. Besides, some recent methods have been proposed to avoid overfitting and improve the accuracy of the networks, as for example, dropout [8] which randomly omits hidden units in the training stage. Another related technique is the so-called Deep Maxout Networks (DMNs) [5] that splits the hidden units at each layer into non-overlapping groups, each of them generating an activation using a max pooling operation. This way, DMNs reduces the size of the parameter space significantly making it very suited for ASR tasks where the training sets and input and output dimensions are normally quite large. For this reason, DMNs have been employed in low-resources speech recognition devices [14] boosting the performance over other methods. We hypothesize that DMNs can improve the recognition rates in noisy conditions given that they are capable to model the speech variability from limited data more effectively [14].

As mentioned before, the number of research works that test DNNs in noisy conditions is still small. Notably, [18] applies DNNs with dropout on the Aurora 4 dataset with encouraging results. Up to our knowledge, the present paper is the first to apply Deep Maxout Networks in combination with dropout strategies in a noisy speech recognition task demonstrating a substantial improvement of the recognition accuracy over traditional DNN and other traditional techniques.

The remainder of this paper is organized as follows: Section 2 introduces deep neural networks and their application under a hybrid automatic speech recognition architecture, Section 3 and Section 4 describe the dropout and maxout methods, respectively. Finally, our results are presented in Section 5 followed by some conclusions and further lines of research in Section 6.

2   Deep Neural Networks and Hybrid Speech Recognition Systems

A Deep Neural Network (DNN) is a Multi-Layer Perceptron (MLP) with a larger number of hidden layers between its inputs and outputs, whose weights are fully connected and are often initialized using an unsupervised pre-training scheme.

As a traditional MLP the feed-forward architecture can be computed as follows:

$$\mathbf{h}^{(l+1)} = \sigma \left(\mathbf{W}^{(l)} \mathbf{h}^{(l)} + \mathbf{b}^{(l)} \right), \quad 1 \le l \le L \tag{1}$$

where $\mathbf{h}^{(l+1)}$ is the vector of inputs to the $l+1$ layer, $\sigma(x) = (1 + e^{-x})^{-1}$ is the sigmoid activation function, L is the total number of hidden layers, $\mathbf{h}^{(l)}$ is the output vector of the hidden layer l and $\mathbf{W}^{(l)}$ and $\mathbf{b}^{(l)}$ are the weight matrix and bias vector of layer l, respectively.

Training a DNN using the well-known error back-propagation (BP) algorithm with a random initialization of its weight matrices may not provide a good performance as it may become stuck in a local minimum. To overcome this problem, DNN parameters are often initialized using an unsupervised technique as Restricted Bolzmann Machines (RBMs) [6] or Stacked Denoising Autoencoders (SDAs) [19]. Nevertheless, as it will be explained later in this paper, pre-training may not be necessary if some recently proposed anti-overfitting techniques are used.

2.1 Hybrid Speech Recognition Systems

In a hybrid DNN/HMM system, just as in classical ANN/HMM hybrids [1], a DNN is trained to classify the input acoustic features into classes corresponding to the states of HMMs, in such a way that, the state emission likelihoods usually computed with GMM are replaced by the likelihoods generated by the DNN.

The DNN estimates the posterior probability $p(s|\mathbf{o}_t)$ of each state s given the observation $\mathbf{o}_t$ at time t, through a softmax final layer:

$$p(s|\mathbf{o}_t) = \frac{\exp \left(\mathbf{W}^{(L)} \mathbf{h}^{(L)} + \mathbf{b}^{(L)} \right)}{\sum_{\bar{s}} \exp \left(\mathbf{W}^{(L)} \mathbf{h}^{(L)} + \mathbf{b}^{(L)} \right)}. \tag{2}$$

In a hybrid ASR system, the HMM topology is set from a previously trained GMM-HMM, and the DNN training data come from the forced-alignment between the state-level transcripts and the corresponding speech signals obtained by using this initial GMM-HMM system.

In the recognition stage, the DNN estimates the emission probability of each HMM state. To obtain state emission likelihoods $p(\mathbf{o}_t|s)$, the Bayes rule is used as follows:

$$p(\mathbf{o}_t|s) = \frac{p(s|\mathbf{o}_t) \cdot p(\mathbf{o}_t)}{p(s)} \tag{3}$$

where $p(s|\mathbf{o}_t)$ is the posterior probability estimated by the DNN, $p(\mathbf{o}_t)$ is a scaling factor constant for each observation and can be ignored, and $p(s)$ is the class prior which can be estimated by counting the occurrences of each state on the training data.

3 Dropout

The most important problem to overcome in DNN training is overfitting. Normally this problem arises when we try to train a large DNN with a small training set. A training method called *dropout* proposed in [8] tries to reduce overfitting and improves the generalization capability of the network by randomly omitting a certain percentage of the hidden units on each training iteration.

When dropout is employed, the activation function of Eq. (1) can be rewritten as:

$$\mathbf{h}^{(l+1)} = m^{(l)} \star \sigma \left(\mathbf{W}^{(l)} \mathbf{h}^{(l)} + \mathbf{b}^{(l)} \right), \quad 1 \leq l \leq L \tag{4}$$

where $\star$ denotes the element-wise product, $m^{(l)}$ is a binary vector of the same dimension of $\mathbf{h}^{(l)}$ whose elements are sampled from a Bernoulli distribution with probability p. This probability is the so called *Hidden Drop Factor (HDF)* and must be determined over a validation set as it will be seen in Section 5.

As the *sigmoid* function has the property that $\sigma(0) = 0$, Eq. (4) can be rewritten as:

$$\mathbf{h}^{(l+1)} = \sigma \left(m^{(l)} \star \left(\mathbf{W}^{(l)} \mathbf{h}^{(l)} + \mathbf{b}^{(l)} \right) \right), \quad 1 \leq l \leq L \tag{5}$$

where dropout is applied on the inputs of the activation function, leading a more efficient way of perform dropout training.

Note that dropout is only applied in the training stage whereas on testing all the hidden units become active. Dropout DNN can be seen as an ensemble of DNNs, given that on each presentation of a training example, a different sub-model is trained and the sub-models predictions are averaged together. This technique is similar to bagging [2] where many different models are trained using different subsets of the training data, but in dropout each model is only trained in a single iteration and all the models share some parameters.

Dropout networks are trained with the standard stochastic gradient descent algorithm but using the forward architecture presented on Eq. (4) instead of Eq. (1). Following [13], we compensate the parameters in testing by scaling the weight matrices taking into account the dropout factor as follows:

$$\overline{\mathbf{W}}^{(l)} = (1 - HDF) \cdot \mathbf{W}^{(l)} \tag{6}$$

Dropout has already successfully tested on noise robust ASR in [18]. Its benefits come from the improved generalization abilities attained by reducing their capacity. Another interpretation of the behaviour of dropout is that in the training state it adds random noise to the training set resulting in a network that is very robust to variabilities in the inputs (in our particular case, due to the addition of noise).

4   Deep Maxout Networks

A Maxout Deep Neural Network (DMN) [5] is a modification of the feed-forward architecture (Eq. (1)) where the maxout activation function is employed. The maxout unit simply takes the maximum over a set of inputs. In a DMN each hidden unit takes the maximum value over the g units of a group. The output of the hidden node i of the layer $l + 1$ can be computed as follows:

$$h_i^{(l+1)} = \max_{j \in 1,...,g} z_{ij}^{(l+1)}, \quad 1 \le l \le L \tag{7}$$

where $z_{ij}^{(l+1)}$ are the lineal pre-activation values from the l layer:

$$\mathbf{z}^{(l+1)} = \mathbf{W}^{(l)}\mathbf{h}^{(l)} + \mathbf{b}^{(l)} \tag{8}$$

As can be observed the max-pooling operation is applied over the $\mathbf{z}^{(l+1)}$ vector. Note that DMNs fairly reduce the number of parameters over DNNs, as the weight matrix $\mathbf{W}^{(l)}$ of each layer in the DMN is $1/g$ of the size of its equivalent DNN weight matrix. This makes DMN more convenient for ASR tasks where the training sets and the input and output dimensions are normally very large. An illustration of a DMN with 2 hidden layers and a group size of $g = 3$ is shown in Figure 1.

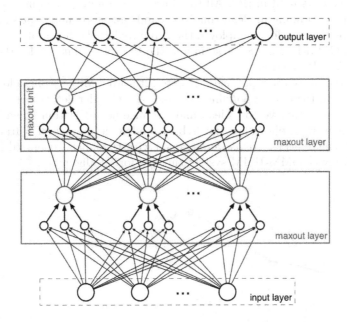

Fig. 1. A Maxout Network of 2 hidden layers and a group size of $g = 3$. The hidden nodes in red perform the max operation.

In [5] a demonstration of the capability of maxout units to approximate any convex function by tuning the weights of the previous layers is included. For this matter, the shapes of activation functions are not fixed allowing the DMNs to model the variability of speech more smoothly. DMNs are commonly applied in conjunction with dropout maximizing the model averaging effects of dropout.

5 Experiments

In this section, we present the experiments carried out for evaluating and comparing the performance of conventional GMM-HMM and the different hybrid deep neural networks-based ASR systems (basic DNN, dropout DNN and DMN). The experiments were performed on the TIMIT corpus [4]; in particular, we used the 462 speaker training set, a development set of 50 speakers to tune all the parameters and finally the 24 speakers core test set. Each utterance is recorded at 16 kHz and the corpus includes time-aligned phonetic transcriptions allowing as to give results in terms of Phone Error Rate (PER).

To test the robustness of the different methods we digitally added to the clean speech four different types of noises (white, street, music and speaker) at four different SNRs using the FANT tool [9] (with G.712 filtering). These noises are the same ones used in [10]. All the noise tests are evaluated in a mismatch condition (i. e. training in clean conditions and testing on noisy speech).

On the technical side we employed the Kaldi toolkit [17] for implementing the traditional GMM-HMM ASR system and the PDNN toolkit [12] for the hybrid DNN-based ASR systems.

In all of the cases, the input features were 12th-order MFCCs plus a log-energy coefficient, and their corresponding first and second order derivatives yielding a 39 component feature vector. Mean and variance normalization on each of the components were applied. For the hybrid models, a context of 5 frames was chosen. All the hybrid systems were trained with the labels generated from the best performance GMM-HMM system through forced alignment.

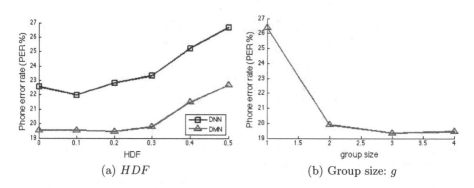

(a) *HDF*   (b) Group size: g

Fig. 2. Results in terms of PER [%] as a function of HDF for DNN and DMN (Figure 2a) and the group size for DMN (Figure 2b) on TIMIT development set. Both nets have 5 layers.

First, we tuned the configuration parameters of the networks (number of hidden layers, HDF and group size, when applicable) under clean conditions. HDF and group size were validated on the development set as can be seen on Figure 2 considering 5 hidden layer networks, yielding an optimal dropout factor of 0.1 for dropout DNNs, 0.2 for DMNs and a group size of $g = 3$. These values of HDR and group size were used throughout the rest of the experiments. DMNs are always employed in conjunction with dropout.

Figure 3 shows the PERs as a function of the number of hidden layers for the development and test sets for different types of hybrid DNN-based ASR systems: randomly initialized, with a pre-training stage, with dropout and maxout networks. The number of hidden nodes in all of the DNNs is 1024. To be fair, we chose 400 hidden maxout units for the DMN since $400 \times 3 = 1200$ yields a number of parameters in the same order as the DNNs. An exploration of the learning rates for the networks without dropout the learning rate started at 0.08 for 30 epochs and was subsequently divided in half while the validation error decreased. For the dropout and DMNs networks we started with a higher learning rate of 0.1. As can be seen in Figure 3 the DMNs outperform clearly the other networks for all the number of layers considered. Best results are obtained in the development set with DMNs of 5 layers.

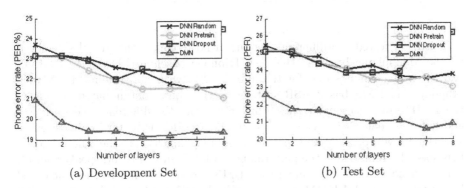

(a) Development Set   (b) Test Set

Fig. 3. Comparison of the performance of the different hybrid DNN-based ASR systems in terms of PER [%] as a function of the number of hidden layers for TIMIT development and test sets

Second, we compared the baseline system (GMM-HMM) with the best configuration of the different hybrid ASR systems under clean conditions: Monophone, Triphone, Triphone with Lineal Discriminant Analysis (LDA), Maximum Likelihood Lineal Transform (MLLT) and Speaker Adaptative Training (SAT). Results for the development and test sets are shown in Table 1.

As can be observed, all of the hybrid systems outperform the different versions of the baseline system, in both development and test sets. DNNs with random initialization, pretraining and dropout achieve similar results whereas with DMN the lowest PER is obtained.

Table 1. Recognition results in terms of PER(%) for the TIMIT development and core test sets in clean conditions

Method	Dev PER %	Eval PER %
Monophone	33.33	34.30
Triphone	28.64	30.42
Triphone + LDA + MLLT	26.44	27.62
Triphone + LDA + MLLT + SAT	23.56	25.79
DNN with random initialization (7 layers)	21.50	23.53
DNN with pretraining (8 layers)	21.05	23.05
DNN with dropout (4 layers)	21.98	23.84
DMN (5 layers)	19.15	21.01

Table 2. Average fine-tuning epoch execution time for a 5 hidden layers networks, 1024 nodes for DNN, 400 nodes and $g = 3$ for DMN

Method	Time(min)
DNN	57.81
DNN with dropout	59.07
DMN	24.10

Third, we tested the different systems in noisy conditions. Results achieved by the Monophone baseline, the best Triphone baseline (LDA+MLLT+SAT) and the best configurations for the hybrid DNN with pre-training, DNN with dropout, and DMN-based ASR systems in the noisy contaminated version of the TIMIT core test set are shown in Figure 4 for the different types of noises and four different SNRs. As can be seen, DMN performs better in almost every situation for white, street and speaker noises in comparison to the other systems. It is specially remarkable the performance of DMN in white and speaker noises. For street noise, results obtained with DMN are very similar to those achieved by the triphone GMM-HMM systems and both DNNs at high and medium SNRs whereas it obtains the lowest PER at low SNRs. For music noise, the results of all of the systems are very similar. As expected dropout performs better than DNN with pre-training at low SNR in all the noises, given that dropout is very robust to the variations of the input.

Fourth, we compared the fine-tunning stage time requirements for the DNNs, DNNs with dropout and DMN. We computed the average epoch time over all the iterations for 5 hidden layers networks with 1024 nodes per layer for the DNNs and 400 maxout units per layer and group size $g = 3$ for the DMN. The resulting times are shown in Table 2. As can be observed the DMN reduce the average epoch time over a half compared with DNNs with and without dropout. making them appealing for ASR tasks where the training set are normally very large.

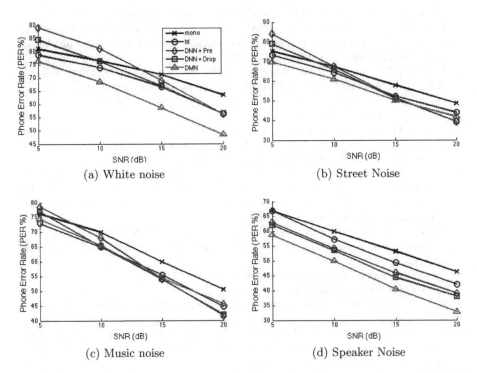

(a) White noise   (b) Street Noise

(c) Music noise   (d) Speaker Noise

Fig. 4. Comparison of the performance of the different systems in terms of PER [%] for TIMIT test set in different noisy conditions

6   Conclusions and Future Work

In this paper Deep Maxout Networks (DMNs) are employed for robust speech recognition using hybrid architecture showing a better performance over standard DNNs. This is due to the DMNs flexibility of the activation functions allowing a better modeling of speech variability. Further lines of research include testing the DMN in a more complete datasets. Other novel machine learning techniques like dropconnect [20] are also interesting candidates not yet been tested in ASR tasks.

Acknowledgements. This contribution has been supported by an Airbus Defense and Space Grant (Open Innovation - SAVIER) and Spanish Government-CICYT project 2011-26807/TEC. We would also like to thank Chanwoo Kim for kindly providing the testing noises.

References

1. Bourlard, H., Morgan, N.: Connectionist Speech Recognition: A Hybrid Approach. Kluwer international series in engineering and computer science: VLSI, computer architecture, and digital signal processing. Springer US (1994)

2. Breiman, L.: Bagging predictors. Machine Learning 24(2) (1996)
3. Dahl, G.E., Yu, D., Deng, L., Acero, A.: Context-dependent pre-trained deep neural networks for large-vocabulary speech recognition. IEEE Transactions on Audio, Speech & Language Processing 20(1) (2012)
4. Garofolo, J.S., Lamel, L.F., Fisher, W.M., Fiscus, J.G., Pallett, D.S., Dahlgren, N.L.: DARPA TIMIT acoustic phonetic continuous speech corpus cdrom (1993)
5. Goodfellow, I.J., Warde-Farley, D., Mirza, M., Courville, A., Bengio, Y.: Maxout Networks. ArXiv e-prints (2013)
6. Hinton, G.E.: A practical guide to training restricted boltzmann machines. In: Montavon, G., Orr, G.B., Müller, K.-R. (eds.) NN: Tricks of the Trade, 2nd edn. LNCS, vol. 7700, pp. 599–619. Springer, Heidelberg (2012)
7. Hinton, G.E., Deng, L., Yu, D., Dahl, G.E., Mohamed, A., Jaitly, N., Senior, A., Vanhoucke, V., Nguyen, P., Sainath, T.N., Kingsbury, B.: Deep neural networks for acoustic modeling in speech recognition: The shared views of four research groups. IEEE Signal Process. Mag. 29(6) (2012)
8. Hinton, G.E., Srivastava, N., Krizhevsky, A., Sutskever, I., Salakhutdinov, R.: Improving neural networks by preventing co-adaptation of feature detectors. CoRR (2012)
9. Hirsch, G.: Fant - filtering and noise adding tool (2005), http://dnt.kr.hsnr.de/download.html
10. Kim, C., Stern, R.M.: Power-normalized cepstral coefficients (PNCC) for robust speech recognition. IEEE Transactions on Audio, Speech, and Language Processing
11. Li, J., Deng, L., Gong, Y., Haeb-Umbach, R.: An overview of noise-robust automatic speech recognition. IEEE/ACM Transactions on Audio, Speech, and Language Processing 22(4) (April 2014)
12. Miao, Y.: Kaldi+PDNN: Building DNN-based ASR systems with Kaldi and PDNN. CoRR (2014)
13. Miao, Y., Metze, F.: Improving low-resource CD-DNN-HMM using dropout and multilingual DNN training. In: INTERSPEECH, pp. 2237–2241. ISCA (2013)
14. Miao, Y., Metze, F., Rawat, S.: Deep maxout networks for low-resurce speech recognition. In: 2013 IEEE Workshop on Automatic Speech Recognition and Understanding, Olomouc, Czech Republic, December 8-12 (2013)
15. Mohamed, A., Dahl, G.E., Hinton, G.E.: Acoustic modeling using deep belief networks. IEEE Transactions on Audio, Speech & Language Processing 20(1) (2012)
16. Morgan, N.: Deep and wide: Multiple layers in automatic speech recognition. IEEE Transactions on Audio, Speech & Language Processing 20(1) (2012)
17. Povey, D., Ghoshal, A., Boulianne, G., Burget, L., Glembek, O., Goel, N., Hannemann, M., Motlicek, P., Qian, Y., Schwarz, P., Silovsky, J., Stemmer, G., Vesely, K.: The Kaldi speech recognition toolkit. In: IEEE Workshop on Automatic Speech Recognition and Understanding. IEEE Signal Processing Society (2011)
18. Seltzer, M.L., Yu, D., Wang, Y.: An investigation of deep neural networks for noise robust speech recognition. In: IEEE International Conference on Acoustics, Speech, and Signal Processing (ICASSP) (2013)
19. Vincent, P., Larochelle, H., Lajoie, I., Bengio, Y., Manzagol, P.A.: Stacked denoising autoencoders: Learning useful representations in a deep network with a local denoising criterion. Journal of Machine Learning Research 11, 3371–3408 (2010)
20. Wan, L., Zeiler, M.D., Zhang, S., LeCun, Y., Fergus, R.: Regularization of neural networks using dropconnect. In: Proceedings of the 30th International Conference on Machine Learning, ICML 2013, Atlanta, GA, USA, June 16-21 (2013)

A Deep Neural Network Approach
for Missing-Data Mask Estimation
on Dual-Microphone Smartphones: Application
to Noise-Robust Speech Recognition[*]

Iván López-Espejo[1], José A. González[2], Ángel M. Gómez[1],
and Antonio M. Peinado[1]

[1] Dept. of Signal Theory, Telematics and Communications,
University of Granada, Spain
[2] Dept. of Computer Science, University of Sheffield, UK
{iloes,amgg,amp}@ugr.es, j.gonzalez@sheffield.ac.uk

Abstract. The inclusion of two or more microphones in smartphones
is becoming quite common. These were originally intended to perform
noise reduction and few benefit is still being taken from this feature
for noise-robust automatic speech recognition (ASR). In this paper we
propose a novel system to estimate missing-data masks for robust ASR
on dual-microphone smartphones. This novel system is based on deep
neural networks (DNNs), which have proven to be a powerful tool in the
field of ASR in different ways. To assess the performance of the proposed
technique, spectral reconstruction experiments are carried out on a dual-
channel database derived from Aurora-2. Our results demonstrate that
the DNN is better able to exploit the dual-channel information and yields
an improvement on word accuracy of more than 6% over state-of-the-art
single-channel mask estimation techniques.

Keywords: Dual-microphone, Robust speech recognition, Mask estimation, Smartphone, Deep neural network, Missing data imputation.

1 Introduction

Robustness in automatic speech recognition (ASR) is still a key issue for enabling
ASR to operate in real world conditions. In fact, with the increasing availability
of ASR software running on mobile devices, this issue is now more important
than ever before. Thus, distortions such as acoustic noise, reverberation, channel
distortion, and so on, which are expected to occur during the normal use of ASR
in mobile platforms, can harm ASR performance to a level that makes it simply
useless.

One way to improve the robustness against noise consists of equipping the device with several microphones. Hardware price decreasing, along with its minia-
turization, has allowed latest smartphones to come with a dual-microphone to

---

[*] This work has been supported by the MICINN TEC2013-46690-P project.

J.L. Navarro Mesa et al. (Eds.): IberSPEECH 2014, LNAI 8854, pp. 119–128, 2014.

perform noise reduction. Recent works propose taking advantage of this new feature in robust speech recognition [1] and speech enhancement [2]. In [2], power level difference (PLD) between the two microphones is used to estimate a spectral gain mask. In a conversational position (i.e. phone loudspeaker placed at the ear) speech power at the primary microphone of the device (related to the first channel) tends to be greater than at the secondary one (related to the second channel), while the noise power received at both microphones is almost the same. Thus, a power level ratio measure (i.e. the ratio between the noisy speech power at the first and second channels) can be used to determine if speech or noise is dominant in each time-frequency (T-F) bin.

Another recent development in the field of ASR has been the application of deep neural networks (DNNs) to improve ASR performance in different ways. Besides their use for acoustic modeling [3, 4], other authors have successfully applied DNNs to the problem of mask estimation in noise-robust ASR [5, 6]. This problem involves identifying the T-F bins in a noisy spectrogram that are dominated by speech or noise. Once the mask is estimated, it can be used either to perform imputation (i.e. spectral reconstruction) on the missing spectral features (i.e. the T-F bins dominated by the noise) [7, 8] or to perform speech recognition with incomplete data, the so-called marginalization approach [9]. In both cases, the performance of these approaches depends heavily on the quality of the estimated binary masks.

In this paper we focus on exploiting the dual-microphone equipped on modern smartphones in order to improve the robustness against acoustic noise of ASR systems. In particular, we propose a novel technique for missing-data mask estimation that takes advantage of the availability of two microphones and the learning capabilities of DNNs. The proposed technique consists of a DNN that is trained on the noisy speech log-Mel features extracted from the signals captured by both microphones. Thus, the DNN is able to estimate a binary mask for a signal acquired by the first channel. Then, the truncated-Gaussian based imputation (TGI) algorithm proposed in [8] is used to compensate the features that are dominated by noise. To assess the performance of the proposed technique, a new database called AURORA2-2C (AURORA2 - 2 Channels - Conversational Position) has been developed [1]. This noisy speech database is based on the well-known Aurora-2 database [10] and tries to emulate speech signals that were recorded with a dual-microphone smartphone in a conversational position. Unlike other related work such as [5, 6] where a wide set of features (amplitude modulation spectrogram, relative spectral transform and perceptual linear prediction, pitch-based features, etc.) is extracted to feed the DNN, in our proposed system the DNN directly provides an estimation of the binary mask by just using dual-channel log-Mel spectral features. Through this approach we can obtain very good results with less computation.

This paper is organized as follows. In Section 2 the spectral imputation technique used here is briefly described. The proposed method for missing-data mask estimation on smartphones with dual-microphone is explained in Section 3. The experiments and results are presented in Section 4. Finally, conclusions and future work are summarized in Section 5.

2   Missing-Feature Compensation

Binary masks allow us to distinguish between spectro-temporal regions dominated by speech or noise, classifying each T-F bin of a noisy speech spectrogram as reliable (speech dominates) or unreliable (noise dominates). Binary masks are very useful in robust speech recognition, since they are used for missing-feature approaches such as marginalization and data imputation. In the case of marginalization, output probabilities for decoding are calculated by only taking into account the reliable features [9]. On the other hand, data imputation (also known as spectral reconstruction) employs reliable spectro-temporal regions in order to estimate values for the unreliable parts of the noisy spectrogram [7, 8].

One of these reconstruction algorithms is the TGI technique [8], which is chosen in this work. This technique is based on the well-known *log-max* model [11] which states that $y \approx \max(x, n)$, where y, x and n represent the noisy speech, clean speech and noise features, respectively, expressed in the log-Mel domain. Thus, y is an upper bound for the masked clean speech energy, i.e. $x \in (-\infty, y]$. This fact is exploited by the TGI method to achieve accurate estimates.

The algorithm operates on a frame-by-frame basis. At time frame t, the mask segregates the noisy observation into reliable and unreliable components, i.e. $\mathbf{y}^{(1)}(t) = \left\{ \mathbf{y}_r^{(1)}(t), \mathbf{y}_u^{(1)}(t) \right\}^1$. Clean speech estimates for reliable elements are the observations themselves, $\hat{\mathbf{x}}_r^{(1)}(t) = \mathbf{y}_r^{(1)}(t)$, while unreliable elements are estimated using minimum mean square error (MMSE) estimation. Taking into account that clean speech is modeled by means of a Gaussian mixture model (GMM) with M components, it can be shown that, for those features labeled as unreliable, the clean speech estimate is

$$\hat{\mathbf{x}}_u^{(1)}(t) = \sum_{k=1}^{M} P\left(k \,\Big|\, \mathbf{y}_r^{(1)}(t), \mathbf{y}_u^{(1)}(t)\right) \hat{\mathbf{x}}_u^{(1,k)}(t), \tag{1}$$

where $\hat{\mathbf{x}}_u^{(1,k)}(t)$ corresponds to the mean of a right-truncated Gaussian distribution defined in the interval $\left(-\infty, \mathbf{y}_u^{(1)}(t)\right]$ given the k-th Gaussian of the clean speech model. The posterior $P\left(k \,\Big|\, \mathbf{y}_r^{(1)}(t), \mathbf{y}_u^{(1)}(t)\right)$ can be understood as the weight of the partial estimate $\hat{\mathbf{x}}_u^{(1,k)}(t)$. Note that correlations between the different elements in the feature vector can be exploited in a precise way, since $\mathbf{y}_r^{(1)}(t)$ conditions the value of $\hat{\mathbf{x}}_u^{(1)}(t)$ according to the posterior probabilities.

3   DNN-Based Proposed System

A DNN, which is an MLP (multilayer perceptron) with many hidden layers, is used here to estimate binary masks from dual-channel noisy speech. Particularly, a feedforward neural network with two hidden layers is employed as in [5, 6]. In order to apply such an approach, the speech features used as input data and

---

[1] Superscript $^{(1)}$ indicates that TGI is applied on the signal from the first (main) channel.

the desired output (target) must be defined. These are described in detail in Subsection 3.1. In addition, to overcome some difficulties in training a neural network with many hidden layers from scratch, the parameters (e.g. weights) of the DNN are initialized according to an unsupervised generative pre-training by considering each pair of layers as restricted Boltzmann machines (RBMs) [12]. These are introduced in Subsection 3.2. The input layer and the first hidden layer behave as a Gaussian-Bernoulli RBM (GRBM), while the rest of pairs of layers (first and second hidden layers, and second and output layers) behave as Bernoulli-Bernoulli RBMs. Features described in Subsection 3.1 are used to train the GRBM, while the inferred states of its hidden units are used to train the second RBM, and so on. The resulting deep belief net (i.e. the multilayer generative model that consists of the stack of RBMs) is used to initialize the feedforward neural network. Then, a fine-tuning second stage is performed in which the DNN is trained in a supervised manner by using the backpropagation algorithm. The cross-entropy criterion was chosen for backpropagation learning.

3.1 Features and Target

Binary mask estimation is performed in the log-Mel domain, where most of the spectral reconstruction algorithms operate. The proposed DNN works on a frame-by-frame basis, i.e. the DNN returns a binary mask for each frame in the utterance. Let the dual-channel noisy speech log-Mel features at time frame t be

$$\mathbf{y}(t) = \begin{pmatrix} \mathbf{y}^{(1)}(t) \\ \mathbf{y}^{(2)}(t) \end{pmatrix}, \tag{2}$$

where $\mathbf{y}^{(i)}(t)$, $i = 1, 2$, is the noisy speech log-Mel feature vector obtained from the signal acquired by the i-th microphone of the device (channel i). Then, the input for the DNN at time t is the stacked vector

$$\mathcal{y} = \begin{pmatrix} \mathbf{y}(t - L) \\ \vdots \\ \mathbf{y}(t + L) \end{pmatrix}, \tag{3}$$

where $L \geq 0$ determines the size of the temporal window around frame t, that is $2L + 1$. Thus, the dimensionality of the input vector is $d = 2 \cdot \mathcal{M} \cdot (2L + 1)$, where $\mathcal{M}$ is the number of channels of the Mel filterbank.

On the other hand, the target is an oracle binary mask vector corresponding to feature vector $\mathbf{y}^{(1)}(t)$. Thus, the size of each output vector is $\mathcal{M} \times 1$. Note that oracle masks were obtained by direct comparison between the clean and noisy utterances using a threshold of 7 dB signal-to-noise ratio (SNR).

3.2 Restricted Boltzmann Machines

A diagram of a restricted Boltzmann machine (that can be seen as a two-layer neural network) is shown in Figure 1. RBMs are mainly used to initialize the set of parameters of a DNN to avoid falling into local minima during backpropagation learning. This could happen because of the complex error surface derived

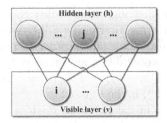

Fig. 1. Example of a restricted Boltzmann machine

from the large number of hidden layers [12]. An RBM consists of a visible layer with stochastic units (that represent input data) which are only connected to the stochastic units in the hidden layer. Hidden units are usually modeled by Bernoulli distributions. On the other hand, visible units can be modeled with either Bernoulli or Gaussian distributions. In the first case the resulting model is referred as Bernoulli-Bernoulli RBM (BRBM), while the second as Gaussian-Bernoulli RBM (GRBM). GRBMs are very useful to model real-valued input data (e.g. input features), so that they are often used as the first level of a multilayer generative model built with stacked RBMs [3].

Let $\mathbf{v}$, $\mathbf{h}$ and θ be the visible units, the hidden units and the set of parameters (e.g. weights) of an RBM, respectively. The probability of a visible vector given the set of parameters is obtained by summing over all hidden vectors as

$$P(\mathbf{v}|\theta) = \frac{1}{Z} \sum_{\mathbf{h}} e^{-E(\mathbf{v},\mathbf{h}|\theta)}, \tag{4}$$

where $Z = \sum_{\mathbf{v}} \sum_{\mathbf{h}} e^{-E(\mathbf{v},\mathbf{h}|\theta)}$ is known as the partition function and $E(\mathbf{v}, \mathbf{h}|\theta)$ is an energy function that defines the joint configuration of the visible and hidden units. For a BRBM, the energy function is

$$E_B(\mathbf{v}, \mathbf{h}|\theta) = -\sum_{i=1}^{V} \sum_{j=1}^{H} w_{ij} v_i h_j - \sum_{i=1}^{V} a_i v_i - \sum_{j=1}^{H} b_j h_j, \tag{5}$$

and in the case of a GRBM,

$$E_G(\mathbf{v}, \mathbf{h}|\theta) = -\sum_{i=1}^{V} \sum_{j=1}^{H} w_{ij} v_i h_j + \frac{1}{2} \sum_{i=1}^{V} (v_i - a_i)^2 - \sum_{j=1}^{H} b_j h_j, \tag{6}$$

where w_{ij} represents the symmetric weight between the visible, v_i, and hidden, h_j, units, and a_i and b_j their respective bias terms. The total number of visible and hidden units are V and H, respectively.

The set of parameters θ is estimated by maximizing $\log P(\mathbf{v}|\theta)$ from training data. For instance, this approach yields the following simple updating equation for the set of weights:

$$\Delta w_{ij} = \epsilon \cdot (\mathbb{E}_{data}[v_i h_j] - \mathbb{E}_{model}[v_i h_j]), \tag{7}$$

where ϵ is the learning rate and $\mathbb{E}[\cdot]$ indicates expectation under the corresponding distribution. To overcome the difficulties in getting samples of $\mathbb{E}_{model}[v_i h_j]$,

Hinton proposed in [13] a fast algorithm called contrastive divergence (CD). Briefly, this algorithm performs alternating Gibbs sampling from visible units initialized to a training data vector [3]. In order to perform the CD algorithm, the following conditional probabilities are employed in the case of a BRBM: $P_B(h_j = 1|\mathbf{v}, \theta) = \sigma(\sum_i w_{ij} v_i + b_j)$ and $P_B(v_i = 1|\mathbf{h}, \theta) = \sigma(\sum_j w_{ij} h_j + a_i)$, where $\sigma(x) = 1/(1 + \exp(-x))$ is the sigmoid function. For the case of a GRBM, conditional probabilities can be calculated as $P_G(h_j = 1|\mathbf{v}, \theta) = \sigma(\sum_i w_{ij} v_i + b_j)$ and $P_G(v_i = 1|\mathbf{h}, \theta) = \mathcal{N}(\sum_j w_{ij} h_j + a_i, 1)$, where v_i is real-valued in this case and $\mathcal{N}$ denotes the normal distribution.

4   Experimental Results

4.1   Experimental Framework

In this work, the European Telecommunication Standards Institute front-end (ETSI FE, ES 201 108) [14] is used to extract acoustic features from the speech signal. Twelve Mel-frequency cepstral coefficients (MFCCs) along with the 0th order coefficient and their respective velocity and acceleration form the 39-dimensional feature vector used by the recognizer. Cepstral mean normalization (CMN) is applied to improve the robustness of the system against channel mismatches. For spectral reconstruction, 23-component log-Mel feature vectors are employed (i.e. $\mathcal{M} = 23$). After reconstruction, the discrete cosine transform (DCT) is applied to obtain the final cepstral parameters.

All the techniques are evaluated on the AURORA2-2C database reported in [1]. AURORA2-2C is generated from Aurora-2 [10] data and emulates speech acquisition using a dual-microphone mobile device in a conversational position. In AURORA2-2C two test sets (A and B) are defined, each one with utterances contaminated with different kind of noises at the same SNRs (referred to the first channel) as in Aurora-2.

The acoustic models used by the recognizer are trained on clean speech. Left to right continuous density hidden Markov models (HMMs) with 16 states and 3 Gaussians per state are used to model each digit. Silences and short pauses are modeled by HMMs with 3 and 1 states, respectively, and 6 Gaussians per state [10].

The binary masks estimated by the proposed DNN-based technique are compared with those calculated by thresholding an estimation of the *a priori* SNR of the first channel and used by the TGI algorithm (T-SNR) [8]. The *a priori* SNR for each T-F bin, $\xi(k,t)$, is approximated by using the following maximum likelihood (ML) estimator [15]:

$$\hat{\xi}(k,t) = \max\left(\frac{|Y_1(k,t)|^2}{|\hat{N}_1(k,t)|^2} - 1, 0 \right), \tag{8}$$

where $|Y_1(k,t)|^2$ is the filterbank output power spectrum of the noisy speech in the first channel at frequency bin k and time frame t, being $|\hat{N}_1(k,t)|^2$ the corresponding noise power spectrum estimate. As in [8], noise estimates are obtained by linear interpolation between the averages of the first and last 20 frames in the log-Mel domain. Finally, each T-F bin of the mask, $\hat{m}(k,t)$, is calculated as

$$\hat{m}(k,t) = \begin{cases} 1 & \text{if } 10\log_{10}\hat{\xi}(k,t) \geq \gamma; \\ 0 & \text{otherwise,} \end{cases} \qquad (9)$$

where $\gamma = 0$ dB is the SNR threshold. This value was experimentally chosen by means of a validation dataset.

The DNN was trained using 19200 sample pairs of input-output vectors. Training input data consisted of a mixture of samples contaminated with the noises of test set A (bus, babble, car and pedestrian street) at several SNRs (-5 dB, 0 dB, 5 dB, 10 dB, 15 dB and 20 dB). Noises of test set B are reserved to evaluate the generalization ability of the DNN when exposed to unseen noises during the training phase (cafe, street, bus station and train station). 100 epochs per each RBM were used during the unsupervised pre-training phase while 1000 epochs were used for the backpropagation algorithm. A learning rate of 0.1 was established and the training dataset was divided into mini-batches (small subsets of training data) of 10 samples by following the recommendations in [16]. Preliminary experiments revealed that increasing L (the number of look-forward and look-backward frames) from zero to a few units provides a better performance. Finally, $L = 2$ was chosen (i.e. temporal window size of 5 frames). Thus, the input layer has 230 units or nodes, both hidden layers have 460 nodes and the output layer has 23 nodes. The DNN implementation was carried out by employing the MatLab toolbox referenced in [17].

TGI is performed using a 256-component GMM with diagonal covariance matrices. GMM training is performed by the expectation-maximization (EM) algorithm on the same dataset used for acoustic model training. The ETSI advanced front-end (AFE) [18], TGI with oracle masks and SPLICE (Stereo-based Piecewise LInear Compensation for Environments) [19] were also evaluated as a reference. SPLICE was included in order to compare with another stereo data technique (as it is the case of our proposal). For this last method, a 256-component GMM with diagonal covariance matrices was trained for each acoustic ambient (noise type & SNR). For a fair comparison, these acoustic ambients were the same as those used for the DNN training phase. Notice that a multi-environment soft-compensation scheme was followed, where every clean speech vector is estimated as a weighted sum of partial clean speech estimates obtained for every acoustic ambient seen during GMM training [20]. Finally, the baseline corresponds to the results obtained when the noisy speech features are employed. For all these cases, only the signals from the first channel were used.

4.2 Results

Figure 2 shows the results on word accuracy for both test sets as well as the averaged results across them. In Table 1, the word accuracy results averaged from -5 dB to 20 dB are shown for the different test sets and techniques evaluated. Similarly, percentages of wrong estimated mask bins with respect to oracle masks are included for our proposal and T-SNR. The DNN-based proposed system outperforms, for all the SNR values, AFE, SPLICE and T-SNR. In addition,

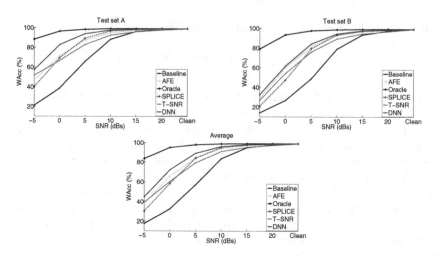

Fig. 2. WAcc results for the different techniques evaluated and for both test sets

Table 1. WAcc results and wrong estimated mask bin percentages for the different techniques evaluated. Results are averaged for SNRs from -5 dB to 20 dB.

	WAcc (%)			Wrong mask bins (%)		
	Test A	Test B	Average	Test A	Test B	Average
Baseline	67.96	59.78	63.87	-	-	-
AFE	82.71	76.37	79.54	-	-	-
Oracle	96.67	94.41	95.54	0	0	0
SPLICE	82.03	72.72	77.38	-	-	-
T-SNR	81.21	72.87	77.04	17.97	19.89	18.93
DNN	88.10	78.07	83.08	10.07	16.19	13.13

and according to the results for the test set B, we can observe that the DNN exhibits some generalization ability. An example of the TGI reconstruction of a dual-channel noisy utterance by using our DNN-based system can be seen in Figure 3.

As mentioned in Subsection 4.1, the DNN could exploit temporal correlations by increasing the frame context through the number of look-forward and look-backward frames, L. The relative improvements in terms of word accuracy (average) over $L = 0$ were 1.43%, 3.17% and 3.47% for L values of 1, 2 and 3, respectively. As could be experimentally checked, the performance tends to saturate for $L = 2$ and greater values. Because of this fact, one can guess that the DNN is mainly exploiting the PLD between the first and second channels. Since most of the information required to provide a PLD-based estimate at frame t is close to that frame, the proposed DNN approach does not benefit of further increasing the length of the analysis window.

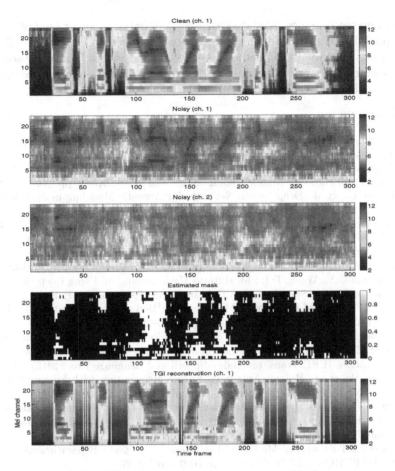

Fig. 3. Example of the TGI reconstruction of an utterance. All the spectrograms are in the log-Mel domain. From top to bottom: clean utterance (1st ch.), corrupted by bus noise at 0 dB (1st & 2nd chs.), mask estimated by the proposed DNN-based system and the resulting reconstruction (over the 1st ch.).

5 Conclusions and Future Work

In this paper we have proposed a new DNN-based system to estimate binary masks for robust speech recognition in the context of a smartphone with a dual-microphone used in a conversational position. The DNN has been able to take advantage of the dual-channel information, providing significant improvements on performance and again confirming the potential of this tool for speech recognition. Furthermore, one of the benefits of the DNN approach, with respect to other mask estimation techniques, is that no assumptions are made as well as it is able to learn complex non-linear dependencies between the input features and the target, thus overcoming the analytical modeling capabilities and allowing better performances.

As future work, an exhaustive search regarding the architecture and training configuration of the DNN should be carried out in order to further improve the system performance. Also, the use of additional or different kind of features (e.g. pitch-based features) could be an interesting research topic. Finally, our objective is to extend this method in order to deal with a hands-free scenario. This scenario is more challenging, as the PLD assumptions are not completely valid since both speech and noise are in far field conditions.

References

1. López-Espejo, I., et al.: Feature Enhancement for Robust Speech Recognition on Smartphones with Dual-Microphone. In: EUSIPCO, Lisbon (2014)
2. Zhang, J., et al.: A Fast Two-Microphone Noise Reduction Algorithm Based on Power Level Ratio for Mobile Phone. In: ISCSLP, Hong-Kong, pp. 206–209 (2012)
3. Hinton, G., et al.: Deep Neural Networks for Acoustic Modeling in Speech Recognition. IEEE Signal Processing Magazine 29(6) (2012)
4. Seltzer, M.L., Yu, D., Wang, Y.: An Investigation of Deep Neural Networks for Noise Robust Speech Recognition. In: ICASSP, Vancouver, pp. 7398–7402 (2013)
5. Wang, Y., Wang, D.L.: Towards Scaling Up Classification-Based Speech Separation. IEEE Trans. on Audio, Speech, and Language Processing 21(7) (2013)
6. Narayanan, A., Wang, D.L.: Ideal Ratio Mask Estimation Using Deep Neural Networks for Robust Speech Recognition. In: ICASSP, Vancouver (2013)
7. Raj, B., Seltzer, M.L., Stern, R.M.: Reconstruction of Missing Features for Robust Speech Recognition. Speech Comm. 48(4), 275–296 (2004)
8. González, J.A., Peinado, A.M., Ma, N., Gomez, A.M., Barker, J.: MMSE-Based Missing-Feature Reconstruction with Temporal Modeling for Robust Speech Recognition. IEEE Trans. on Audio, Speech and Language Proc. 21(3) (2013)
9. Cooke, M., et al.: Robust Automatic Speech Recognition with Missing Data and Unreliable Acoustic Data. Speech Communication 34, 267–285 (2001)
10. Pearce, D., Hirsch, H.G.: The Aurora Experimental Framework for the Performance Evaluation of Speech Recognition Systems Under Noisy Conditions. In: ICSLP, Beijing (2000)
11. Roweis, S.T.: Factorial Models and Refiltering for Speech Separation and Denoising. In: EUROSPEECH, Geneva, pp. 1009–1012 (2003)
12. Hinton, G., Salakhutdinov, R.: Reducing the Dimensionality of Data with Neural Networks. Science 313(5786) (2006)
13. Hinton, G.: Training Products of Experts by Minimizing Contrastive Divergence. Neural Computation 14, 1771–1800 (2002)
14. ETSI ES 201 108 - Distributed speech recognition; Front-end feature extraction algorithm; Compression algorithms
15. Ephraim, Y., Malah, D.: Speech Enhancement Using a Minimum Mean-Square Error Short-Time Spectral Amplitude Estimator. IEEE Trans. on Acoustics, Speech, and Signal Processing ASSP-32(6), 1109–1121 (1984)
16. Hinton, G.: A Practical Guide to Training Restricted Boltzmann Machines. UTML TR 2010-003 (2010)
17. Tanaka, M.: Deep Neural Network Toolbox for MatLab (2013)
18. ETSI ES 202 050 - Distributed speech recognition; Advanced front-end feature extraction algorithm; Compression algorithms
19. Deng, L., et al.: Large-Vocabulary Speech Recognition Under Adverse Acoustic Environments. In: ICSLP, Beijing, pp. 806–809 (2000)
20. González, J.A., et al.: Efficient MMSE Estimation and Uncertainty Processing for Multienvironment Robust Speech Recognition. IEEE Trans. on Audio, Speech, and Language Proc. 19(5), 1206–1220 (2011)

Language Model Adaptation for Lecture Transcription by Document Retrieval

A. Martínez-Villaronga, M.A. del-Agua,
J.A. Silvestre-Cerdà, J. Andrés-Ferrer, and A. Juan

MLLP, DSIC, Universitat Politècnica de València,
Camí de Vera s/n, 46022, València, Spain
{amartinez1,mdelagua,jsilvestre,jandres,ajuan}@dsic.upv.es

Abstract. With the spread of MOOCs and video lecture repositories it is more important than ever to have accurate methods for automatically transcribing video lectures. In this work, we propose a simple yet effective language model adaptation technique based on document retrieval from the web. This technique is combined with slide adaptation, and compared against a strong baseline language model and a stronger slide-adapted baseline. These adaptation techniques are compared within two different acoustic models: a standard HMM model and the CD-DNN-HMM model. The proposed method obtains improvements on WER of up to 14% relative with respect to a competitive baseline as well as outperforming slide adaptation.

Keywords: language model adaptation, video lectures, document retrieval.

1 Introduction

As part of the continuous development and advances in information technologies, new channels and communication possibilities have been established. In the field of education, universities have made a great effort in knowledge dissemination, which has resulted in the creation of large multimedia repositories of lecture recordings [7,2,3] or MOOCs (Massive Open Online Courses) [1,6]. The transcription of these repositories is an increasing necessity so as to achieve their massive dissemination for several reasons: for instance, transcriptions help to improve searchability, classification and analysis within huge repositories; they also help to reach wider audience of students by overcoming linguistic, as well as acoustic, barriers.

Each of these repositories is made up of hundreds or even thousands of videos, rendering manual transcription unfeasible in terms of both time and cost. Despite current state-of-the-art automatic speech recognition (ASR) systems are achieving continuous improvements over time, these repositories can be greatly improved through the use of specifically retrieved in-domain data. For instance, in [15] the video-dependent in-domain data is extracted/retrieved from the slides used in each video. Specifically, a general-purpose ASR system was adapted

J.L. Navarro Mesa et al. (Eds.): IberSPEECH 2014, LNAI 8854, pp. 129–137, 2014.

through language model interpolation from different resources (out-of-domain and in-domain,) including the text of video-dependent slides. The conclusion is that slide-dependent language models could significantly improve the transcription quality.

Unfortunately, it is not always possible to obtain slides for a given video lecture. For instance, it is usual that either the author does not give access to the slide document, or the repository does not keep track of such files. When slides are not available in electronic format, they can be extracted from the video recording using OCR techniques [15]. However, due to the video quality, even this is not possible in many cases.

In addition to slide adaptation, some works have explored language model adaptation by building language models using documents retrieved from the web. Document retrieval techniques are fundamental in gathering relevant in-domain data, a large part of which are based on building search queries to locate documents through common search engines. Previous works have focused on document retrieval for broad and general ASR systems. Some authors have tried to build these queries from a first pass recognition [9,14,18] or from keyword detection [17]. Other works have tried to use the training set itself [23] or the text of the slides [16] to build the query. In summary, previous works have a strong focus on studying how to build the queries in order to have competitive recall and precision trade-off. In contrast, we propose to use the title of each video lecture as the search query, since they tend to be quite descriptive in video lecture repositories.

In this work, we focus on language model adaptation by document retrieval for the automatic transcription of video lectures. We compare our approach with a strong baseline computed from a large collection of out-of-domain and in-domain documents comprising 46 billion words. Furthermore, we compare our results with those obtained by slide adaptation [15], using as slides the text extracted from the video using OCR. We also combine both approaches to further improve adaptation which yields significant improvements with respect to both the baseline model and the slide-adapted model. In order to assess language model adaptation with increasingly better acoustic models, this comparison is made with two different acoustic models: the standard Hidden-Markov-Model (HMM) and the Context-Dependent Deep-Neural-Network Hidden-Markov-Model (CD-DNN-HMM) approach [19]. All these techniques fall within the scope of the European trans**Lectures** [20,4] project whose objective is to develop innovative and cost-effective solutions to produce accurate transcriptions and translations in VideoLectures.NET and poli[Media] [2] through the free and open-source platform Matterhorn [12].

2   Document Retrieval

In this work, we focus on document retrieval from the web by building queries using the title of the video lecture. This is in contrast to other works where more complex techniques are proposed, such as rendering the lines of each slide as queries [16], or extracting keywords from a first pass recognition to build queries [14]. Our method is built on the hypothesis that the title is very informative and tends to contain the most important keywords and they appear in the proper order. The proposed method has several advantages among other works, such as it can be used without the need of slides or a first pass recognition on the video. Furthermore, it is a general and simple technique for this kind of repositories. We should remark that sometimes the paper on which the lecture is based is downloaded. This is very useful for the adaptation, although finding this exact document is not the primary goal of the search.

To ensure that the documents retrieved are of a minimum-required quality, we constrain the search to pdf documents only, and not webpages. Note that typically pdf files are of a higher standard since they are usually papers, books or notes related to the lecture topic. Unfortunately, some of the retrieved documents might be in languages different from that of the video and must be filtered out.

We propose two search methods for retrieving N documents per video:

- **Exact search:** we download documents that exactly match the title of the video lecture, i.e. the title is contained within the text of the document. Sometimes the search produces less than N results. For instance, the lecture "*Especies de interés I. Aromáticas. Lamiaceae. Thymus*" ("*Species of interest I. Aromatic. Lamiaceae. Thymus*") produced 0 results.
- **Extended search:** we perform an exact search and the search is extended with documents that partially match the title if less than N documents are found. The extended search will retrieve all the documents from the exact search plus other documents that contain some of the words of the lecture title, up to N documents.

3   Language Model Adaptation Technique

The language model adaptation technique for video lectures was introduced in [15]. It combines out-of-domain language models, in-domain models and video-specific models by means of a linear interpolation:

$$p(w|h) = \sum_i \lambda_i p_i(w|h)$$

where weights are optimised in a development set according to [11].

This technique is extended to consider language models built from documents retrieved from the web as follows:

$$p(w|h, V) = \sum_i \lambda_i p_i(w|h) + \lambda_D p_D(w|h)$$

where V stands for the current video and $p_D(w|h)$ for the language model trained on the documents retrieved for V.

In this work, we further consider the scenario where the lecture slides can be extracted from the video using OCR and they are available to adapt the models [15], or a mixed scenario that combines both the text in the slides and the retrieved documents as follows

$$p(w|h, V) = \sum_i \lambda_i p_i(w|h) + \lambda_D p_D(w|h) + \lambda_S p_S(w|h)$$

Note that, in the case where no document is retrieved for a given video, the corresponding λ_D is constrained to 0, as done in [15] for slides.

4   Experiments and Results

In this section we compare our approach with a strong baseline language model computed with out-of-domain corpora (Table 1) and in-domain corpus (Table 2). The baseline is tested against three systems: a system adapted with documents, a system adapted with slides, and a mixture thereof. In all cases, two acoustic models are used: a Deep Neural Networks model [19] with 4 hidden layer and a classical HMM with fCMLLR.

4.1   Corpora

Several corpora were used to build the baseline. Regarding the out-of-domain corpora, Table 1 summarises their main statistics. As for the in-domain corpus, we used the poli[Media] corpus, created by manually transcribing a number of video lectures from the Spanish poli[Media] repository for training, adaptation and internal evaluation as part of the trans**Lectures** project. Details of this corpus are given in Table 2.

Table 1. Main statistics of the out-of-domain corpora used by the baseline LM

Corpus	# sentences	# words	Vocabulary
EPPS	132K	0.9M	27K
news-commentary	183K	4.6M	174K
TED	316K	2.3M	133K
UnitedNations	448K	10.8M	234K
Europarl-v7	2 123K	54.9M	439K
El Periódico	2 695K	45.4M	916K
news (07-11)	8 627K	217.2M	2 852K
UnDoc	9 968K	318.0M	1 854K
Google Ngram	–	45 360M	292K

In order to conduct experiments with mixed models (slides and documents), it is necessary to have the text from the slides. However, a correct transcription of the slides (pdf) is not usually available and the text must be extracted automatically using OCR. These OCR slides have been recognised using *Tesseract* OCR tool [21] and applying various preprocessing and postprocessing steps. The

Table 2. Main statistics of the poli[Media] corpus

	Videos	Time (h)	# sentences	# words	Vocabulary
Train	655	96	41.5K	968K	28K
Dev	26	3.5	1.4K	34K	4.5K
Test	23	3	1.1K	28.7K	4K

Table 3. poli[Media] slides details

	# slides	# words	Vocabulary
Dev	107	17.4K	3.9K
Test	363	16.4K	3.1K

final WER of the OCR slides is 40%. Table 3 contains some statistics about the slides.

Regarding the downloaded documents, we performed experiments with models trained with up to 5, 10 and 20 documents per video. As we will see in Section 4.4, the extended search reports significantly better results than the exact search for 5 documents. So for 10 and 20 documents we only considered the extended search. Details of the retrieved documents are depicted in Table 4. As we mentioned, it is possible that the paper the lecture is based on is among the documents downloaded. However, this is not likely to happen in the repository used in this work.

Table 4. Statistics of downloaded documents for poli[Media] development and test sets

			# documents	# words	Vocabulary
5 docs	Exact search	dev	96	1.3M	40K
		test	102	1.2M	41K
	Extended search	dev	130	2.0M	55K
		test	115	1.4M	42K
10 docs	Extended search	dev	260	5.2M	91K
		test	230	2.7M	65K
20 docs	Extended search	dev	515	9.0M	128K
		test	459	6.4M	104K

4.2 Acoustic Models

The language model adaptation techniques are tested with different acoustic models (AMs): standard HMM and deep neural network (DNN). In both cases, the software used to train the systems is the trans**Lectures** -UPV toolkit [5,8], and the data used to train the systems is the poli[Media] corpus training set described in Table 2.

The HMMs are based on triphonemes, modelled with a 3-state left-to-right topology. A decision tree based state-tying is applied, resulting in a total of 5039 triphone states. Each triphoneme was trained for up to 128 mixture components per Gaussian and 4 iterations per mixture. Moreover, in order to reduce the speaker variability, fCMLLR was applied.

Regarding the DNN, we used the hybrid approach proposed by [19]; the so-called CD-DNN-HMM. In this case, we need to train a classical HMM system in order to provide an accurate forced alignment of the input features at triphone state (senone) level. Subsequently, a Deep Neural Network is trained in two steps: pre-training and fine-tuning. With respect to its topology, the output layer was set as large as the number of phonetic targets derived during the previous forced alignment, in this case 5039 classes. After trying several networks configurations, 4 hidden layers of 3000 units each was found to provide the best performance. Finally, the Gaussian mixtures of the acoustic model are replaced with the neural network state posterior probabilities.

4.3   Language Models

As regards the language model, we computed the baseline model as discussed in Section 3, interpolating several individual language models trained on the corpora described in Section 4.1. For each out-of-domain corpora we trained a 4-gram language model with the SRILM [22] toolkit . The individual 4-gram models were smoothed with the modified Kneser-Ney absolute interpolation method [13,10]. Finally, the training set of poli[Media] was used as the in-domain corpus. For the vocabulary, we obtained a base vocabulary using 200K words over all the out-of-domain corpora plus the in-domain vocabulary, resulting in a 205K words vocabulary.

The vocabulary of the adapted models is built extending the base vocabulary with the words in the slides and/or the documents. In the case of the documents, the vocabulary extension will result in much larger vocabularies. From here on, we consider the standard full version of the vocabulary, and a restricted version in which only those words that occur more than three times in the documents are added.

4.4   Experiments

First we run experiments to assess whether the exact or the extended search is better for querying documents. For these experiments the number of documents per video is set to 5. Table 5 depicts these results, in which it is observed that document adaptation significantly improves the baseline results independently of the AM used. The extended search obtains better results than the exact search where the smaller amount of documents retrieved leads to slightly higher WER values. Constraining the vocabulary also results in higher error rates.

After setting the retrieval technique to extended search, we assessed the impact of the number of documents retrieved when using up to 10 and 20 documents, instead of 5. In Table 6 significant improvement is observed for all AMs when using 20 documents. Note that the improvements of up to 10.8% relative WER, depicted in Table 6, can be used to effectively adapt language models for

Table 5. WER (%) on the poli[Media] corpus for the adapted models with 5 documents retrieved per video

Language Model	Acoustic Model			
	HMM		CD-DNN-HMM	
	Dev	Test	Dev	Test
Baseline (BL)	20.4	21.8	14.3	15.7
BL + Exact search	20.3	20.7	14.2	14.6
+ Restricted voc	20.2	20.8	14.1	14.8
BL + Extended search	19.8	20.6	14.0	14.4
+ Restricted voc	19.7	20.6	13.9	14.4

Table 6. WER (%) on the poli[Media] corpus dev and test sets for the adapted models with 10 and 20 documents retrieved by extended search

Language Model	Acoustic Model			
	HMM		CD-DNN-HMM	
	Dev	Test	Dev	Test
Baseline (BL)	20.4	21.8	14.3	15.7
BL + 10 Documents	19.6	20.6	13.8	14.4
+ Restricted voc	19.5	20.5	13.8	14.4
BL + 20 Documents	19.6	20.0	13.8	14.2
+ Restricted voc	19.5	19.9	13.8	14.0

video lectures in those scenarios where no other resources but the lecture title is available.

In cases where slides are available, not only it is possible to perform adaptation by using either the documents or the slides [15], but also a combination of these two resources. These combined results are summarised in Table 7. It is observed that the inclusion of documents significantly improves the results of all the previous systems (adapted or not) where documents were not used. It is also interesting to note that the combination of slides and documents outperforms both the system without slides and the system without documents.

Table 7. WER (%) for the adapted models with documents and slides

Language Model	Acoustic Model			
	HMM		CD-DNN-HMM	
	Dev	Test	Dev	Test
Baseline (BL)	20.4	21.8	14.3	15.7
BL + Slides	19.8	19.4	13.8	13.8
+ Documents	18.7	18.9	13.4	13.5
+ Restricted voc	18.7	19.0	13.4	13.5

5 Conclusions

We have proposed a new simple yet effective method to retrieve documents from the web and use them to build adapted language models for video lecture transcription. These documents have proven to be a very valuable resource for adapting language models, obtaining a WER improvement of up to 1.9 absolute WER points (8.7 % relative) using HMM, and 1.7 points (10.8 % relative) when using DNN, with respect to a strong baseline.

Furthermore, if we combine the document adaptation with slide adaptation the system yields improvements of 2.9 and 2.2 absolute WER points (13.3 % and 14.0 % relative) with respect to a strong baseline, depending on the acoustic model used. If instead we compare these results with the models adapted with slides only, it is observed that documents can still provide improvements of up to 1 absolute WER points for HMMs, and 0.5 for DNNs.

It is worth noting that, in general, the improvements are consistent for all proposed acoustic models, which makes us think that this kind of adaptation will provide significant improvements as the acoustic models get even better.

The documents obtained have led to significant improvements, proving that this method is a good way of retrieving documents for the purpose of adapting language models. However, in the future, we plan to compare this document retrieval method with the alternative methods proposed by ohter authors.

Acknowledgments. The research leading to these results has received funding from the European Union Seventh Framework Programme (FP7/2007-2013) under grant agreement no 287755 (transLectures) and ICT Policy Support Programme (ICT PSP/2007-2013) as part of the Competitiveness and Innovation Framework Programme (CIP) under grant agreement no 621030 (EMMA), the Spanish MINECO Active2Trans (TIN2012-31723) research project and the Spanish Government with the FPU scholarships FPU13/06241 and AP2010-4349.

References

1. coursera.org: Take the World's Best Courses, Online, For Free, http://www.coursera.org/
2. poliMedia: Videolectures from the "Universitat Politècnica de València, http://polimedia.upv.es/catalogo/
3. SuperLectures: We take full care of your event video recordings, http://www.superlectures.com
4. transLectures, https://translectures.eu/
5. transLectures-UPV Toolkit (TLK) for Automatic Speech Recognition, http://translectures.eu/tlk
6. Udacity: Learn, Think, Do, http://www.udacity.com/
7. Videolectures.NET: Exchange Ideas and Share Knowledge, http://www.videolectures.net/

8. del-Agua, M.A., Giménez, A., Serrano, N., Andrés-Ferrer, J., Civera, J., Sanchis, A., Juan, A.: The translectures-UPV toolkit. In: Navarro Mesa, J.L., Giménez, A.O., Teixeira, A. (eds.) IberSPEECH 2014. LNCS (LNAI), vol. 8854, pp. 269–278. Springer, Heidelberg (2014)

9. Chang, P.C., Shan Lee, L.: Improved language model adaptation using existing and derived external resources. In: Proc. of ASRU, pp. 531–536 (2003)

10. Chen, S.F., Goodman, J.: An empirical study of smoothing techniques for language modeling. Computer Speech & Language 13(4), 359–393 (1999)

11. Jelinek, F., Mercer, R.L.: Interpolated Estimation of Markov Source Parameters from Sparse Data. In: Proc. of the Workshop on Pattern Recognition in Practice, pp. 381–397 (1980)

12. Ketterl, M., Schulte, O.A., Hochman, A.: Opencast matterhorn: A community-driven open source solution for creation, management and distribution of audio and video in academia. In: Proc. of ISM, pp. 687–692 (2009)

13. Kneser, R., Ney, H.: Improved Backing-off for M-gram Language Modeling. In: Proc. of ICASSP, pp. 181–184 (1995)

14. Lecorv, G., Gravier, G., Sbillot, P.: An unsupervised web-based topic language model adaptation method. In: Proc. of ICASSP 2008, pp. 5081–5084 (2008)

15. Martínez-Villaronga, A., del Agua, M.A., Andrés-Ferrer, J., Juan, A.: Language model adaptation for video lectures transcription. In: Proc. of ICASSP, pp. 8450–8454 (2013)

16. Munteanu, C., Penn, G., Baecker, R.: Web-based language modelling for automatic lecture transcription. In: Proc. of INTERSPEECH, pp. 2353–2356 (2007)

17. Rogina, I., Schaaf, T.: Lecture and presentation tracking in an intelligent meeting room. In: Proc of ICMI, pp. 47–52 (2002)

18. Schlippe, T., Gren, L., Vu, N.T., Schultz, T.: Unsupervised language model adaptation for automatic speech recognition of broadcast news using web 2.0, pp. 2698–2702 (2013)

19. Seide, F., Li, G., Chen, X., Yu, D.: Feature engineering in context-dependent deep neural networks for conversational speech transcription. In: Proc. of ASRU, pp. 24–29 (2011)

20. Silvestre, J.A., et al.: Translectures. In: Proc. of IberSPEECH 2012, pp. 345–351 (2012)

21. Smith, R.: An overview of the tesseract ocr engine. In: Proc. of ICDAR 2007, pp. 629–633 (2007)

22. Stolcke, A.: SRILM – an extensible language modeling toolkit. In: Proc. of ICSLP, pp. 901–904 (2002)

23. Tsiartas, A., Georgiou, P., Narayanan, S.: Language model adaptation using www documents obtained by utterance-based queries. In: Proc. of ICASSP, pp. 5406–5409 (2010)

Articulatory Feature Extraction from Voice and Their Impact on Hybrid Acoustic Models

Jorge Llombart, Antonio Miguel, and Eduardo Lleida

ViVoLab,
Aragon Institute for Engineering Research (I3A),
University of Zaragoza, Spain
{jllombg,amiguel,lleida}@unizar.es
http://www.vivolab.es

Abstract. There is a great amount of information in the speech signal, although current speech recognizers do not exploit it completely. In this paper articulatory information is extracted from speech and fused to standard acoustic models to obtain a better hybrid acoustic model which provides improvements on speech recognition. The paper also studies the best input signal for the system in terms of type of speech features and time resolution to obtain a better articulatory information extractor. Then this information is fused to a standard acoustic model obtained with neural networks to perform the speech recognition achieving better results.

Keywords: Articulatory features, Neural network, Hybrid models.

1 Introduction

Speech production is a complex process which has attracted a wide research activity in the last decades to obtain articulatory information embedded in the speech signal. The motivation of this work is to study how articulatory information can improve phoneme classification accuracy. As shown in [1], [2] and [3], is possible to take advantage of phoneme similarities to build articulatory class specific classifiers, which we use to provide additional inputs for a phoneme classifier.

To deal with that amount of information and to obtain a better articulatory information representation, we propose to integrate neural networks in a hybrid recognizer. The performance of these models is very sensitive to the input features, therefore in this paper we study two different signal representations, Mel-Frequency Cepstrum Coefficients $MFCC$ and a less processed representation, the Mel scaled Filter Bank. It is also important to study the impact of higher temporal resolution in the feature extraction process, that we think it may help convolutional networks to compensate time label misalignments, which usually degrade the performance of regular networks.

Once a good representation of the articulatory process is obtained as articulatory features, they may be included to get a hybrid model which takes advantage of them to reduce classification errors. We will show in the experimental

J.L. Navarro Mesa et al. (Eds.): IberSPEECH 2014, LNAI 8854, pp. 138–147, 2014.
© Springer International Publishing Switzerland 2014

section that the fusion of the articulatory information with more standard features reduces significantly recognition errors, thus validating the assumption of articulatory information being helpful to improve speech recognition.

This article is organized as follows. Section 2 describes articulatory features used in this work. Section 3 explains our representation of neural networks. Section 4 describes experimental procedure. In Section 5 the results are shown, and in Section 6 are exposed the conclusions extracted from this study.

2   Articulatory Features

Speech production involves three processes; initiation, phonation, and articulation. The first, initiation is the process in which air starts to flow through vocal tract. During the second process, phonation, vocal chords start to vibrate producing the sound. Finally, in the articulation process, some constrictions are made in the oral cavity to modify the produced sound.

During the articulation process, the constrictions made on the vocal cavity perturbate natural air flow. The location and type of constriction imprints specific information in the speech signal that we propose to extract and use to improve speech recognizers.

Constrictions could be done in different places, or by different manners. In order to study the speech production process, articulatory features have been described by phonology, which also studies their relation to human vocal tract. Those articulatory features explain all sounds related with speech and they are pictured on *International Phonetic alphabet (IPA)*. Regarding to the relation between articulatory features, for example the place where the main constriction is made or the shape of lips, they are clustered in independent groups, which offers an opportunity to classify sounds from different points of view and give us additional information to perform the phoneme classification. There are some previous works on speech recognition using only articulatory features to classify phonemes like [1] with good results, or combined with acoustic features [2]. Other works use them for speaker recognition [3]. Besides, there are works that use neural networks for speech recognition with articulatory features like [4].

We consider five different articulatory properties. The first property is **voicing**, which tells if a sound is *voiced* or *unvoiced*, and it is related to vibration of vocal cords. The second property used in this work is **place**, which indicates where is allocated the main constriction. Another property we deal with is the **manner**, which is referred to how the sound is generated, if it is a *nasal* sound or *fricative* and so on. More related to vowel sounds there are two properties, **rounding**, that describes if lips are rounded or not during pronunciation. And finally the **vowel location**, to express the position of the tongue, if it is on the *front* of vocal cavity or on the *back*. Table 1 shows all properties used in this work and the features which are classified in each property. It is important to point that *silence* is included in each property. The class *Silence* does not describe a phoneme but it is included to allow the classifier to deal with audio segments without speech. The same concept is applied to *not representative*, for instance if the sound corresponds to a consonant, it does not make sense to speak in terms of *rounding*, which is a property that only take place on vowel sounds.

Table 1. Articulatory properties and theirs features

Property	Classes	N Classes
Voicing	Unvoiced, Voiced, Silence	3
Place	High, Medium, Low, Labial, Dental, Alveolar, Palatal, Velar, Glottal, Silence	10
Manner	Vowel, Nasal, Fricative, Aproximant-Lateral, Stop, Silence	6
Rounding	Rounded, Not Rounded, Not Representative, Silence	4
Vowel Location	Front, Middle, Back, Not Representative, Silence	5

With those features, now we have to label the database. This process should be done by manual labeling the database, but we propose a simpler labeling process based on the phonetic labels provided by a canonical pronunciation dictionary, since we have word level transcriptions. Then, using the phonetic description of those phonemes we set the attributes which correspond to the articulatory features described on Table 1. In this study it is used the *TIMIT Acoustic-Phonetic Continuous Speech Corpus* in which each phoneme was characterized and pictured in a table with the *Sampa* and *IPA* nomenclatures. The description of the phonemes is based on the work [5] and an extract from this table is shown on Table 2.

Table 2. Extract of *TIMIT* phonemes and their description on *Sampa*, *IPA* and articulatory features. (NR means *Not Representative*).

Mono-phonemes	Sampa	IPA	Voicing	Place	Manner	Rounding	Vowel Location
aa	A:	ɑ	Voiced	Low	Vowel	Not Rounded	Back
ae	{	æ	Voiced	Low	Vowel	Not Rounded	Front
ah	V	ʌ	Voiced	Low	Vowel	Not Rounded	Back
ay	aI	aɪ	Voiced	Low	Vowel	Not Rounded	Front
b	b	b	Voiced	Labial	Stop	NR	NR

3 Artificial Neural Networks

In recent years, there has been an increasing interest in neural networks. This work is based on multi-layer perceptron, a classical architecture of neural networks [6]. Equation (1) describes the mathematical model for an artificial neuron which is given a vector of M elements as input $X = [x_1, x_2, \ldots, x_M]$, where $W = [w_1, w_2, \ldots, w_M]$ are the weights for that input, b is a bias, and $\theta(\cdot)$ is the activation function that applies a non linearity to obtain the output. The training process is based on generalized gradient descent [6].

$$y = \theta \left(\sum_{m=1}^{M} (w_m \cdot x_m) + b \right) \tag{1}$$

The network is composed of tree layers. The input layer, one hidden layer with the internal parameters, and the output layer which transforms the internal parameters to human comprehensive information. Since in this work we use neural networks as classifiers, we choose the cross-entropy as cost function and *softmax*, shown in (2), as activation function for the output layer, where $X = [x_1, x_2, \ldots, x_i, \ldots, x_N]$ is a vector of N elements, where the output vector is normalized and it gives us the probability of being part of each class.

$$\theta(x_i) = \frac{\exp x_i}{\sum_{n=1}^{N} \exp x_n}, \tag{2}$$

Other activation functions used are the *Sigmoid* function for hidden layers, and the *Rectified Linear Unit (ReLU)* on input layer because this type of neurons can regularize the training process both in image [7] and on speech [8].

One of the problems which can be found while processing speech signal with neural networks is that neural networks are prepared for recognizing static patterns, but speech signal is a complex and non stationary signal. One phoneme has a temporal evolution, so in order to recognize better that phoneme it is useful to show to the network the temporal context of the speech signal during the phoneme. That means that it is important to give to the neural network the vector with the calculated features for this time, and a context which consists on the previous and posterior vectors. We suppose that the reference is on central vector, so the label of the overall network input is the label which is referred to the central vector. Using neural networks to learn spectro-temporal patterns makes them very sensitive to the exact label alignment, which can be inaccurate since it is obtained from a reference Hidden Markov Model *HMM*. This effect can be minimized with convolutional neural networks. This type of neural networks can be interpreted as if one neuron is a filter of a windowed input, then this filter is repeated for some displacements of that window. Finally, the maximum activation is selected as output of all those repeated filters. Mathematically, suppose that there is an input composed by feature vectors $X = [x_1, x_2, \ldots, x_M]$ that belongs to K temporal windows, so the input may be written as $X_k = [x_{1,k}, x_{2,k}, \ldots, x_{M,k}]$. There are J filters that we want to compute, therefore the filtering for each time index is $h_k = [h_{k,1}, h_{k,2}, \ldots, h_{k,J}]$ where each filter is represented as (3). To complete the convolutional layer, the output corresponding to the maximum temporal output per each filter as summarized in (4) is called *max pool* stage whose overall output is a vector $P = [p_1, p_2, \ldots, p_J]$ which is the input for the next stages on the neural network.

$$h_{k,j} = \theta \left(\sum_{m=1}^{M} (w_{m,j} \cdot x_{m,k}) + b_j \right) \tag{3}$$

$$p_j = \max_{k=1}^{K} (h_{k,j}) \tag{4}$$

This kind of layer has proved a good behavior on different type of inputs and applications where there is some spatial or temporal variability, and the convolutional mechanism might regularize the input, like in image [9] or in speech in different ways [10] [11].

4   Experiment Description

This work uses the *TIMIT* Acoustic-Phonetic Continuous Speech Corpus, as mentioned on Section 2, and the phonetic classes are referred to that corpus. This corpus consists on 508 speakers from eight United States' regions, 462 on training set and 50 on testing set. As in previous works, we use the 3696 phrases marked as 'si' and 'sx', and in the testing set 192 *core test* phrases [12]. From the training set a 10% has been separated for development and validation set. For all experiments a bigram language model has been used, and the phone alignment has been obtained from reference *HMMs*. The database has 61 phoneme classes, which have been extended up to 183 classes by using the state index in the *HMM* as label, then each of those classes are composed by the phoneme class and the state, using three states per phoneme [11]. However, in the test process the labels are contracted to the 39 to calculate errors, as described on [13], [11] or [10]. One of the benefits of neural networks is that the forward evaluation at test time is inexpensive in computational terms, even though training in this experiments can take up to four days in a *graphic processing unit (GPU)* architecture.

As mentioned before, neural networks have to take care of the influence of temporal displacements. For the time-frequency analysis, a $25ms$ window is taken to get the frequency analysis, and then this window is displaced $10ms$ to calculate the next frame [14]. It has been suggested that there exists a context of $100ms$ with relevant information around each frame, as said in [15], who in [16] used mutual information to check that hypothesis, and [17] with the same method showed that information remains in cepstrum feature space. Therefore, all that information should be shown to the neural network by stacking a time-frequency matrix with 10 frames around the labeled frame, 5 each side to maintain symmetry, for a total of 11 frames, equivalent to $110ms$ of context. The temporal context used by the convolutional networks input is extended to 15 frames, $150ms$, to allow them to realign it while using a comparable effective context of 11 frames.

Another effect that has been taken into account is the time resolution. As mentioned before, the time-frequency analysis is made by transforming a window of the signal of $25ms$ and then displacing it $10ms$. In order to increase time domain resolution the displacement of analysis window is $5ms$, but to maintain the number of labels, and to allow a comparative between this two types of temporal resolution, the separation between two time-frequency matrices is $10ms$. In other words we can say that the time resolution of time-frequency input matrices has been increased but the number of matrices has been maintained as before. We show that effect in Figure 1, where it is pictured the same phoneme, labeled at the same time instant, but each one with different time resolution.

For the experiments, the *TIMIT* audios are processed in eight different ways taking into account the strategies mentioned before. We used the static and dynamic *MFCC*, and the Mel scaled filter bank with static and dynamic coefficients, which are resumed in Table 3

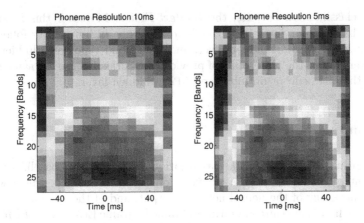

Fig. 1. Time-frequency analysis of a *TIMIT* phoneme. On the left a 10*ms* resolution matrix and on the right the 5*ms* resolution matrix.

Table 3. Input features description

Name			Coefficients description	Analysis displacement
Mfcc	EZ	10	12 Mfcc coefficients, energy and cepstral mean subtraction	10*ms*
Mfcc	EZ	05	12 Mfcc coefficients, energy and cepstral mean subtraction	5*ms*
Mfcc	EACZ	10	12 Mfcc coef., energy, cepstral mean subtraction and dynamic coef.	10*ms*
Mfcc	EACZ	05	12 Mfcc coef., energy, cepstral mean subtraction and dynamic coef.	05*ms*
Fb 26	E	10	26 Mel scaled filter bands with energy	10*ms*
Fb 26	E	05	26 Mel scaled filter bands with energy	05*ms*
Fb 26	EDA	10	26 Mel scaled filter bands, energy and dynamic coef.	10*ms*
Fb 26	EDA	05	26 Mel scaled filter bands, energy and dynamic coef.	05*ms*

The architecture of the system is composed of two different parts. The first part is a classificator, which is a neural network of three layers, an input layer, a hidden layer, and the output layer. For those classificators the first layer has 512 *ReLu* neurons, and it can be of two types: a regular mlp layer or a convolutional layer described in Section 3. The hidden layer is formed by 256 *logistic* neurons. And finally, the output layer has the same neurons than classes to classify, whose output is the probability of membership of the example in the input to the class which this output is referred to. The second part of this architecture is a fusion neural network. Once the classificators of phonemes and articulatory properties are obtained, the information that can be achieved from the articulatory properties is shown to the fusion network to improve the classification result. In this work three fusion philosophies are explored. The first one, *Output-Layer-Fusion*, consist on composing an input with the probabilities of the phoneme states and the articulatory features, then a neural network uses this information to perform a phoneme classification. The second strategy is to use the output of the hidden layer, instead of the output layer, to conform an input vector for the fusion network, the *Previous-Layer-Fusion*. The last strategy used is give to the neural network the context of the classified input by stacking the previous and posterior classification outputs, the *Context-Fusion*. Moreover this fusion network can have two architectures, the fist one is only an input layer followed by an output layer, without hidden layer, and the second type has a hidden layer. These layers follow the philosophy of previous networks and use the same neuron types, with 1024 neurons on input and 512 in hidden layer.

5   Results

The first results obtained are the classification of phonemes as baseline, and the experiment with the first layer as convolutional one. In this experiment we analyzed the accuracy of the neural network output, and of the speech recognition system. The first is measured in terms of Frame by frame Error Rate, *FER*, which counts substitutions, while the second is measured in terms of Phoneme Error Rate, *PER*, which takes into account the substitutions, deletions and insertions. As it is shown on Table 4 a better performance is obtained when convolutional networks are used. Another important point is that when a better time resolution is used a better result is obtained in most of the cases, obtaining the best result, a *PER* of 30.52% on the Fb 26 EDA 05 case in the convolutional case.

Table 4. *FER* and *PER* in phoneme classification. *FER* is calculated for 183 classes and *PER* is calculated for 39 classes.

Features			Baseline		Convolutional	
			$FER[\%]$	$PER[\%]$	$FER[\%]$	$PER[\%]$
Mfcc	EZ	10	49.85	33.55	48.05	32.09
Mfcc	EZ	05	50.18	34.02	48.07	32.27
Mfcc	EDAZ	10	46.57	31.92	47.80	31.94
Mfcc	EDAZ	05	46.25	32.57	47.28	30.72
Fb 26	E	10	49.03	32.57	50.01	32.12
Fb 26	E	05	49.27	32.82	47.90	31.88
Fb 26	EDA	10	45.40	30.90	49.87	32.96
Fb 26	EDA	05	46.12	30.67	46.92	**30.52**

In Table 5 we show the classification *FER* for each articulatory property, for two configurations. In this case the better results are obtained on baseline architecture. This effect can be explained because in these features, the position of events may not be as important as in phoneme classification, since the articulatory classes are less specific. Nevertheless in this case it can be observed as in the phoneme case that using a higher temporal resolution may help classification. As we can see, the best performance has been obtained for higher temporal resolution in almost all cases.

For fusion experiments the Fb 26 EDA 05 convolutional network classificator has been selected to use it as baseline, which provides an accuracy of *PER* of 30.52%, and whose output is fused with the articulatory classificators. For this classificator we used the Fb 26 EDA 05 baseline classificator for each property in order to obtain comparable results and to know which property helps more to the

Table 5. *FER*[%] in articulatory classification. The properties are Voicing, Place, Manner, Rounding and Vowel Location. #Classes means the number of classes of these property.

Features		Baseline					Convolutional				
		Voice	Place	Manner	Roundig	Location	Voice	Place	Manner	Rounding	Location
#Calsses		3	10	6	4	5	3	10	6	4	5
Mfcc EZ	10	9.91	27.59	20.84	14.79	19.93	10.13	25.36	19.64	14.03	16.23
Mfcc EZ	05	9.21	27.23	20.26	14.82	16.60	9.40	25.92	19.32	16.36	16.36
Mfcc EDAZ	10	8.91	24.59	18.54	**13.37**	15.66	9.48	25.23	19.11	14.06	15.92
Mfcc EDAZ	05	8.73	24.63	18.67	13.59	15.24	8.85	25.20	18.20	14.23	15.32
Fb 26 E	10	9.51	26.95	20.05	14.90	17.40	9.66	26.12	17.90	15.14	17.39
Fb 26 E	05	9.67	26.32	20.29	15.13	16.94	9.67	24.90	18.42	13.92	15.82
Fb 26 EDA	10	8.54	**23.90**	18.07	13.51	15.34	9.56	26.09	19.33	14.47	16.65
Fb 26 EDA	05	**8.30**	24.61	**17.59**	13.51	**14.91**	8.96	24.91	18.12	13.62	15.60

Table 6. Fusion experiments. *FER* is calculated for 183 classes and *PER* is calculated for 39 classes.

Properties	Output-Layer-Fusion		Previous-Layer-Fusion		Context-Fusion	
2 Layers	*FER*[%]	*PER*[%]	*FER*[%]	*PER*[%]	*FER*[%]	*PER*[%]
Phoneme + Voicing	45.76	30.01	44.07	27.98	44.68	29.93
Phoneme + Position	45.35	29.92	43.49	27.26	44.39	29.63
Phoneme + Manner	45.31	29.93	43.57	27.79	44.27	29.48
Phoneme + Rounding	45.69	30.37	43.97	27.83	44.24	29.77
Phoneme + Location	45.57	30.12	44.02	28.11	44.10	29.74
Phoneme + All	44.61	29.67	43.21	27.03	43.82	29.66
3 Layers	*FER*[%]	*PER*[%]	*FER*[%]	*PER*[%]	*FER*[%]	*PER*[%]
Phoneme + Voicing	46.27	30.49	44.46	28.20	45.22	30.17
Phoneme + Position	45.67	29.85	43.71	27.64	44.84	29.92
Phoneme + Manner	45.57	29.67	43.61	27.52	44.53	29.77
Phoneme + Rounding	46.02	30.00	44.40	27.97	44.74	29.88
Phoneme + Location	45.92	29.93	44.23	28.09	44.58	29.89
Phoneme + All	45.20	30.06	43.04	**26.96**	44.05	29.86

classification for the same conditions. In Table 6 is shown that *Previous-Layer-Fusion* provides better accuracy than *Output-Layer-Fusion*. Using *Output-Layer-Fusion* might have as drawback that the classification has already been made, and errors can be propagated to the fusion stage. Other interesting effect shown in these results is that the addition of more context to the fusion network, like in *Context-Fusion*, improves the result, even though in these conditions it can not achieve as good results as *Previous-Layer-Fusion*. The motivation of the work is to study how articulatory information can improve phoneme classification accuracy. Since it is harder for a general phoneme classificator to take advantage of phoneme similarities. We propose different methods to train articulatory specific classifiers and to fuse their outputs to improve the accuracy of the system. One last impression of these results may be that *manner* or *position* provide more information for the classification than the other articulatory features. This may be because this two properties are present in all phonemes, so this property add extra information for all phonemes. When we fuse the phoneme classificator, all phonemes have extra information to improve classification. Although it can be seen that the fusion with *manner* or *position* attain the best improvement in accuracy individually. We show that fusion with all articulatory properties provides an $26.96\%PER$ confirming our previous hypothesis. In Table 6 the relative improvement obtained using the different fusion methods ranges from 1% to 11% which is comparable to previous results in similar conditions in the state of the art [2].

6   Conclusions and Future Work

The main motivation of this work is study how articulatory information can improve phoneme classification accuracy, for that we propose to process articulatory information to build specific classifiers which can be used as additional information for the phoneme classifier. The first steps of the current study were to determine the manner in which articulatory features can be extracted from speech signal using neural networks as feature extractor, and use them to complement the acoustic model for using speech recognition. The results of this study indicate that using a less processed input in the frequency domain like Mel scaled filter bank, instead of cepstrum domain input, like $MFCC$, increases accuracy in acoustic neural network models. Moreover it seems that the higher time resolution, the better results, not only in convolutional neural networks which compensate misalignment, but also in simpler architectures, though this may be studied deeper in future works. The other aspect studied in this paper is how articulatory features may perform in an hybrid acoustic model, and the evidence from this study suggests that this kind of models provide a better representation which helps the speech recognition. It is shown that some properties like *position* or *manner* produce a mayor impact on hybrid models, but the relations among all of them in a unified hybrid model achieve the best results.

Further work needs to be done on both lines. It would be interesting to determinate how much time resolution is needed for each type of input to perform articulatory information extraction. The other aspect in which it is appropriated a further research is on fusing this articulatory information. The new techniques on deep neural networks may reach better representation of hybrid models by extracting higher levels of abstraction in the relations between articulatory features and phoneme acoustic models.

Acknowledgments. This work has been supported by the Spanish Government and the European Union (FEDER) through projects TIN2011-28169-C05-02 and INNPACTO IPT-2011-1696-390000.

References

1. Kirchhoff, K.: Robust Speech Recognition Using Articulatory Information. PhD thesis, University of Bielefeld (1999)
2. Kirchhoff, K., Fink, G.A., Sagerer, G.: Combining acoustic and articulatory feature information for robust speech recognition. Speech Communication 37, 303–319 (2002)

3. Leung, K.Y., Mak, M.W., Kung, S.-Y.: Applying articulatory features to telephone-based speaker verification. In: 2004 IEEE International Conference on Acoustics, Speech, and Signal Processing, p. I858. IEEE, Montreal (2004)

4. Yu, D., Siniscalchi, S.M., Deng, L., Lee, C.-H.: Boosting attribute and phone estimation accuracies with deep neural networks for detection-based speech recognition. In: 2012 IEEE International Conference on Acoustics, Speech and Signal Processing (ICASSP), Kyoto, Japan, pp. 4169–4172 (2012)

5. Hieronymus, J.: ASCII phonetic symbols for the world's languages: Worldbet. Journal of the International Phonetic Association (1993)

6. Bishop, C.M.: Pattern Recognition and Machine Learning (Information Science and Statistics). Springer

7. Nair, V., Hinton, G.E.: Rectified Linear Units Improve Restricted Boltzmann Machines. In: Proceedings of the 27th International Conference on Machine Learning, Haifa, Israel, pp. 807–814 (2010)

8. Toth, L.: Phone recognition with deep sparse rectifier neural networks. In: 2013 IEEE International Conference on Acoustics, Speech and Signal Processing, pp. 6985–6989. IEEE, Vancouver (2013)

9. Krizhevsky, A., Sutskever, I., Hinton, G.E.: ImageNet Classification with Deep Convolutional Neural Networks. In: Pereira, F., Burges, C.J.C., Bottou, L., Weinberger, K.Q. (eds.) Advances in Neural Information Processing Systems 25, pp. 1097–1105. Curran Associates, Inc. (2012)

10. Toth, L.: Convolutional Deep Rectifier Neural Nets for Phone Recognition. In: INTERSPEECH, pp. 1722–1726. ISCA, Lyon (2013)

11. Abdel-Hamid, O., Mohamed, A., Jiang, H., Penn, G.: Applying Convolutional Neural Networks concepts to hybrid NN-HMM model for speech recognition. In: 2012 IEEE International Conference on Acoustics, Speech and Signal Processing (ICASSP), Kyoto, Japan, pp. 4277–4280 (2012)

12. Garofolo, J., et al.: TIMIT Acoustic-Phonetic Continuous Speech Corpus LDC93S1. Linguistic Data Consortium, Philadelphia (1993)

13. Lee, K.-F., Hon, H.-W.: Speaker-independent phone recognition using hidden Markov models. IEEE Transactions on Acoustics, Speech, and Signal Processing 37, 1641–1648 (1989)

14. Huang, X., Acero, A., Hon, H.-W.: Spoken Language Processing: A Guide to Theory, Algorithm and System Development. Prentice Hall (2001)

15. Yang, H., van Vuuren, S., Hermansky, H.: Relevancy of time-frequency features for phonetic classification measured by mutual information. In: Proceedings of the IEEE International Conference on Acoustics, Speech, and Signal Processing, ICASSP 1999, vol. 1, pp. 225–228. IEEE, Phoenix (1999)

16. Yang, H.H., Van Vuuren, S., Sharma, S., Hermansky, H.: Relevance of timefrequency features for phonetic and speaker-channel classification. Speech Communication 31, 35–50 (2000)

17. Segura, J., Benitez, M., Torre, A., de la Rubio, A.: Feature extraction from time-frequency matrices for robust speech recognition. In: INTERSPEECH, Aalborg, Denmark (2001)

CVX-Optimized Beamforming and Vector Taylor Series Compensation with German ASR Employing Star-Shaped Microphone Array

Juan A. Morales-Cordovilla[1], Hannes Pessentheiner[1], Martin Hagmüller[1],
José A. González[2], and Gernot Kubin[1,*]

[1] Signal Processing and Speech Communication Laboratory,
Graz University of Technology, Austria
[2] Dept. of Computer Science, University of Sheffield, UK
{moralescordovilla,hannes.pessentheiner,hagmueller,
gernot.kubin}@tugraz.at, j.gonzalez@sheffield.ac.uk

Abstract. This paper addresses the problem of distant speech recognition in reverberant noisy conditions employing a star-shaped microphone array and vector Taylor series (VTS) compensation. First, a beamformer yields an enhanced single-channel signal by applying convex (CVX) optimization over three spatial dimensions given the spatio-temporal position of the target speaker as prior knowledge. Then, VTS compensation is applied over the speech features extracted from the temporal signal obtained by the beamformer. Finally, the compensated features are used for speech recognition. Due to a lack of existing resources in German to evaluate the proposed enhancement framework, this paper also introduces a new speech database. In particular, we present a medium-vocabulary German database for microphone array made of embedded clean signals contaminated with real room impulsive responses and mixed in a 'natural' way with real noises. We show that the proposed enhancement framework performs better than other related systems on the presented database.

Keywords: distant speech recognition, cvx-optimized beamforming, vector Taylor series compensation, star-shaped microphone array, reverberant and noisy environment, natural mixing, German database.

1 Introduction

The distant interaction of a speaker with a dialogue system, which controls some mechanisms of a house, is a difficult challenge because of many reasons: the wake-up of the system (distinction between simple conversations and commands), the

* This work has been supported by the European project DIRHA FP7-ICT-2011-7- 288121, the Austrian COMET project ASD and the Austrian Marshall Plan Foundation.

J.L. Navarro Mesa et al. (Eds.): IberSPEECH 2014, LNAI 8854, pp. 148–157, 2014.

speech variations for the automatic speech recognition (ASR), and the degradation of the speech signal due to background noise, reverberation, or the speaker position. Different projects such as CHIL, DICIT, and the currently finalized CHiME [1] have been proposed to solve this challenge but the Distant-speech Interaction for Robust Home Applications (DIRHA) European project [2] (for people with disabilities) is different from the others in the use of the microphone array technology.

To address the above problems, we propose the enhancement framework depicted in Fig. 1 which is an improved version of the one presented in [12]. Also this framework is part of the distant speech recognition systems presented in [6,7]. This consists of a spatio-temporal localizer (ST-Localizer) which tries to find when the user is speaking and where. Later, a novel convex (CVX)-optimization–based beamformer (BF) attenuates the interference signals different from the user's direction. Finally, a vector Taylor series compensation method further increases the robustness of the ASR on the still degraded signal provided by the beamformer. In this paper, we avoid the problem of the spatio-temporal localization and focuses on the beamformer and the compensation method justifying their proposed configuration with experimental results.

This paper also introduces a new and more realistic German speech database than presented in the previous work [12] to evaluate the proposed enhancement framework. In particular, we present a medium-vocabulary German database for microphone array configuration which contains embedded clean signals contaminated with real room impulsive responses and mixed in a 'natural' way [1] with real noises.

The paper is structured as follows: sections 2 and 3 describe the CVX beamforming and VTS compensation methods respectively. Section 4 explains the proposed BAS-embeded database and the ASR configuration. Section 5 presents and analyses the experimental results, and in section 6 we summarize the most important ideas presented along the paper together with some future works.

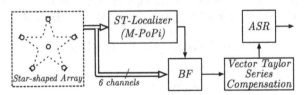

Fig. 1. Block diagram of the proposed system for distant speech recognition which consists of a 6-element star-shaped microphone array, a spatio-temporal localizer (ST-Localizer) of the speaker utterance, a beamformer (BF), a vector Taylor series compensation, and an automatic speech recognition (ASR) system

2   Convex-Optimization–Based Beamformer

In our experiments, we employ a novel CVX-optimization–based beamformer. The beamformer design, first reported in [12], exhibits an improved extension of the design mentioned in [5]. The remarkable improvements of our modified beamformer are null-steering, the compatibility with different array geometries, and an optimization to three spatial dimensions. The last one is a prerequisite to enable beamforming in three spatial dimensions and to reduce the influence of reflections from the ceiling and the floor discussed in [11]. The CVX constrains the white noise gain to be larger than a lower limit γ. It considers the three-dimensional undistorted capturing response with steering direction (φ_s, θ_s) and nulls placed in different directions as constraints. The beamformer design is based on least squares computations that approximate a desired three-dimensional directivity pattern

$$\hat{b}(\omega, \varphi, \theta) = \sum_{n=1}^{N} w_n(f) e^{i\frac{\omega}{c} r_n \cdot \eta(\varphi, \theta, \varphi_n, \theta_n)}$$

with

$$\eta(\varphi, \theta, \varphi_n, \theta_n) = \sin(\theta) \sin(\theta_n) \cos(\varphi - \varphi_n) + \cos(\theta) \cos(\theta_n),$$

or, in vector notation,

$$\hat{\mathbf{B}}(\omega) = \mathbf{G}(\omega) \cdot [\mathbf{w}(\omega) \otimes \mathbf{I}],$$

where f and ω represent the linear and angular frequency, φ and θ are steering-direction–dependent azimuthal and elevation angles, φ_n and θ_n are the angles of a microphone with index n, N is the number of microphones, c is the sound velocity, r_n is the distance between a microphone and the center of the coordinate system, and $\mathbf{w}(\omega) = (w_1(\omega), w_2(\omega), ..., w_N(\omega))^T$ is the beamformer coefficient vector. Moreover, $\mathbf{I}$ is the identity matrix, $\otimes$ denotes the Kronecker product, and $\mathbf{G}(\omega)$ is an $(N_\theta \times [N \cdot N_\varphi])$ capturing response matrix according to $G_{l,m,n}(\omega) = e^{i\frac{\omega}{c} r_n \cdot \eta(\varphi_m, \theta_l, \varphi_n, \theta_n)}$, where N_φ is the number of discretized azimuthal angles φ_m, and N_θ is the number of discretized elevation angles θ_l. The beamformer assumes the same desired response for all frequencies, i.e. $\hat{\mathbf{B}}(\omega) = \hat{\mathbf{B}}$, and

$$\arg\min_{\mathbf{w}(\omega)} \| \mathbf{G}(\omega) \cdot [\mathbf{w}(\omega) \otimes \mathbf{I}] - \hat{\mathbf{B}} \|_F$$

subjected to the white noise gain (WNG), the undistorted capturing response with steering direction (φ_s, θ_s), and the optional null-placement constraints

$$\frac{|\mathbf{w}^T(\omega)\mathbf{d}(\omega)|^2}{\mathbf{w}^H(\omega)\mathbf{w}(\omega)} \geq \gamma, \quad \mathbf{w}^H(\omega)\mathbf{d}(\omega) = 1, \quad \mathbf{w}^H(\omega)\mathbf{V}(\omega) = \mathbf{0},$$

where $\mathbf{d}(\omega) = (d_1(\omega), d_2(\omega), ..., d_N(\omega))^T$ represents the capturing response with steering direction (φ_s, θ_s), and $\mathbf{V} = [\mathbf{v}_1, \mathbf{v}_2, ..., \mathbf{v}_S]$ is a matrix which consists of vectors $\mathbf{v}(\omega) = (v_1(\omega), v_2(\omega), ..., v_{M-1}(\omega))^T$ that describe the capturing response of, e.g., competing speakers or other noise sources, S is the number of nulls, $(\cdot)^T$ is the transpose, $(\cdot)^H$ is the Hermitian-transpose, and $\| \cdot \|_F$ is the Frobenius norm. We set the lower limit γ and the desired response $\hat{\mathbf{B}}$ in a way that we were able to distribute the narrow null-lobe marked in Fig. 2 over frequencies below 1000 Hz. This yields a decreased main-lobe width at lower frequencies without increasing the width at higher ones. Although null-steering is one of the beamformer's big improvements, we did not consider it due to the assumption of unknown noise source positions in our experiments.

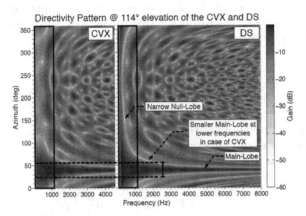

Fig. 2. The directivity patterns of the CVX without null-steering and the DS (delay-and-sum, [14]) based on a 6-element star-shaped array with steering direction $\phi_s = 40°$ and $\theta_s = 114°$

3   Vector Taylor Series Compensation

After applying a beamformer, which yields a single-channel signal, a vector Taylor series (VTS) compensation [10] is used to further enhance the signal and the robustness of ASR. The reason of using VTS rather than other methods, such as marginalization missing data is that it let the final representation of the clean estimated signal be in the cepstral domain, which is a more appropriate representation for a medium or large vocabulary task. In this paper, we apply VTS in the log-Mel domain (i.e. the log-outputs of the Mel filters) and later we apply the cepstrum transformation (Sec. 4.2).

Let $\mathbf{y}_t$, $\mathbf{x}_t$ and $\mathbf{n}_t$ be the feature vectors at time t for the noisy speech, clean speech, and noise signals, respectively, expressed in this domain. Given the noisy observation $\mathbf{y}_t$, VTS estimates the clean feature vector as follows,

$$\hat{\mathbf{x}}_t = \mathbf{y}_t - \sum_{k=1}^{K} P(k|\mathbf{y}_t)\mathbf{g}\left(\boldsymbol{\mu}_X^{(k)}, \hat{\mathbf{n}}_t\right), \tag{1}$$

where $\hat{\mathbf{n}}_t$ is the noise estimate at time t and $\mathbf{g}(\mathbf{x}, \mathbf{n}) = \log(1 + \exp(\mathbf{n} - \mathbf{x}))$ is the so-called mismatch function. To derive the above estimator, a Gaussian mixture model (GMM) with K components is used as the prior speech model. Thus,

$$p(\boldsymbol{x}) = \sum_{k=1}^{K} \pi_X^{(k)} \mathcal{N}\left(\boldsymbol{x}; \boldsymbol{\mu}_X^{(k)}, \boldsymbol{\Sigma}_X^{(k)}\right), \tag{2}$$

with $\pi_X^{(k)}$, $\boldsymbol{\mu}_X^{(k)}$, and $\boldsymbol{\Sigma}_X^{(k)}$ being the parameters of the kth Gaussian component, i.e., its prior probability, mean vector and covariance matrix.

Finally, the noisy speech model $p(\boldsymbol{y}_t)$ is required for computing the posterior probabilities $P(k|\boldsymbol{y}_t)$ in (1). To obtain this model, the clean speech GMM is adapted as follows,

$$\boldsymbol{\mu}_{Y,t}^{(k)} = \boldsymbol{\mu}_X^{(k)} + \boldsymbol{g}\left(\boldsymbol{\mu}_X^{(k)}, \hat{\boldsymbol{n}}_t\right), \tag{3}$$

$$\boldsymbol{\Sigma}_{Y,t}^{(k)} = \boldsymbol{J}_t^{(k)} \boldsymbol{\Sigma}_X^{(k)} \boldsymbol{J}_t^{(k)} + (\boldsymbol{I} - \boldsymbol{J}_t^{(k)}) \boldsymbol{\Sigma}_{N,t}(\boldsymbol{I} - \boldsymbol{J}_t^{(k)}), \tag{4}$$

where $\boldsymbol{\Sigma}_{N,t}$ is the covariance matrix associated to the noise estimate $\hat{\boldsymbol{n}}_t$ and $\boldsymbol{J}_t^{(k)}$ is a diagonal matrix whose elements are given by,

$$\boldsymbol{J}_t^{(k)} = \mathrm{diag}\left(\frac{1}{1 + \exp\left(\hat{\boldsymbol{n}}_t - \boldsymbol{\mu}_X^{(k)}\right)}\right). \tag{5}$$

4   Experimental Framework

4.1   Embedded-BAS Database

Due to a lack of existing resources in German to evaluate the proposed enhancement framework, this paper also introduces a new German database for a star-shaped microphone array. More precisely, this array consists of 6 microphones (1 at the center and 5 on the circle) placed on the ceiling of the living room of the ITEA apartment used by Fondazione Bruno Kessler (FBK) for the DIRHA project [2] (see Fig. 3).

Embedded Noisy Signals Each test multi-chanel signal of this database represents what the microphone array would record if a speaker, in the presence of noise, repeated the action of pronouncing an isolated utterance at a specific position in the room and later moved to another position to pronounce another utterance. We call to this connection of utterances with continuous background noise and with different reverberations, which depend on the speaker position, *embedded noisy signal* .

For the controllability of the experiments, the next 12 speaker position/directions, circled in Fig. 3, are only used: (LA/O8, LB/O8, etc.). To simulate the different SNR noisy conditions in the most possible 'natural' way, we follow the indications of SNR mixture of the CHiME corpus [1] by employing around 3-hours of real noise, recorded by the FBK group with this microphone array.

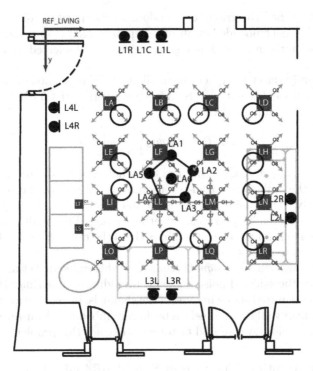

Fig. 3. Living room of the ITEA apartment of Fondazione Bruno Kessler (FBK) with the microphone array at the center and the 12 speaker position/directions employed in this work [provided by FBK].

Table 1. Word accuracies obtained by different configurations of the proposed systems tested over the presented Embedded-BAS database for different SNR values

Systems	Clean	10 dB	0 dB	Average
Baseline (central microphone)	93.24	79.34	43.69	72.09
DS Beamforming	94.73	83.61	51.73	76.69
CVX Beamforming	95.34	83.65	51.98	76.99
Baseline + VTS (FLF noise)	91.60	84.00	53.61	76.40
DS Beamf. + VTS (FLF noise)	93.82	86.83	55.70	78.78
CVX Beamf. + VTS (FLF noise)	93.60	87.29	60.20	80.36
Baseline + VTS (Oracle noise)	92.93	91.75	79.10	87.93
DS Beamf. + VTS (Oracle noise)	94.67	92.42	79.04	88.71
CVX Beamf. + VTS (Oracle noise)	95.19	93.54	80.32	89.68

The way to obtain an embedded noisy signal for a target SNR is summarized in the following steps:

1. We randomly select 7 isolated monaural clean (without reverberation) utterances of one speaker, convolve them with the corresponding impulse responses

(obtained by the FBK group) of 7 random speaker position/directions and obtain a 6-channel embedded clean-reverberant signal by connecting them with a time gap in the middle. These gaps are randomly selected between 0.5 and 5 seconds.

2. We randomly select a segment from all available segments, of the 3-hours of noise, which yields the target SNR within an error of 1.5 dB. The following formula is used for the SNR:

$$SNR = 10 log_{10} \frac{Ex_{central}}{En_{central}} (dB) \qquad (6)$$

where $Ex_{central}$ and $En_{central}$ are the whole energy of the central microphone of the embedded clean-reverberant signal and of the noise segment respectively. If no noise segment is found that yields the target SNR, all channels of the embedded clean-reverberant signal are multiplied by a gain (which depends on the closest found SNR to the target SNR) to find at least an appropriate noise segment.

3. The final *embedded noisy signal* is the sum of this embedded clean-reverberant signal with the selected noise segment. In addition, sometimes this sum can produce a saturated signal in some of the channels. In order to avoid this problem we multiply all the channels of both, the embedded clean-reverberant signal and the noise, by a second factor which avoids this problem.

Database Description The proposed *Embedded-BAS* database exhibits a sampling frequency of 16 kHz and employs the clean sentences of the Bavarian Archive for Speech Signals (BAS) PHONDAT-1 database [13] as its isolated monaural clean utterances (Sec. 4.1) due to their temporal similarity with house control commands. The database consists of the training and test sets.

The training set contains 4999 clean-reverberant isolated utterances corresponding to 50 different-gender speakers (around 100 sentences per speaker) with a reverberation that corresponds to position LA/O8 of Fig. 3. The inclusion of the reverberation in the training set is to reduce the mismatch with the test set. The test set consists of 100 embedded clean-reverberant signals (700 isolated utterances, Sec. 4.1) corresponding to 100 different speakers (half of them are in the training set) contaminated at 10 and 0 dB. Both, the training and test sets share the same medium-vocabulary lexicon and grammar and consist of 1504 words which belong to around 500 different phrases.

4.2   ASR System

Both, the front-end and the back-end, have been derived from the standard recognizer employed in Aurora-4 database [4].

The front-end takes the enhanced signal and obtains mel frequency cepstrum coefficients (MFCCs) using 16 kHz sampling frequency, frame shift and length of 10 and 32 ms, 1024 frequency bins, 26 Mel channels and 13 cepstral coefficients. Then we apply cepstral mean normalization to the MFCCs. Delta and delta-delta features are also appended, obtaining a final feature vector with 39 components.

The back-end employs a transcription of the training corpus based on 34 monophones to train triphone-HMMs. This transcription has been derived from a more detailed transcription (based on 44 SAMPA-monophones) by means of a careful clustering of the less common monophones. Each triphone is modeled by a HMM of 6 states and 8 Gaussian-mixtures/state. By means of a monophone classification (created with the help of a linguistic) a tree-based clustering of the states is also applied to reduce the complexity and a lack of training data. Tree-based clustering also allows to create triphones models for the test stage which have not been observed in the training stage. We train a bigram using the training word transcription. By means of an expansion based on the grammar, the triphone transcription of the test lexicon and the triphones, we obtain the final macro HMMs for the test stage. It is important to point out that only the central microphone of the clean-reverberant training set without any enhancement (beamforming and VTS) is used to train our HMMs-models.

5   Experimental Results

Tab. 1 shows the different Word Accuracies (WAcc, %) achieved by different configurations of the proposed systems tested over the presented Embedded-BAS database for different SNR values.

The *Baseline (central microphone)* results are obtained when no enhancement is performed over the speech signals, i.e., directly the performance of the signal captured by the central microphone of the microphone-array. *DS Beamforming* and *CVX Beamforming* are the results achieved by delay-and-sum [14] and convex-optimization beamformers (Sec. 2). As mentioned in Sec. 1 , we assume that the ST-Localizer of Fig. 1 provides the oracle spatial and temporal localization of the speaker, i. e., we cut the embedded noisy signal in pieces which correspond to the isolated utterances, then each of these pieces together with its spatial position are sent directly to the beamformer. Following, we can see the results of the three previous configurations but when the VTS compensation (Sec. 3) is applied with a First-Last-Frames (FLF) noise estimation. This estimation assumes that the first and last 20 frames of the cut signal correspond to noise and these frames are used to estimate the log-Mel noise (and its corresponding covariance matrix) by means of a linear interpolation to the remaining the frames as shown in [8].

The most significant conclusions which can be drawn from the table are the follows:

1. Using beamformers, specially the CVX, always improves the recognition results (compare the 72.09 of the *Baseline* with the 76.99 % of the *CVX Beamf.*).
2. Considering VTS after applying beamformers additionally improves the results (compare the 76.99 of the *CVX Beamf.* with the 80.36 % of the *CVX Beamf. + VTS (FLF noise)*).

The results with oracle noise are only displayed to show the upper performance of this framework. We can see that we should further improve the noise estimation at 0 dB.

Other compensation mechanisms (such as missing data (MD) imputation based on binary mask) and types of noise estimations (such as pitch-based noise estimations) have been employed in [9]. Due to the techniques' sensitivities to the MD mask and to the pitch estimation errors, the performance of these techniques have been lower.

6   Conclusion and Future Work

This paper presented a system for distant speech recognition in reverberant and noisy conditions, intended to control a room with commands. The proposed system is an improved version of the system presented in [12]. The improvement consists of a recently presented beamformer based on convex optimization, the application of a single-channel enhancement algorithm based on VTS compensation and the presentation of a more realistic database for evaluations. The database consists of embedded noisy signals which represent, with 'natural' noise mixing, what the microphone array would record if the speaker was emitting German commands at different positions of the room. This database is a very suitable challenge for the spatio-temporal localization algorithm of the utterance which is our next future objective. To do it we plan to make use of the pitch information provided by the M-PoPi algorithm [3] .

References

1. Christensen, H., Barker, J., Ma, N., Green, P.: The chime corpus: A resource and a challenge for computational hearing in multisource environments. In: Interspeech (2010)
2. European project FP7. Distant-speech interaction for robust home applications (dirha) (March 2012-2015), http://dirha.fbk.eu
3. Habib, T., Romsdorfer, H.: Concurrent speaker localization using multi-band position-pitch (m-popi) algorithm with spectro-temporal pre-processing. In: Interspeech (2010)
4. Hirsch, H.G.: Experimental framework for the performance evaluation of speech recognition front-ends of large vocabulary task. Technical report, STQ AURORA DSR, Working Group (2002)
5. Mabande, E., Schad, A., Kellermann, W.: Design of robust superdirective beamformers as a convex optimization problem. In: ICASSP (2009)
6. Morales-Cordovilla, J.A., Hagmüller, M., Pessentheiner, H., Kubin, G.: Distant speech recognition in reverberant noisy conditions employing a microphone array. In: EUSIPCO (2014)
7. Morales-Cordovilla, J.A., Pessentheiner, H., Hagmüller, M.M., Kubin, G.: Room localization for distant speech recognition. In: Interspeech (2014)
8. Morales-Cordovilla, J.A., Ma, N., Sánchez, V., Carmona, J.L., Peinado, A.M., Barker, J.: A pitch based noise estimation technique for robust speech recognition with missing data. In: ICASSP, May 22-27, pp. 4808–4811 (2011)

9. Morales-Cordovilla, J.A., Pessentheiner, H., Hagmller, M., Mowlaee, P., Pernkopf, F., Kubin, G.: A german distant speech recognizer based on 3d beamforming and harmonic missing data mask. In: AIA-DAGA (2013)

10. Moreno, P.: Speech Recognition in Noisy Environments. PhD thesis, Carnegie Mellon University (1996)

11. Pessentheiner, H., Kubin, G., Romsdorfer, H.: Improving beamforming for distant speech recognition in reverberant environments using a genetic algorithm for planar array synthesis. In: 10th ITG Symposium on Speech Communication (2012)

12. Pessentheiner, H., Petrik, S., Romsdorfer, H.: Beamforming using uniform circular arrays for distant speech recognition in reverberant environments and double-talk scenarios. In: Interspeech (2012)

13. Schiel, F., Baumann, A.: Phondat 1, corpus version 3.4. Technical report, Bavarian Archive for Speech Signals (BAS) (2006),
http://www.bas.uni-muenchen.de/Bas/BasFormatseng.html

14. Tashev, I.: Sound Capture and Processing: Practical Approaches. John Wiley and Sons (2009)

Flexible Stand-Alone Keyword Recognition Application Using Dynamic Time Warping

Miquel Ferrarons[1,2,*], Xavier Anguera[1], and Jordi Luque[1]

[1] Telefonica Research, Edificio Telefonica-Diagonal 00, 08019, Barcelona, Spain
[2] Universitat Autonoma de Barcelona, Barcelona, Spain
{xanguera,jls}@tid.es

Abstract. We introduce a Query-by-Example (QbE) application for smart-phone devices that implements a recently proposed memory-efficient dynamic programming algorithm [1] for the task of keyword search. The application compares acoustic keywords with the audio input from the microphone and reacts to detected keywords with actions in the phone. These keywords are recorded by the user, who also defines what actions will be performed by each one. One of these keywords is defined to be a trigger keyword, which is used to *wake up* the system and thus reduce false detections. All keywords can be freely chosen by the user. In Monitor mode, the application stays listening to audio acquired through the microphone and reacts when the trigger + some keyword are matched. All processing is done locally on the phone, which is able to react in real-time to incoming keywords. In this paper we describe the application, review the matching algorithm we used and show experimentally that it successfully reacts to voice commands in a variety of acoustic conditions.

Keywords: Mobile search, dynamic time warping, query-by-example, keyword recognition.

1 Introduction

Currently smartphones are found everywhere. The usage of smartphones is not only driven by the need to make phone calls, as more and more people use them for activities like gaming, browsing the internet, reading, etc. Voice recognition is quickly gaining popularity and acceptance among smartphone users, probably due to the small keyboard footprint of these devices which makes it more complicated to type on it than to speak to it. Companies like Google [2] of Microsoft [3] have recently proposed powerful speech-enabled applications in the cellphone that are changing the general public miss-conception that speech recognition *does not work*. Driven by this trend, we decided to experiment with small-footprint but flexible voice-enabled command-and-control applications for the cellphone. In this paper we present one of these experiments. It corresponds to a keyword recognition application we developed for Android devices which

---

* M. Ferrarons was visiting Telefonica Research at the time this work was performed.

J.L. Navarro Mesa et al. (Eds.): IberSPEECH 2014, LNAI 8854, pp. 158–167, 2014.
© Springer International Publishing Switzerland 2014

implements a flexible Query-by-Example (QbE) algorithm to enable many functionalities in the phone by just giving spoken orders to it. QbE algorithms [4] are used to search for matches of a given spoken query within a set of spoken utterances. In this case we use it to match pre-recorded acoustic keywords against online audio captured from the smartphone's microphone. The proposed application is a proof of concept of a totally offline (no server connectivity required) speech enabled tool to control the telephone's functionalities by voice. In addition, recorded keywords can be chosen by the user to be whatever word/sound he/she wants, and each one can be recorded multiple times to improve matching accuracy. There are two kinds of keywords, "trigger" and "action" keywords. A "trigger" keyword is recorded by the user to "wake up" the application (i.e. indicate that an "action" keyword will be spoken next). Then, "action" keywords are detected and associated to actions in the phone. In this proof of concept some actions have been implemented, like taking a picture, recording a voice note or picking up a call.

The rest of the paper is organized as follows: Section 2 describes the application implementation details, including the user interface (Subsection 2.1) and each of the two modes of operation (Subsections 2.2 and 2.3). Then, Section 3 describes and performs an evaluation of usage of the application among real users, to show that it does perform as expected. Finally, in Section 4 we draw some conclusions from the presented work, and draw some lines of future research.

2   System Description

The proposed application has two main modes of operation: Monitor mode, and Recording mode. In Recording mode the user records new acoustic keywords, assigns actions to them, and can set some parameters to each of these keywords. In Monitor mode the application constantly records the ambient sound and reacts accordingly when the user says any of the keywords recorded in the Recording mode. Next we describe the application user interface and how each of these modes works in more detail.

2.1   Application User Interface

We implemented the keyword recognition application in Android. Our development was tested using a Samsung GalaxyS phone, although any smartphone with similar (or superior) capabilities should be able to successfully run the application. Figure 1 shows three screenshots of the application as it is being used. Subfigure 1a shows the main screen for the Recording mode and Subfigure 1c shows the Monitor mode. The user can switch between the two modes by clicking the tab present on top of either of these screens.

Within the Recording mode the user sees the list of keywords that he has already recorded, and has the option (by clicking in "New Recording") to record a new keyword. There is no limit to the number of different keywords that a user can record, although at some point the application might not be able to monitor all of them in parallel (we have experimented with more than 10 concurrent keywords with no felt slowdown on the phone). Clicking an already recorded keyword or in "New Recording" launches a screen similar to Subfigure 1b. This user interface allows the user to record up to two instances of the keyword, define a name with which this keyword will be later identified (or change a current name), select an action to be taken by the phone when this keyword is selected and modify the detection threshold. Although by default every keyword has a precomputed detection threshold, it can be modified by the user whenever it is not producing successful results. Similarly, after the Speech Activity Detection (SAD) module has automatically identified the start-end points of the speech part in the keyword, these boundaries can be played back and modified through this user interface.

Within the Monitor mode the user initially sees a ON/OFF button to toggle the monitoring status. Once ON, the system continuously scans the audio entering the microphone to detect the "trigger" keyword and then, once detected, either of the "action" keywords. All detections are shown on screen as they appear, and actions are then taken on the phone.

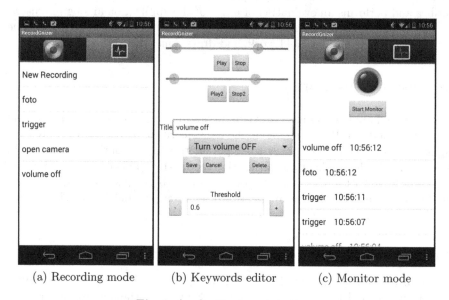

(a) Recording mode   (b) Keywords editor   (c) Monitor mode

Fig. 1. Application user interface

2.2   The Recording Mode

In "Recording mode" the user is able to record up to two speech instances per keyword. These are processed and stored in the system to later compare them with the input audio. The full processing pipeline is shown in Fig. 3 and is described next.

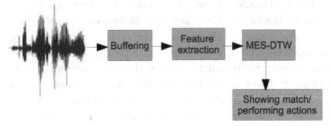

Fig. 2. Online keyword matching in Monitor mode

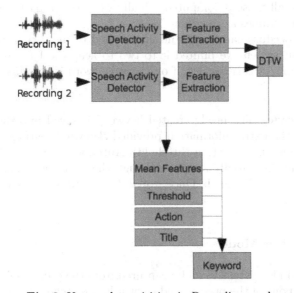

Fig. 3. Keyword acquisition in Recording mode

Speech Activity Detection. A speech activity detector (SAD) is applied to detect start and end points of the spoken keywords. We implemented a simple SAD algorithm described in [5] which focuses on energy and zero crossing rate to determine the endpoints of the speech utterance. The algorithm first automatically determines some parameters using the information provided by the first 100ms of the signal (considering it as noise). Then it uses these values to filter the whole signal and determine correct start (N1) and end (N2) points. However, in some cases N1 and N2 might not be found correctly. To solve this, the user interface depicted in Fig. 1b adds the possibility to manually modify these endpoints.

Feature Extraction. Once we have the SAD endpoints, we extract the features of each keyword. We used standard 39-dimensional MFCCs: 13 statics (12+energy), deltas and acceleration. Input signal is first filtered with a 25ms long Hamming window and features are extracted every 10ms. Global cepstral mean and variance normalization (CMVN) is applied to all features in each keyword.

DTW Alignment. Whenever the user records the keyword twice we apply a DTW alignment to transform both keyword instances into one (stronger) keyword. The purpose of doing so is to improve the system by using a mean keyword, instead of just one instance of that keyword. This can be useful when keywords are recorded in a noisy environment, where the SNR needs to be improved by emphasizing those features in the keyword that are common and averaging out those that belong to noise. In this case, the second keyword instance is aligned to the first at MFCC feature level and then each frame of the second recording is averaged with its corresponding MFCC frames of the first recording. If more than one frame of recording 2 corresponds to one frame of recording 1, then the average between all those is computed. Finally we obtain a mean feature vector that has as many frames as recording 1.

The same procedure can be potentially applied to more than two recorded keywords. In our system we limited it to two to keep the UI and the user interaction pleasant. In this respect, if only one keyword is recorded, this step is skipped.

Keyword Storage. The newly created keyword is saved into the system together with all the extra information provided (keyword features, name, SAD boundaries, action and detection threshold). Automatic values of SAD and detection threshold are initially stored, although these can be manually changed using the interface in Figure 1b. Once stored, the keyword is immediately available for matching.

2.3   The Monitor Mode

The "Monitor Mode" listens to audio captured from the cellphone's microphone and reacts when one of the prerecorded keywords is matched. In order to reduce false alarms and to allow a free selection of keywords leading to actions in the phone, the system first expects to match a "trigger" keyword and then listens for 2 seconds to match either of the "action" keywords. If after 2 seconds no action keyword is detected, the trigger keyword is forgotten and the system goes back to searching for a trigger. Both keyword matching steps are technically identical, as shown in Fig. 2 and described next.

Audio Buffering and Online Feature Extraction. Incoming audio is constantly stored in a circular buffer. Once the buffer contains enough audio, an acoustic feature vector is computed. Note that unlike in the Recording mode, in here, the feature extraction module works online. This affects the way that features are normalized, as we do not have access to the whole signal at once. We use a running mean and variance estimation as follows.

The running mean μ' of a feature vector x is estimated as $\mu' = \alpha\mu + (1 - \alpha)x$ where we set $\alpha = 0.995$ and μ is the running mean value at the previous frame. To compute the running variance, we use a similar approach. Given that $\sigma^2 = E(x^2)' - E(x)^2$, we compute $E(x)^2 = \mu^2$ and $E(x^2)' = \alpha E(x^2) + (1 - \alpha)(x^2)$.

Keyword Matching Algorithm. The core of the application is the keyword matching algorithm. As mentioned above, the system constantly monitors the audio input and only reacts when the "trigger" keyword is detected. Then a span of 2 seconds is allowed to detect any of the "action" keywords, or the system resets and starts again looking for a "trigger" keyword. The use of a "trigger" keyword is used in many modern systems such as [6] , Kinect voice recognition or Google Now. In this application we first run a single keyword matching instance to match the input audio to the "trigger" keyword. Once it is detected, several (one for every "action" keyword) DTW instances are run in parallel to detect whether any of the prerecorded keywords is spoken.

In our application we implement keyword matching by using a modification of the dynamic time warping (DTW) algorithm as proposed in [1]. Standard DTW algorithms cannot be used here as the input audio is not bounded, thus we cannot build standard global alignment matrices to compare both patterns. Instead, we use the MES-DTW algorithm [1] in online mode.

As acoustic frames become available, these are first compared to the "trigger" keyword. The MES-DTW algorithm allows us to perform the comparison by using only 3 support vectors, which is sufficient to find matches when no alignment path (i.e. matrix trackback) is required. The main difference of the current implementation with the MES-DTW algorithm in [1] is that in the later the system tries to align small queries with big references, but in here, we need to align an infinite(online) query with small references.

The matching algorithm works as follows. For every new input feature vector we first compute its distance to all features in the keyword(s) we want to match with. In this work the normalized cosine distance has been used. The distance vector is then used to update the global distance matrix, which in this case is limited to a $2xN$ matrix, where N is the number of frames of a keyword, stored for the previous frames $t-2$ and $t-1$. To update the matrix we use standard DTW local constraints of insertion, deletion and assignment. In addition, a single N-dimensional vector is kept to count how many matching frames each optimum path in position t contains. This is used to perform a local normalization of all values before local constraints are applied. For more details on the MES-DTW algorithm please refer to [1]. In order to impose a local version of the global Sakoe-Chiba band [7], we disallow more than 3 continuous insertions or deletions by keeping a count of previous decisions. After processing every frame we compare the normalized score at position N of time t. If the value is lower than the predefined threshold for that keyword a match is hypothesized. If more than one keyword instance finds a match, the one with the best score is selected. Once a match is granted, all vectors are reset so that a transitory time (of N frames) passes before more matches are allowed.

Showing Matches and Performing Actions. Once a keyword has been detected (i.e. the normalized similarity is better than the selection threshold) if the keyword is one of the "action" keywords and less than 2 seconds passed after the "trigger" keyword was detected, then the action associated to that keyword is launched on the phone. We implemented the following 8 actions through calls to the cellphone core API: Open music player, turn volume ON/OFF, pick up a call, start/end voice note, Open camera and take a photo.

3   Evaluation

In this section we first describe a database we recorded in order to evaluate the system, the evaluation protocol we used and the experimental results we obtained.

3.1   Database Description

In order to obtain experimental results of the accuracy of our system, a database was recorded and labelled. We recruited two users to record a set of keywords in isolation and embedded inside longer utterances, in different acoustic conditions. Every user recorded five keywords and 120 utterances. The keywords were short (less than one second), and the utterances were of around 15 seconds long. Overall we recorded about 30 minutes of audio (15s/utterance * 120 utterances) for each user. The 120 queries were recorded in 4 different backgrounds:

1. Quiet background.
2. Quiet background in a small room (lots of reverberation).
3. Background with music.
4. Street with lots of noise.

In every background condition we recorded the 5 keywords contained in 6 utterances each (totaling 30 utterances recorded per background). The first three recordings contained the keyword alone, with the rest of the utterance containing just background noise. The other three utterances consisted on long sentences that contained the keyword within. In total the database contains around 1h of data. All recordings were done using a smartphone decide, using a standard voice recording application.

For every recording, we manually labelled the time when the user starts and stops saying the keyword. We used that information to evaluate the system, and to determine if a match found was correct or not, or if a miss occurred.

3.2   Evaluation Setup

In this section we're going to explain how the accuracy of the system was evaluated.

All of the 120 recordings available per user were run through the MES-DTW algorithm and compared with the 5 keywords, thus simulating a real use-case scenario (we simulated the process of extracting the live features and computing the live DTW). We did this process for a variety of detection thresholds, trying to find the optimum threshold values and obtaining some curves depending on each threshold. Instead of using a different threshold for each keyword, we used the same threshold for all keywords of each user. Better results would be achieved by using an appropriate threshold for each keyword, but as threshold setting is not a user-friendly activity, and while we do not find a way to automatically set the optimum threshold, we set a unique threshold for all backgrounds.

Then, for a given threshold t and an utterance $q1$ we detect how many matches or false alarms appear. To do this, if a match does not appear when it was expected to appear (between its endpoints previously labelled, plus a margin of 0.2 seconds), we count that as a false negative. If a match appears when it doesn't have to appear, we count that as a false positive. And if a match appears when it has to appear, then we have a true positive. Finally, if a match appears twice within its endpoints, we count one true positive and one false positive.

In order to compute meaningful statistics we also consider the following values:

– The max number of true positives is 120 (the total number of queries)
– The max number of false positives depends on the total length of all the queries. If the total length is 1800s, and we can have an alarm every 1.2s for each reference, we can find up to 1800*5/1.2 alarms, so 7500 alarms, where 120 of them are true positives. So, the difference is the maximum number of false positives. Actually, the total length wasn't 1800s, it depended on every user. The total number of possible alarms was computed for every user.
– The max number of false negatives is 120 (the total number of queries)

We measure performance using standard information retrieval metrics:

$$\text{Precision} = \tfrac{tp}{tp+fp} \qquad \text{Recall} = \tfrac{tp}{tp+fn} \qquad \text{Fscore} = 2\tfrac{\text{Precision}\cdot\text{Recall}}{\text{Precision}+\text{Recall}}$$

$$\text{Misses} = \tfrac{max\_tp-tp}{max\_tp} \qquad \text{FalseAlarms} = \tfrac{fp}{max\_fp}$$

Where tp denotes "true positives", fp denotes "false positives", fn denotes "false negatives", max_tp denotes the possible number of true positives, and max_fp denotes the possible number of false positives, as defined above.

3.3   Experimental Results

We performed experiments individually for each of the two speakers that recorded the database. Table 1 shows results for user 1, and Table 2 shows them for user 2. We show results using just the first recording the user made for each keyword, the second one, or the mix (mean features between the two aligned sets of features). All thresholds were set per speaker and task, using a held-out development set, and are reported in the last column of each table. We can see that results are very different between the two users. While user 1 obtains very satisfactory results (very high Fscore and a low number of misses and false alarms) user 2 obtains much worse Fscore, mostly due to the very high rate of misses (e.g. the application did not detect the right keyword when he spoke it). The reason for this behavior is probably because user 1 knows how to clearly speak to the application and how to use it better (he was involved with the application much more before recording the database) than user 2.

We can also see that the fact of using the mean features is not helping the system to get better results. That probably happened because the keywords in the tests were recorded in clear environments or due to the method we used to align the features from both keywords. More research is due to find out the reasons and to correct them.

Table 1. Results for user 1

Type of test	F score	misses	false alarms	Thres.
Mean Features	0.8559	0.067	0.009	0.43
First Recording	0.8219	0.25	0.001	0.44
Second Recording	0.8642	0.083	0.004	0.45

Table 2. Results for user 2

Type of test	F score	misses	false alarms	Thres.
Mean Features	0.4976	0.5667	0.004259	0.36
First Reference	0.5225	0.5167	0.006033	0.39
Second Reference	0.5804	0.4583	0.0045	0.38

4   Conclusions and Future Work

The use of smartphones is becoming ubiquitous. As the keyboards in these devices are quite small and uncomfortable to use, there is a very good opportunity for speech technology to help users be most efficient when using these devices. In this paper we present a prototype application we developed as a proof of concept of a small-footprint flexible voice-enabled command-and-control application for the cellphone. With the use of the application the user can record acoustic keywords and associate them to actions in the phone. Then the phone can be set to listen to the environment and react whenever one of the keyword is detected. We have implemented the application to work on an Android device totally offline (no connectivity required) and in real-time. In this paper we evaluate the application in terms of matching accuracy in different acoustic environments to see whether it would be useful in a real-live setting. We observe that results are positive but vary a lot depending on the user. Future work will include further quantitative tests with a bigger database as well as a qualitative test to gather insights on how/when users would use this application.

References

1. Anguera, X., Ferrarons, M.: Memory efficient subsequence dtw for query-by-example spoken term detection. In: 2013 IEEE International Conference on Multimedia and Expo (ICME), pp. 1–6. IEEE (2013)

2. Schalkwyk, J., Beeferman, D., Beaufays, F., Byrne, B., Chelba, C., Cohen, M., Kamvar, M., Strope, B.: "your word is my command": Google search by voice: A case study. In: Neustein, A. (ed.) Advances in Speech Recognition, pp. 61–90. Springer US (2010), http://dx.doi.org/10.1007/978-1-4419-5951-5_4
3. Acero, A., Bernstein, N., Chambers, R., Ju, Y., Li, X., Odell, J., Nguyen, P., Scholz, O., Zweig, G.: Live search for mobile: web services by voice on the cellphone. In: IEEE International Conference on Acoustics, Speech and Signal Processing, ICASSP 2008, pp. 5256–5259 (March 2008)
4. Shen, W., White, C.M., Hazen, T.J.: A comparison of query-by-example methods for spoken term detection. DTIC Document, Tech. Rep. (2009)
5. Rabiner, L.R., Sambur, M.R.: An algorithm for determining the endpoints of isolated utterances. Bell System Technical Journal 54(2), 297–315 (1975)
6. Lee, H., Chang, S., Yook, D., Kim, Y.: A voice trigger system using keyword and speaker recognition for mobile devices. IEEE Transactions on Consumer Electronics 55(4), 2377–2384 (2009)
7. Sakoe, H., Chiba, S.: Dynamic programming algorithm optimization for spoken word recognition. IEEE Transactions on Acoustics, Speech and Signal Processing 26(1), 43–49 (1978)

Confidence Measures
in Automatic Speech Recognition Systems
for Error Detection in Restricted Domains

Julia Olcoz, Alfonso Ortega, Antonio Miguel,
and Eduardo Lleida

ViVoLab, Aragon Institute for Engineering Research (I3A)
University of Zaragoza
{jolcoz,ortega,amiguel,lleida}@unizar.es
http://www.vivolab.es/

Abstract. This paper presents the performance achieved using Confidence Measures (CM) in Automatic Speech Recognition (ASR) for the transcription of weather reports from the Spanish public broadcast channel (RTVE). In the CM computation, first Acoustic-Phonetic Decoding (APD) is carried out, then we align reference and hypothesis word sequences through a phone-graph, and finally in this decoding mesh given a time interval, the maximum posterior probability of the hypothesized word is selected as the CM value. The final goal is to use the CM module as an extension of the ASR system to automatically evaluate the reliability of recognition results, discarding low confidence words at the output. These CM can be used as a tool for Unsupervised Learning Techniques, and also for helping human supervision of recognition results. If accurate enough, these CM would increase the usability as well as the robustness of speech applications.

Keywords: Automatic Speech Recognition, Unsupervised Learning Techniques, Confidence Measures, Acoustic-Phonetic Decoding, Error Detection, Restricted Domains.

1 Introduction

In Automatic Speech Recognition (ASR) systems the performance level generally relates to the quality and quantity of training data. If enough, robust models can be trained to achieve better results. Nevertheless, representative databases (DB) are not always available and human interaction for transcribing and labeling is needed, increasing cost and development time.

A possible alternative is to use Unsupervised Learning Techniques to benefit from available audio resources without the need of manual transcriptions, allowing faster and cheaper recognition applications. However, several factors such as the noisy channel or the speaker itself, among others, contribute to get erroneous hypotheses. Therefore, it is often necessary to provide a mechanism for verifying the reliability of recognition results.

J.L. Navarro Mesa et al. (Eds.): IberSPEECH 2014, LNAI 8854, pp. 168–177, 2014.

Confidence Measures (CM) may be used by the ASR system to automatically assess the probability of correctness for each decision increasing its usefulness and intelligence. In the actual state-of-the-art there are several proposals related to the usage of CM, in order to apply unsupervised training of Deep Neural Networks (DNN, [1] and [2]) to manage the wide amount of un-transcribed data available. As it is also shown in the literature, CM can be grouped into three major categories [3]: predictor features, refers to a post-classifier implementation to estimate if a transcribed word is correct or not based on some single features collected within the recognition process [4]; estimation by using the posterior probability [5]; and utterance verification, where a statistical hypothesis test is formulated in a post-processing stage [6].

In this paper we present the performance achieved with CM based on utterance verification, which are computed using Acoustic-Phonetic Decoding (APD), to detect word errors (substitutions and insertions) at the hypothesis given by the recognizer, included in a weather report transcription application. This CM can be used to apply unsupervised training of acoustic models on automatically generated transcriptions discarding low confidence regions, and also to support human supervision of the recognition results.

This work is organized as follows: section 2 describes the task domain, databases used and the methodology steps. In section 3 we explain how CM are computed, and in section 4 the performance achieved using CM to detect errors is presented. Finally, in section 5 we sum up the whole work and discuss future research lines.

2   Task Description

The main goal of the task is to get the transcription of weather reports from the Spanish public broadcast channel (Radio Televisión Española, RTVE). The semantic domain of the task is very restricted most of the time, and the vocabulary is around 5K words. The quality of the audio is good, but one of the main difficulties is the high speech rate of the broadcasters, what makes impossible to use speaker independent models. Our purpose is to develop tools in order to allow us to obtain speaker dependent models for new broadcasters in a fast and easy way, by using the minimum amount of manually transcribed data. These tools can also be used to help human supervision in subtitling applications.

2.1   Speaker Dependent Database

The speaker dependent database used in these experiments corresponds to weather reports of the Spanish public broadcast channel (RTVE) recorded from January 2011 to December 2013, for a given broadcaster. It is an ensemble of 244 TV programs with a total of 43.70 hours of audio (only speech), that have been divided into three different subsets (A, B and C). All subsets must contain a representative sample of files from each month of the year in order to work with a balanced vocabulary. Note that, due to the specificities of the task,

Table 1. Speaker dependent DB subsets

DB subset	methodology stage	#files	#audio hours	%DB audio hours
A	development	32	5.88	13.46
B	test	32	5.93	13.57
C	train	180	31.89	72.97

the vocabulary of each show changes depending on the season (snow in winter, warm weather in summer, rain in spring, wind during autumn). Tab. 1 shows the quantity of files and the amount of audio for each database subset.

2.2   Methodology

In this section we are going to describe the main steps that are followed in order to obtain the transcriptions with CM. A graphical representation of this process can be seen in Fig. 1. First in the train stage, a speaker independent acoustic model λ (AM) is trained using a mixture of three different phonetically balanced DBs (Albayzin [7], SpeechDat-car [8] and Domolab [9]). This AM is built with the HTK Speech Recognition Toolkit [10] and consists of a cross-word tree-based tied-state triphone, with three states in each unit, and sixteen component Gaus-

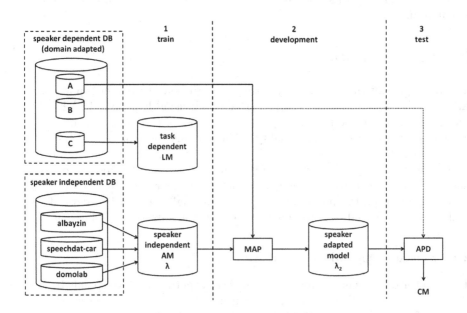

Fig. 1. Methodology block diagram

sian Mixture Models (GMMs) for modeling the observation probability in each
state. The acoustic features extracted from the speech input signal are 39 Mel-
Cepstrum Frequency Coefficients (MFCCs, 12 coefficients plus the energy term
and first and second order derivatives), using a Hamming Window of 25ms. with
a frame rate of 10ms. Moreover, a task adapted language model (LM) is trained
too, using subset C of the speaker dependent DB. This LM consists of a trigram
model trained using the Stanford Research Institute Language Modeling Toolkit
(SRILM) [11], with a vocabulary of 5570 words from the restricted domain.

Second in the development stage, a Maximum A Posteriori (MAP) [12] adaptation is performed using the HTK Toolkit [10], and considering subset A of the
speaker dependent DB, in order to obtain a speaker adapted model λ_2 from the
previous speaker independent AM λ.

Finally in the test step, the transcription along with the proposed CM are
obtained. Note that the main goal is to convert the last stage into an extended
module of the ASR system, in which its free of errors output could be used to
enhance previously existing AM or become helpful in subtitling applications.

3   Confidence Measures Computing

3.1   Acoustic-Phonetic Decoding

Acoustic-Phonetic Decoding (APD) has been considered to compute the CM
at the recognizer output. This technique consists in obtaining the best list of
phonemes fitting the acoustic input signal, aligning the reference and the hypothesis sequences through a phone-graph like the one represented in Fig. 2. In
here, each arc refers to the hypothesis phoneme alternative ph_i and its posterior
probability $P(ph_i)$ associated, obtained using the (lattice-tool) of the SRILM
Toolkit [11]. Given a time interval (t_{ini}, t_{end}), the confidence, which is a normalized value between zero and one, is calculated from the posterior probability

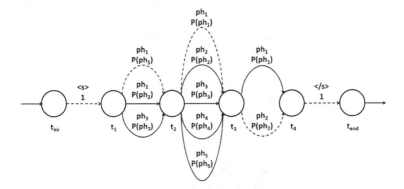

Fig. 2. Decoding mesh

of the decoding lattices. Note that usually, the decoding graph finally used is an equivalent search-mesh to the original one, which has been created using the Finite State Machines (FSM) Toolkit [13] and finally optimized applying its determinization and minimization algorithms to reduce its dimensions, decreasing computation time and complexity. The word-level CM is obtained by averaging the CM values of each phoneme considered in the best sequence alignment (dashed line in Fig. 2).

Each TV program of the speaker dependent DB is about ten minutes duration and it is necessary to split it into shorter segments in order to allow the HTK tools to perform the APD task. As the number of characters in subtitles is restricted, the processing is performed in chunks of ten words, according to the number of words that normally appears in a subtitled line.

4 Experimental Results

4.1 Performance Evaluation

To evaluate the CM performance two sets of experiments have been deployed: error detection in chunks, and burst error detection (consecutive erroneous words) in chunks. The performance measures of the CM will be the probability of false alarm (FA) and the probability of miss (MISS). Note that a FA in this context refers to an erroneous word considered as correct, and a MISS refers to a correct word considered as erroneous. If these CM are used for unsupervised learning, a low FA operating point would be appropriate in order to avoid erroneous transcriptions to modify the AM in an incorrect way.

4.2 Performance of the CM in Non-contiguous Errors

Along this section we present the performance of the CM when the errors in a chunk of words are not required to be contiguous. For this experiment, the

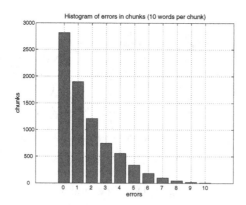

Fig. 3. Histogram of the number of errors in chunks of ten words

transcriptions of subset B obtained using the speaker adapted model λ_2 are considered. In these transcriptions, the Word Error Rate (WER) is 19.97%, and the most of the errors are isolated as it can be seen in Fig. 3, where the histogram of the number of errors in chunks of ten words is presented.

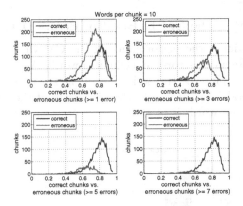

Fig. 4. Distribution of the CM values for correct and erroneous chunks considering different number of errors

Although the most frequent number of errors in a ten words chunk is one, detecting these isolated errors is very difficult since most of the time, one word is replaced by another which is acoustically very similar and grammatically correct in the considered context. What can be more feasible is to detect chunks of words containing several errors. This increase in feasibility can be seen by looking at the distributions of the CM values for correct and erroneous chunks presented in Fig. 4. Distributions are very overlapped when isolated errors are considered

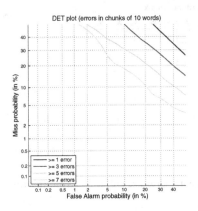

Fig. 5. Detection Error Trade-Off for correct and erroneous chunks considering different number of errors

(only one erroneous word in a ten words chunk), but they progressively separate when the number of errors in the chunk increases. This separation in the distributions helps the error detection task as it can be seen in Fig. 5, where the Detection Error Trade-off (DET) curve is plotted. According to this curve, most of the chunks containing several errors can be detected.

4.3   Performance of the CM in Burst of Errors Detection

In this section we detail the performance of the CM when trying to detect a burst of errors (consecutive errors) in a chunk of words. As in the non-continuous error detection we employ the transcriptions of the subset B obtained using the speaker adapted model λ_2. In Fig. 6, the histogram of the number of burst of errors in chunks of ten words is plotted.

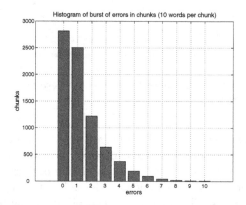

Fig. 6. Histogram of the number of burst of errors in chunks of ten words

Words per chunk   **Type of chunk**

	W_1	W_2	W_3	W_4	W_5	W_6	W_7	W_8	W_9	W_{10}	
Chunk 1	1	1	1	1	1	1	1	1	1	1	Correct
Chunk 2	1	0	1	0	1	0	1	0	1	0	Erroneous: 5 isolated errors / 5 bursts of 1 error
Chunk 3	1	1	1	1	1	0	0	0	0	0	Erroneous: 5 isolated errors / 1 burst of 5 errors
Chunk 4	1	1	0	1	1	1	0	1	1	0	Erroneous: 7 isolated errors / 1 burst of 3 errors
Chunk 5	1	1	0	0	0	1	1	1	1	1	Erroneous: 7 isolated errors / 1 burst of 5 errors

Fig. 7. Correct and erroneous chunks. Different grouping depending on isolated errors and bursts of errors

Note that the number of chunks with bursts of one error is bigger than the number of chunks with one error shown in Fig. 3. The reason for this is that in Fig. 6 we group together the chunks with isolated errors whether there is one or more errors in the chunks. The same would apply to the chunks with a burst of two or more errors. Fig. 7 provides a graphical example of grouping chunks depending on isolated errors and bursts of errors.

As it also happened in the non-contiguous detection, the higher the number of errors considered in the burst the easier to detect, but now the distributions of the CM values for correct and erroneous chunks are even more separated, as it can be seen in Fig. 8.

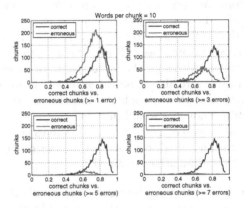

Fig. 8. Distribution of the CM values for correct and erroneous chunks considering different number of errors in a burst

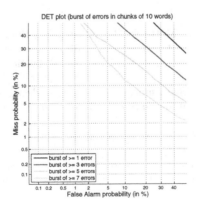

Fig. 9. Detection Error Trade-Off for correct and erroneous chunks considering different number of errors in a burst

Therefore, the capability of detection improves, as it shows the DET curve in Fig. 9. Considering bursts of five errors, we obtain a probability of FA less than ten percent and a MISS probability of less than thirty percent.

5   Conclusions

This paper presents the use of Confidence Measures (CM) in Automatic Speech Recognition (ASR) for a task of transcribing weather reports from the Spanish public broadcast channel (RTVE). CM values are obtained using Acoustic-Phonetic Decoding (APD), and selecting the maximum posterior probability of the hypothesized word in a phone-mesh, where reference and hypothesis word sequences are aligned. The main objective is using these CM module to automatically evaluate the ASR system recognition results. This could be used as a tool for unsupervised learning, as well as for supporting human supervision in subtitling applications. Although the performance of these CM for detecting isolated errors is low, they are able to detect groups of words containing several errors. If CM accurate enough, the usability and the robustness of applications developed by speech technologies would increase.

Future work will be focused on getting new CM values using different Acoustic Models (AMs) than the ones used to obtain the transcriptions using the speaker adapted AM λ_2, and discriminatively trained.

Acknowledgments. This work has been supported by the Spanish Government and the European Union (FEDER) through projects TIN2011-28169-C05-02 and INNPACTO IPT-2011-1696-390000.

References

1. Imseng, D., Potard, B., Motticek, P., Nanchen, A., Bourlard, H.: Exploiting untranscribed foreign data for speech recognition in well-resourced languages. In: Proceedings of the International Conference on Acoustics, Speech and Signal Processing (2014)
2. Vesely, K., Burget, L.: Semi-supervised training of deep neural networks. In: 2013 IEEE Workshop on Automatic Speech Recognition and Understanding (ASRU), pp. 267–272 (2013)
3. Jiang, H.: Confidence Measures for speech recognition: A survey. Speech Communication 45, 455–470 (2005)
4. Cox, S., Rose, R.: Confidence Measures for the switchboard database. In: Proceedings of the International Conference on Acoustics, Speech and Signal Processing, pp. 511–514 (1996)
5. Wessel, F., Schluter, R., Macharey, K., Ney, H.: Confidence Measures for large vocabulary continuous speech recognition. IEEE Transactions on Speech and Audio Processing 9(3), 288–298 (2001)
6. Lleida, E., Rose, R.: Likelihood ratio decoding and confidence measures for continuous speech recognition. In: Proceeding of the Fourth International Conference on Spoken Language Processing, pp. 478–481 (1996)

7. Moreno, A., Poch, D., Bonafonte, A., Lleida, E., Llisterri, J., Mario, J., Nadeu, C.: Albayzin speech database: design of the phonetic corpus. In: EUROSPEECH (1993)
8. Moreno, A., Borge, L., Christoph, D., Khalid, C., Stephan, A., Jeffrey, A.: Speech-Dat Car: a large vocabulary speech database for automotive environments. In: Proceedings II LREC (2000)
9. Justo, R., Saz, O., Guijarrubia, V., Miguel, A., Torres, M., Lleida, E.: Improving dialogue systems in a home automation environment. In: Proceedings of the First International Conference on Ambient Media and Systems (Ambi-Sys), Quebec City (2008)
10. Young, S., Kershaw, D., Odell, J., Ollason, D., Valtchev, V., Woodland, P.: The HTK Book, version 3.4. Microsoft Corporation (1995)
11. Stolcke, A.: An Extensible Language Modeling Toolkit. In: International Conference on Spoken Language Processing (ICSLP 2002), Denver (2002)
12. Gauvain, J., Chin-Hui, L.: Maximum a posteriori estimation for multivariate gaussian mixture observations of markov chains. IEEE Transactions on Speech and Audio Processing 2(2), 291–299 (1994)
13. Mohri, M., Riley, M.: Weighted Finite-State Transducers in Speech Recognition. In: International Conference on Spoken Language Processing (ICSLP 2002), Denver (2002)

Recognition of Distant Voice Commands for Home Applications in Portuguese

Miguel Matos[1,2], Alberto Abad[1,2], Ramón Astudillo[1], and Isabel Trancoso[1,2,⋆]

[1] L²F - Spoken Language Systems Lab, INESC-ID Lisboa
[2] IST - Instituto Superior Técnico, University of Lisbon
{jmatos,alberto,imt}@l2f.inesc-id.pt
http://www.l2f.inesc-id.pt

Abstract. This paper presents a set of exploratory experiments addressed to analyse and evaluate the performance of baseline speech processing components in European Portuguese for distant voice command recognition applications in domestic environments. The analysis, conducted in a multi-channel multi-room scenario, showed the importance of adequate room detection and channel selection strategies to obtain acceptable performances. Two different computationally inexpensive channel selection measures for room detection, channel selection and cluster selection have been investigated. Experimental results show that the strategies based on envelope-variance measure consistently outperformed the remaining methods investigated, and particularly, that channel selection strategies can be more convenient than baseline beamforming methods, such as delay-and-sum, for this type of multi-room scenarios.

Keywords: distant speech recognition, multi-microphone processing, beamforming, microphone selection, home control applications.

1 Introduction

The DIRHA project[1] addresses the challenge of distant-speech recognition in a home environment, with a very realistic and complex application scenario, using a microphone network distributed over the different rooms of an apartment. The system is "always-listening", and an important challenge is to develop a solution that reduces false alarms due to misinterpretation of normal conversations and other generic sounds. Speech enhancement and recognition methods for this type of application have been widely described in the literature, but they do not address the realistic scenario of sound sources occurring in different rooms. The focus of the paper is on multi-room, multi-microphone solutions adequate for the home scenario. The paper starts by describing the data collection process, explaining how simulated corpora were obtained for different languages. The bulk of the paper is devoted to the description of the different experiments on the task of recognizing read commands.

⋆ This work was partially funded by the European Union, under grant agreement FP7-288121. The authors would like to thank their colleagues in the DIRHA consortium.
[1] http://dirha.fbk.eu

J.L. Navarro Mesa et al. (Eds.): IberSPEECH 2014, LNAI 8854, pp. 178–188, 2014.

2   The DIRHA SimCorpus for European Portuguese

The DIRHA SimCorpus is a multi-microphone and multi-language database containing simulated acoustic sequences derived from the microphone-equipped apartment located in Trento (Italy), named ITEA, depicted in Figure 1. The simulated corpora for the different languages -including European Portuguese (EP) - were produced thanks to a technique that reconstructs, in a realistic manner, multi-microphone front-end observations of typical scenes occurring in a domestic environment. For each language, the corpus contains a set of acoustic sequences of duration 60 seconds, at 48kHz sampling frequency and 16-bit accuracy, observed by 40 microphone channels distributed over five rooms. Each sequence consists of real background noise with superimposed localized acoustic events, occurring randomly (and rather uniformly) in time and in space (within predefined positions) with various dynamics. The acoustic wave propagation from the sound source to each single microphone is simulated by convoluting the clean signals with the respective measured impulse response (IR). Acoustic events are divided into two main categories, i.e., speech and non-speech. Speech events include different types of utterances (i.e., phonetically-rich sentences, read and spontaneous commands, conversational speech). Non-speech events have been selected from a collection of high-quality sounds typically occurring within a home environment (e.g., radio, TV, appliances, knocking, ringing, etc.).

For the DIRHA SimCorpus in EP, hereinafter referred to as DIRHA-EP Sim-Corpus, a clean-speech data set of very high quality close-talking speech signals was collected to derive the simulated corpus. The data set contains 20 speakers with an equal gender distribution, ageing between 25 and 50. The EP simulated corpus is divided into two chunks (*dev* and *test*) containing 75 acoustic sequences each, with 10 different speakers in each data set [10].

3   Baseline for Distant Speech Recognition in Portuguese

The baseline ASR system for EP in DIRHA has been developed and assessed with the HTK toolkit [1], using the BD-PUBLICO corpus [2]. The recordings of the newspaper sentences that form this corpus were done in a sound proof room using a high quality microphone at 16kHz sampling frequency. The bi-gram language model contains about 11M words. The selected closed-set vocabulary includes 6,618 unique words. The features used to represent acoustic information are the traditional 13-dimensional MFCCs, augmented by their first and second derivatives, and mean normalized, thus reaching a dimensionality of 39. Following acoustic feature extraction, HMM training was carried out using the typical HTK pipeline toolkit [1]. First, a set of monophone models was trained using "flat-start" initialization (39 phone classes). Then, training of monophones, triphones, state tying, and Gaussian mixture splitting was performed until final cross-word tied-state context-dependent triphones of 3 states and 16 Gaussians per state were built. In the state tying process, a decision tree clustering strategy was applied, using a set of phonetic questions adequate for EP.

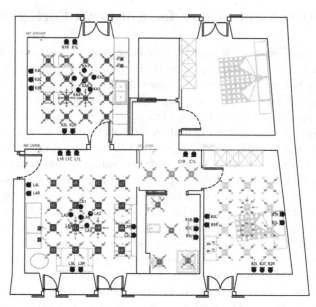

Fig. 1. Outline of the microphone set-up. Black dots represent microphones, while boxes and arrows represent available positions and orientations.

A data-simulation based approach was adopted to evaluate ASR in the DIRHA far-field environment, by artificially convolving the "`clean`" recordings with IRs measured at a number of locations in the apartment, and contaminating them with noise at various SNR values. This resulted in two sets of simulated far-field data, one using a more controlled contamination approach ("`reverb1`"), and another using a wider contamination parameter variability applied in a random fashion ("`reverbR`") [4]. The `dev` set was used for adjusting the decoding parameters which henceforth were kept constant for all experiments. Unfortunately, there is no warranty that the large acoustic variability of the DIRHA multi-room and multi-channel scenario is well-represented by only one of these single environmental conditions. In order to partially mitigate this problem, we followed a quite straightforward approach that consists of using all the training data of the three conditions together to train a single multi-condition acoustic model. This approach yielded a better performance than the single condition models (see [11] for details), yielding WER of 30.04% and 32.67% for the `dev` and `test` "`reverb1`" sets, and 33.07% and 34.53% for the `dev` and `test` "`reverbR`" sets, respectively. The multi-condition models were therefore used in all remaining experiments.

4 Recognition of Voice Commands in Multi-Room Scenarios

This section presents the first exploratory studies conducted on the DIRHA-EP multi-room and multi-channel corpus. The experiments are focused on the task of recognizing read spoken commands. For this purpose, the spoken commands are extracted from the two sets (`dev` and `test`) of the 1 minute DIRHA-EP SimCorpus simulations using the voice activity ground truth information. There are a total of 75 simulations per dataset and each simulation contains one read command, which results in a total of 150 extracted speech segments that are used for evaluation. For the command recognition task, an equally-likely finite state grammar formed by all the unique possible command sentences is used.

4.1 Analysis of Performance in Multi-Room Environments

In contrast to other existing corpora commonly used in the field of robust and far-field speech recognition research, the acoustic events of interest in DIRHA do not always happen in the same room where all the microphones are placed. Instead, acoustic events (speech or any other) may happen anywhere inside the ITEA apartment and they are simultaneously collected by a network of 40 different microphones that are also distributed in the different rooms of the household. Consequently, the challenges faced at the DIRHA project go far beyond the classical problem of far-field speech recognition. Thus, it became first necessary to understand how critical is the selection of a specific microphone or group of microphones in multi-room speech recognition tasks.

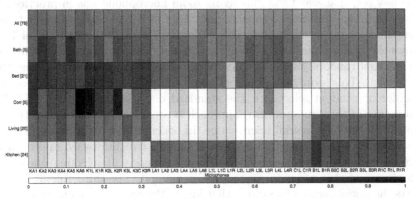

Fig. 2. Pictorial summary of average WER (%) performance obtained for the `dev` set

Figure 2 shows a pictorial summary of the recognition performance for each one of the microphone channels on the `dev` set. The results are the error rates obtained by each channel when recognizing only the speech events taking place in a specific room. The results for all the 75 events are also provided in the first row. The darker (red) each cell is, the larger the corresponding WER is. Notice that the microphone channels have been sorted per room (the first character in the name of each microphone identifies the room). Thus, the pseudo-diagonals of the coloured matrices represent matched conditions in which the speech events occur in the room where the microphone is located. Notice also that the number of spoken commands is not the same in all rooms. This number

Table 1. Average WER (%) performance using different microphone channel selection strategies exploiting knowledge about the room where an event occurs

Microphone selection	testing conditions	
	dev	test
overall best-mic (LA5)	35.28	26.62
room-aware random-mic	11.99	9.64
room-aware best-mic	6.74	8.94 (4.47)
oracle mic per-event	4.94	0.0

is provided in the y-axis together with the name of the room. Consequently, the microphones located in rooms where spoken commands are more frequent obtain better overall performances as it could be expected. One can easily identify the room matched conditions, since they are considerably lighter than the regions outside the pseudo-diagonal. Although there are differences among channels inside the same room, these differences are considerably smaller than the ones observed when compared with the performance of a microphone outside the room. Hence, as it could be expected, the room information is fundamental.

The first row of Table 1 shows the WER results computed in the dev and test datasets using the microphone that obtained the best overall performance in the dev set, that was LA5. This living-room microphone was in practice also the best overall performing channel in test data. A particularity of the data sets is that the test set seems considerably easier than dev. The second row of Table 1 shows the performance of a system that knows the room where an event happens and that randomly selects a microphone of the given room to recognize that speech event. This score has been obtained computing the mean performance of 500 different random selections (the standard deviation was ~ 2 − 3%). The performance of this "room-aware" approach is considerably better than the one obtained by the best overall microphone. In other words, if the room in which an event occurs is a given information, a simple straightforward approach for improved recognition in the DIRHA scenario consists of selecting one of the microphones of that room to process the command. The third row of Table 1 reports the performance of a system that knows the room where an event occurs and that recognizes this event using the microphone that obtained the lowest average error for the events of that room in the dev dataset. While the random microphone selection is clearly outperformed by this oracle approach in dev, the difference in test is not so meaningful. In other words, the best microphone is largely dependent on the specific event and the best average configuration in dev does not necessarily provide better results in test than a simple random selection approach. For comparison purposes, we report in brackets the performance that is obtained in the test if the selected microphone per-room is based on the best average performance on the test set. The considerable improvement reinforces the importance of a microphone selection strategy that depends on the specific event rather than a general per room configuration. Finally, the upper-bound performance that could be attained with a perfect microphone selection algorithm is reported in the last row of Table 1. This perfect oracle was computed by simply selecting the channel that provides the lowest error for any specific speech event. This ideal figure represents the potential of channel selection algorithms, even in the case of extremely challenging multi-microphone and multi-room acoustic environments.

4.2 Beamforming with Multiple Microphone Clusters

The delay and sum beamformer [6] is one of the simplest and most efficient microphone array approaches. It consists of the alignment of the microphone signals to compensate for the different acoustic path lengths from the source to the microphones, followed by the addition of the time-aligned signals. For a multi-channel system with M microphones, this can be expressed as

$$y(t) = \sum_{m=1}^{M} \alpha_m x_m(t - \tau_m) \tag{1}$$

where $x_m(t)$ are the different microphone channels, α_m are the channel gains and τ_m are the time delays of arrival. Typically, one of the microphones is used as the reference channel, and the remaining microphones are compensated with respect to the reference. Simplicity is the most important strength of this approach, making it a practical choice for many microphone array applications. But such a simple spatial filter can only partially suppress directional interference. Given that there is a large amount of microphones in our scenario, our hypothesis is that applying multi-channel processing to specific sub-sets of microphones can be of more benefit than for instance applying beamforming to all the available microphones in a room. In these experiments, we assume that we know the position of the speech source, so the propagation delays can be compensated for all the microphones. Moreover, we consider an equal gain $\alpha_m = \frac{1}{M}$ for all the channels involved in a delay and sum cluster.

Figure 3 shows a pictorial summary of the recognition performance obtained with delay and sum beamformers considering different microphone cluster configurations for the dev set. We have considered 18 delay and sum beamformer configurations: 14 formed by the different microphone clusters of the apartment; 3 beamformers processing all the microphones of the Living-room, Bedroom and Kitchen, respectively; and 1 beamformer that processes the 40 channels. Like in the previous single channel pictures, the cells outside the pseudo-diagonal represent the mismatched scenario in which a beamformer of a different room is selected to process the events of a particular room. Notice that, in contrast to the single channel analysis, this is an awkward scenario, since we are assuming that we have perfect knowledge about the source position to correctly steer the beamformers. Comparing with the previous picture, the colours are "lighter", that is, the overall performance is better when using beamforming signals.

Although in the case of beamforming experiments, the valuable comparisons are between different cluster configurations inside the same room, results obtained with the best overall beamformer when processing all the events are also

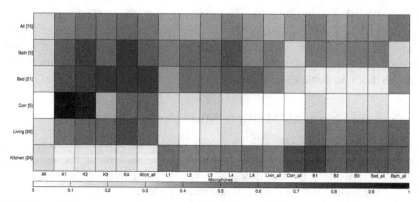

Fig. 3. Pictorial summary of average WER (%) performance obtained with different delay and sum beamformer configurations for the **dev** set.

Table 2. Average WER (%) performance using different cluster selection strategies for beamforming exploiting knowledge about the room where an event occurs.

Cluster selection	testing conditions	
	dev	test
overall best-beamf (`beamf_all`)	17.98	14.95
room-aware allmics_room-beamf	8.54	2.46
room-aware random-beamf	10.08	5.40
room-aware best-beamf	6.74	7.83 (2.46)
oracle beamf per-event	5.17	0.67

reported in the first row of the summary Table 2. Notice the significant improvement with respect to LA5 results of Table 1. Table 2 also summarizes some of the multi-channel "room-aware" speech recognition configurations performance. The second row shows the performance obtained when a delay and sum beamformer of all the microphones of a room is used to spatially filter and later recognize the events occurring in that specific room. From rows 3 to 5, similarly to the previous section 4.1, we report respectively the performance obtained when a random beamformer of the correct room and the best average beamformer of the correct room are selected to process and recognize the speech commands. Notice that the simple delay and sum approach with all microphones achieves excellent results, close to the best cluster selection in **dev**, and equalling its performance in the **test** set. Comparing the "room-aware" delay and sum approaches against the corresponding single channel performances, it is worth noting that there is not a very significant difference if the best cluster or channel is selected. The largest difference is observed mainly in the case of "random" selection. In other words, although the use of delay and sum beamformers in combination with cluster selection provides reduced performance improvements in ideal cluster/microphone selection conditions, they are definitely more robust to erroneous channel selections. Finally, the last row of Table 2 reports again the oracle results in which the appropriate delay and sum cluster is selected per-event. Notice that these results are slightly worse than the ones obtained without beamforming. This may happen because an event that was correctly detected using the channel selection approach is no longer correctly recognized using the beamformed signals.

4.3 Automatic Channel Selection and Room Detection

The two previous sections showed the importance of room knowledge and also the potential of adequate microphone(s) selection strategies. In this section, we explore two simple low-cost methods for automatically selecting either the room, the beamforming cluster or the microphone channel. To the best of our knowledge, this is the first reported work concerning channel selection strategies for multi-room environments.

Channel Selection (CS) Approaches. An overview of some of the most remarkable methods proposed for the microphone selection problem for speech recognition in multi-channel single-room environments can be found in [9]. In practice, the most common approaches are either related to some direct measurement of the signals (SNRs, distortion, correlation, etc.), some indirect relation (knowledge of the position and orientation, knowledge of the room impulse response, etc.) or obtained based on the multi-channel recognition results (likelihood hypothesis, hypothesis combination, etc.). The latter, which are usually named back-end approaches, are able to obtain very competitive performances but they present some limitations: they are computationally inefficient, since they usually need to perform recognition in all channels, and they may suffer from normalization problems due to different acoustic realizations[8]. These problems are in fact exacerbated when many microphones from different rooms are available, like in the case of DIRHA. Consequently, back-end methods are not a convenient solution for our particular task. On the other hand, methods based on indirect relations like position or room impulse responses may be impractical in real world applications due to the difficulty to estimate this type of information. Thus, the focus of this set of exploratory experiments is mainly concentrated in direct measurement based approaches for microphone selection. Particularly, we have considered two alternative signal-based methods based on envelope variance (EV) and universal background model likelihood (UL).

Envelope-variance measure for CS The distortion measure proposed in [7] is extracted directly from the speech signal and it is based on the idea that reverberation smooths the time sequence of speech energy values, so the effect of reverberation may be observed as a reduction in the dynamic range of that envelope. In practice, a vector consisting of the estimated variances of compressed filter-bank energies (FBE) is obtained for each channel in each sub-band. The weighted average variance over all sub-bands is computed as an indicator of the amount of reverberation in each channel: the larger the envelope-variance measure is, the less reverberated is the respective channel.

UBM likelihood measure for CS A new measure for CS that can be partially considered signal- and model- based has been explored. The proposed selection method is based on acoustic likelihoods, but rather than obtaining them from the ASR decoder for the particular recognized hypothesis, a general speech model is used to compute these likelihoods. The concept is similar to the universal background model (UBM) that is common practice in speaker verification [12]. In short, a Gaussian Mixture Model (GMM) is trained with all the data used for training the acoustic models, which is expected to model the general characteristics of the training corpora. Then, in the test phase, the likelihood obtained by each channel with this UBM model is computed. The working hypothesis is that the channels that obtain higher UBM likelihoods will match better the acoustic models and they will likely obtain better recognition performance. In this work, a GMM of 16 mixtures was considered, given that experiences with more mixtures showed no significant improvements.

Channel and Room Selection Strategy. Based on the two above described measures, we propose simple methods for channel, cluster and room selection. In the case of CS, the channel to be recognized is simply the one that obtains the maximum EV or UL measure. In the case of cluster selection for beamforming, since the source position (and consequently, the room) are assumed to be known, we select the cluster of the given room that obtains a maximum EV or UL score. Finally, the room is decided by a simple majority voting approach: the most frequent room out of the 5-most likely channels is the selected room.

Experimental Results. Table 3 shows results exploiting the automatic channel, cluster and room selection strategies previously described. In the first and fourth rows, the results correspond to a random selection of the microphone inside the room that has been automatically identified following the majority voting strategy. Comparing to the results in the second row of Table 1, we observe a constant performance drop due to misidentification of the room. Anyway, the results are still much better than using a single reference microphone for all the events in the house. The second and fifth rows in Table 3 show the ASR performance when the microphone is automatically selected for recognition based on the highest EV or UL score, respectively. The analysis of these results leads us into believing that these methods are not only able to provide meaningful room identification, but also to select individual well-performing microphones. Particularly, the results obtained with the EV measure are remarkably good. None of these approaches makes use of prior knowledge about the position of the sources or about the microphones location. Finally, the third and sixth rows show the performance achieved by the CS methods when they are used to select for each command a specific delay and sum beamformer, knowing the room and position of the speaker. While significant performance gains are obtained with respect to random cluster selection, the method does not outperform the simple delay and sum beamformer that processes all the microphones of each room.

Table 3. Average WER (%) performance exploiting envelope-variance (EV) and novel UBM likelihood-based (UL) microphone selection techniques

CS measure	CS strategy	testing conditions	
		dev	test
EV-based	room-auto random-mic	15.33	12.80
	auto-mic	7.87	5.59
	room-aware auto-beamf	5.62	1.79
UL-based	room-auto random-mic	16.49	14.28
	auto-mic	15.05	9.62
	room-aware auto-beamf	8.99	3.36

5   Conclusions

In this work, we have presented a set of exploratory experiences addressed to analyse and to evaluate the performance of baseline speech processing components in European Portuguese for distant voice command recognition applications in domestic environments. For that purpose, a very realistic multi-channel and multi-room database named DIRHA-EP SimCorpus has been used. The analysis shows the importance of adequate room detection and channel selection strategies to obtain acceptable performances. In practice, according to our results, it seems that channel selection strategies can be more convenient than classical baseline beamforming methods –like the delay-and-sum– for this type of multi-room scenarios. Finally, we have explored two different computationally inexpensive channel selection measures for room detection, channel selection and cluster selection. Experimental results show that the strategies based on envelope-variance measure consistently outperformed the remaining methods investigated.

References

1. Young, S., et al.: HTK – Hidden Markov Model Toolkit, Manual (2006), http://htk.eng.cam.ac.uk/
2. Neto, J.P., Martins, C.A., Meinedo, H., Almeida, L.B.: The design of a large vocabulary speech corpus for Portuguese. In: Proc. Eurospeech, pp. 1707–1710 (1997)
3. Potamianos, G., et al.: Robustness of distant–speech recognition and speaker identification-development of baseline system. Deliverable D4.1, DIRHA Consortium (February 2013)
4. Hagmüller, M., et al.: Experimental task definitions. Deliverable D2.2, DIRHA Consortium (February 2013)
5. Ravanelli, M., et al.: DIRHA-simcorpora I and II. Deliverables 2.1, 2.3, 2.4, DIRHA Consortium (February 2014)
6. Johnson, D., Dudgeon, D.: Array signal processing: concepts and techniques. Prentice Hall (1993)
7. Wolf, M., Nadeu, C.: On the potential of channel selection for recognition of reverberated speech with multiple microphones. In: Proc. Interspeech, pp. 80–83 (2010)

8. Wolf, M., Nadeu, C.: Channel selection using N-Best hypothesis for multi-microphone ASR. In: Proc. Interspeech (2013)
9. Wolf, M.: Channel selection and reverberation-robust automatic speech recognition. PhD, Universitat Politècnica de Catalunya (UPC) (2013)
10. Cristoforetti, L., Ravanelli, M., Omologo, M., Sosi, A., Abad, A., Hagmüller, M., Maragos, P.: The DIRHA simulated corpus. In: Proc. LREC (2014)
11. Abad, A., et al.: First report on novel techniques for distant-speech and speaker recognition. Deliverable D4.2, DIRHA Consortium (February 2014)
12. Reynolds, D.A., Quatieri, T.F., Dunn, R.B.: Speaker Verification Using Adapted Gaussian Mixture Models. Digital Signal Processing, 19–41 (2000)

Assessing the Applicability of Surface EMG to Tongue Gesture Detection

João Freitas[1,2], Samuel Silva[2], António Teixeira[2], and Miguel Sales Dias[1,3]

[1] Microsoft Language Development Center, Lisboa, Portugal
[2] Dep. Electronics Telecommunications & Informatics/IEETA, University of Aveiro, Portugal
[3] Instituto Universitário de Lisboa (ISCTE-IUL), ISTAR-IUL, Lisboa Portugal
t-joaof@microsoft.com, {sss,ajst}@ua.pt,
miguel.dias@microsoft.com

Abstract. The most promising approaches for surface Electromyography (EMG) based speech interfaces commonly focus on the tongue muscles. Despite the interesting results in small vocabularies tasks, it is yet unclear which articulation gestures these sensors are actually detecting. To address these complex aspects, in this study we propose a novel method, based on synchronous acquisition of surface EMG and Ultrasound Imaging (US) of the tongue, to assess the applicability of EMG to tongue gesture detection. In this context, the US image sequences allow us to gather data concerning tongue movement over time, providing the grounds for the EMG analysis. Using this multimodal setup, we have recorded a corpus that covers several tongue transitions (e.g. back to front) in different contexts. Considering the annotated tongue movement data, the results from the EMG analysis show that tongue transitions can be detected using the EMG sensors, with some variability in terms of sensor positioning, across speakers, and the possibility of high false-positive rates.

Keywords: tongue gestures, surface electromyography, ultrasound imaging, synchronization, silent speech interfaces.

1 Introduction

Automatic Speech Recognition (ASR) based on the acoustic signal alone has several disadvantages, such as performance degradation in the presence of environmental noise. Also, if an ASR interface relies only on the acoustic signal, it becomes inappropriate for privacy and non-disturbance scenarios and, importantly, it becomes inadequate for users with speech impairments. These limitations of conventional ASR motivated the Silent Speech Interface (SSI) concept, which is a system that allows for speech communication in the absence of an acoustic signal [1]. One of the most promising technologies used for implementing an SSI is surface ElectroMyoGraphy (EMG), which, according to previous studies, has achieved good performance rates [2]. These studies use EMG electrodes positioned in the facial muscles responsible for moving the articulators during speech, including electrodes in the upper neck area to capture possible tongue movements. Using these approaches, features extracted from

J.L. Navarro Mesa et al. (Eds.): IberSPEECH 2014, LNAI 8854, pp. 189–198, 2014.

the EMG signals are directly applied to the classification problem, in order to distinguish between different speech units (i.e. words or phonemes). However, it is yet unclear what tongue movements are actually being detected, and there is not information about different tongue movements during speech. Finally, we don't know whether these movements can be correctly identified using surface EMG.

To better understand the capabilities of surface EMG, we need reliable data about the articulators' movements, particularly the tongue, which is one of the main articulators in the human speech production process and, for some, the most important of the articulators in speech [3]. There are several technologies that allow obtaining information about the tongue movement during speech (e.g. Real-Time Magnetic Resonance Imaging (RT-MRI) [4], Ultrasound (US) [5], among others [6]). Therefore, one could potentially use this information to provide the grounds for EMG analysis. After analyzing the pros and cons of several modalities, we decided to use US imaging to understand if, by using surface EMG sensors positioned in the neck regions, we are able to detect tongue movements. Thus, by synchronously combining US and the myoelectric signal of the tongue, we would be able to accurately identify tongue movements and develop more informed EMG classifiers that could be easily used to complement a multimodal SSI with an articulatory basis. This way, information about an articulator which is normally hidden by the lips, in the case of a visual approach, or is very difficult to extract, as in the case of Ultrasonic Doppler sensing [7], would be provided. Ideally, one could consider a neckband that detects tongue gestures integrated with other modalities such as video, all of which contribute to a less invasive approach to the characterization of speech production.

The rest of this paper is organized as follows: Section 2 presents a brief background about tongue muscles and a summary of the related work on EMG-based SSI and tongue related studies. Section 3 describes the methodology of this study, namely the corpus, the acquisition system, the applied synchronization solution and the US annotation process. Section 4 reports the first results about tongue movement detection. Finally, section 5 ends the paper with some concluding remarks and future work.

2   Background and Related Work

2.1   Tongue Muscles

The tongue muscles are either classified as intrinsic muscles, which are responsible for changing the shape of the tongue, or extrinsic muscles, which change the position of the tongue in the mouth, as well as the shape the tongue to some extent [8]. The intrinsic muscles are the superior and inferior longitudinal, transverse and vertical. The extrinsic muscles are the *Genioglossus*, *Hyoglossus*, *Palatoglossus* and *Styloglossus*. By working together, these muscles create several type of tongue movements such as: tongue tip elevation, depression and deviation to the left and right, lateral margins relaxation, central tongue grooving, tongue narrowing, protrusion, retraction, posterior elevation and body depression. More details about the function and exact location of these muscles can be found in [3, 8].

2.2   Related Work

As mentioned above, surface EMG is a common approach in SSI. In order to capture tongue information, one of the most important positions for placing the EMG electrodes is in the areas of neck and beneath the chin [2, 9]. Also, in the area of SSI, there are several approaches that use US, combined with video, to get a more complete representation of the human speech production process [10]. Other approaches, able to estimate tongue movements, also used in SSI, include Electromagnetic Articulography (EMA), where magnets glued to the tongue are tracked by magnetic sensors [11].

In the field of phonetics, other studies using intra-oral EMG electrodes attached to the tongue have provided valuable information about the temporal and spatial organization of speech gestures. These studies have analyzed different cases such as vowel articulation [12] or defective speech gestures. An example is the case of aphasia [13]. However, although an electrode directly placed in the articulator would generate more accurate information, avoiding some of the muscle cross-talk and superposition, it would be inadequate and unusable for a natural and non-invasive SSI.

There are also studies of the tongue which use other technologies such as, RT-MRI [14], cinefluorography [15], US using a headset to permit natural head movement [5] and Electropalatography (EPG) [6], which allows us to get a very good understanding of the tongue shapes and movements during speech.

3   Methods

For this study, we started by synchronously acquiring EMG data along with Ultrasound imaging, a modality that is able to provide essential information about tongue movement. For that purpose, we created a corpus where we cover several tongue transitions in the anterior-posterior axis (e.g. front-back and vice-versa) and also elevation and depression of several tongue parts. For future studies, as depicted in Fig. 1, we have also captured three additional modalities: Video, Depth information, and Ultrasonic Doppler sensing. After acquiring the data and synchronizing all data streams, we have determined and characterized the segments that contain tongue movement, based on the US data.

Fig. 1. Recording session and the respective acquisition setup

3.1   Corpus

To define the corpus for our experiment we considered the following goals: (1) record tongue position transitions; and (2) record sequences where the movement of articulators other than the tongue is minimized (lips, mandible and velum). Considering these goals, we selected several /vCv/ contexts, varying the backness and the closeness of the vowels, and tongue transitions between vowels using /$V_1V_2V_1$/ vowel sequences, as presented in Table 1.

Table 1. List of prompts and its respective context

Context	Prompts (using SAMPA phonetic alphabet)
/vCv/	[aka, iki, uku, eko, EkO, iku, aLa, eLe, uLu, ata, iti, utu, eto, EtO, itu, eso, isu, EsO]
/$V_1V_2V_1$/	[iui, ouo, EOE, eoe, iei]

These combinations include the tongue transitions in terms of vowel closeness and backness as well. The selected sequences are composed by the transition /V_1V_2/ and its opposite movement /V_2V_1/. For example, the prompt [iui] is composed of the tongue transition from [i] to [u] and the transition from [u] to [i]). In order to minimize movement of other articulators than the tongue we have not included bilabial and labio-dental consonants. Some exceptions can be found in the corpus for rounded vowels (i.e. vowels that require lip rounding such as [u]) in order to include in corpus the tongue position associated with these sounds.

Based on pilot recordings, we noticed that the speaker would get uncomfortable after a long time using the US headset. As such, we focused on the most relevant transitions in order to minimize the length of the recordings. For each prompt in the corpus three repetitions have been recorded and, for each recording, the speaker was asked to say the prompt twice, e.g. "iiitiii…iiitiii", with around 3 seconds of interval, yielding a total of 6 repetitions per prompt. To facilitate movement annotation we asked the speakers to sustain each phoneme for at least one second. The prompts were recorded in a random order. The prompts were presented on a computer display, and the participant was instructed to read them when signaled (prompt background turned green). For each recorded sequence, EMG recording was started before US recording and stopped after the US was acquired.

The 3 speakers used in this study, were all male native speakers of European Portuguese, with the following ages: 28, 31, and 33 years. No history of hearing or speech disorders is known for any of them. Each speaker recorded a total of 81 utterances containing 2 repetitions each, giving a total of 486 observations (81 utterances x 3 speakers x 2 repetitions of each utterance).

3.2   Ultrasound Acquisition

The ultrasound setup comprises a Mindray DP6900 ultrasound system with a 65EC10EA transducer, an Expresscard/54 Video capture card, to capture the US video, a microphone, connected to a Roland UA-25 external soundcard and a SyncBrightUp unit, which allows synchronization between the audio and ultrasound video, recorded at 30 frames per second. To ensure that the relative position of the ultrasound probe and the head is kept during the acquisition session, a stabilization headset is used [5], securing the ultrasound probe below the participant's chin.

Acquisition is managed by Articulate Assistant Advanced (AAA) [16], which is responsible for recording the audio and ultrasound video and triggering the SynchBrightUp unit. The SyncBrightUp unit, when triggered, introduces synchronization pulses in the audio signal and, for each of those, a white square on the corresponding ultrasound video frames of the sequence.

The synchronization between audio and the US video is tuned after the recording session, in AAA, by checking the pulses in the audio signal and aligning them with the frames containing bright squares.

3.3 Acquisition of Surface EMG and other Modalities

The EMG sensor acquisition system (from Plux [17]), uses 5 pairs of EMG surface electrodes connected to a device that communicates with a computer via Bluetooth. The sensors were attached to the skin considering an approximate 2.0cm spacing between the center of the electrodes for bipolar configurations. Before placing the surface EMG sensors, the sensor location was cleaned with alcohol. While uttering the prompts no other movement besides the one associated with speech production was made. The EMG channels 1 and 4 used a monopolar configuration (i.e. we placed one of the electrodes from the respective pair in a location with low or negligible muscle activity), being the reference electrodes placed on the mastoid portion of the temporal bone. The positioning of the EMG electrodes was based on previous work (e.g. [2, 9]) and was somewhat limited because of the Ultrasound probe placed beneath the chin, as depicted in Fig. 2.

In terms of pre-processing, the EMG signal was normalized, 50 Hz removed with a notch filter and filtered using Single Spectrum Analysis (SSA).

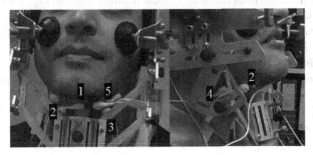

Fig. 2. Frontal (left image) and lateral (right image) view of the positioning of the surface EMG sensors (channels 1 to 5)

For collecting Video and Depth data we used a Microsoft Kinect device. For the ultrasonic Doppler signal we used a custom built device [18], which also contains a microphone besides the ultrasonic emitter and receiver.

The audio from the main microphone (provided by the SyncBrightUp unit), the Ultrasonic Doppler signal, and a synchronization signal programmed to be automatically emitted by the EMG device at the beginning of each prompt were recorded by an external sound card (TASCAM US-1641). The activation of the output bit flag of the EMG recording device generates a small voltage peak on the recorded synchronization signal. To enhance and detect that peak, a second degree derivative is applied to the signal, followed by an amplitude threshold. To be able to detect this peak, the external sound board channel is configured with maximum input sensitivity. Then, after automatically detecting the peak, we remove the extra samples (before the peak) in all channels. More details regarding the setup can be found in [19].

3.4   EMG Synchronization with US

For synchronizing the EMG signals with the US video, we use the audio signal provided by the SyncBrightUp unit, which, as described in section 3.2, contains the synchronization pulses and is captured by both the EMG and US setups. Since, inside each setup, this signal is synchronized with the remaining data, it was used to synchronize data across both. To measure the delay between the two setups, we perform a cross-correlation between the audio tracks, obtaining the time lag between the two, and removing samples from the EMG signals (which always starts first).

3.5   US Data Annotation

The ultrasound was annotated to identify the segments where tongue movement was present. The goal is to examine the video sequence and tag those segments where the tongue is in motion. Given the large amount of US data, we used an automatic annotation method [4]. This method consists in computing the pixel-wise inter-frame difference between each pair of video frames in the sequence. When the tongue moves, the inter-frame difference rises resulting in local maxima (refer to Fig. 3 for an illustrative example). Starting from these maxima, the second derivative is considered, left and right, to expand the annotation. Then, to segment the repetition in each utterance the envelope of the speech signal is used.

Considering, for example, one repetition of the sequence "iiiuuuiii", at least four tongue movements are expected: one at the start for the transition from resting to [i], one for the transition from [i] to [u] (tongue moves backwards), one for the transition from [u] to [i] (tongue moves forward) and one at the end, when the tongue goes from [u] into the resting position. Therefore, the two annotated regions on the middle of each repetition correspond to the transitions between sounds, as depicted in Fig. 3. For the movements outside the utterances no movement direction was annotated. To validate the proposed method, 72 tongue movement segments were manually annotated in several sequences belonging to the three speakers. For additional details, regarding the US sequences automatic annotation, the reader is forwarded to [20].

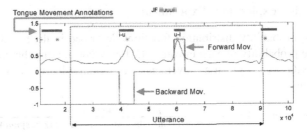

Fig. 3. Inter-frame difference curve (in blue) for a speaker uttering "iiiuuuiii". The automatic annotation identifies all segments with tongue movement, and movement direction for those inside the utterance.

4 Results

To assess detection of tongue movements, the synchronized data was explored for differences on density functions. Additionally, a detection experiment based on the probability of movement was also performed.

4.1 Densities

Using random utterances of each speaker and the annotations from US, the probability mass functions for 3 classes were calculated and compared. Two of these classes represent the tongue movements found in each utterance and the third class denotes no tongue movement. Based on preliminary experiments, we noticed that the statistics for each speaker stabilize after 9 utterances. A Gamma distribution was adopted based on the shape of the histograms. The 2 distribution parameters of this distribution were estimated using Matlab.

As depicted in Fig. 4, differences in distributions were found for all speakers with some variations within EMG channels.

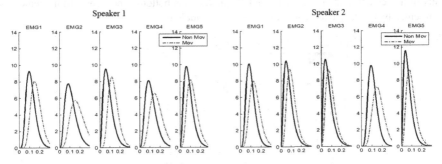

Fig. 4. Density functions for the 5 EMG channels of speaker 1 and 2, including curves for one of the movements (front) and non-movement

4.2   Detection Exploratory Experiment

Based on the probability distribution functions described in the previous section, we estimated the probability of each movement. Hence, considering the probability of the measured EMG (*meas*) given a movement (*mov*), *p(meas|mov)*, we can apply Bayes rules as follows:

$$p(mov|meas) = \frac{p(meas|mov)\,p(mov)}{(1-p(mov))\,p(meas|nonmov)+p(mov)\,p(meas|mov)} \tag{1}$$

The detection threshold was set to 0.5 and p(*mov*) to 0.3, which, based on an empirical analysis, presented a good balance between detections and false positives. Fig. 5 presents the results in a (well behaved) utterance.

To assess the applied technique, we compared the detection results with the US annotation in order to obtain information on correct detections, failures in detection and false detections. As this processing was done for each sample, the outputs were manually analyzed to determine the number of correct detections and number of failures. For false positive (FP) detections, a qualitative assessment was done, quantifying it into 3 classes (0=a few or none; 1= some; 2= many). The best results are attained for Speaker 1 in channel 3 with a detection of 80.0% and an average of 67.1% for the 5 channels. Other 2 speakers attained the best detection result of 68.6% and 66.8% in EMG channels 4 and 5, respectively. There is also a strong variation of results across prompts, as depicted in Fig. 6.

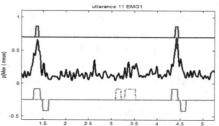

Fig. 5. Example of movement detection. Detected movements are shown at the top, the probability of movement in the middle and the US annotation at bottom, where forward movement is represented by the segments represented above the middle line.

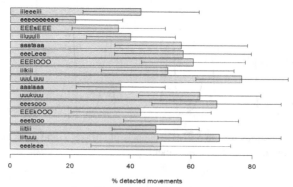

Fig. 6. Detection accuracy results with 95% confidence interval for some of the prompts

In terms of false positives, we noticed that, although speaker 1 presents the best results, it also has a high rate of FP with 38.8% of the utterances having many FP. In that sense, speaker 2 presents the best relation between correct detections and FP with 47.1% of the utterances presenting none or few FP. In terms of sensors the best relation between correct detections and FP was found for channels 2 and 5.

5   Conclusions

This paper describes a novel approach to assess the capability of surface EMG in detecting tongue movements for SSI. The approach uses synchronized US imaging and surface EMG signals to analyze signals of the tongue. For this purpose, a specific corpus, designed with this goal in mind, was collected. After synchronous acquisition modalities and automatically annotating the US data, this new dataset provides the necessary grounds to interpret the EMG data. Results show that tongue movement can be detected using Surface EMG with some accuracy but with variation across speakers and possibility of high FP rates, suggesting the need for an adaptive solution. The work here presented can be used to explore combinations of several sensors and complement existing SSI with articulatory information, about the tongue, using a non-invasive solution. Future work includes detailed analysis of the characteristics of individual movements and to developing an EMG-based tongue movement classifier.

Acknowledgements. This work was partially funded by Marie Curie Actions IRIS (ref. 610986, FP7-PEOPLE-2013-IAPP) and project Cloud Thinking (QREN Mais Centro, ref. CENTRO-07-ST24-FEDER-002031)

References

1. Denby, B., Schultz, T., Honda, K., Hueber, T., Gilbert, J.M., Brumberg, J.S.: Silent speech interfaces. Speech Commun. 52, 270–287 (2010)
2. Wand, M., Schultz, T.: Session-independent EMG-based Speech Recognition. In: International Conference on Bio-Inspired Systems and Signal Processing (BIOSIGNALS), pp. 295–300 (2011)
3. Seikel, J.A., King, D.W., Drumright, D.G.: Anatomy and physiology for speech, language, and hearing. Delmar Learning (2009)
4. Silva, S., Martins, P., Oliveira, C., Silva, A., Teixeira, A.: Segmentation and Analysis of the Oral and Nasal Cavities from MR Time Sequences. In: Campilho, A., Kamel, M. (eds.) ICIAR 2012, Part II. LNCS, vol. 7325, pp. 214–221. Springer, Heidelberg (2012)
5. Scobbie, J.M., Wrench, A.A., van der Linden, M.: Head-Probe stabilisation in ultrasound tongue imaging using a headset to permit natural head movement. In: Proceedings of the 8th International Seminar on Speech Production, pp. 373–376 (2008)
6. Stone, M., Lundberg, A.: Three-dimensional tongue surface shapes of English consonants and vowels. J. Acoust. Soc. Am. 99, 3728–3737 (1996)
7. Livescu, K., Zhu, B., Glass, J.: On the phonetic information in ultrasonic microphone signals. In: IEEE Int. Conf. on Acoustics, Speech and Signal Processing (ICASSP 2009), pp. 4621–4624. IEEE (2009)

8. Hardcastle, W.J.: Physiology of speech production: an introduction for speech scientists. Academic Press, New York (1976)
9. Jorgensen, C., Dusan, S.: Speech interfaces based upon surface electromyography. Speech Commun. 52, 354–366 (2010)
10. Florescu, V.M., Crevier-Buchman, L., Denby, B., Hueber, T., Colazo-Simon, A., Pillot-Loiseau, C., Roussel-Ragot, P., Gendrot, C., Quattrocchi, S.: Silent vs vocalized articulation for a portable ultrasound-based silent speech interface. In: Proceedings of Interspeech 2010, pp. 450–453 (2010)
11. Hofe, R., Ell, S.R., Fagan, M.J., Gilbert, J.M., Green, P.D., Moore, R.K., Rybchenko, S.I.: Evaluation of a silent speech interface based on magnetic sensing. In: Proceedings of Interspeech 2010, pp. 246–249 (2010)
12. Alfonso, P.J., Baer, T.: Dynamics of vowel articulation. Lang. Speech. 25, 151–173 (1982)
13. Shankweiler, D., Harris, K.S., Taylor, M.L.: Electromyographic studies of articulation in aphasia. Arch. Phys. Med. Rehabil. 49, 1–8 (1968)
14. Teixeira, A., Martins, P., Oliveira, C., Ferreira, C., Silva, A., Shosted, R.: Real-time MRI for Portuguese: Database, methods and applications. In: Caseli, H., Villavicencio, A., Teixeira, A., Perdigão, F. (eds.) PROPOR 2012. LNCS (LNAI), vol. 7243, pp. 306–317. Springer, Heidelberg (2012)
15. Kent, R.D.: Some considerations in the cinefluorographic analysis of tongue movements during speech. Phonetica 26, 16–32 (1972)
16. Articulate Assistant Advanced Ultrasound Module User Manual, Revision 212, http://www.articulateinstruments.com/aaa/
17. Plux Wireless Biosignals, http://www.plux.info/
18. Freitas, J., Teixeira, A., Vaz, F., Dias, M.S.: Automatic Speech Recognition Based on Ultrasonic Doppler Sensing for European Portuguese. In: Torre Toledano, D., Ortega Giménez, A., Teixeira, A., González Rodríguez, J., Hernández Gómez, L., San Segundo Hernández, R., Ramos Castro, D. (eds.) IberSPEECH 2012. CCIS, vol. 328, pp. 227–236. Springer, Heidelberg (2012)
19. Freitas, J., Teixeira, A., Dias, M.S.: Multimodal Corpora for Silent Speech Interaction. In: 9th Language Resources and Evaluation Conference, pp. 1–5 (2014)
20. Silva, S., Teixeira, A.: Automatic Annotation of an Ultrasound Corpus for Studying Tongue Movement. In: Campilho, A., Kamel, M. (eds.) ICIAR 2014, Part I. LNCS, vol. 8814, pp. 469–476. Springer, Heidelberg (2014)

Towards Cross-Lingual Emotion Transplantation

Jaime Lorenzo-Trueba[1], Roberto Barra-Chicote[1],
Junichi Yamagishi[2], and Juan M. Montero[1]

[1] Speech Technology Group, ETSI Telecomunicacion,
Universidad Politecnica de Madrid, Spain
[2] National Institute of Informatics, Tokyo, Japan
{jaime.lorenzo,barra,juancho}@die.upm.es
jyamagish@nii.ac.jp

Abstract. In this paper we introduce the idea of cross-lingual emotion transplantation. The aim is to lean the nuances of emotional speech in a source language for which we have enough data to adapt an acceptable quality emotional model by means of CSMAPLR adaptation, and then convert the adaptation function so it can be applied to a target language in a different target speaker while maintaining the speaker identity but adding emotional information. The conversion between languages is done at state level by measuring the KLD distance between the Gaussian distributions of all the states and linking the closest ones. Finally, as the cross-lingual transplantation of spectral emotions (mainly anger) was found out to introduce significant amounts of spectral noise, we show the results of applying three different techniques related to adaptation parameters that can be used to reduce the noise. The results are measured in an objective fashion by means of a bi-dimensional PCA projection of the KLD distances between the considered models (neutral models of both languages, reference emotion for both languages and transplanted emotional model for the target language).

Keywords: Statistical Parametric Speech Synthesis, Expressive Speech Synthesis, Emotion Transplantation, Cross-lingual.

1 Introduction

In nowadays society we can see that computers are increasingly present: internet, smart phones, tablets or virtual agents are just a few examples of machines we have included in our daily life. In consequence, numerous fields of study around these machines have appeared. Among them, the study of human-machine interactions and interfaces pose a challenge, as providing simple and efficient communication interfaces could significantly reduce the gap in technology usability.

Speech synthesis is one of the most natural ways of providing such human-machines interfaces. The objective of speech synthesis systems is to produce artificial human speech by means of either hardware or software technologies. Nowadays speech synthesis can provide very good quality when producing neutral speech regardless of the technology [2] which is ideal for speech interfaces

J.L. Navarro Mesa et al. (Eds.): IberSPEECH 2014, LNAI 8854, pp. 199–208, 2014.
© Springer International Publishing Switzerland 2014

that do not need to engage in a conversation with the user. On the other hand, applications where simulating a more natural behavior is necessary, imbuing the synthetic speech with expressive features (e.g. emotions, speaking styles...) becomes very interesting. This is the role of expressive speech synthesis.

Expressive speech synthesis presents significant challenges: maintaining a good speech quality with traditional systems can be problematic because of how variable some expressiveness are, recording good quality stable expressive data is also difficult because it is difficult for non professionals to maintain stable speaking patterns even while speaking normally, and also as there are so many possible expressiveness that can be produced when talking in real life, it is nearly impossible to cover all of them. In the end, one of the biggest problems is data acquisition. The work proposed in this paper aims to fix one of the main shortcomings of expressive speech synthesis: scalability. We want to obtain a method capable of learning the expressive nuances of emotional speech, and transplant it to different speakers for whom we do not have any expressive information across languages.

One approach to emotion transplantation is the use of projective adaptation techniques such as Cluster Adaptive Training (CAT) [3], Eigenvoices [9] or Multiple-Regression Hidden Semi-Markov Models (MR-HSMM) [6]. These techniques are capable of imbuing emotions into the target adaptation speaker as long as the emotional data was included in the original training process because the output is always a combination of the training models, which at the same time makes them extremely robust and capable of providing very high speech quality transplanted models. As a shortcoming, the output can only take a limited amount of values, so speaker similarity cannot be guaranteed as the transplantation reach is constrained. Another approach is the use of rules to modify the features of the speaker models. This approach should theoretically be capable of modifying any neutral speaker model so that it conveys the desired emotion as long as the correct rules are applied. The truth is that these approaches are tipically capable of correctly imbuing the desired emotion and even provide reasonably good recognition rates [10], but speech quality degradation is a problem because the rules that are applyed are too coarse.

The paper is organized as follows: section 2 provides a brief state of the art of transplantation techniques and introduces the technique used by us in the cross-lingual transplantation, cross-lingual transplantation is introduced in section 3, and section 4 introduces the experimental framework applied to measure the problems of the proposed method. Finally in section 5 we give some brief conclusions and in section 6 we talk about the future work that we expect to carry out regarding the topic at hand.

2 Emotion Transplantation

Emotion transplantation methodologies can be defined as the procedures that allow the modification of a synthetic speech model to incorporate emotional information learned from other speaker models while maintaining the identity of the original speaker as much as possible. By this definition it follows that transplantation is a field of study that aims to solve one of the biggest problems in expressive speech synthesis: scalability.

A successful transplantation system should be capable of learning the paralinguistic nuances of the desired expressive speech model and then convert the target speaker model into a target speaker expressive model. But, as we would want the speaker identity to be maintained as much as possible, there are limitations on how much the features of the target speaker model should be modified [11]. In the end, systems have to reach a compromise between transplanted expressive strength and identifiability, synthetic speech quality and target speaker similarity. The considered transplantation technique attempts to combine the best features of both mainstream approaches to transplantation: adaptation to learn the function that converts a neutral model to substitute the rules while also being stable enough to provide good speech quality and complex enough to maintain the speaker identity.

2.1 Emotion Transplantation through Adaptation

The emotion transplantation process that we will apply in the proposed cross-lingual emotion transplantation system has been proven capable of correctly imbuing emotions into neutral speakers [5]. The system, whose flowchart can be seen in figure 1, relies on adaptation techniques for learning the transformation functions that characterize both speaker identity and emotional information. Then, the system applies both of them, and obtains the desired emotional target speaker model. All of this is done without requiring any kind of emotional information from the target speaker, which greatly helps reduce the scalability problems present in expressive speech synthesis.

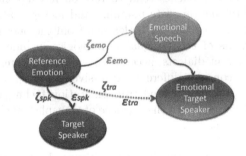

Fig. 1. Step by step block diagram of the emotion transplantation method. The spheres represent the speaker models and the arrows the adaptation transforms.

3   Cross-Lingual Emotion Transplantation

Cross-lingual processing is always difficult because of inter-language differences. Traditional approaches rely on phonetic mapping between the source and target

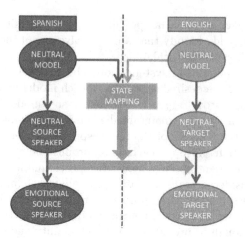

Fig. 2. Step by step block diagram of the emotion transplantation method. The spheres represent the speaker models and the thin arrows the adaptation transforms. The state mapping process is represented by the rectangle and the result of the mapping as the thick arrow. The two colors also represent the different languages.

languages at different levels in order to do a correspondence between what is done in the source language in hopes that if the same is done for the destination language, the results will be acceptable.

The first attempts at phonetic mapping relied on monophones or triphones without contextual information in order to establish direct relationships between languages [4,8], and evolved to using contextual information by exploiting the decision tree structures by measuring distances between tree nodes of both languages [14]. Different approaches tend to rely on having bilingual data for a single speaker and relying on state mapping and factor analysis techniques to extrapolate the knowledge that can be learned from the one speaker [16,17].

Typical applications of cross-lingual technologies include adapting speaker models between different dialects, accents, or variants of languages [12,13]. We believe that we can consider different expressiveness or speaking styles in the same fashion, and use our proposed transplantation technique combined with cross-language technologies with the purpose of transplanting paralinguistic features between languages.

3.1 Proposed Cross-Lingual Emotion Transplantation Method

The proposed cross-lingual emotion transplantation method is based on the state mapping principle [7]. The method begins by obtaining the mapping of the closest states amongst all states by means of the Karhunen-Loeve Divergence (KLD). Then, the emotional adaptation function obtained by means of the transplantation method is converted from the source model and source language to the target model and target language. Finally we apply the emotional transformation to the target language. A flowchart overviewing the complete process can be seen in figure 2.

4   Experimental Evaluation

Informal evaluations of the initial implementation of the cross-lingual emotion transplantation system showed that it is already capable of successfully transplanting the prosodic features between languages thanks to the state mapping technique, but a feature stream by feature stream transplantation showed that there is a significant amount of spectral noise introduced when transplanting the Cepstral information, specially in fundamentally prosodic emotions such as anger, which we will be using for the rest of the experimental evaluation section.

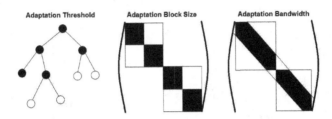

Fig. 3. Illustrations of the three different considered experimental variations. Black filled surfaces represent nonzero values.

In an attempt to quantify and lessen the effects of the introduced spectral noise we tried a number different experiments: increase the minimum number of frames per adaptation node, reduce the adaptation covariance transformation matrix block size and reduce the covariance adaptation bandwidth. We also developed an objective method to compare the results of the different approaches based on a combination of KLD and Principal Component Analysis (PCA). KLD is used to obtain the distances between all the speaker models used in the cross-lingual emotion transplantation process. PCA is used to project the KLD values into a bi-dimensional space that allows us to easily measure the distances in an objective way. This process is only done to the spectral features stream of the models as we want to measure the spectral distortion introduced to the process. In the ideal environment, the distance between the transplanted model (Korin-anger-S in the figures) and the target language model (Korin-neutral) should be the same as the distance between the source model (joa-anger-S) and the source language model (joa-neutral), which means obtaining a ratio of 1 in equation 1. The Spanish source data is a subsection of the SEV database [1], while the English target data was recorded in CSTR, University of Edinburgh.

4.1   Adaptation Function Occupancy Threshold

The first approach increased the adaptation function occupancy threshold. The purpose of this is to reduce the size of the decision tree used for the adaptation process in the source language by increasing the number of frames that must be present for each node (represented graphically in the first graph of figure 3). This produces more global transformation functions that convert the target language in a less complex fashion, potentially reducing the spectral noise introduced in the transplantation process. On the other hand, making use of more global adaptation functions means that there is less specificity in the transplantation, which could have an effect in the perceived emotion after transplanting.

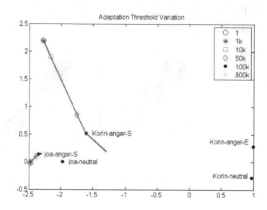

Fig. 4. PCA projection of the different adaptation threshold experiments in the anger cross-lingual extrapolation between joa (Spanish speaker) and Korin (English speaker). The prefix S stands for Spanish and E for English source data. The black dot is the reference system constant across experiments.

The results of this first experiments can be seen in figure 4, where it can be seen that while for lower threshold values there is no variation, for a very high value the distances between models clearly shrink, particularly between the emotional and neutral models of both languages. This means that using a higher threshold reduces the differences between the emotional and the neutral models.

4.2   Adaptation Variance Block Size

The second analysis aims to reduce the nonzero values in the adaptation function variance matrix by reducing the amount of intra-feature coefficients that influence each other (second illustration in figure 3). This means that, if in the standard block size every coefficient of a feature stream is able to influence each other, a smaller block size prevents the higher order coefficients from affecting lower ones.

The projection of the models obtained by manipulating the size of the blocks in the adaptation matrix can be seen in figure 5, and they show that both a

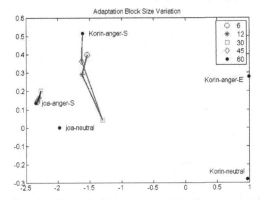

Fig. 5. PCA projection of the different adaptation block size experiments in the anger cross-lingual extrapolation between joa (Spanish speaker) and Korin (English speaker). The prefix S stands for Spanish and E for English source data. The black dot is the reference system constant across experiments.

big block size and a very small block size do not provide the optimal results, while an intermediate value provides less distant models. This is because a too small block size removes too many coefficients in the adaptation variance matrix, which results in a very coarse adaptation unable to deal correctly with emotional data [15].

4.3   Adaptation Variance Bandwidth

The final variant controls the values in the adaptation function variance matrix by only allowing a certain bandwidth of them around the diagonal to be nonzero as seen in the third illustration in figure 3. This approach also aims to reduce the interaction between higher and lower order coefficients in the adaptation of the feature streams, and it is supposedly smoother because there are no abrupt cuts in which coefficients affect each other. This approach makes special sense when using Linear Spectral Pairs (LSP) as the spectral features instead of Cepstral features, as the order of the coefficient correlates with the central frequency of the LSP. Thus, this approach directly limits the bandwidth that is considered in the adaptation process.

In the case of controlling the bandwidth of the adaptation variance matrix (figure 6) we can see that the lower the adaptation bandwidth the closest all the models become between each other. This translates into less noisy transplanted models but at the same time less expressive and identifiable models. This is also expected to give less expressive models as in the block size case.

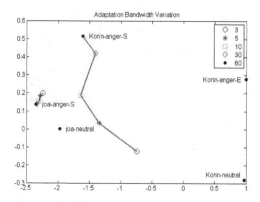

Fig. 6. PCA projection of the different adaptation bandwidth experiments in the anger cross-lingual extrapolation between joa (Spanish speaker) and Korin (English speaker). The prefix S stands for Spanish and E for English source data. The black dot is the reference system constant across experiments.

4.4 Perceptual Evaluation and Covariance Analysis

In an attempt to verify the validity of the objective measures, we carried out a small perceptual evaluation which aimed to obtain subjective speech quality results for all the considered systems. In this evaluation we presented the listeners with 14 different audio samples (one per system and only one at a time), and asked them to rate the perceived speech quality from 1 (very bad) to 5 (very high). A total of 14 utterances were synthesized according to the Latin square evaluation strategy in order to remove any bias in the evaluation process. Finally, we measured the correlation between a ratio of the model distances and the speech quality as follows:

$$corr(\frac{dist(TransplantedEnglish_i - NeutralEnglish)}{dist(EmotionalSpanish_i - NeutralSpanish)}, SpeechQuality_i) \quad (1)$$

In the results of measuring said correlation (table 1) we can see that there is a very strong relationship between the ratio of the distances between transplanted and source models and the perceived speech quality. This means that the proposed objective measure is a good tool of measuring how much we can improve speech quality compared to the initial cross-lingual transplantation system.

Table 1. Covariance analysis results for the three experimental environments

Evaluation System	Threshold	Block Size	Bandwidth
Measured Correlation	-0.948	-0.952	-0.893

5   Conclusions

We have set the foundations for a cross-lingual emotion transplantation system, where we are able to successfully convert the adaptation functions that convey emotional information from a source language (Spanish) to the desired target language (English) by means of a state mapping technique based on minimizing the KLD between neutral language models. This has enabled us to correctly modify the prosody and spectral components of the target speaker in the target language in the same fashion that we would have done in the source language, conveying then the desired emotion.

Preliminary evaluations show that there is a significant amount of spectral distortion introduced in the transplantation process. By measuring the KLD distance and projecting it into a bi-dimensional space with PCA we plotted the distances between the source and the transplanted models, providing us with an easy way of measuring the effects of our experiments. The experiments aimed to reduce the spectral noise by means of controlling different adaptation parameters such as the adaptation threshold or limiting the non-zero values of the adaptation variance matrix. The experiments showed that we should minimize the distances across neutral speaker models in both languages in order to obtain a really successful emotion transplantation across languages. We have also carried out a perceptual evaluation of the speech quality of the transplanted models that, by means of a correlation analisis, helped prove that the proposed objective measure is a good way of visualizing the transplantation results.

6   Future Work

Future work can be separated into two sections: first of all we want to record a bilingual neutral corpus in a controlled environment that we can use to evaluate the successfulness of the proposed technique when there are no environmental differences present. Secondly we also want to try different ways of minimizing the model variability such as applying Cepstral variance and mean normalization to the neutral speakers, or implementing environmental factoring in the average voice model training process.

Acknowledgements. Part of this work has been funded by, and carried out during the research stay of Jaime Lorenzo-Trueba at the National Institute of Informatics (NII) in Spring 2014. The work leading to these results has also received funding from the European Union under grant agreement 287678. It has also been supported by TIMPANO (TIN2011-28169-C05-03), INAPRA (MICINN, DPI2010-21247-C02-02), and MA2VICMR (Comunidad Autonoma de Madrid, S2009/TIC-1542) projects. Jaime Lorenzo has been funded by Universidad Politécnica de Madrid under grant SBUPM-QTKTZHB. The authors want to thank the other members of the Speech Technology Group, ARABOT and Simple4All projects for the continuous and fruitful discussion on these topics.

References

1. Barra-Chicote, R., Montero, J.M., Macias-Guarasa, J., Lufti, S., Lucas, J.M., Fernandez, F., D'haro, L.F., San-Segundo, R., Ferreiros, J., Cordoba, R., Pardo, J.M.: Spanish expressive voices: Corpus for emotion research in spanish. In: Proc. of LREC (2008)
2. Barra-Chicote, R.: Contributions to the analysis, design and evaluation of strategies for corpus-based emotional speech synthesis. Ph.D. thesis, ETSIT-UPM (2011)
3. Gales, M.J.: Cluster adaptive training of hidden markov models. IEEE Transactions on Speech and Audio Processing 8(4), 417–428 (2000)
4. Liang, H., Dines, J.: Phonological knowledge guided hmm state mapping for cross-lingual speaker adaptation. In: INTERSPEECH, pp. 1825–1828 (2011)
5. Lorenzo-Trueba, J., Barra-Chicote, R., Yamagishi, J., Watts, O., Montero, J.M.: Towards speaking style transplantation in speech synthesis. In: 8th ISCA Speech Synthesis Workshop (2013)
6. Nose, T., Kato, Y., Kobayashi, T.: Style estimation of speech based on multiple regression hidden semi-markov model. In: INTERSPEECH, pp. 2285–2288 (2007)
7. Oura, K., Yamagishi, J., Wester, M., King, S., Tokuda, K.: Analysis of unsupervised cross-lingual speaker adaptation for hmm-based speech synthesis using kld-based transform mapping. Speech Communication 54(6), 703–714 (2012)
8. Qian, Y., Xu, J., Soong, F.K.: A frame mapping based hmm approach to cross-lingual voice transformation. In: 2011 IEEE International Conference on Acoustics, Speech and Signal Processing (ICASSP), pp. 5120–5123. IEEE (2011)
9. Shichiri, K., Sawabe, A., Yoshimura, T., Tokuda, K., Masuko, T., Kobayashi, T., Kitamura, T.: Eigenvoices for hmm-based speech synthesis. In: INTERSPEECH (2002)
10. Takeda, S., Kabuta, Y., Inoue, T., Hatoko, M.: Proposal of a japanese-speech-synthesis method with dimensional representation of emotions based on prosody as well as voice-quality conversion. International Journal of Affective Engineering 12(2), 79–88 (2013)
11. Togneri, R., Pullella, D.: An overview of speaker identification: Accuracy and robustness issues. IEEE Circuits and Systems Magazine 11(2), 23–61 (2011)
12. Toman, M., Pucher, M., Schabus, D.: Multi-variety adaptive acoustic modeling in hsmm-based speech synthesis. In: 8th ISCA Speech Synthesis Workshop (2013)
13. Toman, M.E., Pucher, M.: Structural kld for cross-variety speaker adaptation in hmm-based speech synthesis. In: Proc. SPPRA, Innsbruck, Austria (2013)
14. Wu, Y.J., Nankaku, Y., Tokuda, K.: State mapping based method for cross-lingual speaker adaptation in hmm-based speech synthesis. In: INTERSPEECH, pp. 528–531 (2009)
15. Yamagishi, J., Kobayashi, T., Nakano, Y., Ogata, K., Isogai, J.: Analysis of speaker adaptation algorithms for hmm-based speech synthesis and a constrained smaplr adaptation algorithm. IEEE Transactions on Audio, Speech, and Language Processing 17(1), 66–83 (2009)
16. Yoshimura, T., Hashimoto, K., Oura, K., Nankaku, Y., Tokuda, K.: Cross-lingual speaker adaptation based on factor analysis using bilingual speech data for hmm-based speech synthesis. In: 8th ISCA Speech Synthesis Workshop (2013)
17. Zen, H., Braunschweiler, N., Buchholz, S., Knill, K., Krstulovic, S., Latorre, J.: Hmm-based polyglot speech synthesis by speaker and language adaptive training. In: Seventh ISCA Workshop on Speech Synthesis (2010)

A Preliminary Study of Acoustic Events Classification with Factor Analysis in Meeting Rooms

Diego Castán, Alfonso Ortega, Antonio Miguel,
and Eduardo Lleida

ViVoLab
Aragon Institute of Engineering Research (I3A)
University of Zaragoza
{dcastan,ortega,amiguel,lleida}@unizar.es
http://www.vivolab.es/

Abstract. The classification of acoustic events is useful to describe the scene and can contribute to improve the robustness of different speech technologies. However, the events are usually overlapped with speech or other sounds. This work proposes an approach based on Factor Analysis to compensate the variability of the acoustic events due to overlap with speech. The system is evaluated in the CLEAR evaluation database composed of recordings in meeting rooms where the acoustic events have been spontaneously generated in five different locations. The experiments are divided in two sets. Firstly, isolated acoustic events are used as development to analyze and evaluate parameters of the Factor Analysis system. Secondly, the system is compared to a baseline based on Gaussians Mixture Models with Hidden Markov Models. The Factor Analysis approach improves the total error rate due to the variability compensation of overlapped segments.

Keywords: Acoustic Events, Factor Analysis, Meeting Rooms, CLEAR Evaluation.

1 Introduction

Speech can be considered the most informative part of the audio. However, non-speech sounds can be useful to characterize situations of people, places or objects. These sounds are known in the literature as *acoustic events* (AEs) and can be critical to understand human activities or to describe the scene. *Acoustic Event Detection* (AED) aims at processing a continuous audio stream and determine what event has been produced and when. Therefore, the system must be able to produce labels to understand the concept behind the event. The symbolic description provided by the AED systems has been used in a wide variety of applications. For example, in [1] the authors detect events for surveillance. AED has been also widely used for monitoring people with disabilities. An example of this is given in [2] where people with dementia can be monitored in the bathroom to generate an automatic hygiene behavioral report.

J.L. Navarro Mesa et al. (Eds.): IberSPEECH 2014, LNAI 8854, pp. 209–218, 2014.

AED is very useful in the task of audio indexing and retrieval of multimedia documents or related tasks like multimedia event detection (MED) since it is an important resource of semantic description. For example, in [3], the authors combine the AEs with speech to detect five different multimedia events. Therefore, some approaches in this field try to compensate the variability with factor analysis (FA) techniques [4] or model the temporal relationship between events [5] to provide robustness to the AED system.

Another challenging field is the AED in meeting rooms because the AEs have low SNR and are overlapped with speech or other AEs. The 2007 AED CLEAR Evaluation [6] was performed on a database recorded in real seminars (five different locations) where the AEs were spontaneously generated, most of them are not highlighted and overlapped with speech. In this evaluation, the submitted systems showed low accuracies and high error rates (the winning system [7] got around 30% of accuracy and 99% of error rate) where the overlapping segments represent more than 70% of the errors. Subsequent investigations have dealt with the overlap problem in different ways. Since the meeting rooms in the evaluation are equipped with multiple cameras and multiple microphone arrays, in [8] the authors propose a multi-modal system because some of the AEs have a visual correlate and, therefore, the video modality can be exploited to enhance the detection rate. Also the authors use multiple microphones to know the position of the AE since some events can only occur at particular locations like "door slam". Another popular solution is the separation of overlapped signals with signal processing techniques. In [9], an approach based on partial signal separation using multiple array beamformers was proposed previously to an HMM-GMM classification system.

Since the CLEAR evaluation database was recorded in five different rooms with different furniture, the AEs present some variability that can be compensated. This work studies variability compensation techniques based on factor analysis with one microphone in this meeting room environment. The main goal is to increase the robustness in the classification of the AEs for each microphone so it does not interfere with multimodal or multichannel techniques that could be applied later. Due to the extremely high error rate shown in the CLEAR evaluation, this paper proposes a preliminary study where the segmentation is given by the labels to evaluate the classification of the proposed system and leaving the detection as a future work.

The remainder of the paper is organized as follows: section 2 describes the database and the metric for this task. The FA framework is described in section 3. Section 4 shows a comparative of the proposed system with a baseline and, finally, the conclusions are presented in section 5.

2   Database and Metric

2.1   Database

The database used in the CLEAR evaluation is composed of 25 meetings of approximately 30 minute long recorded in five different meeting rooms (AIT,

ITC, IBM, UKA and UPC). One meeting from each location have been used as training set and the rest of the meetings represents the test set. Also, a database with isolated AEs recorded at UPC [10] has been used to get some preliminary results, but these isolated events have not been used to train the final system.

The set of AEs composed of 12 semantic classes is summarized in Table 1. The classes of "speech", "unknown" and "silence" are not evaluated. 11% of the database is silence, 53% are "speech" and "unknown" classes and 36% of the time are AEs where most of them are overlapped with "speech" (64%) or other AEs (3%).

Table 1. Acoustic event classes with the corresponding annotation label and the number of the events in the train and test set

Event name	Label	Train	Test
Knoch in door or table	[kn]	82	152
Door slam	[ds]	73	75
Step	[st]	72	496
Chair moving	[cm]	238	226
Cup jingle	[cl]	28	27
Paper wrapping	[pw]	130	88
Key jingle	[kn]	22	32
Keybord typing	[kt]	72	105
Phone ringing or music	[pr]	21	25
Applause	[ap]	8	13
Cough	[co]	54	36
Laugh	[la]	37	154
Unknown (Unidentified sounds)	[un]	-	-
Speech	[sp]	-	-
Silence	[ ]	-	-

2.2 Classification Metric

In these experiments, the system has to classify correctly the segment which boundaries are given by the reference labels. The segments where two AEs are overlapped count twice (one for each event). The error rate for the acoustic event classification (AEC-ER) can be written as:

$$AEC - ER = \frac{number\ of\ segments\ incorrectly\ classified}{number\ of\ total\ segments} \qquad (1)$$

3 Factor Analysis Framework

We propose a framework for AED system that deals with the problem of assigning a class label to each fixed-length window using Factor Analysis (FA) models.

The FA approach has been successfully used in speaker recognition/verification, speaker diarization and in language recognition. In these tasks, the systems have to face several sources of variability such as speaker, channel and environment. The variability of the same class segments is known as *within-class variability*. The goal of these systems is to model or compensate the *within-class variability* to reduce the mismatch between training and test. In our task, the variability comes from the overlap of the AEs with speech and the different locations where the database has been recorded. The functionality of this system is described in the next subsections step by step.

3.1 Acoustic Feature Extraction

In this work we extract 16 MFCCs (including the zeroth order cepstrum) computed in 25 ms frames with a 10 ms frame step, their first and second derivatives. The feature vectors are normalized in mean for each file.

3.2 Channel Compensation

A particular class is modeled by a GMM defined by a set of mean vectors $m_1, m_2, ..., m_C$, weights $w_1, w_2, ..., w_C$ and covariance matrices $\Sigma_1, \Sigma_2, ..., \Sigma_C$ where C is the number of Gaussians. We can concatenate all GMM mean-vectors to one mean supervector m of dimension $CF \times 1$ where F is the feature vector length:

$$m = [m_1^T, m_2^T, ..., m_C^T]^T. \tag{2}$$

The Factor Analysis model is the adaptation of a general GMM model (known as Universal Background Model or UBM in the literature) where the supervector of means is not fixed and it can vary from segment to segment due to several sources that increase the within-class variability. We assume that these GMMs have segment and class dependent means but fixed weights and covariances chosen to be equal to the UBM weights and covariances. Specifically, we use a Factor Analysis model for the mean vector of the kth component of the GMM for segment s:

$$m^s = t^{c(s)} + Ux_s, \tag{3}$$

where $c(s)$ denotes the class of segment s. The class-location vector $t^{c(s)}$ is obtained by using a single iteration of relevance-MAP adaptation from the UBM. U is known as the *within-class variability matrix* and x_s is a vector of L *segment-dependent-within-class-variability factors* assumed to follow a normal distribution $(N(0, I_L))$. The columns of the U matrix are the basis spanning the subspace of the within-class variability and the *within-class variability factors* are the coordinates defining the position of the supervector in the subspace. The *within-class variability factor* dimension (L) is smaller than CF so U has low rank ($CF \times L$ dimensions). This paper does not aim to deepen in the FA theory and more details with an exhaustive description can be found in [11].

3.3   Class/Non-Class Models

Most of the approaches based on FA are implemented with a single U matrix because the segments are well-delimited (typically in separate files) and the nature of the within-class variability is similar for all the classes. However, in [12], an approach based on FA was proposed with class/non-class vectors (one class vector and one non-class vector for each class) and specific matrices modeling the within-class variability of each pair class/non-class as follows:

$$T = [t^{class}, t^{\overline{class}}] \tag{4}$$

$$U = U^{class - \overline{class}} \tag{5}$$

The main advantage of these models is that the final scoring can be more discriminative. For example, in the speaker ID tasks, the score to detect a speaker is the log-likelihood ratio test (LLRT):

$$LLRT_{class} = log \frac{P(\chi/class)}{P(\chi/UBM)}, \tag{6}$$

where the numerator is the likelihood for the class model and the denominator the likelihood for the UBM. Note that the UBM is used as a general model to describe the alternative hypothesis which is appropriate for speaker identification where the hypothesized speaker is not in the UBM. However, in a problem with a small number of classes, a non-class model can be trained to be used as the alternative hypothesis as:

$$CLLRT_{class} = log \frac{P(\chi/class)}{P(\chi/\overline{class})}, \tag{7}$$

where the alternative hypothesis is the likelihood for the non-class model which is compensated also with the with-in class variability matrix.

4   Experimental Results

Two different set of experiments have been carried out with a clear increase in the difficulty of the task. The first set is composed of isolated AEs with oracle boundaries and the second set verifies the quality of the models to classify the overlapped AEs when the boundaries are given. Only one microphone located in the center of the room (on the table) was used for both experiments to be able to capture all the activity of the meeting.

4.1   Classification of Isolated Acoustic Events

The AEs used in this experiments were recorded in the UPC smart-room for development. Although the AEs are the same than the CLEAR AEs shown in Table 1, these isolated AEs are not used in the posterior experiments because the AEs are not generated in an spontaneous way and they are not overlapped with speech or other AEs. However, this experiment is useful to study the behavior of the proposed system, to set some parameters and it shows how the errors are distributed among different AEs. The database is divided into three groups: two of them are used to train the model and the third one is used to test.

A GMM with 128 components has been used as a baseline system. Table 2 shows the error rate given by the metric of eq.(1). The same experiment has been done with FA where the UBM was also trained with 128 Gaussians over all the train set to be able to compare the results with the baseline. Table 2 shows the results of this experiment with the baseline and with FA for different values of τ. This parameter is known as *relevance factor* (τ) and it controls the MAP adaptation of the means of the model. If we increase the τ to infinite, the MAP will remain in the original UBM. On the other hand, if we decrease τ, the means will be more affected by the new frames. The results show that it is better to be more restrictive in movements of the means and, therefore, a $\tau = 250$ is chosen for the next experiments.

Table 2. Classification error rate for CHIL acoustic events with oracle segmentation

System	Error Rate %
GMM-128G	3.26
FA $\tau = 10$	5.22
FA $\tau = 30$	4.47
FA $\tau = 50$	4.24
FA $\tau = 100$	4.24
FA $\tau = 250$	3.26
FA $\tau = 500$	3.26

The error rate is equal with GMM and FA and no relevant conclusions can be drawn. However, this experiment allows to chose the τ parameter for next experiments with overlapped AEs. Also, Figure 1 shows the error of the classes with GMM and FA for different values of τ and, as it can be seen, only half of the AEs are not correctly classified once or more. Also, increasing τ, the classification accuracy improves. Finally, some AEs are better classified with GMM ([pw] and [pr]) and others are better classified with FA ([co] and [st]). We can conclude that both systems classify the isolated events easily because these AEs are artificially generated and there is not overlap with speech or other events. Therefore, the variability of each AE is very reduced and both systems classify with the same accuracy.

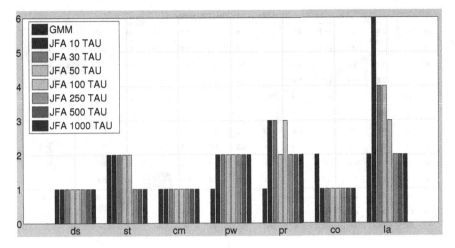

Fig. 1. Number of errors for each acoustic event

4.2   Classification of Spontaneous Acoustic Events

Following the procedure presented in the last subsection, this experiment is carried out with oracle segmentation over the CHIL database where the events can be overlapped with speech or other events increasing the difficulty dramatically. In addition, the audio has been recorded in five different locations which increase the variability of each event.

Table 3. Classification error rate for CHIL acoustic events with oracle segmentation

System	Error Rate %
GMM-128G	70.95
GMM-128G / one state HMM	70.88
FA-CLNoCL-10Chnf	75.71
FA-CLNoCL-10Chnf / one state HMM	75.57
FA-CL-10Chnf	71.09
FA-CL-10Chnf / one state HMM	**70.11**

Table 3 compares a baseline based on GMM, with FA system. The parameters for this experiment are the values fixed in the last subsection: 128 Gaussian for GMMs and UBM and $\tau = 250$ for the MAP adaptation. The first two rows show the error rate for a GMM-128G and the same GMM inside a one-state HMM where the transition probabilities have been estimated with the training labels improving slightly the results compared to the GMM system. The remaining rows show the error rate for the FA systems with two different scores: the FA-CLNoCL approaches employ eq.7 while the FA-CL approaches employ eq. 6. The results clearly show that the FA-CL approaches are more discriminative than the FA-CLNoCL since the model and the anti-model share common information due to

Confusion matrix GMM-128G HMM-1st

	kn	ds	st	cm	cl	pw	kj	kt	pr	ap	co	la	sp	si
kn	26.3	3.9	5.3	14.5	4.6	11.2	4.6	1.3	0.0	0.0	2.6	11.2	11.2	3.3
ds	1.3	40.0	13.3	21.3	0.0	1.3	0.0	0.0	0.0	0.0	1.3	6.7	2.7	12.0
st	0.8	0.2	22.8	13.9	1.4	6.2	0.0	0.6	0.0	0.2	0.0	1.8	32.5	19.6
cm	3.1	0.9	19.5	27.4	0.9	8.8	0.4	0.4	0.0	0.0	0.4	5.8	23.5	8.8
cl	11.1	7.4	3.7	14.8	18.5	11.1	7.4	0.0	0.0	0.0	0.0	18.5	3.7	3.7
pw	0.0	0.0	20.5	21.6	0.0	30.7	1.1	2.3	0.0	0.0	0.0	4.5	12.5	6.8
kj	0.0	0.0	0.0	21.9	0.0	31.2	31.2	3.1	0.0	0.0	3.1	9.4	0.0	0.0
kt	1.9	0.0	17.1	5.7	1.9	8.6	0.0	6.7	0.0	0.0	0.0	1.0	25.7	31.4
pr	0.0	0.0	12.0	8.0	24.0	0.0	0.0	0.0	8.0	0.0	4.0	8.0	24.0	12.0
ap	7.7	7.7	7.7	7.7	0.0	0.0	0.0	0.0	0.0	69.2	0.0	0.0	0.0	0.0
co	0.0	0.0	2.8	8.3	2.8	2.8	0.0	0.0	0.0	0.0	47.2	22.2	11.1	2.8
la	1.3	0.0	4.5	13.6	0.6	4.5	0.0	0.6	0.0	0.0	0.6	61.0	9.1	3.9
	kn	ds	st	cm	cl	pw	kj	kt	pr	ap	co	la	sp	si

(a)

Confusion matrix FA-CL-10Chnf HMM-1st

	kn	ds	st	cm	cl	pw	kj	kt	pr	ap	co	la	sp	si
kn	36.8	6.6	6.6	2.6	4.6	7.2	5.9	5.3	0.0	2.6	5.9	5.3	5.9	4.6
ds	2.7	42.7	5.3	9.3	5.3	0.0	0.0	4.0	0.0	0.0	20.0	2.7	6.7	1.3
st	6.2	1.8	26.8	8.5	3.2	3.6	1.8	5.8	2.0	1.2	6.2	3.2	17.1	12.3
cm	12.4	2.7	16.4	14.2	4.9	4.9	0.4	8.8	1.8	0.0	6.2	8.8	12.4	6.2
cl	7.4	3.7	14.8	0.0	33.3	7.4	7.4	11.1	0.0	0.0	0.0	3.7	3.7	7.4
pw	8.0	1.1	12.5	8.0	2.3	30.7	1.1	3.4	1.1	0.0	5.7	5.7	11.4	9.1
kj	0.0	3.1	9.4	0.0	6.2	18.8	28.1	0.0	0.0	3.1	9.4	6.2	3.1	12.5
kt	5.7	1.0	18.1	1.0	2.9	4.8	1.0	24.8	1.0	1.0	2.9	1.9	15.2	19.0
pr	8.0	8.0	12.0	0.0	24.0	0.0	0.0	4.0	8.0	0.0	0.0	16.0	16.0	4.0
ap	7.7	7.7	0.0	0.0	7.7	7.7	0.0	0.0	0.0	69.2	0.0	0.0	0.0	0.0
co	13.9	5.6	5.6	8.3	5.6	0.0	2.8	5.6	2.8	0.0	38.9	11.1	0.0	0.0
la	6.5	1.3	4.5	3.9	3.9	5.2	1.9	4.5	0.6	0.0	5.8	46.8	9.1	5.8
	kn	ds	st	cm	cl	pw	kj	kt	pr	ap	co	la	sp	si

(b)

Fig. 2. Confusion matrices for (a) GMM-128G / HMM-1st and (b) FA-CL-10Chnf / HMM-1st

events overlapped with speech. Therefore, the best result is given for the system FA-CL which slightly improves the final result with the transition probabilities compared to the HMM-GMM.

Finally, Figure 2 shows the confusion matrices with the classification percentage in each event combination for the best two systems: GMM-128G with one state HMM approach and the FA-CL with one state HMM approach. Some conclusion can be drawn from these figures. First, the GMM system tends to classify the AEs as "speech" [sp] or "silence" [si] more easily than the FA which shows that the FA system compensates the variability due to the speech in the overlapped AEs. Also, the FA system classifies better the events "Door Knock" [kn], "Door Slam"[ds], "Steps" [st], "Cup Jingle" [cl] and "Keyboard Typing" [kt].

On the other hand, the events "Chair Moving" [cm], "Key Jingle" [kj], "Cough" [co] and "Laugh" [la] have been better classified with GMM. The rest of the AEs have been classified with identically accuracy. A final count shows that the GMM and the FA have correctly classified 416 and 421 AEs respectively from a total of 1429 AEs.

5 Conclusions

The presented work focuses on the classification of AEs that may happen in a meeting room when the segmentation is given using the CLEAR evaluation database. Since the database is composed of tracks recorded in five different locations and the events can be overlapped with speech, the AEs present a variability that can be compensated with FA techniques. Two sets of experiments have been carried out in this work. The first one evaluates the FA system over isolated AEs. This isolated AEs database has been used as a development to choose the *relevance factor* (τ) of the MAP adaptation for the FA systems. The second set of experiments evaluates the FA system with spontaneous generated AEs that can be overlapped with speech or other AEs. The proposed system improves the results of a baseline system based on GMM/HMM slightly. The confusion matrices of both systems suggest that the FA system compensates the variability due to the speech in the overlapped AEs. However, there is still a big room from improvement since the classification error is very high. Therefore, further work needs to be done to improve the classification of overlapping sounds and the application of FA techniques to the detection problem.

Acknowledgements. This work has been funded by the Spanish Government and the European Union (FEDER) under the project TIN2011-28169-C05-02 and INNPACTO IPT-2011-1696-390000.

References

1. Atrey, P.K., Maddage, N.C., Kankanhalli, M.S.: Audio Based Event Detection for Multimedia Surveillance. In: 2006 IEEE International Conference on Acoustics Speed and Signal Processing Proceedings, pp. V–813–V–816 (2006)
2. Chen, J., Zhang, J., Kam, A.H., Shue, L.: An Automatic Acoustic Bathroom Monitoring System. In: 2005 IEEE International Symposium on Circuits and Systems, pp. 1750–1753 (2005)
3. van Hout, J., Akbacak, M., Castan, D., Yeh, E., Sanchez, M.: Extracting Spoken and Acoustic Concepts For Multimedia Event Detection. In: IEEE International Conference on Acoustics, Speech, and Signal Processing (ICASSP), pp. 2–6 (2013)
4. Huang, Z., Cheng, Y.-C., Li, K., Hautamaki, V., Lee, C.-H.: A Blind Segmentation Approach to Acoustic Event Detection Based on I-Vector. In: Proc. Interspeech, pp. 2282–2286 (August 2013)
5. Castan, D., Akbacak, M.: Indexing Multimedia Documents with Acoustic Concept Recognition Lattices. In: Interspeech, pp. 3–7 (2013)

6. Temko, A., Malkin, R., Zieger, C., Macho, D.: Acoustic event detection and classification in smart-room environments: Evaluation of CHIL project systems. IV Jornadas en Tecnología del Habla, 1–6 (2006)
7. Zhou, X., Zhuang, X., Liu, M., Tang, H., Hasegawa-Johnson, M., Huang, T.: HMM-based acoustic event detection with AdaBoost feature selection. In: Stiefelhagen, R., Bowers, R., Fiscus, J. (eds.) RT 2007 and CLEAR 2007. LNCS, vol. 4625, pp. 345–353. Springer, Heidelberg (2008)
8. Butko, T., Camprubí, C.N.: Detection of overlapped acoustic events using fusion of audio and video modalities. In: Proc. FALA, pp. 165–168 (2010)
9. Chakraborty, R.: Acoustic Event Detection and Localization using Distributed Microphone Arrays. PhD thesis (2013)
10. Temko, A., Macho, D., Nadeu, C., Segura, C.: UPC-TALP Database of Isolated Acoustic Events. In: Internal UPC report (2005)
11. Kenny, P., Boulianne, G., Ouellet, P., Dumouchel, P.: Joint Factor Analysis Versus Eigenchannels in Speaker Recognition. IEEE Trans. Audio Speech Lang. 15(4), 1435–1447 (2007)
12. Castan, D., Ortega, A., Villalba, J., Miguel, A., Lleida, E.: Segmentation-By-Classification System Based on Factor Analysis. In: IEEE International Conference on Acoustics, Speech, and Signal Processing (ICASSP) (2013)

A Spoken Language Database for Research on Moderate Cognitive Impairment: Design and Preliminary Analysis

Fernando Espinoza-Cuadros[1], Marlene A. Garcia-Zamora[2], Dania Torres-Boza[3],
Carlos A. Ferrer-Riesgo[3], Ana Montero-Benavides[1], Eduardo Gonzalez-Moreira[3],
and Luis A. Hernandez-Gómez[1]

[1] Departamento de Señales, Sistemas y Radiocomunicaciones,
Universidad Politécnica de Madrid, Madrid, Spain
{fernando,ana.montero,luis}@gaps.ssr.upm.es
[2] Center for Elderly Adults #2, Santa Clara, Cuba
garcia.zamora@capiro.vcl.sld.cu
[3] Center for Studies on Electronics and Information Technologies,
Universidad Central "Marta Abreu" de Las Villas, Santa Clara, Cuba
{moreira,dtb}@uclv.edu.cu

Abstract. This paper addresses the use of spoken language technologies to identify cognitive impairment through the degree of speech deficits. We present the design of a spoken language database where patients' voices are collected during regular clinical screening tests for cognitive impairment. Three different speaking styles are recorded: dialogues during structured interviews, readings of a short-passage and verbal picture descriptions. We hope these different spoken materials will help promoting the research on a wide range of spoken language technologies in assessing Moderate Cognitive Impairment (MCI). To illustrate this, a preliminary analysis on the speech recorded from a small group of MCI patients and healthy elder controls is also presented. A Random Forest classifier working on seven prosodic measures extracted from the reading task achieved 78.9% accuracy for MCI detection when compared with a control group, suggesting that these measures can offer a sensitive method of assessing speech output in MCI. This experimental framework shows the potential of the presented spoken language database for the research on automatic and objective identification of early symptoms of MCI in elderly adults.

Keywords: moderate cognitive impairment, spoken language database, prosodic analysis.

1 Introduction

Cognitive impairment is a syndrome with largest impact among elderly people, leading to dependency of the patient from their families or caregivers. Beyond all reasonable doubt cognitive impairment affects in an enormous way the quality of life of patients and their families due to the impossibility of patients to carry out their daily tasks. A general agreement of the experts in the field revealed that not only 36 million

J.L. Navarro Mesa et al. (Eds.): IberSPEECH 2014, LNAI 8854, pp. 219–228, 2014.
© Springer International Publishing Switzerland 2014

people live with mild or moderate cognitive impairment worldwide but 4.6 million new cases appear annually [1].

Moderate Cognitive Impairment (MCI) is one of the earliest, and generally underdiagnosed, stages of cognitive decline where sustained decrease of cognitive functions is insufficiently severe to warrant a diagnosis of MCI [2]. Since MCI often progress to Alzheimer's disease (AD), its detection in early or prodromal phase is a current challenge. Also an early detection of the MCI becomes an important goal, allowing either the use of alternative non-pharmacological therapies or short periods of pharmacological treatments, to slow down the development of cognitive deterioration.

Although several neurophysiological tests exists (e.g. using MRI [3] or CSF biomarkers [4]), patients generally attend consultations with memory complaints, and the first step usually involves a screening test based on structured interviews. A questionnaire test such as the Mini-Mental State Examination (MMSE) [5], Clinical Dementia Rating (CDR) [6] or Memory Impairment Screen (MIS) [7] are commonly used.

It is at these early screening stages where we think that spoken language technologies can contribute to explore new automated methods for screening and characterizing MCI. Due to the fact that one of the most significant areas affected by MCI disease is language, many researches have been settled in this direction, showing that language impairment is strongly related to cognitive impairment some years before patient is clinically diagnosed [8] [9].

In [10] authors propose assessing MCI through automatic analysis of patients' spoken productions while retelling of a brief narrative previously read by a clinician. This is done according the Wechsler Logical Memory (WLM) subtest of the Wechsler Memory Scale; a test used for memory and language functioning assessment. Speech recordings from both a story-recall test and a picture description test were used in a speech-based automated method for cognitive status assessment presented in [11]. In this work, manual and automatic transcriptions of the speech from these two types of tests were compared for detecting how many semantic content units the speaker has uttered. Speech analysis techniques for early detection of cognitive impairment have also been tested on segments of dialogue collected during structured interviews, as, for example, in [12], where authors analyze speech corresponding to the HDS-R questionnaire test about time orientation and number counting. However, as stated in [12], the language used in structured interviews cannot capture the richer information that spontaneous conversations provides, so spontaneous speech has also been researched for automatic detection and rating of dementia of Alzheimer type (see for example [13] [14]). In some other studies, as [15] and [16], prosodic analysis of speech samples recorded from short-text passage readings, including the analysis of pause and utterance duration distributions, has been proposed for differentiating between cognitively healthy and impaired older adults.

It is in line with these previous studies on spoken language technologies to assess MCI, that we present (Section 2) the design of a spoken language database directed to collect different speaking styles from populations with different stages of cognitive decline. We believe this database will foster the research on the potential for different spoken language technologies in this field. After presenting our database we also illustrate, in Section 3, some preliminary results of MCI detection using a Random Forest classifier working on prosodic measures extracted from speech corresponding to the reading task. Conclusions and future research lines are given in the last section of the paper.

2   Spoken Language Database to Study MCI

2.1   Protocol and Speaking Styles

Two major conflicting criteria were considered for the design of the recording protocol in our database. On the one side, it should represent the minimum possible burden on the busy schedules of daily clinical practices, while on the other side it should collect the richest variety of speaking styles which can result in a notable increase in testing time.

Consequently we decided to design a protocol consisting on three sequential parts. During the first part we recorded the speech productions from both clinician and patient during structured interviews commonly used in clinical assessment procedures. More specifically we considered the *Mini Examen Cognoscitivo* (MEC) which is the Spanish version of the Mini-Mental State Examination (MMSE) [2].

As pointed out in the Introduction, other speaking styles beyond dialogues in structured interviews can provide more valuable information. Therefore a second part was included to collect speech while patients read a short-passage. In particular we selected a Spanish version of the paragraph "The Grandfather Passage" [17] (see Figure 2). This text is a short reading that has evolved into a ubiquitous metric of reading ability and speech intelligibility. Finally, in the third part of our database protocol, the picture in Figure 2 is shown to patients asking them to describe it in detail. This picture is included in standard aphasia evaluation instruments, such as the WAB test [4]. In this way during a single clinical session not only conversational speech from structured interviews but also read and spontaneous speech is recorded.

2.2   Recording Tools and Procedures

Also trying to make the process of speech recording the less annoying as possible for a daily clinical practice, two different tools were developed. The first one consisted on the use of a standard laptop equipped with two headworn condenser C520L AKG microphones for capturing both clinician and patient voices. Each microphone was connected to a different channel (left or right) of an M-audio ADC device connected to the laptop through an USB port. This configuration provides some acoustic separation, although no complete isolation, of patient and clinician voices thus making it easier their further processing. A specific software DCGrab v3.0, shown in Figure 1, was created by the authors to allow an easy recording of the audio signals during each one of the three parts in the recording protocol. The speech sound was recorded in stereo format with 16 bits of resolution and 44.1 KHz of sampling rate. The DCGrab v3.0 software also allows storing clinical data and demographic information for each patient.

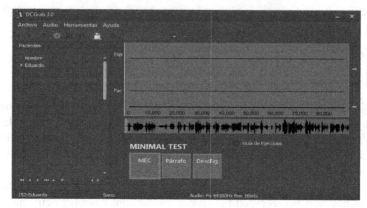

Fig. 1. DCGrab v3.0 software

A second tool, DCTest App (see Figure 2), was developed for Android tablets trying to have a more portable device suitable for some specific clinical practice environments. In this case audio from both patient and clinician is recorded using a single AKG CBL 410 Conference microphone. The Android App also allows the clinician to annotate her results from the MEC test.

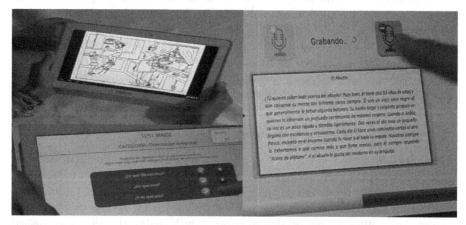

Fig. 2. DCTest App for Android Tablets

3   Preliminary Analysis

3.1   Experimental Setup

To have a first insight on the possibilities of the speech material collected using the protocol previously described, we present a preliminary experiment for a sample of nineteen subjects with more than sixty years of age, including MCI patients and healthy subjects (Non-MCI). Other inclusion criteria were basic reading skills and no significant visual impairments. Demography data are shown in Table 1 and no significant differences between groups were found in terms of gender, age or years of education.

Table 1. Subject demographic data

Item	Group	
	MCI	Non-MCI
Number of patients	8	11
Male	6	5
Female	2	6
Average Age (Years)	80.3	78.9
Average Education (Years)	5	8

For this experimental study only the speech recorded while reading the Spanish version of the paragraph "The Grandfather Passage" was used.

3.2   Prosodic Analysis

Following an approach similar to [16], we explored the capabilities of using some prosodic features to detect patients with cognitive impairment and healthy controls. For each subject seven prosodic features were obtained from the speech recorded during the reading test by using the prosogram program [19]:

1. speech time (**SPT**): total time from first syllable to last syllable produced.
2. number of pauses (**NPU**): total number of silences over 0.3s.
3. proportion of pause (**PPU**): total number of pauses over 0.3s divided by the total amount of time spent speaking expressed in seconds.
4. phonation time (**PHT**): total time of all syllables produced plus silences lower than 0.3s.
5. proportion of phonation (**PPH**): total time of all syllables produced plus silences lower than 0.3s divided by the amount of time.
6. speech rate (**SPR**): total number of syllables produced in a given speech sample divided by the amount of total time (including pause time).
7. articulation rate (**ARR**): total number of syllables produced in a given speech sample divided by the amount of time taken to produce them in seconds.

Table 2 shows the mean, standard deviation, and range for every prosodic measure on both groups (MCI and non-MCI). Visual inspection reflects that differences between subjects with MCI and healthy subjects could be found on some measures like NPU and ARR. Other measures like PPU and PPH show small differences suggesting further discriminant analysis to corroborate whether the measures have power to discriminate between classes.

Table 2. Prosodic features for MCI and heathy controls (Non-MCI)

Features	MCI		Non-MCI	
	Mean(SD)	Range	Mean(SD)	Range
SPT	177.3(47.8)	119.1-235.8	128.3(63.7)	59.2-249.7
NPU	107.2(21.7)	78.0-130.0	61.9(33.3)	27.0-124.0
PPU	58.8(14.2)	45.3-75.0	47.4(10.9)	30.7-64.8
PHT	69.3(20.4)	57.2-99.9	62.1(20.6)	33.5-107.2
PPH	41.1(14.2)	24.9-54.6	52.5(10.9)	35.1-69.2
SPR	2.1(0.6)	1.4-2.7	2.5(0.6)	1.6-3.6
ARR	5.3(0.4)	4.9-5.9	4.7(0.5)	4.3-6.3

In order to determine if both groups of prosodic measures differ significantly the Kolmogorov-Smirnov test (KS-test) was employed [20]. The KS-test has the advantage of making no assumption about the distribution of data. The decision to reject the null hypothesis occurs when the significance level (0.05) equals or exceeds the p-value. Summary of results for Kolmogorov-Smirnov test are shown in Table 3 using the p-values to sort measure's relevance to differentiate between both groups.

Table 3. Statistic analysis results for Kolmogorov-Smirnov test

Features	Kolmogorov-Smirnov	
	h	p-values
NPU	1	0.016
ARR	1	0.044
SPT	0	0.235
PPU	0	0.235
PPH	0	0.235
SPR	0	0.584
PHT	0	0.728

3.3   Cognitive Impairment Detection

In order to explore the capabilities of the extracted prosodic features for cognitive impairment detection, they were used as inputs to a Random Forest (RF) trained to predict the group (MCI or healthy patients) of the subject under analysis. A Random Forest is an ensemble of classifiers $\{h(x,\Phi_k), k =1,...\}$ where $\{ \Phi_k \}$ are independent identically distributed random vectors and each tree cast a vote for the most popular class at input x [21].

In experimental contexts with small data sets, as is our case, a Random Forest would be able to keep the probability of over-fitting low by using different subsets of the training data and different subsets of features for each tree of the forest. The Random Forest performance depends on a fixed set of parameters but doesn't require much tuning.

For this experiment, different values of RF parameters were tested regarding those that have high dependence on classification performance. The parameters selected were the number of trees to grow and the number of features randomly sampled as candidates at each split. In addition, to include additional protection against over-fitting, throughout this work the standard leave-one-out cross-validation was used. Specifically this technique sequentially discards one subject and uses it as a test sample; the remaining subjects are used as training data. The process is repeated for each sample (*n times*) and the percentage of correct classifications is generated through averaging for the *n* trials. In our case *n* is equal to the total number of participants (*n* = 19), and in each iteration of the cross-validation method, one fold is used for testing and the other eighteen folds are used for training the RF classifier.

Running the random forest in 100 repetitions the best average classification rate (78.9 %) was achieved by using 20 trees and 4 variables randomly sampled. The computed results are summarized in Table 4.

Table 4. Random forest classification results for all features

Group	Correct	Error	Correct Classification (%)
Non-MCI	9	2	81.8
MCI	6	2	75
Total	15	4	78.9

An important feature of random forests is the possibility to measure the relevance of each attribute (or input variable). There are two methods to measure this attribute relevance [21]. The first method analyzes each attribute and reveals its importance in predicting the correct classification of the random forest classifier. The analysis is made by using internal out-of-bag examples. Then the attribute under analysis is random permuted in the out-of-bag examples. The new data set is then tested in the random forest classifier. The importance attribute is the average over all trees of the difference between the number of correct classification of the original out-of-bag examples and the number of correct classification of the new data set created as from the modified attribute. The second method is based on the Gini coefficient, which measures how each variable contributes to impurity of the nodes and leaves in the resulting random forest. Figure 3 shows the variable importance measured by both methods.

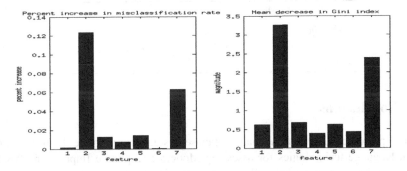

Fig. 3. Measure of variable importance

Figure 3 shows that the features NPU (variable 2: number of pauses) and ARR (variable 7: articulation rate) are the most significant attributes. In order to go in depth about the influence of the most significant attributes on the random forest classifier, the prediction experiments were repeated running the random forest in 100 repetitions, with 20 trees, 4 variables randomly sampled and using the most significant attributes random permuted (NPU, AAR).

Table 5. RF classification results for sigfinicant features

Trial	Correctly Classified Instances (%)
All attributes	78.9
NPU	66.5
NPU, ARR	57.4
All others	74.0

Table 5 shows a strong influence between the classification performance and the attribute selected. Randomly permuting only NPU the incorrect classification rate increases to 33.4 %, compared to 21.1 % when using all attributes. But when attribute ARR is also permuted the error raises to 42.5 %. In contrast, just permuting the values of all others attributes the incorrect classification rate is almost close to the one obtained when all variables are used. This results show that the variables NPU and ARR carry significant predictive information at the moment of classify a subject. These results confirm the previous analysis made by means Kolmogorov-Smirnov test (KS-test) (Table 3).

Finally the results of this study are compared against the findings of previous works where prosodic speech features are used to identify cognitive impairment. Table 6 summarizes the classification accuracies for the Random Forest and other published methods notwithstanding the data and features selection were different in each case.

Table 6. Comparison of the performance of different databases and classifiers

Classifier	Correct Classification (%)
Random Forest MCI	78.9
SVM [10]	80.9
CNG [13]	69.6
CCV [12]	87.5

4   Conclusions

We have presented a spoken language database designed to promote the research on spoken language technologies for assessing Moderate Cognitive Impairment (MCI). Patients' voices were recorded during a structured interview, a short-passage reading and the verbal description of a picture. A preliminary analysis using prosodic parameters extracted from the reading task and a Random Forest classifier achieved a 78.9 % of correct classification between healthy controls and MCI patients. Future efforts will be focused on expanding the sample of subjects under study and to explore the possibilities of applying different spoken language technologies to this field.

Acknowledgements. This research was supported in part by "CMC-V2: Caracterización, Modelado y Compensación de Variabilidad en la Señal de Voz" TEC2012-37585-C02-02 and "Herramienta de Apoyo al Diagnóstico Médico del Deterioro Cognitivo mediante el Procesamiento Digital de Voz" award. Furthermore the authors thank the Center for Elderly Adults #2 from Santa Clara, Cuba, for their meticulous care and effort in collecting the data. Finally authors acknowledge Carmen Pardo Noguera for the development of DCTest App for Android Tablets.

References

1. Llibre, J.J.: Aging and dementia: implications for the scientist community, public health and Cuban society. Rev. Academia de Ciencias de Cuba 2(2), 36–54 (2012)
2. Montenegro Peña, M., Montejo Carrascoa, P., LlaneroLuquea, M., Reinoso García, A.I.: Evaluación y diagnóstico del deterioro cognitivo leve. Revista de Logopedia, Foniatría y Audiología 32, 47–56 (2012)
3. De Leon, M.J., De Santi, S., Zinkowski, R., Mehta, P.D., Pratico, D., Segal, S., Clark, C., Kerkman, D., De Bernardis, J., Li, J., Lair, L., Reisberg, B., Tsui, W., Rusinek, H.: MRI and CSF studies in the early diagnosis of Alzheimer's disease. Journal of Internal Medicine 256, 205–223 (2004)
4. De Leon, M.J., Mosconi, L., Blennow, K., DeSanti, S., Zinkowski, R., Mehta, P.D., Rusinek, H.: Imaging and CSF studies in the preclinical diagnosis of Alzheimer's disease. Annals of the New York Academy of Sciences 1097(1), 114–145 (2007)
5. Folstein, M.F., Folstein, S.E., McHugh, P.R.: Mini-mental state. A practical method for grading the cognitive state of patients for the clinician. J. Psychiatr. Res. 12(3), 189–198 (1975)
6. Morris, J.C.: The Clinical Dementia Rating (CDR): current version and scoring rules. J. Neurology 43, 2412–2414 (1993)
7. Buschke, H., Kuslansky, G., Katz, M., Stewart, W.F., Sliwinski, M.J., Eckholdt, H.M., Lipton, R.B.: Screening for dementia with the Memory Impairment Screen. Neurology 52(2), 231–238 (1999)
8. Deramecourt, D., Lebert, F., Debachy, B., Mackowiak-Cordoliani, M.A., Bombois, S., Kerdraon, O., et al.: Prediction of pathology in primary progressive language and speech disorders. Neurology 74, 42–49 (2010)
9. Mesulam, M., Wicklund, A., Johnson, N., Rogalski, E., Léger, G.C., Ra-demaker, A., et al.: Alzheimer and frontotemporal pathology in subsets of primary progressive aphasia. Annual Neurology 63, 709–719 (2008)
10. Lehr, M., Prud'hommeaux, E., Shafran, I., Roark, B.: Fully automated neuropsychological assessment for detecting mild cognitive impairment. In: Interspeech 2012 (2012)
11. Hakkani-Tür, D., Vergyri, D., Tür, G.: Speech-based automated cognitive status assessment. In: INTERSPEECH, pp. 258–261 (2010)

12. Kato, S., Endo, H., Homma, A., Sakuma, T., Watanabe, K.: Early detection of cognitive impairment in the elderly based on Bayesian mining using speech prosody and cerebral blood flow activation. In: 2013 35th Annual International Conference of the IEEE Engineering in Medicine and Biology Society (EMBC), pp. 5813–5816 (2013)
13. Thomas, C., Keselj, V., Cercone, N., Rockwood, K., Asp, E.: Automatic detection and rating of dementia of Alzheimer type through lexical analysis of spontaneous speech. In: 2005 IEEE International Conference on Mechatronics and Automation, vol. 3, pp. 1569–1574 (2005)
14. Bucks, R.S., Singh, S., Cuerden, J.M., Wilcock, G.K.: Analysis of spontaneous, conversational speech in dementia of Alzheimer type: Evaluation of an objective technique for analysing lexical performance. Aphasiology 14, 71–91 (2000)
15. Rochford, I., Rapcan, V., D'Arcy, S., Reilly, R.B.: Dynamic minimum pause threshold estimation for speech analysis in studies of cognitive function in ageing. In: 2012 Annual International Conference of the IEEE Engineering in Medicine and Biology Society (EMBC), pp. 3700–3703 (2012)
16. Martínez-Sánchez, F., Meilán, J.J.G., García-Sevilla, J., Carro, J., Arana, J.M.: Análisis de la fluencialectora en pacientes con la enfermedad de Alzheimer y controles asintomáticos. Neurología 28(6), 325–331 (2013)
17. Darley, F.L., Aronson, A.E., Brown, J.R.: Motor speech disorders, 3rd edn. W.B. Saunders Company, Philadelphia (1975)
18. Risser, A.H., Spreen, O.: The western aphasia battery. Journal of Clinical and Experimental Neuropsychology 7(4), 463–470 (1985)
19. Mertens, P.: Automatic segmentation of speech into syllables. In: Laver, J., Jack, M. (eds.) Proceedings of the European Conference on Speech Technology, Edinburgh, vol. 2, pp. 9–12 (1987)
20. Massey Jr., F.J.: The Kolmogorov-Smirnov test for goodness of fit. Journal of the American Statistical Association 46(253), 68–78 (1951)
21. Breiman, L.: Random Forest. Machine Learning 45, 5–32 (2001)

Towards Customized Automatic Segmentation of Subtitles

Aitor Álvarez, Haritz Arzelus, and Thierry Etchegoyhen

Human Speech and Language Technologies, Vicomtech-IK4, San Sebastián, Spain
{aalvarez,harzelus,tetchegoyhen}@vicomtech.org
http://www.vicomtech.org/

Abstract. Automatic subtitling through speech recognition technology has become an important topic in recent years, where the effort has mostly centered on improving core speech technology to obtain better recognition results. However, subtitling quality also depends on other parameters aimed at favoring the readability and quick understanding of subtitles, like correct subtitle line segmentation. In this work, we present an approach to automate the segmentation of subtitles through machine learning techniques, allowing the creation of customized models adapted to the specific segmentation rules of subtitling companies. Support Vector Machines and Logistic Regression classifiers were trained over a reference corpus of subtitles manually created by professionals and used to segment the output of speech recognition engines. We describe the performance of both classifiers and discuss the merits of the approach for the automatic segmentation of subtitles.

Keywords: automatic subtitling, subtitle segmentation, machine learning.

1 Introduction

Automatic subtitling has recently attracted the interest of the speech and natural language processing research communities, notably after the adoption of new audiovisual legislation by the European Parliament in 2007. This legislation regulates the rights of people with disabilities to be integrated in the social and cultural life of the Community, through accessible audiovisual contents by means of sign-language, audio-description and subtitling. As a result, the demand for automatic subtitling has grown rapidly, with public and private TV channels moving to produce subtitles for larger volumes of their content. The effort has focused on quantity in a first step, in order to match legislative requirements, but there is an increasing demand for an improvement in the quality of automatically generated subtitles as well.

The quality of subtitles involves several parameters linked to subtitle layout, duration and text editing. Layout parameters include: the position of subtitles on screen; the number of lines and amount of characters contained in each line; typeface, distribution and alignment of the text; colors for front and

J.L. Navarro Mesa et al. (Eds.): IberSPEECH 2014, LNAI 8854, pp. 229–238, 2014.

background; different colors per speaker; and transmission modes, i.e. blocks or scrolling/word-by-word. Duration parameters involve delay in live subtitling and the persistence of subtitles on screen. Finally, text editing parameters are related to capitalization and punctuation issues, segmentation and the use of acronyms, apostrophes and numerals.

Among these quality features, the strong need for proper segmentation is supported by the psycholinguistic literature on reading [11], where the consensual view is that subtitle lines should end at natural linguistic breaks in order to favor readability and minimize the cognitive effort produced by poorly segmented text lines [21].

In order to address the need to tackle subtitle quality aspects beyond bare speech recognition and to provide solutions adaptable to the standard guidelines and specific rules of companies, we explored a flexible approach based on machine learning techniques and tested it on the automated segmentation task. Specifically, we trained Support Vector Machines and Logistic Regression classifiers on subtitle corpora created by professional subtitlers and used the resulting models to filter and select optimal segmentation candidates. The results we present involve the use of these two classifiers for the automatic segmentation of subtitles in Basque, although the approach is not language-specific as it only requires properly segmented training material of the type created by subtitling companies under their own guidelines.

This processing pipeline for segmentation has been integrated into the automatic subtitling system described in [3], taking the output of speech processing engines to provide customized segmented subtitles.

The paper is structured as follows. Section 2 describes existing solutions and studies regarding automatic subtitling and segmentation. Section 3 looks at standard issues and considerations for the segmentation of subtitles. Section 4 describes the machine learning approach we implemented. Section 5 presents the experiments and evaluation results. Finally, Section 6 draws conclusions and describes future work.

2 Related Work in Automatic Subtitling

There is extensive research focused on automatic subtitling, mainly through the using of Automatic Speech Recognition technology for the recognition and alignment tasks [2,6,13]. Most of the work in the area has centered on improving recognition accuracy and producing well-synchronized subtitles. Audimus [17] is a reference system in the field, as it provides a complete framework for automatic subtitling of broadcast news contents with low error rates in both batch and live modes. It includes an automatic module for subtitle generation and normalization aimed at improving readability, but segmentation is performed minimally, using only information about the maximum amount of characters permitted per line. The Audimus system was improved and extended to several languages within the European project SAVAS[1]. Many quality features were considered in

---

[1] http://www.fp7-savas.eu/

the development of the new systems, but technology for automatic segmentation was not included.

Although considerable importance is commonly placed on most of the quality parameters described above, proper line-breaking has generally been disregarded [20]. A survey of the literature in the field actually provides no references on the topic of automatically segmenting subtitles. A few studies were carried out on related topics, as can be found for instance in [20], which explores the way line-breaking is commonly performed, and in [21] which studies the impact of arbitrary segmented subtitles on readers. The importance of segmentation has been noted by [23], a study whose aim was to verify whether text chunking over live re-spoken subtitles had an impact on both comprehension and reading speed. They concluded that even though significant differences were not found in terms of comprehension, a correct segmentation by phrase or by sentence significantly reduced the time spent reading subtitles.

3 Subtitle Segmentation

3.1 Standard Guidelines

A number of guidelines for subtitling have been published over the years. Among well-known ones are: Ofcom's Guidance on Standards for Subtitling[2]; BBC's Online Subtitling Editorial Guidelines[3] ; ESIST's Guidelines for Production and Layout of TV Subtitles[4], the Spanish UNE 153010 norm [1] on subtitling for the deaf and hard of hearing and a reference textbook on generally accepted subtitling practice published in 2007 by Jorge Diaz-Cintas and Aline Remael [10]. Standard guidelines cover the various aspects of subtitle quality, such as subtitle segmentation, and standard practices along these recommendations are shared among subtitling companies and broadcasters.

In terms of segmentation, all standard recommendations conclude that it must benefit and improve readability. For this purpose, considering syntactic information to create linguistically coherent line-breaks is the preferred and most adopted solution in the community. This follows from results in psycholinguistic research, which show that readers analyze texts in terms of syntactic information [9], grouping words corresponding to syntactic phrases and clauses [8]. Reading subtitles is a similar task and subtitles for which segmentation is not based on coherent syntactic groups can thus be assumed to trigger sub-optimal reading [15]. In order to facilitate readability, subtitle lines should thus be split according to coherent linguistic breaks, and the generally accepted solution is to operate the splits at the highest possible syntactic node. This ensures that fragments split along these lines encompass the largest possible amount of related semantic information.

---

[2] http://www.ofcom.org.uk/static/archive/itc/itc_publications/
codes_guidance/standards_for_subtitling/subtitling_1.asp.html
[3] http://www.bbc.co.uk/guidelines/futuremedia/accessibility/
subtitling_guides/online_sub_editorial_guidelines_vs1_1.pdf
[4] http://www.translationjournal.net/journal/04stndrd.htm

3.2   Issues in Automatic Segmentation

Although the strong need for proper segmentation and the general constraints that apply to it are clear, there are issues regarding the implementation of automated segmentation.

First, as the previously described guidelines are fairly general in terms of what constitutes a proper subtitle split, there is actual variation among professional subtitlers when it comes to executing the actual segmentation. These variants are usually reflected as distinct sets of company-specific rules, which makes a generic automated solution all the more difficult to achieve as such a solution would have to either disregard company-specific rules or require resource-consuming adaptation of syntactic rule sets on a case by case basis.

Secondly, the automatic detection of the highest syntactic node requires language processing tools for sentence analysis. For major languages like Spanish or English, several such tools are available, e.g. Freeling [18], OpenNLP [4] or the parsers developed by the Berkeley [22] and Stanford [5] groups. For other languages, particularly under-resourced ones, there can be a lack of robust natural language analyzers, which would limit the possibilities of using a syntax-based approach for segmentation.

Finally, a correct syntactic analysis and detection of the highest nodes in subtitles does not guarantee proper segmentation. Several other features have to be considered simultaneously, such as the amount of characters, timing issues and, as previously mentioned, the specific splitting rules used by each subtitling company. All these features have a clear impact on proper subtitle segmentation and need to be taken into account for each specific subtitle.

An ideal solution for the automatic segmentation of subtitles would thus have to (1) correspond to the specific rules used by each subtitling company, and (2) simultaneously consider all relevant information like character sequence length and timing.

In the remainder of the paper, we present a possible solution that involves the use of machine learning classifiers to create segmentation models adapted to each company's needs, thus providing a highly customizable and language-independent solution. This approach has the additional advantage of allowing the simultaneous integration of different features to reach optimal segmentation.

4   Machine Learning for Automatic Segmentation

This section describes the core components of the machine learning approach we followed. We define the automatic segmentation problem as a binary classification task, where subtitles with correct or incorrect segmentation are split into two classes. Positive (correct) feature vectors were extracted from professionally-created subtitle data and contain the segmentation marks found in the corpus; negative (incorrect) vectors were generated by automatically inserting improper segmentation marks. Classifiers were then trained on balanced sets formed with these two types of vectors and used for the segmentation task.

4.1 Corpus Characteristics

The corpus used to train and test the classifiers was composed of subtitles that were manually created by professional subtitlers for TV cartoon programs in Basque, for a total amount of 158,011 subtitles. The files were provided in SRT format, indicating start and end time codes for each subtitle and presented in blocks of a maximum of two lines. The corpus was split between training and test sets containing 80% and 20% of the data, respectively. The subtitles in the corpus were manually generated considering subtitle layout, duration and text editing features. In particular, the segmentation rules followed by the subtitlers focused on maintaining linguistic coherence, splitting subtitles according to the highest possible syntactic node.

4.2 Corpus Processing

In order to train classifiers, both positive and negative examples are necessary, from which to extract feature vectors suitable for the task. We thus prepared a balanced set of positive and negative sets by transforming the original subtitles into a task-specific format. Positive examples were generated by merging consecutive lines in reference subtitles into a single sentence containing the original segmentation mark. Each such transformed sentence was then used as a basis to generate a set of negative examples, by moving the original correct segmentation symbol to other positions in the sentence. All possible negative training examples were generated in a first step, each with a different segmentation point, and a randomly selected subset of these possible incorrect examples was used to balance the amount of positive and negative training elements.

Table 1 provides examples of transformed subtitles, including positive and negative candidates.

Table 1. Training data. The #S# mark denotes a segmentation symbol. The <S1> and <S2> marks correspond to speaker information marks.

Reference subtitles	Transformed data (examples)	Label
1 00:00:47,430 → 00:00:49,448 <S1>Lapitza eta erregela. 2 00:00:51,283 → 00:00:54,660 <S2>Ez dira berdinak, ezta pentsatu ere.	Lapitza eta erregela. #S# Ez dira berdinak Ez dira berdinak, #S# ezta pentsatu ere. Lapitza #S# eta erregela. Ez dira berdinak Lapitza eta #S# erregela. Ez dira berdinak Lapitza eta erregela. Ez #S# dira berdinak ...	Correct Correct Incorrect Incorrect Incorrect ...

Training sentences were thus composed of two parts corresponding to each line in a subtitle and divided by the #S# symbol. Features were computed on each of the parts and on the entire sentence as well. Each feature vector was then categorized with the corresponding label.

4.3   Feature Vectors

The features extracted from the transformed data can be divided into four types of characteristics related to (1) timing, (2) number of characters, (3) speaker change and (4) perplexity as given by a language model built over the training data. A feature vector was calculated for each of the sentences in the transformed data and used to train the classifiers.

The timing feature involved the time difference between the first and second parts of each sentence in the transformed data. It was calculated from the start time of the first word of the second part and the end time of the last word of the first part. Since the reference subtitles provided just the time-codes of the first and last words at subtitle level, the forced alignment system for Basque presented in [3] was used to obtain the start and end times-codes for all the words.

To characterize aspects related to the number of characters, three features were calculated from the transformed data. The first two contained the amount of characters of the first part and second part of each sentence, respectively, and the third feature indicated the total number of characters in the entire (bi-)sentence.

Speaker change information was available in the reference subtitles and converted into a boolean value: speaker changes were defined to have value 1 if true and 0 otherwise.

The last feature indicated the perplexity value given by a language model built on the correct sentences in the transformed data. Given that Basque is a morphologically rich language and considering the scarcity of the training data, the language model was built using part-of-speech (POS) information. For this end, the Eustagger [12] toolkit was used, which includes a morphological analyser and a POS tagger for Basque. An unpruned 9-gram language model was estimated using the KenLM toolkit [14], with modified Kneser-Ney smoothing [16]. The average perplexity value was 24.25 on the test set.

4.4   Segmentation Algorithm

As previously mentioned, the automatic segmentation module was integrated into our automatic subtitling system for Basque. This system produces alignments between audio signal and transcripts, thus producing time-codes for each word and providing a basis for the complete generation of subtitles. The segmentation module benefits from the automatically aligned and time-coded words to create candidates for segmentation. These candidates are then measured against the machine-learned models and optimal candidates selected according to the score obtained by their feature vectors. The algorithm for candidate generation and selection is described below.

```
INITIALIZE start_index to zero;
INITIALIZE end_index to one;
SET max_length to maximum length of characters per subtitle;
CALL get_words() RETURNING words;
while end_index is less than length of words do
    COMPUTE generate_candidates(start_index,end_index);
    if exist_valid_candidates() then
        CALL get_best_candidate() RETURNING cut_index;
        COMPUTE insert_cut (cut_index);
        SET previous_maxindex to end_index + 1;
        SET start_index to cut_index + 1;
        SET end_index to start_index + 1;
        SET right_block to words (start_index...end_index);
    else
        if length of right_block is greater than one then
            COMPUTE insert_cut (previous_maxindex);
            SET start_index to previous_maxindex + 1;
            SET end_index to start_index + 1;
        else
            SET start_index to start_index + 1;
            SET end_index to start_index + 1;
        end
    end
end
```

Algorithm 1: Segmentation procedure

The procedure for the generation and selection of segmentation candidates is shown in Algorithm 1. Processing of the text to be segmented is iterative, with validated insertion points taken as new starting points for further processing of the remainder of the text. In other words, we compute segmentation points through short windows of text and repeat the process on the yet unprocessed text after an optimal segmentation has been found for the current window.

Potential points of segmentation are inserted between sequences of consecutive words, where the sole constraint is a maximum allowed sequence length before and after segmentation points. That is, neither sequence on either side of a potential segmentation point can have more characters than this fixed value, which is computed at the beginning of the process and comes from the maximum length in characters for a subtitle line, as observed in the training data. The candidates are created through the subroutine generate_candidates(). The initial candidates correspond to all combinations of the current sequence of words and segmentation points. Each candidate thus includes only one segmentation point and the set of all candidates covers the space of potential segmentation points for the current window of words. Feature vectors are then extracted for each candidate and classified according to the previously trained models. In order to reduce the list of current candidates into a more manageable set, we only retain candidates with a model-predicted probability above a fixed threshold. Empirical determination for the task at hand yielded a fixed value of 0.7 for this threshold.

The sub-function exist_valid_candidates() checks for the existence of any valid candidate in the filtered set. If the test is positive, the best candidate is selected through the sub-routine get_best_candidate(), which returns the candidate with the highest probability according to the model. In case of a tie, the longest candidate is selected. The sequence of words to the right of the last segmentation point is then stored for the next iteration. As this sequence has already been determined to be a an autonomous sequence at this point, it is taken as an indivisible block in the next iteration, i.e. no new segmentation points can be set between the words that compose it.

If exist_valid_candidates() indicates no candidates at all, the last stored sequence is considered. If this sequence consists of more than one word, a segmentation point is inserted by default; if it contains just one word, the case is taken to be identical to processing the first word of the text: new sequences and candidates are generated from the sequences that include this word and the next ones.

5   Experiments and Evaluation

Several experiments were carried out using Support Vector Machines (SVM) and Logistic Regression (LR) classifiers using the LibSVM [7] and Scikit-learn [19] toolkits respectively. For the SVM classifier, after testing and comparing different combinations of Kernel functions and methods to perform multi-class classification, the Radial Basis Function (RBF) kernel with nu-support vector classification (nu-SVC) algorithm was selected, as this setup gave the best results. The LR classifier was trained through Stochastic Gradient Descent (SGD). Fig. 1 presents results in terms of F-1 measure for each of the test files for both classifiers.

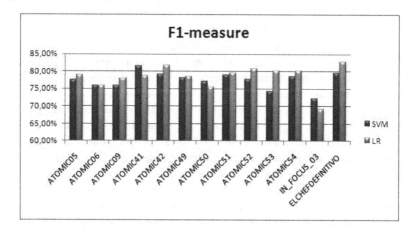

Fig. 1. Segmentation accuracy using SVM and LR classifiers

The results demonstrated similar performance for the two classifiers, with an average score of 74.71% and 76.12% for the SVM and LR classifiers, respectively. In terms of precision and recall, the SVM classifier obtained scores of 82% and 69%. In contrast, the LR classifier achieved a precision of 85% and a recall of 69%. Interestingly, both classifiers reached identical recall, showing that on average almost seven out of ten segmentation points are correctly identified in this approach. Combining this result with precision scores above 80%, the general approach can be seen as promising.

6   Conclusions and Future Work

We presented a novel approach to automatic subtitle segmentation which generates and selects optimal segmentation points according to the predictions made by machine-learned classifiers. This method provides a customized solution to company-specific segmentation guidelines and rules, as the models are strictly induced from existing segmented corpora and generate similar segmentation on new input. Additionally, the approach fills a void as far as generating quality subtitles is concerned, given that automatic subtitle segmentation, which is a crucial quality feature, has been somewhat neglected within the research community. Finally, the method offers a versatile solution as it permits the addition of new features to further tune and improve classification models and subsequent segmentation accuracy.

The preliminary results we have presented are quite satisfactory, with an average recall of nearly 70% and precision above 80% on the test set of a professionally-created corpus of TV cartoon programs in Basque.

In future work, we will pursue experiments on additional corpora, to further evaluate the approach with different domains. More languages will also be tested, as different linguistic characteristics can have an impact on segmentation results, notably in terms of language-dependent infelicitous line endings. We will also explore the impact of including additional features to train classifiers, and evaluate the performance of different feature sets. For instance, incorporating perplexity scores from additional language models trained on surface forms and morphemes might prove beneficiary, as the models would thus include a measure of superficial linguistic knowledge which can be assumed to further improve the proper segmentation of subtitles.

References

1. AENOR: Spanish Technical Standards. Standard UNE 153010:2003: Subtitled Through Teletext, http://www.aenor.es
2. Álvarez, A., del Pozo, A., Arruti, A.: APyCA: Towards the Automatic Subtitling of Television Content in Spanish. In: Proceedings of IMCSIT, pp. 567–574. IEEE, Wisla (2010)
3. Álvarez, A., Ruiz, P., Arzelus, H.: Improving a Long Audio Aligner through Phone-Relatedness Matrices for English, Spanish and Basque. In: Sojka, P., Horák, A., Kopeček, I., Pala, K. (eds.) TSD 2014. LNCS (LNAI), vol. 8655, pp. 473–480. Springer, Heidelberg (2014)

4. Baldridge, J.: The OpenNLP Project (2005), http://opennlp.sourceforge.net/
5. Baldridge, J.: Stanford Parser 1.6 (2007),
   http://nlp.stanford.edu/software/lex-parser.shtml
6. Bordel, G., Peñagarikano, M., Rodríguez-Fuentes, L.J., Varona, A.: A Simple and Efficient Method to Align Very Long Speech Signals to Acoustically Imperfect Transcriptions. In: Proceedings of INTERSPEECH, Portland (2012)
7. Chang, C.C., Lin, C.J.: Libsvm: A Library for Support Vector Machines. ACM Transactions on Intelligent Systems and Technology (TIST) 2(3), 27:1–27:27 (2011)
8. Coltheart, M.: What Would We Read Best? Attention and Performance II: The Psychology of Reading. Lawrence Erlbaum Associates, London (1987)
9. D'Arcais, F., Giovanni, B.: Syntactic Processing during Reading for Comprehension. Attention and Performance II: The Psychology of Reading, pp. 619–633. Lawrence Erlbaum Associates, London (1987)
10. Díaz-Cintas, J., Orero, P., Remael, A.: Media for All: Subtitling for the Deaf, Audio Description, and Sign Language, vol. 30. Rodopi (2007)
11. D'Ydewalle, G., Rensbergen, J.V.: Developmental Studies of Text-Picture Interactions in the Perception of Animated Cartoons with Text. Advances in Psychology, vol. 58, pp. 233–248. Elsevier, Amsterdam (1989)
12. Ezeiza, N., Alegria, I., Arriola, J.M., Urizar, R., Aduriz, I.: Combining Stochastic and Rule-based Methods for Disambiguation in Agglutinative Languages. In: Proceedings of the 36th Annual Meeting of the Association for Computational Linguistics, vol. 1, pp. 380–384, Montreal (1998)
13. Automatic Captions in YouTube (2009),
    http://googleblog.blogspot.com/2009/
    11/automatic-captions-in-youtube.html
14. Heafield, K.: KenLM: Faster and Smaller Language Model Queries. In: Proceedings of the Sixth Workshop on Statistical Machine Translation, pp. 187–197, Edinburgh (2011)
15. Karamitroglou, F.: A Proposed Set of Subtitling Standards in Europe. Translation Journal 2(2), 1–15 (1998)
16. Kneser, R., Ney, H.: Improved Backing-off for n-gram Language Modeling. In: Proceedings of ICASSP, pp. 181–184, Detroit (1995)
17. Neto, J., Meinedo, H., Viveiros, M., Cassaca, R., Martins, C., Caseiro, D.: Broadcast News Subtitling System in Portuguese. In: Proceedings of ICASSP, pp. 1561–1564, Las Vegas (2008)
18. Padró, L.: Stanilovsky. E.: FreeLing 3.0: Towards Wider Multilinguality. In: Proceedings of the 8th Language Resources and Evaluation Conference, Istanbul (2012)
19. Pedregosa, F., et al.: Scikit-learn: Machine Learning in Python. The Journal of Machine Learning Research 12, 2825–2830 (2011)
20. Perego, E.: Subtitles and line-breaks: Towards improved readability. In: Between Text and Image: Updating Research in Screen Translation, vol. 78, pp. 211–223. John Benjamins Publishing (2008)
21. Perego, E., Del Missier, F., Porta, M., Mosconi, M.: The Cognitive Effectiveness of Subtitle Processing. Media Psychology 13(3), 243–272 (2010)
22. Petrov, S., Klein, D.: Improved Inference for Unlexicalized Parsing. In: Proceedings of HLT-NAACL, pp. 404–411, Rochester (2007)
23. Rajendran, D.J., Duchowski, A.T., Orero, P., Martínez, J., Romero-Fresco, P.: Effects of Text Chunking on Subtitling: A Quantitative and Qualitative Examination. Perspectives 21(1), 5–21 (2013)

Bootstrapping a Portuguese WordNet from Galician, Spanish and English Wordnets*

Alberto Simões[1] and Xavier Gómez Guinovart[2]

[1] Centro de Estudos Humanísticos
Universidade do Minho, Portugal
ambs@ilch.uminho.pt
[2] Seminario de Lingüística Informática
Universidade de Vigo, Spain
xgg@uvigo.es

Abstract. In this article we exploit the possibility on bootstrapping an European Portuguese WordNet from the English, Spanish and Galician wordnets using Probabilistic Translation Dictionaries automatically created from parallel corpora.

The process generated a total of 56 770 synsets and 97 058 variants. An evaluation of the results using the Brazilian OpenWordNet-PT as a gold standard resulted on a precision varying from 53% to 75% percent, depending on the cut-line. The results were satisfying and comparable to similar experiments using the WN-Toolkit.

Keywords: WordNet, Portuguese, probabilistic translation dictionaries, parallel corpora, knowledge acquisition.

1 Introduction

For the Portuguese community there is a lack of a good, complete and free accessible WordNet. There are lot of different projects whose main goal is to construct such a resource, but most are incomplete, not free, or heavily based on machine translation.

We propose and evaluate a method to bootstrap an European Portuguese WordNet using the Galician, Spanish and English wordnets as guidance, and using Probabilistic Translation Dictionaries (PTDs) for their Portuguese translation. The main difference on this approach when compared with others, namely the Unified Wordnet [12] or the WN-Toolkit [15], is the use of probabilistic translation dictionaries that, being probabilistic and automatically generated, give a wider set of translations, rather than the small set of possible translations usually presented on standard bilingual lexicons.

Also, we want to exploit the proximity of the Portuguese language with the Galician language. Although we do not have access to a big bilingual lexicon for

---

* This research has been carried out thanks to the Project SKATeR (TIN2012-38584-C06-01 and TIN2012-38584-C06-04) supported by the Ministry of Economy and Competitiveness of the Spanish Government.

J.L. Navarro Mesa et al. (Eds.): IberSPEECH 2014, LNAI 8854, pp. 239–248, 2014.
© Springer International Publishing Switzerland 2014

these two languages, a rewriting method to bring Portuguese closer to Galician was used [19].

This bootstrapped version will be incorporated into Multilingual Central Repository [9,1]. From this base work we plan corrections and different expansion works, using similar approaches to the ones being taken by GalNet [4].

This document is structured as follows: first we discuss briefly similar approaches to this task (Section 2), followed by a presentation on the resources that were used in our experiments (Section 3). In Section 4, the algorithm used in this research is explained using a specific synset example. Section 5 evaluates the obtained results, and in Section 6 we draw some conclusions and point some directions in our future work.

2   Similar Approaches

There are different initiatives on the creation or enlargment of wordnets and similar lexical databases. In this section we will focus mainly three of these initiatives.

Onto.PT [7] includes more than 117,000 synsets. These synsets were computed using different mechanisms, and incorporating data from different sources. A big amount of relations were computed using patterns over conventional electronic dictionaries [8]. Some other were extracted processing Wikipedia [6]. The authors also incorporated data from other lexical resources, like TeP 2.0 [11], OpenWordNet-PT [17] or OpenThesaurus.PT.

WN-Toolkit [15] is a lexical extraction tool for the creation of wordnets from bilingual resources, including lexical resources (such as bilingual dictionaries) and textual resources (such as parallel corpora), which has already been used for expanding the Catalan, Spanish and Galician wordnets [5].

Universal WordNet [12] initiative used the Princeton WordNet, other monolingual wordnets, bilingual dictionaries and parallel corpora to bootstrap wordnets in more than 200 languages. The resulting resource, looking to the Portuguese language, includes only 23,500 synsets. Unfortunately the resulting resource was only used for some cross-lingual text classification, and no results are presented for the Portuguese language.

3   Used Resources

This section describes the resources used in our experiments, namely the English, Galician and Spanish wordnets, a set of probabilistic translation dictionaries, a dynamic Portuguese-Galician dictionary and the *Vocabulário Ortográfico do Português* (Portuguese Orthographic Vocabulary or VOP).

3.1   English, Spanish and Galician Wordnets

The English WordNet, known as Princeton WordNet [13], was used to guide our extraction as other languages wordnets usually rely on the Interlingual Index (ILI) to synchronize concepts with it. We used the English WordNet version 3.0 as it is the base for the current Spanish and Galician wordnets.

The Spanish [2] and Galician [4] wordnets were obtained from the Multilingual Central Repository [9,1]. This project aims to integrate the wordnets for the languages of Spain in a similar repository, together with the English WordNet 3.0.

Table 1 presents some statistics on English, Galician and Spanish wordnets.

Table 1. Number of synsets and variants of English, Galician and Spanish wordnets, distributed by part-of-speech

		Nouns	Verbs	Adjectives	Adverbs	Total
English	Syn.	82 889	13 769	18 156	3 621	118 435
	Var.	147 358	25 051	30 004	5 580	207 993
Galician	Syn.	16 812	1 413	4 962	223	23 419
	Var.	22 186	3 996	7 884	253	34 319
Spanish	Syn.	26 594	6 251	5 180	677	38 702
	Var.	39 142	10 829	6 967	1 051	57 989

3.2   Probabilistic Translation Dictionaries

PTDs (or probabilistic translation dictionaries) are dictionaries obtained with NATools [20] by the word-alignment of parallel corpora. Unlike other tools, like Giza++ [14] that aims on extracting a relationship between each occurrence of a word and a specific occurrence of its translation, NATools extracts a single mapping for each source-language word. Each mapping associates a set of possible translations (in the parallel corpora) together with a probability measure of it being a correct translation.

Consider the following example of a PTD entry:

$$
\mathcal{T}(\text{codificada}) = \begin{cases} \text{codified} & 62.83\% \\ \text{uncoded} & 13.16\% \\ \text{coded} & 6.47\% \\ \dots \end{cases}
$$

This example states that the Portuguese word *codificada* is usually co-ocurrent with the English words *codified*, *coded* and *uncoded*. Other than this co-ocurrence information, the dictionary adds a probability measure to each possible co-ocurrent word. When these resources are extracted from aligned parallel corpora, it is usual that this co-occurrence can be seen as a translation measure. Nevertheless, and as presented in the example, it might happen that some relations are not really translations of each other: they might be related (like the fact of *uncoded* being the antonym of *codificada*), or not related at all. Nevertheless, as a statistical measure, we expect it to be have a small probability for these situations.

The PTDs used in this experiment were extracted both from the Per-Fide corpora[1] and the CLUVI [3] corpus. From the Per-Fide project we extracted dictionaries between Portuguese–Spanish and Portuguese–English. From the CLUVI corpus we extracted a Spanish–Galician dictionary. Using the composition [18] of PT–ES and ES–GL dictionaries we obtained a PT–GL dictionary.

Given that wordnets do not include word forms, the corpora were lemmatized and tagged using FreeLing [16]. Thus, the corpora words were replaced by the pair `lemma/pos` before the PTD extraction. This results on a better translation dictionary.

3.3 Portuguese–Galician Dictionary

There is not a wide translation dictionary for the PT–GL languages. Nevertheless, given the big proximity of the two languages, and despite the fact of existing some false friends, it is possible to rewrite, with a reasonable precision, Portuguese words in their Galician counterparts [19].

This kind of approach can be seen as a dynamic dictionary, as new words, as far as they follow the usual pattern, can be translated by the tool without the need of a lexicon.

3.4 Portuguese Orthographic Vocabulary

The *Vocabulário Ortográfico do Português* (VOP)[2] is a list of 182 012 lemmas of Portuguese words, together with their part-of-speech. For our work we just considered the list of lemmas, discarding all other information.

4   Algorithm

The bootstrapping algorithm uses a "score" approach. Different variants are generated, together with an associated score. As other languages or heuristics are analyzed, the system adapts the variant score accordingly. The variants with higher score are then returned.

In order to explain the approach we will explain the process for a specific synset, reference `00008007-r`, that corresponds to an adverb.

The first step is to search, in each wordnet, for this synset. The Spanish WordNet does not include this synset, but it exists for the other two languages:

$$variants_{EN} = \{all, altogether, completely, entirely, totally, whole, wholly\}$$
$$variants_{GL} = \{completamente, totalmente\}$$

---

[1] The corpora available in the Per-Fide project includes most of the free available corpora in the Web, like EuroParl, JRC-Acquis or the DGT Translation Memories, as well as corpora computed from the Vatican or European Central Bank websites.

[2] http://www.portaldalinguaportuguesa.org/vop.html

For each language the probabilistic translation dictionary is queried, searching for translations for these words, although maintaining the same part-of-speech. Table 2 and table 3 show the contents of the probabilistic translation dictionaries for each original variant[3]

Table 2. Result of translating the Galician synset

completamente	totalmente
completamente 0.48523	simplemente 0.00746
totalmente 0.14573	totalmente 0.53396
plenamente 0.06537	completamente 0.10343
absolutamente 0.01693	plenamente 0.04045
simplemente 0.00204	absolutamente 0.01739
definitivamente 0.00025	no 0.00002

Table 3. Result of translating part of the English synset

completely	totally
completamente 0.350345	totalmente 0.728418
totalmente 0.332604	inteiramente 0.056268
inteiramente 0.096318	completamente 0.052408
plenamente 0.091360	plenamente 0.022330
absolutamente 0.045507	absolutamente 0.012403
perfeitamente 0.005288	perfeitamente 0.008233
ainda 0.004253	não 0.002670
definitivamente 0.000979	ainda 0.002226
integralmente 0.000152	integralmente 0.000173

For each different Portuguese variant candidate (for each source language) the maximum value is chosen.

If the translation is symmetric, the score is incremented by 0.5. For example, consider the Portuguese variant *completamente* obtained using the English–Portuguese dictionary, by translating the English variant *completely*.

If the Portuguese–English dictionary also maps the word *completamente* into the English word *completely*, this variant score is incremented. So, for example, the new score for *completamente* would be 0.850345, but for *ainda* it will be maintained, as the word *completely* does not occur as its translation. The words with a star (⋆) in table 4 are reflexive.

The next step is to find out how many language wordnets generated each of the Portuguese variants. For example, looking to Table 4 we can notice that the word *no* is generated only in the Galician side. In the other hand, the word *totalmente* is generated from both languages.

---

[3] The described process needs to be performed to every word of the presented set. Nevertheless, for simplicity, we chose only two of the seven English variants.

Table 4. Result after scoring the Portuguese candidate words

Galician			English		
Variant	Max	Sym.	Variant	Max	Sym.
completamente 0.48523	0.98523	⋆	completamente 0.350345	0.850345	⋆
simplesmente 0.00746	0.50746	⋆	totalmente 0.728418	1.228418	⋆
totalmente 0.53396	1.03396	⋆	inteiramente 0.096318	0.596318	⋆
plenamente 0.06537	0.56537	⋆	plenamente 0.091360	0.591360	⋆
absolutamente 0.01739	0.51739	⋆	absolutamente 0.045507	0.545507	⋆
definitivamente 0.00025	0.50025	⋆	perfeitamente 0.008233	0.508233	⋆
no 0.00002	0.00002		ainda 0.004253	0.004253	
			não 0.002670	0.002670	
			definitivamente 0.000979	0.500979	⋆
			integralmente 0.000173	0.500173	⋆

So, for each Portuguese variant candidate we will multiply the maximum probability found (1.728418 for the *totalmente* word) by the number of wordnets that generated this candidate: $1.228418 \times 2 = 2.456836$. Table 5 show the result of this step ($score_1$).

Table 5. Portuguese variants, the maximum score obtained from the English or Galician wordnets, $score_1$ and $score_2$

Variant	Max Score	$Score_1$	$Score_2$
totalmente	1.228418	2.456836	3.456836
completamente	0.985230	1.970460	2.970460
plenamente	0.591360	1.182720	1.182720
absolutamente	0.545507	1.091014	1.091014
inteiramente	0.596318	0.596318	0.596318
perfeitamente	0.508233	0.508233	0.508233
definitivamente	0.500979	1.001958	1.001958
integralmente	0.500173	0.500173	0.500173
simplesmente	0.507460	0.507460	0.507460
ainda	0.004253	0.004253	0.004253
não	0.002670	0.002670	0.002670
no	0.000020	0.000020	0.000020

This next step tries to take advantage of the Portuguese–Galician proximity. It uses the Portuguese–Galician dictionary (not the probabilistic dictionary) for each one of the Portuguese variant candidates. If any of its translations occurs in the Galician set of variants, then the variant candidate score is incremented by 1. Table 5 shows what happens to our candidate set (column $score_2$).

Finally the VOP is used to decrease by 1 point all words that are not part of the Portuguese vocabulary. In our example nothing changes, as all words are present in VOP.

The top classified variant candidates are then returned. At the moment the number of words to return is the size of the biggest set of variants for the source languages (English, Spanish or Galician). Therefore, considering the example above is complete, the first seven candidates would be returned.

Note that we do not define any kind of cut-line, other than suggesting that it is not probable to compute more variants than the number of existing variants for other languages. The threshold should be defined later, accordingly with a specific goal. In the evaluation section different cut-lines will be used, and the results analyzed.

5 Evaluation

This section presents an automatic evaluation of the obtained results, first using OpenWordNet-PT [17] as a gold standard, and then a comparing with the results obtained by WN-Toolkit in a similar experiment [5].

Given one of our work motivation is the lack of a good wordnet for the Portuguese language, it gets hard to have a gold standard to evaluate our work with[4]. Nevertheless, and although it contains only half the synsets created by our tool, we used the Brazilian OpenWordNet-PT [17] as our gold standard. The OpenWordNet-PT version used in these experiments contains 43 895 synsets, with a total of 74 012 variants.

After running the tool we obtained 56 770 synsets (33 275 nouns, 10 803 verbs, 10 733 adjectives and 1 959 adverbs) with a total of 97 058 variants. From these synsets, only 49.6% are available on OpenWordNet-PT (28 156 synsets).

These candidates synsets were tested using different heuristics to select which variants to test.

Heuristic A: Evaluate variants with a score greater or equal to 2.5;
Heuristic B: Evaluate variants with a score greater or equal to 2.0;
Heuristic C: Evaluate variants with a score greater or equal to 1.5;
Heuristic D: Evaluate the higher score variant for all synsets, and any other variant with a score greater or equal to 2.0;

Table 6 summarizes the obtained results. For each test it includes the number of variants tested, the average score for these variants, the number of correct variants, accordingly with OpenWordNet-PT, and, finally, the percentage of the tested variants that are correct[5].

When analyzing the results we noticed that there were some false negatives. As OpenWordNet-PT is based on Brazilian Portuguese, and the corpora used by us if from European Portuguese, there were some words that did not match (for example, "ação" vs "acção"). Therefore, in top of the previously described

---

[4] Unfortunately all freely available wordnets follow the automatic generation of synsets, without any real, thorough, manual evaluation. They do not, even, have some kind of score to be used to know each synset variant expected quaity.

[5] Note that it does not make much sense to compute the recall, as we are not trying to generate the complete Gold standard.

Table 6. Result of the four approaches for the synsets evaluation

Heuristic	Nr. Variants	Average Score	Correct Variants
A	9 307	3.0005	6 813 (73.20%)
B	13 785	2.8501	9 426 (68.38%)
C	19 315	2.7360	11 189 (57.93%)
D	31 526	2.1180	16 424 (53.37%)

heuristics we used the Levenshtein algorithm [10], and decided to accept candidate variants as if they are at an edit distance of 1. Table 7 show the values obtained with this approach.

Table 7. Result of the four approaches for the synsets evaluation, with Levenshtein distance of 1

Heuristic	Nr. Variants	Average Score	Correct Variants
A'	9 307	3.0001	6 996 (75.17%)
B'	13 785	2.8477	9 747 (70.71%)
C'	19 315	2.7312	11 662 (60.38%)
D'	31 526	2.0970	17 726 (56.23%)

Finally, we did an extra manual evaluation on the obtained variants, both by an author of this paper, and an external researcher[6]. Table 8 summarizes the results.

E_1 In the first evaluation we selected 100 variants not present in OpenWordNet-PT, but which respective synsets are. When looking for the number of variants approved by both evaluators there is a correctness of 41%.

E_2 For the second evaluation we selected 100 variants which synsets are not present in OpenWordNet-PT. In this case we selected the higher scoring variant for each of these synsets. There is a correctness of 45% when looking to the two evaluators agreement.

Table 8. Manual evaluation for 200 variant candidates

Evaluation	Internal Evaluator	External Evaluator	Common Overally
E_1	46 OK	54 OK	41 OK
E_2	54 OK	53 OK	45 OK

These results are very similar to those obtained with the WN-Toolkit [5] using data for candidates acquired from only one resource. In this case, the automatic precision value was 77.02%, with a real precision (calculated with human revision) of 70% for new variants for empty synsets and 53% for the candidate variants for not empty synsets.

---

[6] Our deepest thanks to Hugo Gonçalo Oliveira for his evaluation of our candidate variants.

6 Conclusions and Future Work

We presented a quick way to bootstrap a wordnet for Portuguese. Although the initial results are not satisfactory, we were still able to extract about 56,700 synsets. An automatic evaluation to part of these synsets measure a correctness of 54.87%. If this ratio is maintained for every extracted synset, it means there are 31,000 correct synsets, which is already 3,000 more than the total number of synsets in OpenWordNet-PT.

Nevertheless, this was a primary study on the process. We will perform an evaluation on the set of synsets not present on OpenWordNet-PT, as well as the variants from synsets on OpenWordNet-PT that are not recognized. Finally, the use of TeP or Onto.PT will allow the automatic enlargement of the synsets.

References

1. Atserias, J., Villarejo, L., Rigau, G., Agirre, E., Carroll, J., Magnini, B., Vossen, P.: The MEANING Multilingual Central Repository. In: Second International Word-Net Conference, pp. 80–210 (2004)
2. Fernández Montraveta, A., Vázquez, G.: La construcción del wordnet 3.0 en español. In: Castillo, M.A., Platero, J.M.G. (eds.) La Lexicografía en su Dimensión Teórica, pp. 201–220. Universidad de Málaga, Málaga (2010)
3. Gómez Guinovart, X.: A hybrid corpus-based approach to bilingual terminology extraction. In: Fandiño, I.M.S., Crespo, B. (eds.) Encoding the Past, Decoding the Future: Corpora in the 21st Century, pp. 147–175. Cambridge Scholar Publishing, Newcastle upon Tyne (2012)
4. Gómez Guinovart, X., Clemente, X.M.G., Pereira, A.G., Lorenzo, V.T.: Galnet: WordNet 3.0 do galego. Linguamática 3(1), 61–67 (2011)
5. Gómez Guinovart, X., Oliver, T.: Methodology and evaluation of the Galician WordNet expansion with the WN-Toolkit. Procesamiento del Lenguaje Natural 53, 43–50 (2014)
6. Gonçalo Oliveira, H., Costa, H., Gomes, P.: Extracção de conhecimento léxico-semântico a partir de resumos da Wikipédia. In: Proceedings of INFORUM 2010, Simpósio de Informática. Braga, Portugal (September 2010)
7. Gonçalo Oliveira, H., Gomes, P.: Towards the automatic creation of a wordnet from a term-based lexical network. In: Proceedings of the ACL Workshop TextGraphs-5: Graph-based Methods for Natural Language Processing, pp. 10–18. ACL Press (July 2010)
8. Gonçalo Oliveira, H., Gomes, P.: Automatic discovery of fuzzy synsets from dictionary definitions. In: Proceedings of 22nd International Joint Conference on Artificial Intelligence, IJCAI 2011, pp. 1801–1806. AAAI Press, Barcelona (2011)
9. González, A., Laparra, E., Rigau, G.: Multilingual central repository version 3.0: upgrading a very large lexical knowledge base. In: 6th Global WordNet Conference, Matsue, Japan (2012)
10. Levenshtein, V.I.: On the minimal redundancy of binary error-correcting codes. Information and Control 28(4), 268–291 (1975)
11. Maziero, E.G., Pardo, T.A.S., Di Felippo, A., Dias-da Silva, B.C.: A base de dados lexical e a interface Web do TeP 2.0: Thesaurus eletrônico para o português do brasil. In: Companion Proceedings of the XIV Brazilian Symposium on Multimedia and the Web, WebMedia 2008, pp. 390–392. ACM, New York (2008)

12. de Melo, G., Weikum, G.: Towards a universal wordnet by learning from combined evidence. In: Proceedings of the 18th ACM Conference on Information and Knowledge Management, CIKM 2009, pp. 513–522. ACM, New York (2009)
13. Miller, G.A.: WordNet: A lexical database for English. Commun. ACM 38(11), 39–41 (1995)
14. Och, F.J., Ney, H.: A systematic comparison of various statistical alignment models. Computational Linguistics 29(1), 19–51 (2003)
15. Oliver, A.: Wn-toolkit: Automatic generation of wordnets following the expand model. In: Proceedings of the 7th Global WordNetConference, Tartu, Estonia (2014)
16. Padró, L.: Analizadores multilingües en FreeLing. Linguamática 3(2), 13–20 (2011)
17. de Paiva, V., Rademaker, A., de Melo, G.: OpenWordNet-PT: An open Brazilian WordNet for reasoning. In: Proceedings of the 24th International Conference on Computational Linguistics (2012)
18. Simões, A., Almeida, J.J., Carvalho, N.R.: Defining a probabilistic translation dictionaries algebra. In: Correia, L., Reis, L.P., Cascalho, J., Gomes, L., Guerra, H., Cardoso, P. (eds.) XVI Portuguese Conference on Artificial Inteligence - EPIA, pp. 444–455. Angra do Heroismo, Azores (2013)
19. Simões, A., Guinovart, X.G.: Dictionary Alignment by Rewrite-based Entry Translation. In: Leal, J.P., Rocha, R., Simões, A. (eds.) 2nd Symposium on Languages, Applications and Technologies. OpenAccess Series in Informatics (OASIcs), vol. 29, pp. 237–247. Schloss Dagstuhl–Leibniz-Zentrum fuer Informatik, Dagstuhl (2013)
20. Simões, A.M., Almeida, J.J.: NATools – a statistical word aligner workbench. Procesamiento del Lenguaje Natural 31, 217–224 (2003)

ATVS-CSLT-HCTLab System for NIST 2013 Open Keyword Search Evaluation

Javier Tejedor[1], Doroteo T. Toledano[2], and Dong Wang[3]

[1] GEINTRA, University of Alcalá, Spain
javier.tejedor@depeca.uah.es
[2] ATVS-Biometric Recognition Group, Universidad Autónoma de Madrid, Spain
doroteo.torre@uam.es
[3] Center for Speech and Language Technologies (CSLT), Tsinghua University, China
wangdong99@mails.tsinghua.edu.cn

Abstract. This paper presents the ATVS-CSLT-HCTLab spoken term detection (STD) system submitted to the NIST 2013 Open Keyword Search evaluation. The evaluation consists of searching a list of query terms in Vietnamese conversational speech data. Our submission involves an automatic speech recognition (ASR) subsystem which converts speech signals into word/phone lattices, and an STD subsystem which indexes and searches for query terms. The submission is a hybrid approach which employs a word-based system to search for in-vocabulary (INV) terms and a phone-based system to search for out-of-vocabulary (OOV) terms. A term-dependent discriminative confidence estimation is employed to score confidence of detections. Although the ASR performance is not state-of-the-art, our submission achieves a moderate STD performance in the evaluation.

Keywords: spoken term detection, evaluation, N-gram reverse indexing, term-dependent discriminative confidence.

1 Introduction

The increasing volume of speech information stored in audio repositories motivates the development of automatic audio indexing and spoken document retrieval systems. Spoken Term Detection (STD), defined by NIST as 'searching vast, heterogeneous audio archives for occurrences of spoken terms' [7] is a fundamental block of those systems, and significant research has been conducted on this task [12,11,4,3,1,8].

In STD, a hypothesized occurrence is called a *detection*; if the detection corresponds to an actual occurrence, it is called a hit, otherwise it is a false alarm (FA). If an actual occurrence is not detected, this is called a miss.

To evaluate STD performance, NIST defines a metric called average termweighted value (ATWV) [7], which integrates the miss rate and false alarm rate of each term into a single metric and then averages over all search terms:

J.L. Navarro Mesa et al. (Eds.): IberSPEECH 2014, LNAI 8854, pp. 249–258, 2014.
© Springer International Publishing Switzerland 2014

$$ATWV = \frac{1}{|\Delta|} \sum_{K \in \Delta} (\frac{N_{hit}^K}{N_{true}^K} - \beta \frac{N_{FA}^K}{T - N_{true}^K}), \tag{1}$$

where Δ denotes the set of search terms and $|\Delta|$ is the number of terms in this set. N_{hit}^K and N_{FA}^K respectively represent the numbers of hits and false alarms of term K and N_{true}^K is the number of actual occurrences of K in the audio. T denotes the audio length in seconds, and β is a weight factor.

In addition, NIST proposed a detection error tradeoff (DET) curve [6] to evaluate the performance of an STD system working at various miss/FA ratios. Both ATWV and DET curves are used for performance evaluation.

Finally, an auxiliary metric called maximum term-weighted value (MTWV) was proposed by NIST. Different from ATWV which depends on a pre-defined threshold, MTWV assumes an oracle threshold and corresponds to the best ATWV on the DET curve.

This paper presents the ATVS-CSLT-HCTLab STD system submitted to the NIST 2013 Open Keyword Search evaluation. It is a collaborative work of three research groups, including ATVS-Biometric Recognition Group and Human Computer Technology Laboratory (HCTLab)[1] from Universidad Autónoma de Madrid, and Center for Speech and Language Technologies (CSLT) at Tsinghua University.

The submission involves an automatic speech recognition (ASR) subsystem, and an STD subsystem. The ASR subsystem converts input speech signals into word/phone lattices, and the STD subsystem integrates a *term detector* which searches for putative occurrences of query terms, and a *decision maker* which decides whether a detection is reliable enough to be considered as a hit or should be rejected as a false alarm. A tool provided by NIST is used to evaluate system performance.

The ASR subsystem is based on Gaussian mixture models (GMM) and was built using the Kaldi toolkit [9]. The training process largely followed the Switchboard s5 recipe, and the same tool was used to conduct decoding and produce word or phone lattices.

The STD subsystem employs an n-gram reverse indexing approach [5] to achieve fast term search. This approach indexes word/phone n-grams retrieved from lattices, and term search is implemented as retrieving n-gram fragments of a query term. Comparing to search in lattices, reverse indexing is much faster and may achieve higher recalls. The confidence score of a hypothesized detection is computed as the averaged lattice-based score of the n-grams of the detection.

A drawback of this scoring method is that the scores are term-independent. In other words, if two detections are assigned the same score, their confidences are considered to be the same, no matter how much the two terms differ. This is not certainly desirable since detections of low-frequency terms are more precious than those of high-frequency terms, and thus need to be treated differently.

---

[1] Javier Tejedor was with HCTLab research group during the evaluation period of time.

This 'term preference' is essentially related to the fact that the evaluation metric (ATWV) prefers recalls rather than FAs. A term-dependent discriminative confidence estimation proposed in [14] was adopted. First, the lattice-based confidence is fed into a multiple-layer perceptron (MLP) to produce a discriminative confidence; second, this discriminative confidence is further normalized by taking into account term frequencies. This score normalization approach significantly improved system performance of our submission.

The rest of the paper is organized as follows: Section 2 describes the system submitted to the evaluation; Section 3 presents the experiments, the results and some discussion; Section 4 concludes the paper.

2   System Description

Our submission involves an ASR subsystem and an STD subsystem. This section will describe these two components in sequence. In addition, we note that the submission is a hybrid approach which employs a word-based system to deal with in-vocabulary (INV) terms and a phone-based system to treat out-of-vocabulary (OOV) terms. The two systems are largely identical except that the word-based system uses a word-based lexicon and a word-based language model (LM), and the phone-based system uses a phone-based lexicon (i.e., a trivial lexicon where each entry is a phone and the pronunciation is the phone itself) and a phone-based LM. The whole system architecture is depicted in Figure 1.

The evaluation task involves searching for some terms from speech data in Vietnamese. However, the language of the data profile was completely unknown until data were released. The participants therefore had to prepare their submission on the data provided in English from the task at NIST STD'06, and once the data were released, the tools, algorithms, recipes, configurations, etc, were quickly migrated to the evaluation data. We selected the Switchboard corpus[2] to conduct the pre-evaluation development.

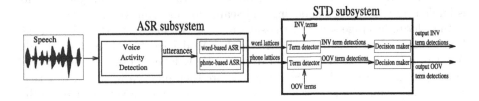

Fig. 1. System architecture. 'ASR' stands for Automatic Speech Recognition, and 'STD' for Spoken Term Detection. 'INV' stands for in-vocabulary, and 'OOV' for out-of-vocabulary.

---

[2] https://catalog.ldc.upenn.edu/LDC98S75

2.1   Automatic Speech Recognition Subsystem

The Kaldi toolkit [9] was used to build the ASR subsystem, and we largely follow the Switchboard s5 recipe, except some minor changes in the configurations. Specifically, the acoustic features are 13-dimensional Mel-frequency cepstral coefficients (MFCCs), with cepstral mean and variance normalization (CMVN) applied to mitigate channel effects. The normalized MFCC features then pass a splicer which augments each frame by its left and right 4 neighboring frames. A linear discriminant analysis (LDA) is then employed to reduce the feature dimension to 40, and a maximum likelihood linear transform (MLLT) is applied to match the diagonal assumption in the GMM acoustic modeling.

The acoustic model training procedure starts from constructing context-independent phone models, based on which context-dependent (CD) phone models are trained by state cloning and clustering. The speaker adaptive training (SAT) technique is applied to improve model robustness, and a discriminative training approach based on the maximum mutual information (MMI) criterion is adopted to produce the final models.

Based on the acoustic models, a word-based ASR system was built for searching INV terms and a phone-based system was built for searching OOV terms. Here OOV terms are defined as those involving words absent from the word lexicon. The word-based system uses a 3-gram word-based LM, and the phone-based system uses a 3-gram phone-based LM.

An energy-based voice activity detection (VAD) implemented in SoX[3] is used to segment speech signals into utterances. Some heuristics of utterance and silence duration are employed to constraint the VAD process, where the heuristic parameters are optimized on a development set. The segmented utterances are then fed into the decoder implemented in Kaldi, which produces word or phone lattices (depending on the type of the system).

2.2   Spoken Term Detection Subsystem

Term Detector - Indexing and Search. The STD stage detects potential occurrences from word/phone lattices obtained within the ASR subsystem. This is implemented as reverse indexing and search in our submission.

In order to leverage some off-the-shelf toolkits, we first convert lattices in the Kaldi format to lattices in the Hidden Markov Model Toolkit (HTK) format [16]. A list of n-grams is then generated from the HTK lattices using the *lattice-tool* of the SRI LM toolkit [10]. These n-grams are then indexed in such a way that the keys are spelling forms of n-grams and the value of each key involves all the occurrences of the n-grams corresponding to the key. This approach is denoted as 'reverse indexing'. We used a toolkit provided by CSLT at Tsinghua University to conduct the reverse indexing[4]. More details of the tool can be found in [5].

Once the reverse indices are constructed, a query term can be searched quickly by looking for occurrences of its word/phone n-gram fragments, constrained

---

[3] http://sox.sourceforge.net/

[4] http://homepages.inf.ed.ac.uk/v1dwang2/public/tools/index.html

by the vicinity in time of the fragments. A detection is hypothesized if its n-gram fragments form the spelling of the query term and their timestamps form a reasonably connected time sequence. The initial and end timestamps of a detection are found to be the initial time of the first n-gram and the end time of the last n-gram. The confidence score of a detection is computed as the average of the confidences of the n-gram segments it involves, and the confidence of an n-gram fragment is computed as the posterior probability of the fragment in the lattice [15]. Since phone sequences are much more flexible than word sequences, the n-gram order of the phone-based indexing should be larger than that of the word-based indexing. In our submission, the order of word n-grams is set to 1 whereas the order of phone n-grams is set to 2. This selection is based on a development set.

We highlight that the OOV issue is critical for STD: search terms usually involve some words that are unknown to the system. In order to deal with OOV terms, the phone-based approach is adopted in our submission. By resorting to phone n-grams instead of word n-grams, it is possible to discover any words including those that did not appear during the construction of the system. This advantage, however, is at the cost of a huge number of false alarms. We therefore treat the phone-based system as a complement to the word-based system, and it is used only for retrieving OOV terms.

Another difficulty for the phone-based approach consists in predicting pronunciations for unknown words, i.e., letter-to-sound (LTS) conversion. Our submission employs a fully automatic approach that combines a joint-multigram model and a conditional random field (CRF) model [13]. This approach first employs a joint-multigram model to align the grapheme/phone sequences of the words in a lexicon, and then derives a CRF model based on the alignment. The CRF model is finally used to generate pronunciations for OOV terms. In OOV search, the 2-best pronunciation predictions of every OOV term are used in phone n-gram search.

Decision Maker - Confidence Measure. Our submission adopts the discriminative normalization approach proposed in [14] for confidence score measuring and decision making. This approach involves two components: an MLP-based discriminative score normalization and a term frequency-based metric-oriented score normalization.

First, an MLP model is used to convert the lattice-based confidence scores (refer to the previous section) to discriminative scores which are more suitable for hit/FA decision making. The MLP model in our submission involves three layers: an input layer consisting of a single unit corresponding to the lattice-based confidence score, a hidden layer consisting of 5 units in the case of the word-based system and 3 units in the case of the phone-based system, and an output layer consisting of two units corresponding to hit and FA respectively. The number of units of each hidden layer was optimized on a development set.

Taking the word-based STD system as an instance, the MLP training procedure is sketched as follows: a subset of 2000 words presented in the lexicon was used as query terms to conduct STD on a development set. Hits and FAs

254 J. Tejedor, D.T. Toledano, and D. Wang

were assigned to each detection according to the label file, and an MLP model was trained by using the hits as positive samples and FAs as negative samples. The WEKA toolkit [2] was used to conduct the training. For the phone-based STD system, the MLP model was trained in a similar way except that the query terms were selected to be lexical words that involve 4 or more phones.

The discriminative confidence of detection d, denoted by $c_{disc}(d)$, is then compensated by a linear transform followed by an ATWV-oriented non-linear transform. The linear transform is given by:

$$c'_{disc}(d) = \alpha c_{disc}(d) + \gamma, \tag{2}$$

where $c'_{disc}(d)$ is the linearly transformed confidence, and α and γ are two term-independent factors which are selected based on a development set. For simplification, we merge γ into the global threshold θ', and optimize α and θ' together with respect to ATWV, based on a development set.

The ATWV-oriented transform is given by:

$$\zeta_K(c_{disc}(d)) = c'_{disc}(d) - \frac{\beta \sum_i c'_{disc}(d_i^K)}{(\beta - 1) \sum_i c'_{disc}(d_i^K) + T}, \tag{3}$$

where $\zeta_K(c_{disc}(d))$ represents the transformed confidence for detection d, and K, β, and T denote the same as in Equation 1. Essentially, the linear and ATWV-oriented transforms function to regularize the confidence scores by a word-frequency-dependent term so that the detections of less frequent terms are treated more seriously, and then hits and FAs are better traded off with respect to the evaluation metric (ATWV).

The decision making process defines a global threshold θ' and simply compares the regularized confidence $\zeta_K(c_{disc}(d))$ with θ', formally formulated as:

$$assert(d) = \begin{Bmatrix} 1 \; if & \zeta_K(c_{disc}(d)) > \theta' \\ 0 \; if & \zeta_K(c_{disc}(d)) \le \theta' \end{Bmatrix}. \tag{4}$$

Note that θ' in the word- and phone-based systems was optimized individually. Since an STD system requires a unique threshold for ATWV computation, the hybrid system threshold is that of the word-based system due to its better performance over the phone-based system when both systems are evaluated individually.

The entire confidence measurement can be seen as a non-linear score mapping, and more information can be found in [14].

3 Experiments

3.1 Data Profile

The system development started by building an English ASR component with the Switchboard II Phase I corpus. The training set for the acoustic and language models involves 120 hours of speech data and the development set involves 5

Table 1. ASR performance of the English system and the Vietnamese system on the development sets. 'WER' stands for Word Error Rate, 'PER' stands for Phone Error Rate, and 'fMMI' stands for feature maximum mutual information.

	English		Vietnamese	
ASR configuration	WER	PER	WER	PER
CD phones (20GMMs)	46.5%	54.5%	77.45%	N/A
+LDA and MLLT	42.3%	51.4%	N/A	N/A
+SAT	35.6%	N/A	N/A	N/A
+100K Gaussians	31.3%	43.3%	71.63%	N/A
+MMI training	27.9%	41.0%	69.77%	N/A
+fMMI training	N/A	N/A	68.80%	N/A

hours of speech data. This development set was used to optimize ASR parameters and to evaluate system performance.

The 'real' evaluation task is to search in Vietnamese speech signals, and the organizer released a training set, a development set and a test set. The training set consists of 17 hours of scripted speech and 73 hours of conversational speech. The development set contains 9 hours of conversational speech, and the evaluation set involves 67.66 hours of conversational speech. All data were telephone speech. We used the speech data in the training set to train the Vietnamese ASR system acoustic models, while the conversational speech of the training set was used to train its language models. For STD, we used the development set to train the MLP model and adjust hyperparameters. Note that the speech data mentioned above do not include non-speech segments identified by the VAD component and segments labeled as unintelligible voice, truncated, foreign words, overlapping, and with high non-stationary noise.

Besides the speech data, the organizer also provided a lexicon that consists of 10600 pronunciations of 6800 words. There are also 200 query terms provided for system development in which 2 terms are OOV, and 864 occurrences in total in the development set. The query terms provided for STD evaluation involve 3978 INV terms and 87 OOV terms (4065 terms in total), and these terms appear 277030 times in the evaluation set.

3.2   Results and Discussion

Automatic Speech Recognition. Table 1 shows the ASR results of the English system and the Vietnamese system.

For the English system, we note that the Word Error Rate (WER) result is not the best among the results reported by other researchers on the same database, but it is still reasonably good; particularly for STD tasks, 27.9% is acceptable in many situations [12]. Some results of the English system are missed in Table 1 because we received the Vietnamese data in the process of English system development and switched to the real evaluation task.

Due to the limited amount of time given to system construction, we just evaluated some 'key steps' when building the Vietnamese system. The WER of the final system is 68.80%. This number is surprisingly high compared to that of the English system, perhaps attributed to the fact that words in Vietnamese are actually syllables and most of them involve just 3 or less phones, as shown in Table 2. The short word length may lead to less discrimination between words and this results into a low ASR performance.

Spoken Term Detection. Table 3 presents the results of the Vietnamese STD systems in terms of MTWV and ATWV. Performance on both development and evaluation sets is reported. We first observe that the hybrid system does not provide any gain over the word-based system on development data. This can be explained by the fact that there are only 2 OOV terms so the phone-based system contributes little.

To measure the performance of the phone-based system in a reasonable way, we conducted an experiment on the development set where the terms involving 5 or more phones (regardless of being INV or OOV terms) were searched with the phone-based system. The results are reported in the second row of Table 3. It can be seen that the phone-based system performs much worse than the word-based system. Note that this does not mean that the phone-based system is useless since OOVs are inevitable in practice, and so a phone-based system is a necessary complement to a word-based system.

Results on the evaluation data presented in Table 3 show a similar pattern in that the hybrid system does not outperform the word-based system, although there are 72 OOV terms (only the OOV terms with 5 or more phones were searched). Further analysis shows that the threshold obtained from the word-based system on the development set does not work well in the hybrid system on the evaluation set, so almost all the detections were rejected. The performance gap between MTWV and ATWV suggests a better score calibration is necessary.

DET curves of the phone-based and the word-based systems with the development set are presented in Figure 2. Note that the DET curve of the hybrid system completely overlaps with that of the word-based system. It is clear that the word-based system outperforms the phone-based system, which can be largely attributed to the extra lexical information that is used in word-based ASR.

Table 2. Percentage of Vietnamese words of various lengths

Word length in phone #	Percentage in lexicon
1	1.25%
2	31.5%
3	57.86%
4	3.48%
5	2.66%
5+	3.24%

Table 3. STD results of the Vietnamese system

	Development data		Evaluation data	
	MTWV	ATWV	MTWV	ATWV
word-based system	0.1180	0.1180	0.1055	0.0772
phone-based system	0.0227	0.0227	N/A	N/A
hybrid system	0.1180	0.1180	0.1055	0.0772

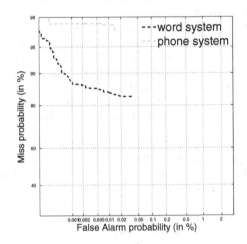

Fig. 2. DET curves of the word- and phone-based STD systems with the development set

4   Conclusions

We presented the ATVS-CSLT-HCTLab STD system submitted to the NIST 2013 Open Keyword Search evaluation. The system involves an ASR subsystem which is based on the GMM architecture and an STD subsystem which employs n-gram reverse indexing for term search and discriminative confidence normalization for decision making. A word-based system and a phone-based system were constructed, and the two systems were combined into a hybrid system where the word-based system deals with INV terms and the phone-based system works on OOV terms. The evaluation results show that this system achieves moderate STD performance comparing to other participants (7th position out of 11 participants).

A particular weakness of our system is the low ASR performance, which may have seriously deteriorated the ATWV results. Future work will migrate the GMM-based ASR system to a Deep Neural Network (DNN)-based ASR system, which has been widely adopted by the speech recognition community. Additionally, more informative factors (e.g., detection duration, phone-based features, etc) will be considered in the discriminative confidence estimation.

Acknowledgements. This work has been partly supported by project CMC-V2 (TEC2012-37585-C02-01) from the Spanish Ministry of Economy and Competitiveness.

References

1. Abad, A., Rodríguez-Fuentes, L.J., Peñagarikano, M., Varona, A., Bordel, G.: On the calibration and fusion of heterogeneous spoken term detection systems. In: Proc. of Interspeech, pp. 20–24 (2013)
2. Hall, M., Frank, E., Holmes, G., Pfahringer, B., Reutemann, P., Witten, I.H.: The WEKA data mining software: An update. SIGKDD Explorations 11(1) (2009)
3. Katsurada, K., Miura, S., Seng, K., Iribe, Y., Nitta, T.: Acceleration of spoken term detection using a suffix array by assigning optimal threshold values to subkeywords. In: Proc. of Interspeech, pp. 11–14 (2013)
4. Li, H., Han, J., Zheng, T., Zheng, G.: A novel confidence measure based on context consistency for spoken term detection. In: Proc. of Interspeech, pp. 2429–2430 (2012)
5. Liu, C., Wang, D., Tejedor, J.: N-gram FST indexing for spoken term detection. In: Proc. of Interspeech, pp. 2093–2096 (2012)
6. Martin, A., Doddington, G., Kamm, T., Ordowski, M., Przybocki, M.: The DET curve in assessment of detection task performance. In: Proc. of Eurospeech, pp. 1895–1898 (1997)
7. NIST: The spoken term detection (STD) 2006 evaluation plan, 10 edn. National Institute of Standards and Technology (NIST), Gaithersburg, MD, USA (September 2006), http://www.nist.gov/speech/tests/std
8. Norouzian, A., Rose, R.: An approach for efficient open vocabulary spoken term detection. Speech Communication 57, 50–62 (2014)
9. Povey, D., Ghoshal, A., Boulianne, G., Burget, L., Glembek, O., Goel, N., Hannemann, M., Motlicek, P., Qian, Y., Schwarz, P., Silovsky, J., Stemmer, G., Vesely, K.: The KALDI speech recognition toolkit. In: Proc. of ASRU (2011)
10. Stolcke, A.: SRILM - an extensible language modeling tool. In: Proc. of ICSLP, pp. 901–904 (2002)
11. Szoke, I.: Hybrid word-subword spoken term detection. Ph.D. thesis, Brno University of Technology (June 2010)
12. Wang, D.: Out-of-vocabulary Spoken Term Detection. Ph.D. thesis, University of Edinburgh (December 2009)
13. Wang, D., King, S.: Letter-to-sound pronunciation prediction using conditional random fields. IEEE Signal Processing Letters 18(2), 122–125 (2011)
14. Wang, D., Tejedor, J., King, S., Frankel, J.: Term-dependent confidence normalization for out-of-vocabulary spoken term detection. Journal of Computer Science and Technology 27(2), 358–375 (2012)
15. Wessel, F., Macherey, K., Schluter, R.: Using word probabilities as confidence measures. In: Proc. of ICASSP, pp. 225–228 (1998)
16. Young, S., Evermann, G., Gales, M., Hain, T., Kershaw, D., Liu, X., Moore, G., Odell, J., Ollason, D., Povey, D., Valtchev, V., Woodland, P.: The HTK v3.4 Book. Engineering Department, Cambridge University (March 2006)

Speech Watermarking Based on Coding of the Harmonic Phase

Inma Hernaez[1], Ibon Saratxaga[1], Jianpei Ye[1],
Jon Sanchez[1], Daniel Erro[1,2], and Eva Navas[1]

[1] Aholab (UPV/EHU), ETSI Bilbao, Alda. Urquijo s/n, Bilbao, Spain
[2] IKERBASQUE, Alda. Urquijo, 36-5, Bilbao, Spain
{inma,ibon,jianpei,ion,derro,eva}@aholab.ehu.es

Abstract. This paper presents a new speech watermarking technique using harmonic modelling of the speech signal and coding of the harmonic phase. We use a representation of the instantaneous harmonic phase which allows straightforward manipulation of its values to embed the digital watermark. The technique converts each harmonic into a communication channel, whose performance is analysed in terms of distortion and BER. The developed tests show that with a simple coding scheme a bit rate of 300bps can be achieved with minimal perceptual distortion and almost zero BER.

Keywords: Data Hiding, Digital Speech Watermarking, Relative Phase Shift.

1 Introduction

Digital data hiding consists in a set of technologies aimed to conceal information in a host digital signal like image, video, audio, speech or text. They are also named digital watermarking techniques, for purposes like data authentication or copyright protection. The hidden information (or watermark) embedded in the host signal should be perceptually and statistically undetectable and should be recoverable after any unintentional processing or intentional attack [1].

Watermarking of speech signals is a very challenging task because the human auditory system operates over a wide dynamic range [2], thus, it is really difficult to develop a robust data hiding technique without degrading the perceptual quality of the host speech signal [3].

In recent years, digital speech watermarking techniques have achieved a significant progress [4]. Some of these techniques operate in the time domain to embed the watermark signal. Others are based on slight modifications in the quantization process [5] [6] [7]. Many other techniques rely on the transformed domain to embed the changes in an imperceptible way. Using the Fourier transform, some methods modify the spectral module, like [8] or [9]. The human auditory system is not very sensitive to phase modifications, especially in medium to high frequencies [10] and thus phase coding is considered one of the most effective data hiding method in terms of signal-to-perceived noise ratio. Examples of use

J.L. Navarro Mesa et al. (Eds.): IberSPEECH 2014, LNAI 8854, pp. 259–268, 2014.

of phase techniques can be found in [11] [12] [13] [14] [15]. Most of these techniques modify the instantaneous phase of some frequencies of the signal. Other transform domains have also been proposed, like wavelet [16] or DCT [17].

More recently, some authors have explored techniques which code the hidden data by modifying a parameter of a model of the host signal. For instance, in [18] pitch and duration of the speech signal is used for this purpose, in [19] a statistical model of the signal is used, in [20] the LSP values representing the vocal tract are changed. Depending on the parameter used these methods are often more robust to usual noise and conventional signal processing degradation.

In this paper we propose a new method for data hiding which falls in this last category: it uses a phase related parameter of the harmonic model of the speech signal to encode the watermark. We will show that this method combines the inaudibility of the phase techniques with the robustness of the model based methods. In [21] we proposed a representation, the Relative Phase Shifts (RPS), which reflects the phase shift between harmonic components of the speech signal, and consequently the waveform of the signal. Manipulating this parameter provides a way to hide information in a speech signal, affecting only to its waveform, and producing an almost imperceptible impairment in it.

The paper is organized as follows: In Section 2 the fundamentals of the proposed watermarking technique are presented. This technique provides what could be seen as a set of hidden communication channels whose features are analyzed in section 3. This analysis leads to the choice of some design parameters and the resulting signals are evaluated from the quality and perceptual points of view in section 4. Finally some conclusions are derived.

2   Watermarking Architecture

2.1   Watermark Embedding

Harmonic models for speech have been successfully applied to a wide range of applications, including data hiding applications. The Harmonic plus Stochastic Model [22] (HSM) assumes that the speech signal can be represented as a sum of a time-varying number of harmonically related sinusoids and a noise-like component:

$$\hat{s}(t) = \sum_{k=1}^{N(t)} a_k(t) \cdot \cos(\phi_k(t)) + r(t) \ . \tag{1}$$

The model parameters in equation (1) are the harmonic amplitudes $a_k(t)$, the instantaneous phases $\phi_k(t)$ and the stochastic component $r(t)$ which accounts for all non-sinusoidal signal components caused by friction of the articulators, breathing noise, etc. $N(t)$ is the number of harmonics, which can vary from frame to frame according to the fundamental frequency value. In the implementation of the model presented in this work, we do not use the stochastic component, in order to focus on the phase coding process. However, any other harmonic representation could be used.

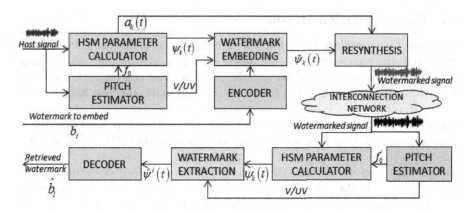

Fig. 1. Architecture of the speech watermarking system

The above mentioned RPS representation [21] transforms the instantaneous phases of the harmonic components into the Relative Phase Shifts using the following equation:

$$\psi_k(t) = \phi_k(t) - k \cdot \phi_1(t) \quad 1 < k \leq N(t) . \tag{2}$$

Where $\phi_1(t)$ is the instantaneous phase of the fundamental frequency component and $\phi_k(t)$ and $\psi_k(t)$ are the instantaneous phase and the RPS value of the kth harmonic. The RPS transformation reveals a meaningful and structured pattern in the phase information and allows a straightforward way to manipulate the phases of the harmonic components, making it easy to embed watermarks into a speech signal. As shown in Fig. 1 the embedding process consists in modifying the RPS value of the kth harmonic component by encoding the binary data (b_i) to be transmitted. We have chosen a simple binary encoding system where the transmitted RPS values (transmitted symbols) will be $\pm\pi/2$:

$$\tilde{\psi}_k^i = (2b_i - 1)\frac{\pi}{2} \quad b_i = \{0,1\} . \tag{3}$$

The watermarked signal is obtained after resynthesis using the original amplitudes and f_0 as well as the new values of the RPSs. The recovering of the embedded data from the received watermarked speech signal implies a new harmonic analysis to get the received RPSs, $\tilde{\psi}_k^i$. Decoding is performed using a threshold at 0 radians.

Theoretically, we could use all the harmonics present in the signal as a communication channel, each channel conveying digital binary data at one symbol per frame. However, the number of harmonics can vary significantly not only from speaker to speaker, but also in the course of one only utterance. Also, some channels will perform better than others, either offering a more reliable transmission performance or just in terms of auditory perception. Thus, we propose the use of only a selected number of channels, as we will see in the next section.

2.2 Phase Distortion Measure

One important consideration in the design of the system is the fact that once watermarked, the reconstructed signal differs from the original, and consequently both the voice/unvoiced analysis and the pitch analysis can return a value different from the one used at the transmission. Still more, this can happen even if no watermarking is used, because the reconstructed signal and the original signal are of course not identical. As a result, the recovered phase value differs from the original value, which can cause detection errors if the differences are sufficiently important.

Also important when using the harmonic phase to embed the watermark is the fact that only the voiced segments of speech can be used for the transmission. Indeed, unvoiced segments are noisy in nature, and they will show random phase during analysis and recovery. Thus, the transmission channel has a discontinuous nature and some recovery mechanisms will have to be used for reliable transmission. We do not treat this sync problem in this paper and we will assume that the voiced/unvoiced decision taken at the transmitter side is known by the receiver in such a way that perfect synchronism is achieved.

To measure the differences between transmitted and received phase values we will use the mean square error of the RPS values as shown by the following equation:

$$d_k = \sqrt{1/L \cdot \sum_{i=1}^{L} |\text{wrap}\,(\psi'_k[i] - \psi_k[i])|^2} \; . \tag{4}$$

This measure is defined for each communication channel (i.e. for each harmonic) as the quadratic mean of the differences between the L transmitted RPS values of the original host signal ψ_k, and the L estimated RPS values of the received signal ψ'_k.

3 Hidden Channel Characterization

3.1 Database

To set the parameters of the system and evaluate its performance, a database consisting on all voiced sounds has been used [10]. It contains 20 sentences uttered by 12 speakers (6 males, 6 females) thus with a total of 240 sentences. Although the texts contain only voiced phones, silences and some plosive segments result in unvoiced frames. The signals are sampled at 16 kHz. To obtain the watermarked signals for the following measures and experiments, 2000 random binary sequences were embedded into randomly selected sentences from the database. The harmonic analysis was performed at a frame rate of 10 ms.

3.2 Analysis of the Distortion

Prior to the introduction of the watermarking signal into the host signal, it is necessary to know the intrinsic distortion of the system, that is to say, the inherent distortion obtained just by coding-decoding the signal. Fig. 2 shows the intrinsic distortion of the system calculated under different conditions. The discontinuous (blue) line corresponds to the values obtained when the pitch values used during the analysis are transmitted, i.e. the original pitch values are used to calculate the received phase value. This can be taken as baseline system with ideal working conditions. When the pitch is calculated from the received signal (as it will normally be), the distortion increases an average of 0.0324 radians over all the channels (continuous green line).

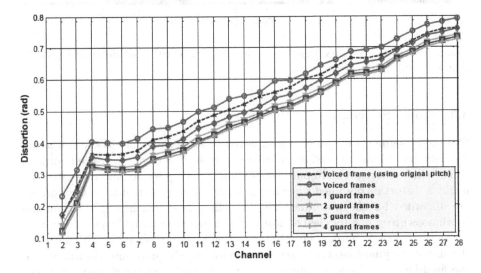

Fig. 2. Intrinsic distortion in radians as a function of the harmonic number and the number of guard frames used

As can be seen in Fig. 2, the distortion is larger at higher channels, which will also be larger frequencies. This was expected, as lower harmonics will have in general larger energy, and will allow a more robust estimation of the RPS value. Additionally, at high frequencies the evolution of the phase is also faster, making high frequencies more error prone.

Also of interest is the statistical distribution of the inherent distortion values. Fig. 3 shows the Probability Density Function of those values. As expected, the values are symmetrically distributed around zero.

As shown in Fig. 3, the variance of the distortion increases when the watermarking is introduced. This was expected, as during the watermarking the RPS value will vary rapidly from one extreme value to the other, thus complicating a true estimation. This fact brought us to propose a system with redundancy, i.e., a system where M consecutives frames are used for each information bit. At the receiver, a majority vote will be applied to make a decision. In the following subsections, the influence of this parameter M on the final BER will be further treated.

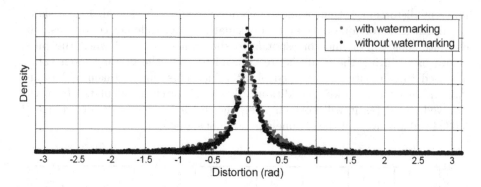

Fig. 3. Probability Density Function of the distortion with (red dots) and without (black circles) watermarking

3.3 Frame Selection

Stationary segments of speech are expected to be more robust to the sinusoidal analysis than frames located at the voiced/unvoiced or unvoiced/voiced borders, which will be more prone to phase distortion. This is why we have evaluated the intrinsic distortion obtained when one or more voiced frames at the VUV borders are discarded for the watermarking. The effect is shown in Fig. 2. From the continuous green line (circles) almost 0.05 radians are won by leaving one guard frame at the VUV border, but the distortion goes further down by increasing the size of the guard interval. However, the use of this guard interval will reduce the final bit rate. Thus, for our further experiments we have chosen a value of $N = 2$ guard frames.

3.4 Channel Selection

As commented before, not all the channels are equally suitable for transmission. The harmonics located at the low and medium bands will in general have more energy and consequently the distortion introduced by the watermarked phase will be noticed. We also know that the human auditory system is more sensitive to phase changes at low and medium bands. This is an important aspect to consider at the time of selecting the transmission channel. On the other hand, as previously seen, the intrinsic distortion of the system is very high at the higher channels. Fig. 4 shows how the Bit Error Rate (highly correlated with the phase distortion) increases at the higher channels. This figure also shows the beneficial effect of introducing redundancy. As it can be seen, a factor of $M = 5$ (i.e., using 5 repeated samples per input symbol) reduces the BER practically to zero in all channels. However, this will also reduce the bandwidth by the same amount. In the experiments that follow, we have used a redundancy value of M=3.

For the results shown in Fig. 4 the watermarking data have been transmitted over one channel at a time. However, more channels can be used simultaneously

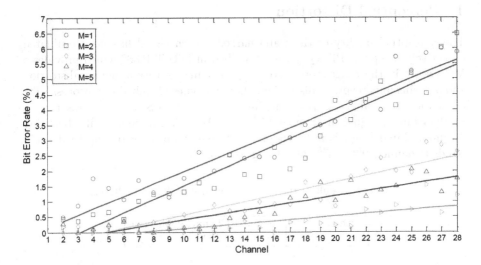

Fig. 4. Bit Error Rate for every channel and (only one channel used at a time). The colored lines show a linear estimation.

to increase the system transmission rate. We have experimented using different number of channels simultaneously and the results show that low and medium bands are able to convey the hidden data without significantly increasing the BER. Fig. 5 shows the averaged BER obtained when we use from 1 to 9 simultaneous channels randomly chosen at the medium frequency bands (from the 9th to the 17th channel, $M = 1$). As it can be seen, the BER remains constant in practice, so there is no damage in terms of BER. However, the perception quality must also be considered, which will be analysed in the last section of this paper.

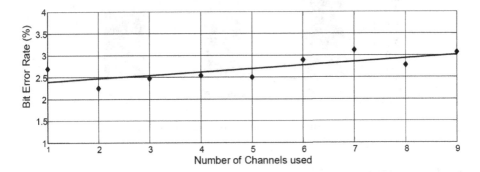

Fig. 5. Bit Error Rate using 1 to 9 simultaneous channels

4   Perceptual Distortion

The perceptual quality of the watermarked speech signal has been evaluated objectively using the PESQ system described in ITU-T P.862 which provides a MOS score in the range from 1 to 5, where 1 means very annoying distortion and 5 means imperceptible distortion. Different types of embedding process were chosen for the evaluation: i) No modification of the RPS values. ii) Inserting a random binary signal in channel 14th with $M = 3$ redundancy. iii) Inserting 9 random binary signals in 9 randomly selected channels belonging to the mid bands (Channels 9th - 17th) also using $M = 3$.

Table 1. Result of the objective quality evaluation (PESQ)

Method	No WM	1 Channel	9 Channels
Averaged MOS	4.1057	4.1022	4.0948

Table 1 shows the statistical average value of the MOS score obtained by evaluating the degradation of the resynthesized speech signals with respect to the original host signal. These results show that the embedding process using method *ii* is almost perfectly transparent.

To obtain an accurate and reliable value of perceptual distortion, apart from the objective speech quality assessment, some resynthesized speech signal have been tested subjectively by different listeners (a total of 11). The subjective evaluation test consisted in rating the quality of a resynthesized speech signal generated using methods *i*, *ii* or *iii* described above. The output of the subjective test is also a MOS score on a scale from 1 to 5. Fig. 6 shows the results, from which we can conclude that the proposed scheme is imperceptible when one only channel is used.

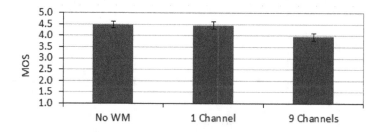

Fig. 6. Result of the subjective quality evaluation

5   Conclusion

In this paper, a new method to hide data into a speech signal has been described. Using the Relative Phase Shift of the harmonic phases of the signal, binary data have been embedded using a simple coding scheme. Although many other existing coding strategies can be applied, a very simple one has been chosen in order to evaluate the physic layer performance. At a bit rate of 100/3 bps (160 samples/frame at 16 kHz and 3 samples/symbol), the technique has proven to offer BER close to zero and degradation equivalent to that of the harmonic vocoder. If a slightly higher degradation is accepted and 9 channels are used, the BER is still very low and bit rate grows proportionally to 300bps which is a reasonable achievement considering the simple coding system.

One important feature of this technique is that it can be used even when the most common speech coding algorithms are present in the communication channel. Although not shown in this paper, informal experiments have demonstrated the RPS robustness to MP3 or OPUS coding algorithms. On the other hand, the robustness of the system to intentional attacks has not yet been analysed.

Future works will focus on introducing suitable synchronization systems, which is essential for the correct operation of a real application.

Acknowledgments. This work was supported in part by the Spanish Ministry of Economy and Competitiveness (SpeechTech4All, TEC2012-38939-C03-03), the Basque Government (Ber2tek, IE12-333).

References

1. Nematollahi, M., Al-Haddad, S.: An overview of digital speech watermarking. International Journal of Speech Technology 16(4), 471–488 (2013)
2. Bender, W., Gruhl, D., Morimoto, N., Lu, A.: Techniques for data hiding. IBM Syst. J. 35(3-4), 313–336 (1996)
3. Arnold, M.: Audio watermarking: features, applications and algorithms. In: Proc. of IEEE Int. Conf. on Multimedia and Expo, vol. 2, pp. 1013–1016 (2000)
4. Cox, I.J., Miller, M.L., Bloom, J.A., Fridrich, J., Kalker, T.: Digital Watermarking and Steganography, 2nd edn. The Morgan Kaufmann Series in Multimedia Information and Systems. Morgan Kaufmann (2008)
5. Bai, Y., Bai, S., Zhu, G., You, C., Liu, B.: A blind audio watermarking algorithm based on fft coeficients quantization. In: Proceedings of the Int. Conf. on Artificial Intelligence and Education (ICAIE), pp. 529–533 (2010)
6. Chen, S., Leung, H.: Speech bandwidth extension by data hiding and phonetic classification. In: Proceedings of the IEEE Int. Conf. on Acoustics, Speech and Signal Processing (ICASSP), vol. 4, pp. IV593–IV596 (2007)
7. Sakaguchi, S., Arai, T., Murahara, Y.: The efect of polarity inversion of speech on human perception and data hiding as an application. In: Proceedings of the IEEE Int. Conf. on Acoustics, Speech, and Signal Processing (ICASSP), vol. 2, pp. II917–II920 (2000)
8. Hsieh, C.T., Sou, P.Y.: Blind cepstrum domain audio watermarking based on time energy features. In: Proc. of the 14th Int. Conf. on Digital Signal Processing, vol. 2, pp. 705–708 (2002)
9. Megías, D., Serra-Ruiz, J., Fallahpour, M.: Efficient self-synchronised blind audio watermarking system based on time domain and FFT amplitude modification. Signal Processing 90(12), 3078–3092 (2010)

10. Saratxaga, I., Hernaez, I., Pucher, M., Navas, E., Sainz, I.: Perceptual importance of the phase related information in speech. In: Proceedings of the 13th Annual Conference of the International Speech Communication Association, pp. 1448–1451 (2012)

11. Ansari, R., Malik, H., Khokhar, A.: Data-hiding in audio using frequency selective phase alteration. In: Proc. of the IEEE Int. Conf. on Acoustics, Speech, and Signal Processing (ICASSP), vol. 5, pp. V389–V392 (2004)

12. Dong, X., Bocko, M., Ignjatovic, Z.: Data hiding via phase manipulation of audio signals. In: Proc. of the IEEE Int. Conf. on Acoustics, Speech, and Signal Processing (ICASSP), vol. 5, pp. V377–V380 (2004)

13. Liew, P., Armand, M.: Inaudible watermarking via phase manipulation of random frequencies. Multimedia Tools and Applications 35(3), 357–377 (2007)

14. Kuo, S., Johnston, J.D., Turin, W., Quackenbush, S.R.: Covert audio watermarking using perceptually tuned signal independent multiband phase modulation. In: Proc. of the Int. Conf. on Acoustics, Speech and Signal Processing, vol. II, pp. 1753–1756 (2002)

15. Hofbauer, K., Kubin, G., Kleijn, W.B.: Speech Watermarking for Analog Flat-Fading Bandpass Channels. IEEE Trans. on Audio, Speech, and Language Processing 17(8), 1624–1637 (2009)

16. Chen, S.H., Yu, S.Y., Chang, C.H.: Speech watermarking based on wavelet transform and bch coding. In: Proc. of the IEEE Int. Conf. on Sensor Networks, Ubiquitous and Trustworthy Computing (SUTC), pp. 507–512 (2008)

17. Huang, J., Wang, Y., Shi, Y.: A blind audio watermarking algorithm with self-synchronization. In: Proc. of the IEEE Int. Symposium on Circuits and Systems, vol. 3, pp. 627–630 (2002)

18. Celik, M., Sharma, G., Tekalp, A.: Pitch and duration modification for speech watermarking. In: Proc. of the IEEE Int. Conf. Acoustics, Speech, and Signal Processing (ICASSP), vol. 2, pp. 17–20 (2005)

19. Akhaee, M., Kalantari, N., Marvasti, F.: Robust multiplicative audio and speech watermarking using statistical modelling. In: Proc. of the IEEE Int. Conf. on Communications (ICC), pp. 1–5 (2009)

20. Hatada, M., Sakai, T., Komatsu, N., Yamazaki, Y.: Digital watermarking based on process of speech production. In: Proc. SPIE Multimedia Systems and Applications V, vol. 4861, pp. 258–267 (2002)

21. Saratxaga, I., Hernaez, I., Erro, D., Navas, E., Sanchez, J.: Simple representation of signal phase for harmonic speech models. Electronics Letters 45(7), 381–383 (2009)

22. Stylianou, Y.: Harmonic Plus Noise Models for Speech, Combined with Statistical Methods, for Speech and Speaker Modification. Ph.D. thesis, Ecole Nationale Superieure des Telecommunications, Paris, France (1996)

The Translectures-UPV Toolkit

M.A. del-Agua, A. Giménez, N. Serrano, J. Andrés-Ferrer,
J. Civera, A. Sanchis, and A. Juan

MLLP, DSIC, Universitat Politècnica de València (UPV)
Camí de Vera s/n, 46022 València, Spain
{mdelagua,agimenez,nserrano,jandres,jcivera,josanna,ajuan}@dsic.upv.es

Abstract. Over the past few years, online multimedia educational repositories have increased in number and popularity. The main aim of the transLectures project is to develop cost-effective solutions for producing accurate transcriptions and translations for large video lecture repositories, such as VideoLectures.NET or the Universitat Politècnica de València's repository, poliMedia. In this paper, we present the transLectures-UPV toolkit (TLK), which has been specifically designed to meet the requirements of the transLectures project, but can also be used as a conventional ASR toolkit. The main features of the current release include HMM training and decoding with speaker adaptation techniques (fCMLLR). TLK has been tested on the VideoLectures.NET and poliMedia repositories, yielding very competitive results. TLK has been released under the permissive open source Apache License v2.0 and can be directly downloaded from the transLectures website.

Keywords: TLK, ASR toolkit, transLectures, HMM.

1 Introduction

Online multimedia repositories are on the rise and becoming evermore consolidated as key knowledge assets. This is particularly true in the educational arena where large repositories of video lectures are being established on the back of increasingly available and standardized infrastructures. A well-known example of this is VideoLectures.NET, a free and open access web portal that has so far published more than 15K educational videos. VideoLectures.NET is a major player in the diffusion of the open source Matterhorn platform currently being adopted by many institutions and organizations within the Opencast community [3]. Other examples include massive open online course (MOOCs) aggregators, such as Coursera, Udacity, EdX, Udemy, iVersity, UPV[x] and others.

The generation of subtitles for these repositories is a costly task, both in terms of time and money, which prohibits many repositories from having their videos transcribed. Most of the video lectures available on VideoLectures.NET and MOOC aggregators, for instance, are not transcribed, despite the obvious benefits of doing so, including the incorporation of search and analysis functions. In order to overcome this deficit, the transLectures project aims to develop innovative, cost-effective solutions for producing accurate transcriptions and translations for video lectures. The project has two case studies: the aforementioned

J.L. Navarro Mesa et al. (Eds.): IberSPEECH 2014, LNAI 8854, pp. 269–278, 2014.

VideoLectures.NET, and poliMedia, a Spanish and Catalan video lecture repository developed at the Universitat Politècnica de València (UPV).

An important area of work at transLectures is to develop solutions that can be easily transferred to other repositories beyond VideoLectures.NET and poliMedia. With this in mind, the transLectures-UPV team has developed a whole series of transferable tools, including online applications. This paper is focused on just one of these tools, the transLectures-UPV toolkit (TLK). TLK implements all the functionalities required to develop an automatic speech recognition (ASR) system. Although developed as part of the transLectures project to meet the specific requirements of video lecture transcription, it can also be used as a conventional ASR toolkit, like HTK [20], RASR [17] or KALDI [15]. In this paper, we go into more detail about this toolkit, which can be freely downloaded [6] under the permissive (for research and commercial purposes alike) Apache License v2.0.

This paper is organised as follows. Section 2 describes the different tools forming part of TLK that can be used either to build an ASR system or simply to transcribe input media files. A practical guide to the development of an ASR system using TLK is given in Section 3. Finally, the performance of TLK is assessed in Section 4, and some conclusions are given in Section 5.

2   Overview of the Toolkit

TLK can be divided into three major components: the library, the basic command line tools and the high-level command line tools. The library, named libTLK, is an ANSI C library and implements the core functionalities of TLK (feature extraction, parameter estimation, decoding, adaptation, etc.). A set of basic command line tools have been defined to use libTLK. Based on these basic tools, high-level command line tools have also been developed in order to carry out the main steps involved in building an HMM-based ASR system: preprocessing, training and decoding.

2.1   Building an ASR System Using TLK Tools

As illustrated in Fig. 1, an ASR system can be built using three high-level TLK tools: tLtask-preprocess, tLtask-train and tLtask-recognise.

tLtask-Preprocess. This tool takes time-segmented audio signals and the corresponding transcriptions as input and performs feature extraction and phonetic annotation. It also extracts clusters from the input audio, which can be used for speaker or video adaptation, and other useful data like the original or non-punctuated text.

tLtask-preprocess uses the tLextract basic command tool to perform the Mel-Frequency Cepstral Coefficients (MFCC) feature extraction process as described in [20]. tLextract supports a large number of audio file formats since it uses the libsox library. The parameters involved in the extraction process

High-level tools   **Basic tools**

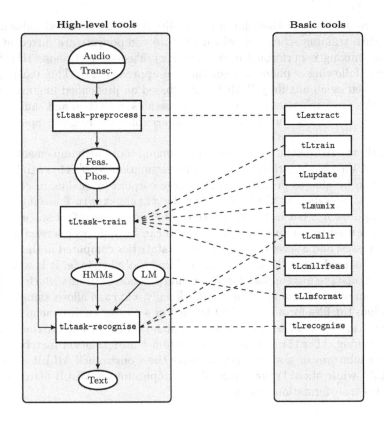

Fig. 1. Building an ASR system using TLK tools

are easy to configure: sampling frequency, duration of the extraction window, number of cepstral coefficients, etc. Furthermore, `tLextract` also allows the application of a mean variance normalization to the input samples.

The phonetic transcription is obtained using different auxiliary scripts depending on the input language. The current release supports Spanish and Catalan.

tLtask-Train. This tool takes the output from `tLtask-preprocess` and performs the following training schema to estimate the HMMs:

1. Standard model training: monophone training, triphone training, transformation of the triphone model to a tied phoneme model, tied phoneme training.
2. Estimation of CMLLR matrices and CMLLR features.
3. CMLLR model training: CMLLR monophone training, CMLLR triphone training, CMLLR transformation of the triphone model to a tied phoneme model, CMLLR tied phoneme training.

This is the training schema for a two-step recognition system using fCMLLR features [9], and tied-state triphone HMMs. The final standard and CMLLR models are made up of Gaussian mixture distributions estimated following on an iterative training schema in which mixture components are mixed at each iteration (mixing is performed using `tLmumix`). Tied-state triphone HMMs are estimated following a phonetic decision tree approach [21]. This technique is implemented as an auxiliary Python script based on predefined linguistic rules. These rules are implemented as regular expressions in Python and can be easily defined by users. The current release includes rules for English, Spanish and Catalan.

`tLtask-train` uses the `tLtrain` basic command tool which implements Baum-Welch and Viterbi algorithms for parameter estimation [7,19]. `tLtrain` has been designed to be able to properly manage large corpora by scaling in cluster environments. Specifically, `tLtrain` is used by `tLtask-train` following a Map-Reduce approach. That is, training is split into two stages: a first stage in which `tLtrain` is used to compute statistics, which can be split over several independent processes; and a second stage where the statistics computed in the previous stage are merged using the basic command line tool `tLupdate`. It is worth noting that `tLupdate` has support for linear interpolation of counts which might be useful in an online learning schema. Additionally, `tLtrain` allows samples to be packed into tar files for a better I/O latency in a cluster environment.

`tLtask-train` uses additional basic command tools to complete the CMLLR model training. `tLcmllr` is used to calculate a transformation matrix over all Gaussian mixtures of a simple HMM using the Constrained MLLR algorithm (CMLLR), while `tLcmllrfeas` transforms samples into fCMLLR features using a CMLLR transformation matrix.

tLtask-Recognise. This tool transcribes audio samples produced by `tLtask-preprocess` using HMM models estimated by `tLtask-train` following a two-step recognition schema:

1. Recognition using the standard tied phoneme HMMs.
2. Estimation of CMLLR matrices.
3. CMLLR transformation of input samples.
4. Recognition using the CMLLR tied phoneme HMMs.

`tLtask-recognise` uses the basic tool `tLrecognise`, which implements the well-known Viterbi algorithm, to obtain the most probable hypothesis [19]. In addition to HMMs, a language model and a pronunciation dictionary must be provided for decoding. `tLrecognise` allows two different language model representations. If the language model is a wordnet (without back-off), decoding is carried out over a huge finite state model built by embedding HMMs into the states of the wordnet [20]. In contrast, if the language model is in ARPA format (back-off), the decoder follows a word-conditioned tree search approach [12]. Specifically, a prefix tree with all the possible pronunciations is pre-calculated. To speed up the process, prior to decoding (`tLtask-recognise` or `tLrecognise`), the language model must be transformed into an internal format. This transformation is carried out by the basic tool `tLlmformat`. `tLrecognise` implements several well-known pruning techniques: beam search, histogram pruning, word end pruning and look-ahead. Although look-ahead is not exactly a pruning technique, its use is highly recommended when pruning techniques are applied in conjunction with a prefix tree approach [13]. tLrecognise also supports the generation of lattices following the technique described in [14]. Two formats for lattices are supported: the TLK format and the HTK format [20]. If desired, lattices can be generated including information related to time alignment at phoneme level.

As with tLtask-train, tLtask-recognise has been designed to work well in cluster environments. Specifically, it can be configured to split recognition into parallel processes, and cache big files (like models) on host machines.

The output of tLtask-recognise is given in different formats: plain text, recognise output, CTM format [4], etc.

2.2 Using TLK Tools for Decoding Only

TLK includes a high-level tool named tLtranscribe that allows users to directly transcribe media files. This tool reads a preinstalled system, freeing the user from all the technical details. As illustrated in Fig. 2, tLtranscribe makes use of the high-level tools tLtask-recognise and tLtask-segment. The tool tLtask-segment uses tLextract to automatically perform the segmentation of the audio signal. For the purposes of testing the tLtranscribe tool, a system for Spanish transcription has been released under a Creative Commons Attribution 4.0 International License.

3 Using TLK

This section describes how an ASR system can be built using TLK following the process depicted in Fig. 1. A more detailed version of this tutorial is available on the transLectures website [6].

1. TLK installation and data preparation.
   - The current version of TLK runs on Linux and Mac OS X, and can be easily installed from the transLectures website.
   - Acoustic data is also available on the transLectures website and can be downloaded by executing:
     ```
     wget translectures.eu/files/tlk/tlk-tutorial-data.tgz
     tar -xzvf tlk-tutorial-data.tgz
     ```
     This will create the directory tlk-tutorial-data, which itself contains several directories. The train directory contains the data that will be used to train HMMs, while the test directory contains the data that will be used to asses the system. These data correspond to Spanish lectures recorded at Universitat Politècnica de València and their annotations in .trs and .dfxp format.

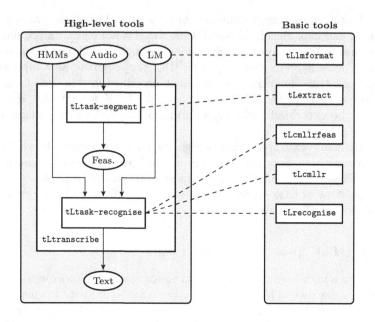

Fig. 2. Transcribing media files with `tLtranscribe`

- Now, running `tLtask-preprocess` the data is preprocessed obtaining
  the required files for training and evaluation:
  `tLtask-preprocess es dfxp tlk-tutorial-data/train preprocess-train`
  `tLtask-preprocess es dfxp tlk-tutorial-data/test preprocess-test`
  Note that the configuration options (i.e. `es` and `dfxp`) indicate the language and the file format, respectively.

2. HMM training:
   - First of all, a directory should be created to store the training files:
     `mkdir training; cd training`
   - Then, the two directories inside `preprocess-train` need to be linked to
     the training directory:
     `ln -s ../preprocess-train/samples ../preprocess-train/lists .`
   - Next, a template of the tool's configuration file `tLtask-train` should be
     generated:
     `tLtask-train --write-example-config-file > config-file.ini`
     This configuration file contains the default parameters needed to train
     standard HMMs for the Spanish language. In order to use previously
     preprocessed acoustic data, the `Lists` section of this configuration file
     has to be changed:
     `[Lists]`
     `set_name = lists/samples`
     `...`
     `[General]`
     `...`
     `prefix-name = training-tutorial`

- Finally, the following command runs the tool `tLtask-train` to perform the HMM training:

```
tLtask-train config-file.ini --log-folder log
```

The tool `tLtask-train` will execute all necessary commands to train HMMs following the training schema described in previous section Note that, although certain processes are executed in parallel depending on the computer, this process might take some time.

3. Automatic transcription:
   - As in the case of training, a directory should be created in the base directory for storing the automatic transcriptions:

```
mkdir recognition; cd recognition
```

   - Also, some links must be created to the acoustic data and models:

```
ln -s ../preprocess-test/samples ../preprocess-test/lists \
      ../preprocess-test/references ../training/models \
      ../tlk-tutorial-data/misc/mono.lex \
      ../tlk-tutorial-data/misc/mlm.gz .
```

   - The tool `tLtask-recognise` needs a configuration file, easily generated by running:

```
tLtask-recognise --write-example-config-file > config-file.ini
```

Some changes need to be made to this file in order to use previously preprocessed test data:

```
[General]
prefix-name = tutorial
...
[HMM]
prefix-name = training-tutorial
...
[LM]
language-model = mlm.gz
lexicon = mono.lex
```

   - Finally, upon executing the following command, the test audio samples will be automatically transcribed following the two-step recognition schema described in previous section:

```
tLtask-recognise config-file.ini --log-folder log
```

4. Measuring the transcription quality:
   - The sclite tool in SCTK is used to compute the Word Error Rate (WER) of the automatic transcriptions [4]:

```
sclite -r references/035040d6-7fd4-ab4a-80ff-e87d3a5d84db.stm \
       stm -h tutorial/cmllr_step2/transcription.ctm ctm
```

4   Empirical Results

TLK has been developed within the framework of the transLectures project to deal with the transcription of video lectures. Specifically, ASR systems have been developed for three languages: English, Spanish and Catalan. The English ASR system has been developed for the transcription of English lectures from the VideoLectures.NET repository. The Spanish and Catalan ASR systems have been developed for the poliMedia repository. For training and evaluation purposes, three databases have been developed by manually transcribing video lectures from these repositories. The main statistics of these speech databases are shown in Table 1.

Table 1. Main statistics of the English, Spanish and Catalan speech databases used in the transLectures project

	English	Spanish	Catalan
Videos	28	704	210
Speakers	104	83	53
Hours	26.6	114.2	25.8
Sentences	7.3K	41.6K	13.7K
Running Words	192K	1M	198K
Vocabulary Size	13K	35.9K	24.4K

From each database some lectures were selected for evaluation purposes: 3.4h for Spanish and English, and 2.1h for Catalan. However, since video lectures from VideoLectures.NET are longer ($\approx$ 50min) than poliMedia lectures ($\approx$ 10min), this means just 4 videos were selected for English in absolute terms, while 23 and 16 videos were selected for Spanish and Catalan, respectively. The remaining data were used for training and development. For tasks where there was a lack of training data, as was the case for English and Catalan, the training data was increased by out-of-domain corpora.

The progress of the ASR systems developed within the transLectures project using TLK for each language is depicted in Fig. 3. As can be observed, the performances of the three systems have improved continuously throughout the project. In particular, very high performance levels have been achieved in Spanish (12.8% WER). Work began on the English and Catalan systems later than on the Spanish system (specifically, one year later). However, big improvements in WER have been achieved in the six-month period (20.1% in Catalan and 22.7% in English). In all languages, the performance is close or below 20% WER, which has been reported as the threshold under which ASR output becomes useful for users [11]. All these improvements can in part be explained by the fact that TLK has been under active development since the beginning of the project. This includes some features currently being tested, for example, hybrid models with deep neural networks (DNNs) [16,8,18], and multilingual DNNs [10]. It is worth noting that, in all cases, the language model used has about 200K words. Moreover, the percentage of out-of-vocabulary words is below 2% (1.7% for Spanish). For further details on the development of these systems, please refer to the public transLectures reports [2,5,1].

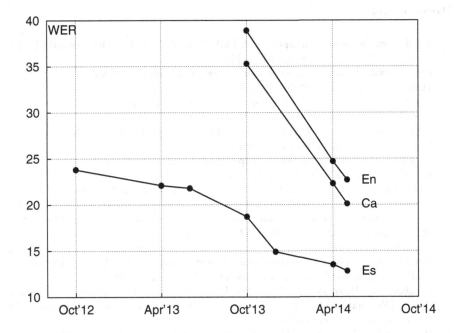

Fig. 3. Progress measured in WER of the TLK ASR systems developed within the transLectures project for Spanish (Es), English (En) and Catalan (Ca)

5   Conclusions and Further Remarks

In this paper we have presented the transLectures-UPV ASR toolkit (TLK) based on HMMs. TLK implements well-known ASR features and released under the open source Apache License 2.0. The functionality of TLK has been recently extended, adding a new component that supports Deep Neural Networks (DNNs) following a hybrid decoding approach [8]. Although the current release does not include DNN training, with this still being at an experimental stage, it does include DNN support for recognition. In fact, beside the standard Gaussian HMM based Spanish system, we have also released a Spanish system based on DNNs. Both systems can be downloaded from the transLectures website [6].

As future work, we plan to improve TLK further by adding new state-of-the-art features, such as convolutional NNs or recurrent NNs. Also, we plan to carry out extensive, comparative tests with other toolkits.

Acknowledgments. The research leading to these results has received funding from the European Union Seventh Framework Programme (FP7/2007-2013) under grant agreement no 287755 (transLectures) and ICT Policy Support Programme (ICT PSP/2007-2013) as part of the Competitiveness and Innovation Framework Programme (CIP) under grant agreement no 621030 (EMMA), and the Spanish MINECO Active2Trans (TIN2012-31723) research project.

References

1. Final report on massive adaptation (M36). To be delivered on October 2014 (2014)
2. First report on massive adaptation (M12),
   https://www.translectures.eu/wp-content/uploads/2013/05/
   transLectures-D3.1.1-18Nov2012.pdf
3. Opencast Matterhorn, http://opencast.org/matterhorn/
4. sclite - Score speech recognition system output,
   http://www1.icsi.berkeley.edu/Speech/docs/sctk-1.2/sclite.htm
5. Second report on massive adaptation (M24),
   https://www.translectures.eu//wp-content/uploads/2014/01/
   transLectures-D3.1.2-15Nov2013.pdf
6. TLK: The transLectures-UPV Toolkit, https://www.translectures.eu/tlk/
7. Baum, L.E., Petrie, T., Soules, G., Weiss, N.: A Maximization Technique Occurring in the Statistical Analysis of Probabilistic Functions of Markov Chains. The Annals of Mathematical Statistics 41(1), 164–171 (1970)
8. Dahl, G.E., Yu, D., Deng, L., Acero, A.: Context-Dependent Pre-Trained Deep Neural Networks for Large-Vocabulary Speech Recognition. IEEE Transactions on Audio, Speech, and Language Processing 20(1), 30–42 (2012)
9. Digalakis, V., Rtischev, D., Neumeyer, L., Sa, E.: Speaker Adaptation Using Constrained Estimation of Gaussian Mixtures. IEEE Transactions on Speech and Audio Processing 3, 357–366 (1995)
10. Huang, J.T., Li, J., Yu, D., Deng, L., Gong, Y.: Cross-language knowledge transfer using multilingual deep neural network with shared hidden layers. In: Proc. of ICASSP (2013)
11. Munteanu, C., Baecker, R., Penn, G., Toms, E., James, D.: The Effect of Speech Recognition Accuracy Rates on the Usefulness and Usability of Webcast Archives. In: Proc. of CHI, pp. 493–502 (2006)
12. Ney, H., Ortmanns, S.: Progress in dynamic programming search for LVCSR. Proceedings of the IEEE 88(8), 1224–1240 (2000)
13. Ortmanns, S., Ney, H., Eiden, A.: Language-model look-ahead for large vocabulary speech recognition. In: Proc. of ICSLP, vol. 4, pp. 2095–2098 (1996)
14. Ortmanns, S., Ney, H., Aubert, X.: A word graph algorithm for large vocabulary continuous speech recognition. Computer Speech and Language 11(1), 43–72 (1997)
15. Povey, D., et al.: The Kaldi Speech Recognition Toolkit. In: Proc. of ASRU (2011)
16. Rumelhart, D., Hintont, G., Williams, R.: Learning representations by back-propagating errors. Nature 323(6088), 533–536 (1986)
17. Rybach, D., et al.: The RWTH Aachen University Open Source Speech Recognition System. In: Proc. Interspeech, pp. 2111–2114 (2009)
18. Seide, F., Li, G., Chen, X., Yu, D.: Feature engineering in Context-Dependent Deep Neural Networks for conversational speech transcription. In: Proc. of ASRU, pp. 24–29 (2011)
19. Viterbi, A.: Error bounds for convolutional codes and an asymptotically optimum decoding algorithm. IEEE Transactions on Information Theory 13(2), 260–269 (1967)
20. Young, S., et al.: The HTK Book. Cambridge University Engineering Department (1995)
21. Young, S.J., Odell, J.J., Woodland, P.C.: Tree-based state tying for high accuracy acoustic modelling. In: Proc. of HLT, pp. 307–312 (1994)

The AhoSR Automatic Speech Recognition System

Igor Odriozola, Luis Serrano, Inma Hernaez, and Eva Navas

Aholab Signal Processing Laboratory,
University of the Basque Country (UPV/EHU),
Urkixo zumarkalea z/g, Bilbao, Basque Country
{igor,lserrano,inma,eva}@aholab.ehu.es
http://aholab.ehu.es

Abstract. AhoSR is a hidden Markov model based speech recognition system developed in the *Aholab* Signal Processing Laboratory research group of the University of the Basque Country. It has been modularly devised for ASR-based tools and applications to be easily implemented and tested, being also particularly interesting for research in the field of language model optimization of agglutinative languages like Basque. The system relies on the use of a static search graph where decoupled language model information is incorporated at run-time. This paper introduces the basic architecture as well as the most relevant aspects of the AhoSR speech recognition system. Besides, this paper compiles the results of several experiments which validate the system for its use in different tasks: phonetic, grammar-based and LM-based recognition. Two CALL/CAPT applications that use AhoSR are also described.

Keywords: speech recognition, Basque ASR, software.

1 Introduction

This paper presents a new tool for Automatic Speech Recognition (AhoSR) which has been developed at the Aholab Laboratory during the last years. AhoSR is a modular speech recognition decoder written in C++, which aims at providing a flexible computing environment for ASR based applications. It is based on HMMs (Hidden Markov Models) and it uses MFCCs (Mel Frequency Cepstral Coefficients) as acoustic features. Although several open-source toolkits are nowadays available for researchers working on the field of automatic speech recognition (ASR), among them HTK [1], Julius [2], Kaldi [3], RWTH ASR [4] and Sphinx-4 [5], some important gaps moved us to develop our own toolkit. The main motivation is that all of them need to be tuned when a specific use in a non-classical ASR application is required. For example, CALL (Computer Assisted Language Learning) and CAPT (Computer Assisted Pronunciation Training) applications make use of verification scores which can not be easily obtained with such a toolkit. Indeed, a parallel graph must be built in order to compute the GOP (Goodness of Pronunciation) in a CAPT system, which is of course

J.L. Navarro Mesa et al. (Eds.): IberSPEECH 2014, LNAI 8854, pp. 279–288, 2014.

not available. In many cases, the effort to tune the existing toolkits can be as important as building them from scratch.

On the other hand, these systems are optimized to work with word-based language models (LM), typically N-grams, which are useful for languages with no overt inflection -e.g. Chinese-, with minimal inflection -e.g. English-, or not highly inflected -e.g. Spanish-. However, in highly inflective or agglutinative languages (like Basque, among many others), words are built concatenating several prefixes and/or suffixes to the word roots, leading to millions of different but still frequent word forms [6]. Different approaches are being tested, mostly based on using sub-word units as basic speech recognition units, as explained in [7] for Turkish, in [8] for Arabic, in [9] for Hungarian, in [10] for Tamil or in [11] for Basque. The introduction of such a subword units based LM requires the modification of the search space and fine control of the propagating paths.

There is also the issue of availability for commercial uses, which varies from one toolkit to another. If a CALL/CAPT tool is to be integrated in an existing language learning tool, or a migration to an embedded system is foreseen, full availability of the source code is crucial. Taking all these aspects into account, we considered it very convenient to develop an adaptable recognition system where different approaches could be applied and tested, and which would keep all the doors open for future developments.

The paper is organized as follows: in the next section (section 2) the system architecture is described in detail. It is followed by showing several experimental recognition results that validate the recognition system for Basque (section 3). Then, some applications and research work developed using AhoSR are briefly explained (section 4). Finally, some conclusions are presented (section 5).

2   System Architecture

The overall architecture of AhoSR is modular, so that modifications and adaptations can be easily applied in each block separately without affecting the rest of the modules. The overall block diagram of AhoSR is shown in Fig. 1.

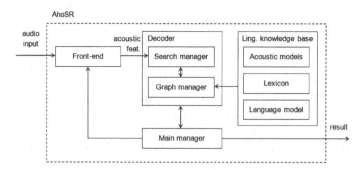

Fig. 1. System architecture of AhoSR. The main blocks are the Main Manager, the Front-End, the Linguistic Knowledge Base, and the Decoder. The communication between these modules is depicted.

2.1   Main Manager

The Main Manager is responsible for managing the communication between the different parts of the recognizer. Firstly, it reads a configuration file where the user sets the values of different parameters regarding the acoustic analysis, the input/output formats etc., and most important, the recognition task mode as a phonetic, grammar-based or continuous speech, as well as the possibility of using verification scores. The Manager checks for potential incompatibilities among all the parameters values and according to them, it configures and initializes each module, and decides which execution sequence must the decoding process follow. It also initiates the decoding process.

During the decoding process, the Main Manager controls the communication between the different parts of the recognizer, and when the decoding process is finished, it processes the data received from the Decoder and yields a final result. The results can be shown or stored in different formats in accordance with the requirements of the user.

2.2   Front-End

The purpose of the Front-End is to perform the feature extraction process, converting the input audio data (both direct audio and wav files) into classic MFCC vectors. Several parameter values can be set: frame rate, frame length, number of mel bins, minimum and maximum frequency cutoffs, etc. The generation of features and the management of the stack they are stored in is controlled by the Main Manager, which sends a message to the Decoder when new data are available.

The Front-End also supports other helpful techniques like different implementations of voice activity detection (VAD) [12], and cepstral mean and variance normalization (CMVN) for noise robust performance [13].

2.3   Linguistic Knowledge Base

Three different knowledge sources are used to create the search graph of the recognition decoding process:

Acoustic Models. HMMs [14] are used to model the acoustic sequential structure of speech signals, with local spectral variability modelled using mixtures of Gaussian densities (continuous density HMMs).

AhoSR can manage HMMs modelling different types of word or subword units. Nevertheless, it is optimized for triphones, which account for the left and right context of a phone. AhoSR allows the use of tied-state (also known as senone) HMMs, which are created by clustering similar states together [15]. The format of the acoustic models is HTK-compatible. This means that HMMs generated with the HTK toolkit can be used in AhoSR.

Lexicon. The lexicon is a file that contains the mapping between the written representation and the pronunciation of a word. The pronunciations must be depicted as a sequence of units (words, syllables, phones etc.), all of which must match a given HMM. As a result, each word in the lexicon is described as a sequence of HMM states.

AhoSR also manages alternative pronunciations of words beyond the canonical representation, thus taking into account pronunciation variations due to, for instance, dialectal variations. The alternative pronunciations must be included in the lexicon as different entries with the same lexical word (and the corresponding pronunciation).

Language Model. Two types of language models are managed: context-free grammars and n-gram language models. The standard adopted for context-free grammars in AhoSR is the Augmented BNF (Backus-Naur Form) notation [16], which defines a syntax for representing grammars to use in speech recognition. On the other hand, ARPA format N-gram backoff LMs can also be used to implement a statistical language model [17], which can be generated, for instance, with the SRILM tool [18].

The modular nature of AhoSR allows new grammar formats to be easily added to the system, without deep knowledge of the internal representation of the search space. This provides the possibility of easily testing new solutions for different tasks or for researching on agglutinative languages like Basque.

2.4   Decoder

The Decoder is composed of two primary modules: the Graph Manager, which controls the construction of the specific search graph for the required task; and the Search Manager, which picks up the incoming acoustic features from the Front-End and manages the decoding process over the search graph created by the Graph Manager. The results obtained by the Search Manager are sent to the Main Manager.

Graph Manager. The primary function of the Graph Manager is to create a search graph suitable for the task. Firstly, it translates the information of the Linguistic Knowledge Base into an internal data structure. Then, it creates the search graph by means of the information of the Linguistic Knowledge Base: using the LM information, the Graph Manager creates a suitable word-level net, composed of nodes and arcs, where each node represents a word and each arch the relationship between nodes. Then, each node of the word-level net is substituted by the corresponding HMM sequence representation given by the lexicon (alternative pronunciations are allowed). Finally, each HMM representation is linked with its corresponding HMM, thus obtaining a state-level net or final search graph comprised of nodes and arcs. For phonetic recognition, a special way of creating the search graph is used, where HMMs are considered as if they were representing a word.

The search graph can be compressed in order to obtain a significant reduction in the acoustic search effort. AhoSR allows prefix-suffix tree compression to be performed over the search space [19] [20]. In this search space topology, the LM is a separate module which is consulted at run-time by the Search Manager. This characteristic makes AhoSR not only memory efficient, but also flexible in use.

In case utterance verification is needed as well, the Graph Manager is the responsible for creating a parallel search graph, through which verification scores will be obtained.

Search Manager. The Search Manager uses the token-passing algorithm [21] for the decoding process. It expands tokens through the search graph, making use of the standard Viterbi algorithm. Each token contains information about the search and provides a complete history of all active paths in the search. Besides, each token stores the overall acoustic and language scores of the path at a given point. During the search, each incoming feature frame is scored against the acoustic models associated with each token state, and low scoring branches are pruned. Two types of pruning have been implemented, which can also be combined: global beam pruning, which retains only paths with a likelihood score close to the best partial path hypothesis; and the histogram pruning, which limits the number of active paths at each time frame by retaining only a predefined number of best paths [22]. A configurable number of tokens propagates in each state node or in each auxiliary node of the graph so that, for instance, an N-Best list can be obtained.

When choosing the verification performance mode, the search manager also computes GOP scores, which are calculated as the duration normalized log of the posterior probability of a phone or sequence of phones over the acoustic segment [23]. To compute the GOP, two groups of scores are used: on the one hand the ones obtained in the main search graph during the recognition process, and on the other hand those obtained in a secondary graph, which consists of a free phone loop.

3   Experimental Evaluation

Several experiments have been carried out using AhoSR. The following are the most significant experiments:

3.1   Phonetic Test

Phonetic recognition experiments have been done in order to validate several acoustic models trained from the *Basque Speecon-like* database [24]. Different acoustic models have been created regarding the subset of the Train part (155 sessions out of 230, each session containing one speaker): *a*) the read subset; *b*) the read subset with the phonetic transcriptions of the 16 % of its sessions manually corrected. Different number of gaussians have also been used. 300 files from the Test part (75 sessions), 4 files per speaker, have been tested with each set of HMMs, containing phonetically rich read sentences. Results show that a phone error rate (PER) of 12.33 % is achieved using subset *b* with mixtures of 32 gaussians (see Table 1).

Table 1. Phone error rates (PER) for different number of gaussians with training sets *a* and *b* (see text), using AhoSR and the *Basque Speecon-like* database

	2 g.	4 g.	8 g.	16 g.	32 g.	64 g.
Exp. *a*	18.02	16.28	15.04	14.08	13.34	14.17
Exp. *b*	16.76	15.01	13.67	12.91	12.33	12.90

3.2 Grammar-Based Tests

AhoSR has been also used to validate a speech database using grammar-based LMs. That database is the *Basque SpeechDat MDB-600*, which was recorded through mobile telephones according to the SpeechDat specifications. The experiments follow the recommendations of the *RefRec* (the COST 249 SpeechDat Reference Recogniser) procedure [25], and must be done over different subcorpora representing typical test applications. Used dictionary sizes and obtained word error rates (WER) are shown in Table 2, both for non-normalized cepstra and normalized (CMVN) cepstra. Further details can be found in [24].

Table 2. Dictionary sizes and WERs of the speech recognition experiments on different test subsets (Refrec), for *Basque SpeechDat MDB-600*

Test subcorpus	Dict. size	WER %	WER % (CMVN)
Isolated digits	12	12.73	3.25
Yes/no	2	7.47	1.18
Isolated application words	42	18.14	7.18
Connected digit strings, unknown length	12	4.06	2.58
City names	1352	38.53	20.79
Phonetically rich words	1055	37.65	18.76

3.3 Tests Using an External LM

The objective of this experiment was to perform a continuous speech recognition test by using the acoustic models obtained from the *Basque Speecon-like* database along with an external LM. The acoustic models (HMMs) were trained using the subset of read speech from the training set, whereas the LM was created from the CRP (Contemporary Reference Prose) [26], a textual corpus which contains about 25.1 million words. Thus, a N-gram model of 984 238 unigrams, 12 558 022 bigrams and 3 004 799 trigrams was created.

To compensate for the difference between the acoustic models source and the LM source, an α weight factor is applied to the LM log-probability prior to add it to the acoustic log-probability. This weight is usually calculated empirically [27]. 275 files from the test set were tested using different LM weights. The WERs obtained for the different weights values are shown in Fig. 2. As can be seen the best results were obtained for $\alpha = 30$.

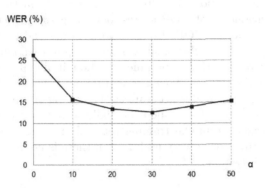

Fig. 2. WERs obtained using different α weight factors to compensate for the difference of origins between the acoustic models and the LM

With the calculated value of α, a continuous speech recognition experiment was performed. 2950 speech files containing phonetically rich sentences from the test set were tested, using all the training set vocabulary (23 243 words) and the external LM. A coverage analysis showed that the test set contained 40.71 % of out-of-vocabulary (OOV) words, which was expected due to the agglutinative nature of Basque. So a second experiment was carried out adding those words to the vocabulary (26 624 in total). In both experiments a set of 31 phonemes was used. Another experiment was carried out reducing the phoneme set to 24 and removing pronunciation alternatives from the training dictionary. The results are shown in Table 3. Further details can be found in [24].

Table 3. Dictionary size, number of phonemes and WER of three experiments on the phonetically rich sentences subset of the *Basque Speecon-like* database

	Dict.size	# Phonemes	WER (%)
Exp. 1	23 243	31	30.62
Exp. 2	26 624	31	20,44
Exp. 3	26 624	24	19.47

4 Applications of AhoSR

Some research work has already been developed with AhoSR, mainly on the field of utterance verification for CALL and CAPT applications. All the following experiments were carried out using the *Basque Speecon-like* database to train the acoustic models.

4.1   CAPT System for Basque

In [28], a method to build a CAPT system for low-resourced languages is proposed, using a general purpose ASR speech database. The method automatically determines the thresholds of GOP scores, obtaining the distribution of incorrectly pronounced phones' GOPs by simulating errors and evaluating them in forced alignment mode. The threshold corresponding to each phone is calculated using the equal error rate (EER) parameter. The initial experiments show that the discernment of the Basque phonemes that do not belong to the student's native language inventory is not as accurate as the scoring of the ones belonging to both phoneme inventories. This issue is partially solved by removing the speech of non-native speakers from the training set and creating new acoustic models. The method proves to be very useful when there is no database specifically designed for CAPT systems.

4.2   Message Verification Tool for CALL Systems

In [29] basic research for the development of a message verification system is introduced, which proves to be very useful to be implemented in CALL applications. The system aims to verify a sentence uttered by the user in real time, word by word, in order to display the verified word as soon as it is detected. Thus, it provides the student with real-time feedback. The behaviour of the whole system is tested inserting erroneous extra words by the users (insertion errors). The results of the experiments show that the proposed system is suitable for this kind of tasks, specially for those languages in which the meaning of a sentence depends of its word order.

5   Conclusions

This paper describes the AhoSR speech recognition system for Basque. Its modularity allows to test and develop ASR based applications, as well as its use for research in the field of continuous speech recognition for Basque, a minority language with scarce resources and a very complex morphological structure. Two developed tools in the field of language learning for Basque have demonstrated its usefulness for the foreseen tasks. On the other hand, basic speech recognition experiments have also proved the validity of the implemented software. In the near future it is planned to deliver the software as open source code. Now, our present and future work is mainly focused on the development of a continuous speech recognition for Basque making use of subword units for language modelling which will exploit all the potential of the system.

Acknowledgements. This work has been partially funded by the Spanish Ministry of Economy and Competitiveness (SpeechTech4All project, TEC2012-38939-C03-03) and the Basque Government (Ber2tek project, IE12-333).

References

1. Young, S.J., Evermann, G., Gales, M.J.F., Hain, T., Kershaw, D., Liu, X., Moore, G., Odell, J., Ollason, D., Povey, D., Valtchev, V., Woodland, P.C.: The HTK Book Version 3.4.1 (2009), http://htk.eng.cam.ac.uk/
2. Lee, A., Kawahara, T.: Recent Development of Open-Source Speech Recognition Engine Julius. In: Asia-Pacific Signal and Information Processing Association Annual Summit and Conference (APSIPA ASC), Sapporo, Japan (2009)
3. Povey, D., Ghoshal, A., Boulianne, G., Burget, L., Glembek, O., Goel, N., Hannemann, M., Motlicek, P., Qian, Y., Schwarz, P., Silovsky, J., Stemmer, G., Vesely, K.: The Kaldi Speech Recognition Toolkit. In: IEEE Workshop on Automatic Speech Recognition and Understanding (ASRU), Waikoloa, USA (2011)
4. Rybach, D., Gollan, C., Heigold, G., Hoffmeister, B., Lf, J., Schlter, R., Ney, H.: The RWTH Aachen University Open Source Speech Recognition System. In: Conference of the International Speech Communication Association (Interspeech 2009), Brighton, United Kingdom, pp. 2111–2114 (2009)
5. Walker, W., Lamere, P., Kwok, P., Raj, B., Singh, R., Gouvea, E., Wolf, P., Woelfel, J.: Sphinx-4: A flexible open source framework for speech recognition. Technical report (2004)
6. Hirsimki, T., Creutz, M., Siivola, V., Kurimo, M., Virpioja, S., Pylkknen, J.: Unlimited vocabulary speech recognition with morph language models applied to Finnish. Computer Speech and Language 20(4), 515–541 (2006)
7. Sak, H., Saraclar, M., Gngr, T.: Morphology-based and sub-word language modeling for Turkish speech recognition. In: IEEE International Conference on Acoustics, Speech, and Signal Processing (ICASSP 2010), Dallas, USA, pp. 14–19 (2010)
8. Choueiter, G., Povey, D., Chen, S.F., Zweig, G.: Morpheme-based language modeling for Arabic LVCSR. In: IEEE International Conference on Acoustics, Speech and Signal Processing (ICASSP 2006), Toulouse, France, pp. 14–19 (2006)
9. Mihajlik, P., Fegy, T., Tske, Z., Ircing, P.: A morpho-graphemic approach for the recognition of spontaneous speech in agglutinative languages - like Hungarian. In: Conference of the International Speech Communication Association (Interspeech 2007), Antwerp, Belgium, pp. 27–31 (2007)
10. Thangarajan, R.: Speech Recognition for agglutinative languages. In: Modern Speech Recognition Approaches with Case Studies, ch. 2, pp. 37–56 (2012)
11. Guijarrubia, V.G., Torres, M.I., Justo, R.: Morpheme-based automatic speech recognition of basque. In: Araujo, H., Mendonça, A.M., Pinho, A.J., Torres, M.I. (eds.) IbPRIA 2009. LNCS, vol. 5524, pp. 386–393. Springer, Heidelberg (2009)
12. Luengo, I., Navas, E., Odriozola, I., Saratxaga, I., Hernaez, I., Sainz, I., Erro, D.: Modified LTSE-VAD Algorithm for Applications Requiring Reduced Silence Frame Misclassification. In: International Conference on Language Resources and Evaluation (LREC 2010), Valletta, Malta, pp. 1539–1544 (2010)
13. Viikki, O., Laurila, K.: Cepstral domain segmental feature vector normalization for noise robust speech recognition. Speech Communication 25(1-3), 133–147 (1998)
14. Rabiner, L.R.: A tutorial on HMM and selected applications in speech recognition. IEEE 77, 257–286 (1989)

15. Young, S., Odell, J., Woodland, P.: Tree-based state tying for high accuracy acoustic modelling. In: ARPA workshop on Human Language Technology (HLT), Plainsboro, USA, pp. 307–312 (1994)
16. Hunt, A., McGlashan, S.: Speech Recognition Grammar Specification. World Wide Web Consortium (2004), http://www.w3.org/TR/speech-grammar/
17. Xiaolong, L., Yunxin, Z.: A fast and memory-efficient N-gram language model lookup method for large vocabulary continuous speech recognition. In: Computer Speech & Language, pp. 1–25 (2007)
18. Stolcke, A.: SRILM – an extensible language modeling toolkit. In: International Conference on Spoken Language Processing (ICSLP), Denver, USA, vol. 2, pp. 901–904 (2002)
19. Cardenal, A.: Realización de un reconocedor de voz en tiempo real para habla continua y grandes vocabularios. PhD. Thesis, Universidad de Vigo, Spain (2001) (in Spanish)
20. Demuynck, K., Duchateau, J., Compernolle, D., Wambacq, P.: An efficient search space representation for large vocabulary continuous speech recognition. Speech Communication 30(1), 37–53 (2000)
21. Young, S.J., Russell, N.H., Russell, J.H.S.: Token passing: A simple conceptual model for connected speech recognition systems. Cambridge University Engineering Dept. Tech. Rep. (1989)
22. Ortmanns, S., Ney, H.: Look-ahead techniques for fast beam search. Computer Speech and Language 14, 15–32 (2000)
23. Kanters, S., Cucchiarini, C., Strik, H.: The Goodness of Pronunciation algorithm: a detailed performance study. In: ISCA International Workshop on Speech and Language Technology in Education (SLaTE 2009), Warwickshire, United Kingdom, pp. 49–52 (2009)
24. Odriozola, I., Hernaez, I., Torres, M.I., Rodríguez-Fuentes, L.J., Penagarikano, M., Navas, E.: Basque Speecon-like and Basque SpeechDat MDB-600: speech databases for the development of ASR technology for Basque. In: International Conference on Language Resources and Evaluation (LREC 2014), Reykjavik, Iceland, pp. 2658–2665 (2014)
25. Johansen, F.T., Warakagoda, N., Lindberg, B., Lehtinen, G., Kacic, Z., Zgan, A., Elenius, K., Salvi, G.: COST 249 SpeechDat Multilingual Reference Recogniser. In: International Conference on Language Resources and Evaluation (LREC 2000), Athens, Greece, pp. 1351–1354 (2000)
26. Contemporary Reference Prose (Ereduzko Prosa Gaur) corpus, http://www.ehu.es/euskara-orria/euskara/ereduzkoa/ (in Basque)
27. Ogawa, A., Takeda, K., Itakura, F.: Balancing acoustic and linguistic probabilities. In: IEEE International Conference on Acoustics, Speech and Signal Processing (ICASSP 1998), Seattle, USA, pp. 181–184 (1998)
28. Odriozola, I., Navas, E., Hernaez, I., Sainz, I., Saratxaga, I., Snchez, J., Erro, D.: Using an ASR database to design a pronunciation evaluation system in Basque. In: International Conference on Language Resources and Evaluation (LREC 2012), Istanbul, Turkey, pp. 4122–4126 (2012)
29. Odriozola, I., Hernaez, I., Navas, E.: Design of a message verification tool to be implemented in CALL systems. In: Advances in Speech and Language Technologies for Iberian Languages (IberSPEECH 2012), Madrid, Spain, pp. 251–259 (2012)

Author Index